D1551687

Library of
Davidson College

The Illyrians

The Peoples of Europe

General Editors
James Campbell and Barry Cunliffe

This series is about the European tribes and people from their origins in prehistory to the present day. Drawing upon a wide range of archaeological and historical evidence, each volume presents a fresh and absorbing account of a group's culture, society and sometimes turbulent history.

Accessible and scholarly, the volumes of 'The Peoples of Europe' will together provide a comprehensive and vivid picture of European society and the peoples who formed it.

Already published

The Mongols
David Morgan

The Basques
Roger Collins

The Franks
Edward James

The Bretons
Patrick Galliou and Michael Jones

The Illyrians
John Wilkes

In preparation

The Picts
Charles Thomas

The Armenians
Elizabeth Redgate

The Celts
David Dumville

The Gypsies
Angus Fraser

The Huns
E. A. Thompson

The Spanish
Roger Collins

The Turks
C. J. Heywood

The Sicilians
David Abulafia

The Goths
Peter Heather

The Early Germans
Malcolm Todd

The Early English
Sonia Chadwick Hawkes

The Irish
Francis John Byrne and Michael Herity

The Etruscans
Graeme Barker and Thomas Rasmussen

The English
Geoffrey Elton

The Lombards
Neil Christie

The Hungarians
Michael Hurst

The Norsemen
John Haywood

The Illyrians

John Wilkes

BLACKWELL
Oxford UK & Cambridge USA

939.8
W 682i

Copyright © John Wilkes 1992

John Wilkes is hereby identified as author of this work in accordance with Section 77 of the Copyright, Designs and Patents Act 1988.

First published 1992
First published in USA 1992

Blackwell Publishers
108 Cowley Road, Oxford, OX4 1JF, UK

3 Cambridge Center
Cambridge, Massachusetts 02142, USA

All rights reserved. Except for the quotation of short passages for the purposes of criticism and review, no part may be reproduced, stored in a retrieval system, or transmitted, in any form or by any means, electronic, mechanical, photocopying, recording or otherwise, without the prior permission of the publisher.

Except in the United States of America, this book is sold subject to the condition that it shall not, by way of trade or otherwise, be lent, re-sold, hired out, or otherwise circulated without the publisher's prior consent in any form of binding or cover other than that in which it is published and without a similar condition including this condition being imposed on the subsequent purchaser.

Library of Congress Cataloging in Publication Data
A CIP catalogue record for this book is available from the Library of Congress.

British Library Cataloguing in Publication Data
A CIP catalogue record for this book is available from the British Library.

ISBN 0631 14671 7

Typeset in 11 on 12½ pt Sabon
by Photo·graphics, Honiton, Devon
Printed in Great Britain by Biddles Ltd, Guildford

This book is printed on acid-free paper.

ACU- 7943

93-9049

For Susan and Nicholas

The extracts on pp.91 and 110 from *Appian's Roman History*, vols. 2 and 3, translated by Horace White, are reprinted by kind permission of Harvard University Press.

Contents

Illustrations

Maps

Preface

The purpose of this book is to present the current state of knowledge regarding peoples known to the Ancient World as Illyrians. During the past two decades a large amount of work has taken place on known prehistoric and historic sites in Albania and Yugoslavia, while many new finds have been reported. Here annotation of the text and the accompanying bibliography are intended as a guide only to recent publications. In this respect I acknowledge my debt to the Illyrian bibliographies compiled by Aleksandar Stipčević and his colleagues. Research on the origins and identity of Illyrians continues to be infected by the politics of today. That is no novelty for this region of Europe but in recent years much has been gained through the open debates in symposia organized by Alojz Benac of Sarajevo and in the Illyrian congresses in Albania. Moreover, at a time when the political future of the Yugoslav and Albanian peoples seems so uncertain, it is right for the outsider to pay tribute to the scholarly integrity of many colleagues in these lands as they confront the myths and falsehoods relating to the remote past which are deployed in modern political contests.

I am grateful to the Editors and to the Publishers for their invitation to contribute to this series, and no less for their patience and forbearance in the face of delay and procrastination. I am grateful also for the help and support of my London colleagues, Mark Hassall and Richard Reece, which allowed me to enjoy the hospitality of the British School at Athens and the use of its excellent library for two months early in 1990. Colleagues in Yugoslavia and Albania have responded generously to my requests for illustrations. Sheppard Frere kindly read a part of the text and offered many helpful criticisms and suggestions, as have also the editorial and production staff at Blackwell Publishers. I am also indebted to my colleague Judith Higgens for help and advice at the proof-reading stage. My greatest debt, signalled in the dedication, is to my family, for their unfailing encouragement and support.

List of Abbreviations

AAnt. *Hung.*	*Acta Antiqua Academiae Scientiarum* *Hungaricae*, Budapest
AArch. *Hung.*	*Acta Archaeologica Academiae Scientiarum* *Hungaricae*, Budapest
AI	*Archaeologia Iugoslavica*, Beograd
AJA	*American Journal of Archaeology*, New York
ANUBiH	Akademija Nauka i Umjetnosti Bosne i Hercegovine (Académie des Sciences et des Arts de Bosnie-Herzegovine), Sarajevo
Arch. Anz.	*Archäologischer Anzeiger*, berlin
AV	*Arheološki Vestnik*, Ljubljana
BAR	British Archaeological Reports, Oxford
BRGK	*Bericht der Römisch-Germanischen Kommission* *des Deutschen Archäologischen Instituts*, Mainz
BUST	*Buletin i Universitet Shtetëror te Tiranes* *(Bulletin of the State University Tirana)*, Tirana
BzN	*Beiträge zur Namenforschung*, Heidelberg
CBI	Centar za Balkanološka Ispitivanja (Centre d'Études Balkaniques), Sarajevo
CRAI	*Comptes rendus de l'Académie des Inscriptions* *et Belles Lettres*, Paris
FGrHist	*Fragmente der griechischen Historiker*, ed. F. Jacoby, Berlin 1923
FHG	*Fragmenta Historicorum Graecorum*, ed. C. Müller, Paris 1841–70
GCBI	*Godišnjak (Annuaire) CBI*, Sarajevo
GGM	*Geographi Graeci Minores*, ed. C. Müller, Paris,

	1855-61
GZMS	*Glasnik Zemalskog Muzeja u Sarajevo*, Sarajevo
Inv. Arch.	*Inventaria Archaeologica* (Corpus des Ensembles Archéologiques)
JFA	*Journal of Field Archaeology*, Boston
JHS	*Journal of Hellenic Studies*, London
JÖAI	*Jahreshefte des Österreichischen Archaeologischen Instituts*, Wien
JRGZM	*Jahrbuch des Römisch-Germanischen Zentralmuseums Mainz*, Bonn
JRS	*Journal of Roman Studies*, London
LCL	Loeb Classical Library
LF	*Listy Filologické*, Praha
MAA	*Macedoniae Acta Archaeologica*, Prilep
MGH	*Monumenta Germaniae Historica*, Berlin
PZ	*Prähistorische Zeitschrift*, Berlin
Rev. Arch.	Revue Archéologique, Paris
SA	*Studia Albanica*, Tirana
SAZU	Slovenska Akademija Znanosti in Umetnosti (Slovene Academy of Sciences and Arts), Ljubljana
SF	*Studime Filologjike (Philological Studies)*, Tirana
SH	*Studime Historike (Historical Studies)*, Tirana
VAHD	*Vjesnik za Arheologiju i Historiju Dalmatinsku (Bulletin d'Archéologie et d'Histoire Dalmate)*, Split
VAMZ	*Vjesnik Arheološkog Muzeja u Zagrebu (Bulletin of the Archaeological Museum in Zagreb)*, Zagreb
WMBH	*Wissenschaftliche Mitteilungen aus Bosnien und der Hercegovina*, Wien
WMBHL	*Wissenschaftliche Mitteilungen des Bosnisch-herzegowinischen Landesmuseums*, Sarajevo
ŽA	*Živa Antika (Antiquité Vivante)*, Skopje
ZPE	*Zeitschrift für Papyrologie und Epigraphik*, Bonn

Map 1 Illyrian Lands

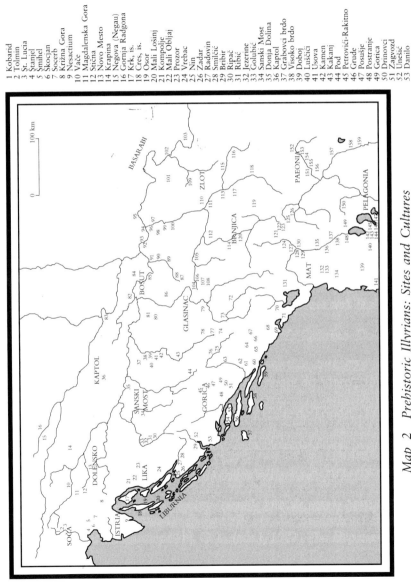

Map 2 *Prehistoric Illyrians: Sites and Cultures*

1 Kobarid	54 Vičja Luka
2 Tolmin	55 Brač, is.
3 St. Lucia	56 Hvar, is.
4 Štanjel	57 Vis, is.
5 Šmihel	58 Korčula
6 Skocjan	59 Mljet
7 Socerb	60 Ston
8 Križna Gora	61 Radimlja
9 Nesactium	62 Ošanići
10 Vače	63 Gubavica
11 Magdalenska Gora	64 Kačanj
12 Stična	65 Ljubomir
13 Novo Mesto	66 Mosko
14 Krapina	67 Plana
15 Negova (Negau)	68 Crvena Stijena
16 Gornja Radgona	69 Glogovik
17 Krk, is.	70 Lipci
18 Cres, is.	71 Budva
19 Osor	72 Gotovuša
20 Mali Lošinj	73 Barakovac
21 Kompolje	74 Butmir
22 Mali Obljaj	75 Orahovica
23 Prozor	76 Lisičići
24 Vrebac	77 Debelo brdo
25 Nin	78 Obre
26 Zadar	79 Glasinac
27 Radovin	80 Tuzla
28 Smilčić	81 Dvorovi
29 Bribir	82 Bosut
30 Ripač	83 Vučedol
31 Ribić	84 Gomolava
32 Jezerine	85 Šabac
33 Golubić	86 Belotić
34 Sanski Most	87 Godljevo
35 Donja Dolina	88 Ražana
36 Kaptol	89 Rožanci
37 Grabovci brdo	90 Barajevo
38 Visoko brdo	91 Rudovci
39 Doboj	92 Vinča
40 Lušćići	93 Starčevo
41 Usova	94 Židovar
42 Kamen	95 Bela Crkva
43 Kakanj	96 Vranovo
44 Pod	97 Aljudov Manastarica
45 Petrovići-Rakitno	98 Umčari
46 Grude	99 Mramorac
47 Posušje	100 Žirovnica
48 Postranje	101 Zlot
49 Gorica	102 Balta Verde
50 Drinovci	103 Basarabi
51 Zagvozd	104 Užice
52 Unešić	105 Atenica
53 Danilo	106 Pilatovići

107 Kriva Reka	134 Zadrimë
108 Srpci	135 Bellovë
109 Rtanj	136 Burim
110 Bubanj	137 Debar
111 Vrtište	138 Rajce
112 Josajnička Banj	139 Pazhok
113 Gornja Stražav	140 Symize
114 Novi Pazar	141 Çakran
115 Dub	142 Maliq
116 Vranište	143 Dunavec
117 Donja Toponic	144 Barç
118 Konopnica	145 Bilisht
119 Donja Brnjica	146 Kuç i Zi
120 Karagač	147 Tren
121 Suva Reka	148 Trebenište
122 Belaćevac	149 Ohrid
123 Siroko	150 Visoi
124 Romaja	151 Stip
125 Dibičak	152 Donje Orizare
126 Skopje	153 Kunovi Čuki
127 Kruma	154 Radanje
128 Kolsh	155 Gorno Pole
129 Çinamak	156 Orlovi Čuki
130 Kenetë	157 Demir Kapija
131 Nezir	158 Gevgheli
132 Burrel	159 Chauchitsa
133 Zadrimë	

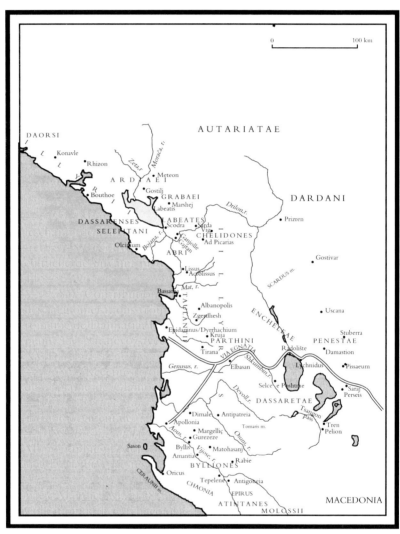

0   100 km

DAORSI

AUTARIATAE

Konavle

Rhizon

Meteon

A R D I A E I

Gostilj

GRABAEI

DARDANI

Marshej

Bouthoe

Labeatis

Prizren

DASSARENSES

LABEATES

SELEPITANI

Scodra

Sarda

CHELIDONES

Ganjolle

Vig

Gostivar

Olcinium

Gajtan

Ad Picarias

ABRI

Drilon. r.

Lissus

Acrolissus

SCARDUS m.

Bassania

Mat, r.

Albanopolis

Uscana

Zgerdhesh

ENCHELEAE

Stuberra

Epidamnus/Dyrrhachium

Kruja

PENESTAE

PARTHINI

Radolište

Damastion

Tirana

VIA EGNATIA

Shkumbin r.

Lychnidus

Pissaeum

Genusus, r.

Elbasan

Devoll r.

Saraj

Selce e Poshtme

Perseis

DASSARETAE

Dimale

Antipatreia

Tsangon Pass

Apollonia

Tomaris m.

Tren

Margelliç

Osum. r.

Pelion

Sason

Gurezeze

Byllis

Matohasanj

Amantia

Rabie

BYLLIONES

Oricus

CERAUNII m.

Vijosë, r.

Tepelene

Antigoneia

CHAONIA

EPIRUS

ATINTANES

MACEDONIA

MOLOSSII

Map 3   The Kingdom of the Illyrians

Map 4   Roman Illyricum

Part I

The Search for Illyrians

1

Rediscovery of Illyrians

Illyrian studies

For more than a thousand years before the arrival of the Slavs in the sixth century AD, the lands east of the Adriatic were the home of peoples known to the ancient world as Illyrians. Their territory comprised much of what is now occupied by the Yugoslavs, along with northern and central Albania. They spoke a language of which almost no trace has survived. That it belonged to the 'family' of Indo-European languages has been deduced from the many names of Illyrian peoples and places preserved in Greek and Latin records, both literary and epigraphic. We cannot be sure that any of them actually called themselves Illyrians: in the case of most of them it is near certain that they did not. In general the Illyrians have tended to be recognized from a negative standpoint, in that they were manifestly not Celts, Dacians or Thracians, or Greeks or Macedonians, their neighbours on the north, east and south respectively.[1]

Not merely do all the surviving descriptions of Illyrians and their ways derive from 'external' sources, but what has made matters much worse, for history's verdict upon them, is that many Greek and Roman writers seem to vie with each other in expressing their contempt and detestation for Illyrians. Even though they have escaped the sort of lasting infamy attached

---

[1] Trbuhović 1971, Stipčević 1986.

to the name of the German Vandali, they have fared little better in the historical record. As 'savages' or 'barbarians' on the northern periphery of the classical world, even today Illyrians barely make the footnotes in most versions of ancient history, and more often than not they are simply ignored. Readers generally familiar with the worlds of ancient Greece and Rome are likely to suspect, and rightly so, an attempt to adjust this balance of the historical record, not least because, as the playwright said, it is the only version they know. There seems little to be gained from seeking to create a picture of Illyrians that does not adopt a perspective of them as peoples on the periphery of the Mediterranean worlds of Greece and Rome. On the other hand, it is now less acceptable to order descriptions of such geographically marginal societies according to such categories as 'Hellenized', 'part-Hellenized' and 'Romanized'. These labels convey simplistic notions of a diffusion of all material innovation and development from an advanced centre to a more primitive periphery, through varieties of direct or indirect contact. Happily, we can now seek an escape from such narrow confines through the increasing archaeological evidence for Illyrians and their way of life. Not that it can be claimed that archaeologists and other students of prehistoric societies are free from a liking for traditional explanations of change and development, among which diffusion and migration continue to enjoy special favour. While we have to accept that an authentic and comprehensive account of Illyrians will remain out of reach for the foreseeable future, the evidence now available justifies an interim statement. We may best begin with a reconnaissance of progress in Illyrian studies.[2]

For all that William Shakespeare's *Twelfth Night* was set in a 'city in Illyria', two centuries were to elapse before that name appeared on the map of Europe. By the Treaty of Schönbrunn on 14 October 1809 a large tract of land east of the Adriatic, including Carinthia, the Istrian peninsula and the Dalmatian coast, was ceded by Austria to the Napoleonic kingdom of Italy to be ruled with the title of the Illyrian Provinces. In the

[2] Salmon 1986 (Roman image of Illyrians), Irmscher 1986 (Illyrians in Classical scholarship).

early nineteenth century the stirrings of Slav national feeling began to be translated into political manifestos more specific to the established order of Europe as constituted by the Congress of Vienna in 1815. Among the Slav subjects of the Austro-Hungarian Empire of the Hapsburgs the Illyrian name was invoked by a movement in Croatia, centred on its capital Agram, the Zagreb of today. Here the continued dominance of the Hungarian language set off a movement among the 'Illyrian Slavs', the Slovenes in the northwest around Laibach (Ljubljana), the Croats and the independent Serbs further east. It was from this feeling of cultural oppression that assertions of close links between the ancient Illyrians and the southern ('jugo-') Slavs began to be vigorously promoted, notably by Ljudevit Gaj and the Illyrian Movement. Though their arguments lacked the support of scientific evidence their widespread currency as political slogans awakened the sense of an Illyrian heritage from the remote past. Moreover, it happened that around this period, in the middle decades of the nineteenth century, the foundations of the modern historical and archaeological traditions of Illyrian studies were being laid.[3]

In Dalmatia historians and antiquaries of the Renaissance, notably Marko Marulić (1450–1524), had already begun to observe and record the abundant ancient remains. In the seventeenth century Vičko Prodić included an account of the Illyrian burial mounds on Brač in his chronicle of the island's history. In Croatia and Dalmatia, an Austrian territory after the defeat of Napoleon, the collection and study of ancient remains began with the foundation of archaeological museums at Split in 1818–21, at Zadar in 1830 and in the Croatian capital Zagreb in 1846. The first detailed account of the ancient Illyrians appeared in the *Albanesische Studien* of J. G. von Hahn, published at Jena in 1854, in which the author advanced the proposition that modern Albanians were descended from ancient Illyrians. In Austria imperial patronage of archaeology and ancient monuments was formally signalled in 1856 with the establishment in Vienna of the Central Commission for the

---

[3] Archaeological Museum Pula 1986a (exhibition on the Illyrian Movement).

Study and Preservation of Artistic and Historical Monuments. In Zagreb the Croatian Archaeological Society was re-established in 1878. Around this time also some of the pioneers of Illyrian studies in Croatia began long and industrious careers, Frane Bulić in Split and at Zagreb, Šime Ljubić in the Museum and Josip Brunšmid in the University. In the Austrian port of Trieste the British consul Richard Burton contributed a study of ancient hill settlements (gradina) and other prehistoric remains in the Istrian peninsula (see figure 25), to be followed 30 years later by the major synthesis of Carlo Marchesetti.[4]

At the Congress of Berlin in the summer of 1878 the Great Powers of Europe sought to resolve the Eastern Question, specifically the wretched condition of Christian Slavs in the European territories of Ottoman Turkey. By assigning to Austria the troubled provinces of Bosnia and Hercegovina, the lot of the Slav population may not have been greatly improved but the heartlands of the ancient Illyrians were laid open to historical and archaeological exploration. A vivid account of the archaeology of Austria's new territories, interspersed with comments on the political questions of the time, is provided by the works of the young Arthur Evans, later famous for his excavations at Knossos, centre of the Minoan civilization of Bronze Age Crete. In the late summer of 1875 the 25-year old Evans (see figure 1) made a journey across Bosnia and Hercegovina from Zagreb to Ragusa (Dubrovnik) on the Adriatic. As he and his brother Lewis moved south, news reached them of uprisings by Christian peasants in Hercegovina and of the atrocities committed by the irregular troops sent to quell them. Though on a lesser scale than the Bulgarian atrocities of the following year, the sufferings of the South-Slav peasants described in Evans' lurid and frankly sensationalized account produced an outburst of indignation in England. It had been his ambition to discover forgotten and exciting civilizations but his search for Illyrians soon became bound up with the cause of Slav freedom, a movement in which he now began to play a leading part. As a special correspondent of the *Manchester Guardian* based at Ragusa from 1877 he reported in unflatter-

---

[4] Burton 1874, Marchesetti 1903.

Figure 1 Arthur Evans in 1878

ing terms the imposition of Austrian rule after the Berlin Congress. His intemperate assertions that the Emperor's regime was no better than that of the Moslem Turk, and in some respects was worse, evoked little response in England. In 1881 he published a sympathetic account of the activities of Slav dissidents in the nearby mountains and, after a spell in prison, he was deported from Austrian territory in April 1882.[5]

Though they ended in ignominy, his years of residence at Ragusa allowed Evans to travel widely throughout the Illyrian lands, to collect and study antiquities. His 'Antiquarian Researches in Illyricum', published in four parts by the Society of Antiquaries of London in its *Archaeologia* (1883–5), still repay study for their wealth of information and observation of detail at first hand. He described a society which had been largely cut off from the rest of Europe during nearly five centuries of Ottoman rule. His discursive and enthusiastic accounts of prehistoric and classical remains and the ancient customs of the contemporary Slavs were not composed in a scholarly seclusion but amid a career of political journalism and agitation. The achievements of Illyrians in the remote past were deployed in order to emphasize to his readers how dark and regressive had been the era of Turkish rule.

Though castigated for its insensitive ways the Austrian regime in Bosnia and Hercegovina transformed the archaeological picture of those areas from one of near total darkness after the centuries of Turkish rule into one of the best observed regions of Europe. The advance began with the foundation of the provincial museum in Sarajevo (Bosnisch-Hercegovinische Landesmuseum). Several major programmes of excavation were soon under way; the Neolithic settlement at Butmir near Sarajevo; the great Bronze and Iron Age burial grounds on the Glasinac plateau in eastern Bosnia; in the west the Iron Age cemetery at Jezerine near Bihać in the Una valley and the pile-dwellings at Donja Dolina on the river Sava. The results and finds were published in the museum Bulletin (*Glasnik*) in Serbian, and in German in the volumes of Scientific Reports (*Wissenschaftliche Mitteilungen aus Bosnien und der*

[5] Wilkes 1976.

Herzegovina) which appeared between 1893 and 1916 along with several monographs on major sites. In addition to the archaeological papers these volumes also included many pioneering studies by anthropologists and ethnologists who seized the chance to work in this little known area of Europe.[6]

In Yugoslavia the second half of the twentieth century has seen many important discoveries and numerous publications relating to the Illyrian past. Most of this work has been undertaken by specialists in the universities and in the national museums of Belgrade, Zagreb, Skopje, Sarajevo and Ljubljana. In addition much important evidence that might have been lost through new building and other development has been rescued by the hard-pressed antiquities services of the Republics. Several of the long-established periodicals were reconstituted after the Second World War and continue to be published, including the *Starinar* of Belgrade, the *Glasnik* of the Sarajevo museum, and the *Vjesnik* of the Zagreb and Split museums. Some important new periodicals have issued from the new state academies for scientific research at Zagreb, Ljubljana (the Slovenian journal *Arheološki Vestnik*) and more recently Sarajevo. Here the Centre for Balkan Studies (*Centar za balkanološka ispitivanja*) of the Academy of Sciences in Bosnia and Hercegovina, under the inspiration of Alojz Benac, has published an Annual (*Godišnjak*), numerous monographs and a massive synthesis of Yugoslav prehistory in several volumes now nearing completion (*Praehistorija Jugoslavenskih Zemalja*). With the international community in mind, the Archaeological Society of Yugoslavia has since 1954 published *Archaeologica Iugoslavica* containing brief reports on major new finds and important research in English, French or German, followed later by *Arheološki Pregled* (Archaeological Preview) with annual summaries of recent field-work. The same body has also initiated a series of monographs for major excavation reports or archaeological syntheses. At the time of writing political tensions appear to have made concerted publication at the federal level more difficult, but the quality of archaeological publication remains high,

---

[6] Stipčević 1977a, 3–13; Munro 1900 for a first-hand account of work in progress at these sites and of the Sarajevo congress of 1894.

notably in the flow of volumes from Sarajevo, while the proceedings (*Materijali*) of the annual conference of the Yugoslav
Archaeological Society continue to appear.[7]

In Albania the first systematic record of ancient sites was
made before the First World War by Carl Patsch (1904) and
subsequently by Camillo Praschniker and Arnold Schober
(1919). Their topographical studies remain the basis of modern
studies of Illyrian sites, while between the wars Italian
expeditions tended to be focused on classical sites on the coast,
notably Apollonia where major excavations were directed by
Leon Rey. Since the Second World War archaeological exploration has been impelled by a national policy to establish
the link between modern Albanians and ancient Illyrians. The
investigation of both prehistoric and classical sites, well
underway during the fifties and sixties, gained impetus in the
seventies through a heightened political interest in the Albanian
Illyrian heritage. Research was centred on the archaeological
and ethnographical museum in Tirana from 1948 until 1976
when the Albanian Academy of Sciences created its Centre for
Archaeological Research in Tirana with eight regional offices
covering the entire country. In addition to the National
Museum in Tirana, major museums have been organized at
Durrës, Apollonia, Fieri, Saranda and Butrint. Since 1971 all
major archaeological research in Albania, including several
conferences and colloquia attended by foreign specialists, has
been published in the periodical *Iliria*, while the many activities
of the Monuments Protection Service are recorded in *Monumentet*.[8]

A welcome development has been the publication of general
works on Illyrians, notably that by Aleksandar Stipčević, which
first appeared in 1968 in an Italian edition and subsequently
in Yugoslav (1974) and American (1977) versions. A more
technical study by the Polish scholar W. Pajakowski is more
accessible in a German edition published in Sarajevo (1980).
Several general works on Illyrians have appeared in Albania,

---

[7] Now registered in the bibliographies of Stipčević (1967, 1977b, 1978,
1984a) and Škegro 1988.
[8] Bibliography for 1945–71 in Jubani 1972a and survey for 1945–86 in
Cabanes 1988c.

among which one may include the proceedings of the 1972 Illyrian congress published in volumes 4–6 of *Iliria*. A major compilation is *Les Illyriens: aperçus historiques* (1985) edited by Selim Islami, with other contributors including S. Anamali, M. Korkuti and the doyen of Albanian archaeology F. Prendi. German technology has now furnished more than one fine visual record of Albanian archaeology: one is the lavishly illustrated catalogue (edited by A. Eggebrecht) produced for an exhibition at Hildesheim during the summer of 1988, while the monuments of Albanian Illyria are well presented in a guidebook by Guntram Koch (1989).[9]

The current version of the Albanian theory of their Illyrian origins is centred on the unbroken descent of modern Albanians from an Illyrian people already formed in Bronze Age times and in a geographical area that coincided with that occupied today by Albanian speakers, the modern state of Albania and the Yugoslav region of Kosovo. The guiding principles of archaeological research are the following: excavation of prehistoric burial tumuli to supplement evidence for prehistoric Illyrians from the Korcë basin and to define more clearly the relations with prehistoric cultures of Greece, Italy and Yugoslavia; the growth of Illyrian urban settlements in the Hellenistic period (fourth to second centuries BC) and their relations with the Greek colonies on the coast; and studies in the late Roman and early medieval periods to demonstrate the links between Illyrians under Roman rule and Albanians, who first appear during the second half of the eleventh century.[10]

The continuing political collisions between Albanians and the Yugoslav Serbs have had a marked impact on Illyrian studies. It is no novelty that debates over the ethnic affinities of ancient peoples in southeast Europe should be bound up with the antipathies of Serbs, Bulgars, Greeks and Albanians but the question of Kosovo has become more serious than at any time since it was first posed at the break-up of the Ottoman Empire. After the First World War the area moved between Albania and Yugoslavia according to the balance of Great-

[9] Also the 1984 Clermont-Ferrand colloquium, Cabanes 1987.
[10] Buda 1984.

Power politics, though for most of the period it has remained
under Yugoslav control while the population has become more
and more Albanian. For this reason the ethnic affinities of the
Dardanians, ancient inhabitants of Kosovo, northern Macedonia and southern Serbia, have attracted attention. Albanians
hold them to be Illyrians, ethnically homogeneous with the
rest, while a Serbian view argues that Dardanians represent an
intermingling of both Illyrian and Thracian elements. There is
little danger of lasting damage being caused by arguments being
conducted on these lines when the evidence is historical or
epigraphic and remains in the public domain, but the damage
is done when archaeological evidence is successively deployed
to support one hypothesis with another. These reconstructions
of prehistory – 'houses of cards' according to one scholar –
prove suprisingly difficult to demolish even long after their
foundations have been shown not to exist. Similar problems
arise regarding the peoples of ancient Epirus, now divided
between Albania and Greece. Against a widespread view that
they spoke a form of Greek the Albanians argue that the
Epirotes were one with the rest of the Illyrians.[11]

   If we set aside some of the themes inspired by modern politics
we are still left with several worthwhile areas of enquiry for
which much new evidence is to hand. Who were the Illyrians
and how valid are suggested definitions of Illyrians on the basis
of archaeological and linguistic evidence, taken together or
separately? How were Illyrians linked with other inhabitants
of the Danube lands, Thracians, Daco-Moesians, Italic peoples,
Greeks and Celts, in their material culture and language? What
happened to the Illyrians under Roman rule and how were
they affected by the process known as Romanization? What
connection did the 'Illyrian emperors' of the third and fourth
centuries AD have with the peoples conquered by the first
Roman emperor Augustus? Is there evidence for the survival of
an Illyrian native culture during the Roman and early Byzantine
periods? What traces of Illyrians can be detected today in the
culture of the South Slavs and Albanians? Before we tackle the

[11] For the Albanian view see Hadri 1976 and for the Serbian response M.
Garašanin 1980 and the comments of Benac 1987b on Islami et al. 1985.

prehistoric origins of Illyrians and their evolution down to the fifth century BC we must consider the lands in which they lived, since Illyrian landscapes exhibit several distinctive features that imposed a pattern of life on the inhabitants that was very different from even the adjacent parts of Europe.

Illyrian landscapes[12]

The Illyrian lands are dominated by the results of Europe's most recent phase of mountain building. The extensive sedimentary beds of limestone, clay and sandstone created in the Palaeozoic period were raised into a series of complex folds to create the Alpine systems of relief. On the east the main Alpine system divides, the northern to form the Carpathians of Czecho-Slovakia and Romania which then double back as the Stara Planina of Bulgaria. The southern branch continues southeastwards, parallel with the Adriatic, as the Dinaric system of Yugoslavia and then into Albania and Greece as the Pindus range. Between the two Alpine systems lies the great Hungarian or Pannonian plain, divided by the Bakony hills, where the Danube turns south at the great bend north of Budapest, into a smaller northwestern plain (Kiss-Alföld) and the great plain (Nagy-Alföld) to the southeast. Drainage of this area is entirely to the Danube, which exits from the plain by the Iron Gates gorge through the Carpathians east of Belgrade. Europe's greatest river, navigable from Ulm in southern Germany, flows for 1725 miles from its source in the Black Forest to its delta on the Black Sea. Its major tributaries drain most of the Illyrian lands, from the Julian Alps in the northwest to the Alps of northern Albania. From this quarter heavy winter rains contribute to a sustained flow, partly cancelling out the summer maximum from the melting snow of the Alps and the summer rainfall of the plains. Compared with this vast system the rivers which flow into the Mediterranean are insignificant. Along the Adriatic only the Drin and the Neretva are permanent rivers,

---

[12] Accounts of historical geography are furnished by Pounds 1969 and Turnock 1988.

the rest being little more than seasonal torrents, and even those are navigable for light craft only in their lowest courses. At the same time these lesser Adriatic rivers are important because they offer a means of passage through intractable country, and the most notable in this regard is the Vardar of Macedonia for passage between the Aegean and the Danube basin. The route along the Neretva between the Adriatic and central Bosnia is not easy but was evidently used already in prehistoric times.

In Albania the Mediterranean rivers are altogether more significant. Flowing mainly in a northwesterly direction between parallel ranges, some of the larger streams, including the Drin, Mat and Shkumbin, cut through some hills to reach the sea by meandering courses across the coastal plain. The largest system is that of the Drin, which as the Black Drin (Drin i Zi) flows through a deep valley northwards to Kukës, where it is joined by the White Drin (Beli Drin) from the Metohija basin. The united stream flows west through the mountains for 25 miles in a deep gorge but at the edge of the plain divides between a westward course into the Lake of Shkodër and a tortuous southern course to the sea at the ancient and modern port of Lezha. Within the bend of the Drin the river Mat flows northwestwards through lower hills before turning west to cut through the last range of hills bordering the plain. In central Albania the Shkumbin rises close to Lake Ohrid and then turns west towards the sea, while the Devoll, which once drained Lake Prespa and the Ohrid basin, takes a zig-zag course following and crossing several mountain ranges. In contrast the more southerly Osum and Vijosë flow northwestwards in their main courses parallel with the ranges. Throughout this area there occur abrupt changes in river character at the meeting of mountain and plain. The flows become slower and great quantities of alluvium bring braided streams, flood plains and frequent changes of course among the malarial marshlands that dry out in the hot summers.

The Cretaceous limestones of the Dinaric ranges are not acutely folded and present a uniquely dry surface devoid of vegetation over large areas; they comprise the most extensive and spectacular example of the karst land-formation. Three regions can be distinguished: the Julian Alps and Karawanken in the northwest; the western Dinara 40 to 70 miles broad, extending from Istria to Greece and falling steeply in many places to the Adriatic where it is screened by long and narrow islands belonging to the fold-lines of the Dinaric system; and the eastern Dinara, lower and dissected by valleys of rivers flowing across it to the Sava and Danube, where the hills fall away gently to the Pannonian plain. South of this plain and to the east of the Dinaric system lies an area dissected by two major rivers and their tributaries, the Morava flowing north to the Danube and the Vardar (Axios) south to the Aegean. This region contains many plains and basins, usually with lacustrine deposits, separated by high but generally isolated mountain masses, notably the great Šar planina (2702 m). Through the valleys and basins of this region pass several major routes between the Danube and the Mediterranean, the so-called Morava-Vardar corridor.

In Albania a coastal plain, north of the Shkumbin the Kavaje, south of it the Myzeqeja, extends north from Cape Linguetta (Kepi Gjuhezés) for more than 100 miles until the border with Montenegro, after which the coastline turns northwestwards and the Dinaric ranges approach the sea. In places the plain is over 30 miles wide but elsewhere is interrupted as the hills come within a few miles of the sea. Flat and only a few metres above sea-level, the surface consists mainly of layers of sand and alluvium deposited by the rivers in the manner described above. As a whole the line of the coast is advancing and has moved more than three miles since classical times. The area has always provided excellent winter grazing but is now extensively exploited for the irrigated cultivation of rice and cotton. Major settlements have developed either as coastal ports (Durrës and Vlora) or important towns on the inland margins (Shkodër, Tirana, Elbasan and Berat) but rarely in between.

In Yugoslavia the karst is everywhere close to the coast, most dramatically in the Velebit range in the north which falls almost sheer into the sea. Except for the central stretch between Zadar and Split there are no significant areas of lowland adjoining the sea north of the plain of the Bojana which drains the Lake of Shkodër. From here to the Neretva some small and isolated areas of flat land have supported the settlements of Dubrovnik, Herceg-Novi, Kotor, Budva and Ulcinj. Behind the last lies the basin of the Lake of Shkodër, into which the Montenegrin

rivers Zeta and Morača flow through an alluvial plain. The
coastal ranges are next interrupted by the basin of the Neretva,
the only river to cross the karst from a source which lies to
the north of it. After flowing through several basins linked by
narrows the stream reaches the sea through a small delta. At
Makarska south of Split the high ranges retreat inland and the
highly indented coast as far as the Zrmanja estuary beyond
Zadar has always been intensively settled, notably around the
Bay of Castles (Kaštelanski zali) on which lay Salona, the
largest ancient settlement of the area and precursor of medieval
and modern Split (Spalato). North of the Krka estuary at
Šibenik the limestone plateau rises towards the interior but
contains several bands of alluvial basins which have long been
settled and cultivated. Between the Zrmanja and the head of
the Quarnero (Kvarner) gulf the coast is barred by the Velebit
range, and even the great port of Rijeka at its northern
extremity is confined to a narrow shelf between mountains and
sea. The Istrian peninsula is formed of a low limestone platform
linked to the higher Julian karst along a line roughly between
Trieste and Rijeka. On the west and a part of the east coast
areas of lowland border the sea. Though karst features pre-
dominate, and there are few rivers, the lower altitude and a
higher water-table has inhibited the more severe conditions of
the Dinaric region.

Behind the coastal plain of Albania lies a belt of hills formed
for the most part by the folding of sedimentary sandstone,
shale and limestone. The greater resistance of the last to surface
erosion has resulted in steep ridges separated by softer, more
eroded hills. In the north this zone confines the river Mat but
further south the Shkumbin cuts through several ridges in
gorges. Further south again this zone of hills broadens to more
than 50 miles to reach the coast and contains up to eight steep-
sided ridges running parallel with the coast, most rising to
around 1500 metres, although the Nëmërckë range between
the Vijosë and the Drino attains 2486 metres. On the north
the valleys open to the coastal plain and their courses alternate
between narrows and wide basins containing the major settlements such as Gjirokastra, Tepeleni and Berat. These valleys
offer several routes to the south, in marked contrast with
northern Albania where the mountains rise steeply from the

plain to bar passage to the interior. This distinction has resulted in major differences of historical development between northern and southern Albania, a divide which, as we shall see later, marked also a southern limit of Illyrian peoples.

Behind this intermediate range of mountains, the highlands of eastern Albania are divided by the steep-sided and narrow passages of the Drin, Shkumbin, Devoll and Osum. In the north a great arc of Albanian Alps rises to around 2500 metres, among which are areas of summer pasture and near inaccessible, though inhabited valleys. To the east of the upper Drin the high mass of Korab (2764 m) is no less rugged. Between these masses the alternating gorges and small basins of the Black Drin have never been a route in modern times. South of the Shkumbin the hills are less rugged and there occur several upland plains where cultivation is possible. Here the existence of the transverse valleys has allowed the passage between east and west and for that reason has always been the highly strategic area of the southern Balkans. The lake region which straddles the Albanian–Yugoslav border consists of several alluvial basins formed by north–south faulting, containing Lakes Ohrid, Prespa and Little Prespa, all once much larger than they are today. South of Ohrid the extensive Korcë basin is dotted with marshes and relict lakes, and a similar, smaller basin exists around Bilisht south of Lake Prespa.

East and northeast of the Albanian highlands there lies a maze of river valleys and alluvial basins, drained by rivers flowing in all directions. This region, comprising southern Serbia and Yugoslav Macedonia, includes in the valleys of the Morava, Vardar and Ibar some of the major routes between the Mediterranean and central Europe used since Neolithic times. To the west there is no way across the Dinaric region until the Julian karst plateau at the head of the Adriatic. The area belongs to the Pelagonian massif that remained unaffected by the later Alpine folding which produced the high mountain chains to the east and west, although it is extensively faulted and has been affected by volcanic activity. The lakes which once filled the basins have long since drained away and narrow channels that once joined lake with lake form the modern pattern of drainage.

The Tertiary basins of the Vardar valley around Titov Veles

and Skopje are the largest and most important of the region. The former is more hilly and comprises treeless ridges which rise to around 700 metres, settlements and cultivation being for the most part confined to the river valley. Between the two basins the river flows in a gorge that is followed by the railway but not by the modern road. Above this the triangular Skopje basin is bounded by steep-sided faulted mountains but is accessible by routes from three directions, from the northwest by the Vardar flowing from the Tetovo basin (see below), from the north where a route enters from Kosovo via the Kačanik gorge and the tributary Lepenac between the massifs of the Šar and the Skopska Crna Gora and from the northeast along the river Pčinja and the Kumanovo basin to the Morava system. The upper course of the Vardar forms an arc that encloses the Jakupnica massif (2540 m), from which the ridges of Nidže and Kozuf extend southwards to enclose the Bitola-Prilep basin. This extends from north to south more than 60 miles and is drained by the Crna Reka (Black River) which, after exiting from the southern limit of the plain, doubles back to a northeastward course through an area of mountains to join the Vardar below Titov Veles near the ancient Paeonian capital of Stobi (Gradsko). Though marshy in some areas this plain – the ancient Pelagonia – has supported a large population from prehistoric times and contains two of the major cities of Yugoslav Macedonia, Prilep and Bitola (formerly Monastir).

West and northwest of this area the districts of Ohrid and Tetovo are dominated by the north–south ranges of the Pindus system, notably the Šar planina and its southward continuation formed by the Korab, Bistra (2163 m) and Karaorman (2242 m). Together they form a barrier to east–west movement more than 100 miles long. East of the Šar lies the roughly parallel Suva Gora to the southwest of Skopje which is continued southwards as the ranges of Plakenska and Pelister, between which lie (from south to north) the basins of Prespa, Ohrid, Debar (on the Black Drin between the Jablanica and Stogovo ranges), Kičevo and Gostivar-Tetovo, the last drained to the north by the upper Vardar. Much of the Ohrid and Prespa basins are covered by lakes that still in places reach to the foot of steep mountains. Ohrid, drained northwards by the Drin, has contracted and is now bordered with marshes, notably around Struga in the north. Prespa is 160 metres higher than Ohrid, from which it is divided by the Galičica range, and was once drained westwards via Little Prespa and the Albanian Devoll, but its level has long since sunk and there is now no discharge to the sea. At the same time its recorded fluctuations in level are caused by drainage into underground passages dissolved in the limestone of the Pindus. Unlike the isolated basins to the north the Ohrid basin has always been an important centre of the southern Balkans. Once the domain of the Enchelei and crossed by the Roman Via Egnatia, it was the site of one of the early Slav settlements and then for a time heartland of the First Bulgarian Empire.

The gently rolling terrain of the linked basins of Kosovo and Metohija is bounded by steep-sided mountains formed along fault-lines. On the southwest lie relatively low ranges (*c.* 1500 m) northeast of the united Drin, on the northwest Koprivnik (2530 m) and Mokra Gora (2155 m), while to the southeast lie the northern heights of the Šar massif. The Metohija basin in the west is drained by the White Drin which exits through a gorge to meet the Black Drin at Kukës in northern Albania. The two hills which define the Metohija on the east, Crnoljeva and Čičevica, are no barrier to communication with the Kosovo basin around Priština, which is smaller and more elongated. This is drained by the northwards-flowing Sitnica which joins the Ibar, itself a tributary to the Morava, at Kosovska Mitrovica at the northern edge of the basin, where the united stream follows a gorge between the massifs of Rogožna (1504 m) and Kopaonik (2017 m). Towards the south of the plain, around the town of Uroševac, there lies an area between the drainage of the Sitnica/Ibar system and that of the Nerod-imka, which feeds the Vardar via the Lepenac at Kačanik. This is the crucial area of a major north–south passage between the upper Vardar and the Morava basin around Niš. It was in Kosovo that the advancing Turks destroyed the forces of Serbia in 1389, and in more recent times, as a part of the Sanjak of Novi Pazar, the region was a subject of dispute between Austria and Turkey.

North of the Kumanovo basin rises the Morava, whose northward course links a string of small basins that once con-tained lakes. As the Southern (Južna) Morava the stream crosses

the Rhodope plateau by a long gorge, linking Vranje and Priboj
to the major basin of Leskovac around 25 miles long. From
there it passes into a more dramatic gorge to reach the great
basin of Niš, cross-roads of the central Balkans. After yet
another defile at Stalać comes the meeting with the Western
(Zapadna) Morava, which has also flowed through several
gorges linking the basins of Požega, Čačak, Kraljevo and Kruševac. The united river then passes through a final defile in the
Rhodope system at Bagrdan to the final broad valley where
the now puny relic of a great river gently meanders through
marshes to the Danube. In spite of the gorges and defiles that
had to be by-passed through the surrounding hills, the Morava
up to Leskovac has been the favoured route for passage towards
the Aegean. The railway and the main modern road now
continue along the river via Vranje and Priboj and cross by a
dry valley into the Kumanovo basin and from there reach the
Vardar. An alternative route, avoiding the detour of the gorge
at Grdelica, follows the Jablanica from the Leskovac basin into
the Kosovo basin. A longer but easier detour, avoiding the
Southern Morava altogether, follows the Western Morava up
to Kraljevo and then the Ibar to Kosovo, a line now also taken
by railway and modern road. The area east of the Ibar around
the massif of Kopaonik is still covered with dense forests of
oak and beech. Several of the smaller basins within this area
contained cultivable land, including Prokuplje drained by the
Toplica into the Southern Morava, Gnjilane, where rises the
Southern Morava, and, further north, the Malo (Little) Kosovo
basin.

For a distance of around 450 miles an uninterrupted system
of mountains, high plateaus, deep valleys and gorges extends
from northern Albania to the head of the Adriatic. Becoming
steadily broader towards the south, this Dinaric system consti-
tutes a near-impassable barrier between the Adriatic and the
Pannonian plain. Most of the rock is limestone of the Trias
and Cretaceous ages and has no surface drainage except for
the streams that cross the clay floor of a basin (polje) before
vanishing underground. The surface of the limestone plateau
in the karst is quite dry and there is no accumulation of red
soil to sustain even a cover of scrub vegetation. Cultivation is
impossible, while travel in the region is made difficult by ser-

rated ridges caused by uneven erosion. The most conspicuous surface formations are the depressions (dolina), where a heavy residual clay can retard the drainage of rainwater. These depressions can unite to form dry valleys, but the most significant formations are the karst basins or polje, a level area of alluvium between ridges on which rainwater can seasonally accumulate to form a lake. Some of the higher polje remain dry but those nearer the coast at a lower level usually have lakes for some months of the year, while the Lake of Shkodër is in fact a polje whose surface lies below sea-level and is permanently inundated. These areas afford the only place for permanent settlement in the karst, with most of the villages being spread around the margins. Towards the northeast of the Dinaric system the karst becomes discontinuous, interrupted by beds of sandstone and shale. While the lines of relief follow the same northwest to southeast axis, the ridges are broader and less rugged and the surface greener with more extensive forests. There is also more surface drainage to the few major rivers which cut across the lines of relief through deep valleys and gorges to link narrow basins of cultivated land. The Dinaric region of Yugoslavia comprises some of the most impenetrable country anywhere in Europe. Its inhabitants have never submitted to a central authority, as local loyalties prevail and the fragmented terrain hinders contact even between adjacent communities. By the same token, resistance to the would-be conqueror has always been determined; the struggles of the Pannonian Illyrians against the Romans and those of the Montenegrins against the Turks were emulated by Yugoslavs during the Second World War.

Beyond the high karst plateaus and the adjacent high mountains lies a mountainous region where heights rise to between 1300 and 1600 metres. Here the valleys are broader and offer easier passage, while there are long-established major centres in Sarajevo, Višegrad and Novi Pazar. East of the Drina an area of broad valleys and rounded hills ends at the Golija planina (1833 m) and the Ibar valley. On the west lie several plateaus, including the great prehistoric centre of Glasinac, that reach to the basin of Sarajevo, once a great lake and bordered on the southwest by the fault-line of the Vranica (2112 m) and Bjelašnica (2067 m) ranges. This area is the physical centre of

Bosnia and the source of the river Bosna which forms the axis of the basin as far as Zenica, where the river enters a tortuous defile between the volcanic massifs of northern Bosnia. The next river to the west is the Vrbas, which rises on the west slopes of Vranica. After the broad high basin of Bugojno the river enters a gorge, with dramatic falls at Jajce, until Banjaluka. This densely forested area in the Middle Ages formed a nucleus of the short-lived independent state of Bosnia and later of Serbia. In addition to the timber that away from the gorges can be floated down the major rivers, the area has rich mineral deposits, including lead, silver and iron ore, most of which have been worked since Roman times.

The main eastward continuation of the Alpine system is the Karawanken, a steep-sided ridge that reaches over 2000 metres and separates the upper Drau (Drava) basin around Klagenfurt from that of the upper Sava around Ljubljana. This range, which is crossed by several passes, notably the Wurzen and Lubelj (Loibl), terminates in the high Savinski mountains, but the line of relief is continued into the Pannonian plain with some lower hills above Maribor on the Drava. The upper course of the Sava follows a valley that has continued eastward from Friuli, where it is drained by the Tagliamento, and then turns southeastwards into the Ljubljana basin, around 30 miles long. Several small but steep-sided hills rise from this plain, around one of which is situated the city of Ljubljana, founded as the Roman colony Emona although an inhabited area from at least the Late Bronze Age. On the east a limestone plateau rises in places to above 1000 metres but has been dissected by the Sava, Krka and their tributaries. Only in modern times has the gorge of the Sava across this area become a route, for all of its length by the railway and in part by a modern road. North of the Karawanken the river Drau rises in the High Tauern of Austria and at Maribor emerges from a gorge through the Pohorje plateau into the broad basin around Ptuj, site of a Roman fortress and veteran colony. Later it is joined by the Mur, flowing from the area of Prekomurje, some way below Varaždin. With its gentle relief and broad alluvial valleys this region marks the transition from the high Alpine mountains to the flat Pannonian plain, which lies mostly below the 150 metre contour and is drained by the Danube and its two principal tributaries Tisa (Tisza) and Sava. The part of the plain which lies south of the Drava is the historic region Slavonia, through which a double line of hills passes from northwest to southeast. The southern range commences with the hills north of Zagreb which rise here and there above 1000 metres, while further east the line is continued by the slightly lower Moslavačka and Psunj hills. The northern range commences with the Kalnik hills (643 m) and broadens eastwards to form the Papuk and Ravna Gora which partly enclose the basin of Slavonska Požega. Around 70 miles east of this area the narrow range of the Fruška Gora (539 m) is forested on the north face and falls steeply to the Danube, but the gentler southern slopes have long been cultivated and support large villages with vineyards.

The loess plateaus which rise from the plains between the major rivers to heights of more than 60 metres appear to be formed of wind-blown deposits from the northeast. There is little surface drainage and wells must be dug deep. Although now fertile and intensively cultivated in some areas, for example around Vukovar, in the Bačka and Banat plains the settlements tend to be located around the margins. The old Tertiary basins around the Drava and Sava have been overlaid with masses of sediment borne down from the Alps. Now both rivers meander sluggishly, with many cut-offs and occasional changes of course. Both have flood-plains up to five miles across, bordered by rising terraces to the respective plains of Podravina and Posavina. Here settlements were set well back from the river with meadows reaching to the bank and fields extending across the valley floor.

The Illyrian lands experience a wide range of climate. The northern plains and the mountains have the cold winters and short hot summers of the continental climate, while the coast enjoys the more amenable regime of hot summers and mild wet winters. During winter much of the plain and mountains have freezing temperatures, although snowfall is comparatively light, except towards the Adriatic. Snow is rarely seen on the coast except on high ground. Summer temperatures are everywhere high, especially in the karst hollows near the Adriatic and in the alluvial basins of Macedonia, though even here night-time cooling is significant. Rain is borne to the area on westerly winds and is consequently higher in the mountainous west and southwest, with from around 1200 to 2000 mm, than areas further east such as the Morava-Vardar corridor with around 750 mm. The Mediterranean receives the bulk of its rainfall during autumn and early spring, the plains in late spring and early autumn. In the matter of winds the Illyrian lands experience the consequences of lying astride the boundary between the Mediterranean and continental systems. High pressure in central Europe and lower pressure in the Mediterranean produces the notorious winter bura (bora), a cold dry wind which sears down the Adriatic from Istria to Albania. Locally it can become a great danger to shipping at anchor and is totally destructive of any tree- or vegetation-growth, especially in the northern Adriatic. Similar conditions produce the Vardarac which blows down the Vardar during winter, cold and dry like the bura but much less violent.

Except on the dry karst towards the Adriatic and the loess platforms around the Danube the Illyrian lands tend to be tree-covered, though a good deal of this has been removed through human activity since prehistoric times. Towards the Mediterranean the characteristic cover is the maquis, a combination of drought-resistant shrubs which is widespread between the mountains and the coast. At higher levels this can turn into light deciduous woodland. Where some soil is retained in the limestone karst an open woodland of broad-leaved trees, including hornbeam and varieties of oak, can develop, and towards the north the karst areas tend to be more densely wooded with oak and beech. The interior mountains of Bosnia and Old Serbia are densely forested with oak and beech, a huge natural resource for long barely exploited. In Macedonia woodland is now confined to the higher ridges and plateaus but evidently never extended to the alluvial plains. Towards the north, areas such as Šumadija, whose name means 'woodland', have now largely been cleared for cultivation. In the plains few trees are to be seen, except for the stands of willow and poplar which cover the wetlands near the rivers. On the whole the Illyrian lands are among the least favoured areas of Mediterranean Europe in the matter of soils. These, when present, originate from the rock and are generally shallow with little formation of humus. The karst limestone is bare save for a few pockets of clay, but alluvium, albeit badly drained, covers the basins. In the plains of Albania the cultivation of alluvial deposits requires irrigation during the hot summers. Some valleys contain cultivable soils but many are narrow and the soils have been covered with stony deposition. In some upland basins of the mountainous and lake region the alluvial and other deposits of dried-out lakes have produced soils of a high quality, though often amounting to only a small proportion of the Ohrid, Korcë, Debar and Kukës basins. The forest soils of the belt of lower hills to the north of the high mountains offer a better reward for cultivation, while the most recent loess and alluvial deposits of the plains are now fully cultivated.

The united state of the South Slavs proclaimed on 1 December 1918 comprised all the Illyrian lands except for Albania, where a boundary line defined with Montenegro in 1913 was retained. The predominantly Albanian Kosovo region was also assigned to Yugoslavia. At the time Albania was in no position to press her claim, while the Yugoslavs were eager to gain northern Albania itself for its easier passage to the Adriatic. In the northwest the border with Italy was no less a problem, in a manner which mirrored the conflicting needs of those who inhabited the Illyrian karst plateaus and the population of the plains in northeast Italy in ancient times. The east coast of the Adriatic had for centuries been under Italian influence. Until Napoleon most of it had belonged to the Republic of Venice and in 1815 it passed under Austrian rule. An undisclosed pact in 1915 promised most of the coast and islands to Italy but in the final treaty Italy was confined to the Istrian peninsula, including the ports of Trieste and Pula, and further south Zadar and some minor islands. The Italian grievance focused on Fiume (Rijeka), an Italian port in a Croatian hinterland, which in 1919 was siezed by an expedition of Italian patriots. After the Treaty of Rapallo (1920) had proclaimed it a free city Fiume was eventually annexed to Italy under Mussolini (1924), leaving merely the eastern suburb of Susak as the wholly inadequate Adriatic harbour for northwest Yugoslavia. After the Second World War the Yugoslav need for an adequate Adriatic port was acknowledged with the award of almost all Istria, along with the Julian Alps. Unfortunately, Trieste was denied and a wholly artificial frontier line from Gorizia on the Isonzo to Koper (Capodistria) ten miles behind the coast left the once-great port of Trieste bereft of its natural hinterland. Along the Dalmatian coast all Italian possessions were assigned to Yugoslavia, the first occasion since the end of the Roman Empire when the entire area was politically integrated with the interior.

The stirring of Albanian nationalism in the late nineteenth century was prompted less by a desire for freedom than by the fear of being partitioned between an enlarged Greece and Serbia. They resisted the encroachments of the Montenegrins sanctioned by the Congress of Berlin in 1878, while their hostility to an increasingly oppressive Turkish regime culminated in the rebellion of 1912 which brought a declaration of Albanian independence before the end of the year. The Greeks and Slavs objected to the new state, the latter eager to join Serbia with the Adriatic via the route from Ohrid. The Montenegrins had designs on the north, while the Greeks were more than willing to take over southern Albania with its large Orthodox population. Across the Adriatic, Italy was a supporter of the new state, confidently anticipating the prospect of increased influence across the strait. Though the Great Powers consented, Albanian independence remained precarious until 1920 when it was formally accepted by Italy, which retained possession of the small island Sazani (Saseno) in the Bay of Vlora (Valona). Kosovo and the Metohija, which in 1912 the Turks had been prepared to include with their offer of an autonomous Albanian province, was in 1920 finally ceded to Yugoslavia. During the Second World War the Albanians gained temporary control of the area while under Italian rule but gave it up in 1945 without protest, in spite of its Albanian majority. The rupture of relations between Yugoslavia and the rest of the communist bloc in 1948 was marked by a renewed hostility towards the Yugoslavs, a change which, in the eyes of most Albanians, was a satisfactory return to the natural state of affairs. At the time of writing the old dispute has once more reached a state of crisis. Federal Yugoslavia faces disintegration while a bid for autonomy, or even independence, by Kosovo has been suppressed by an increasingly nationalistic Serbian Republic. The battleground of this conflict has now been extended to the area of prehistory. The long-standing Albanian claim for a continuity of descent from the ancient Illyrians is now accompanied by arguments that Kosovo and Metohija form parts of an ancient Illyrian homeland that should naturally be joined with the rest of modern Albania.

2

Prehistoric Illyrians

Illyrian origins: Stone and Bronze Ages[1]

The earliest testimony of man's presence in the Illyrian lands are stone hand-axes and pebbles broken for use as chopping tools. Elsewhere in Europe these are dated to 200,000–100,000 BC, in the Lower Palaeolithic era. These, however, are merely scattered finds and the earliest traces of occupation come from several caves used at intervals over many thousands of years. In Montenegro, Crvena Stijena, at Petrovići near Nikšić, was found to contain 9 metres of debris in which were 31 levels of deposition with 15 'cultural horizons'. More than 23,000 stone objects were found bearing signs of having been struck or worked. In Level 24 (counting from the top where the latest deposit belonged to the Bronze Age) there was a thick interglacial deposit which could be dated to the Last Interglacial period, that is before the advances of the great Alpine ice caps dated 200,000 to 100,000 BC. From the levels beneath came the flint-making flakes of the Levalloisian technique, industries of the Proto-Mousterian and Mousterian types. From the end of the Last Interglacial (65,000 BC) a rock shelter in a sandstone bluff above a tributary of the river Drava at Krapina, not far from Zagreb, has an accumulation of 8 metres, with the lower 6 metres being sealed by a later stalagmite deposit. Around

[1] Prehistory of Albania: Prendi 1982, 1988, Korkuti 1983b and Cabanes 1986; of Yugoslavia: Novak et al. 1971, Alexander 1972, Benac et al. 1979a–c, 1983.

600 fragments of human bones included the remains of at least 13 men, women and children. Their teeth indicated a similarity to Neanderthal Man but in other respects they resembled modern man (*homo sapiens*). Their tools were flakes of flint and other local rocks.[2]

From the Upper Palaeolithic (*c.*40,000–8000 BC) no bones of modern man have yet come to light, but his presence is attested in several places by blade industries. The known sites have been identified with the principal divisions of the West European Palaeolithic, Aurignacian, Gravettian and Magdalensian, but so far few scientific dates have been obtained through Carbon 14. The general character of these industries has suggested links with the northeast, namely Hungary and western Romania. In Crvena Stijena the most widespread and oldest Aurignacian had been found along with the remains of red deer, wild cattle and goats. The Aurignacian and Gravettian industries which occur on the plains and in northern Bosnia (Kamen, Doboj, Grabovca brdo, Lušcići, Usova and Visoko brdo) are generally linked with hunting of the mammoth. The caves used by early man in these lands are devoid of paintings or carvings, though there may well be some in areas yet to be fully explored. This prospect is encouraged by finds of carvings on a rock face at Lipci, near Risan and Morinj on the Gulf of Kotor in Montenegro. The subjects include deer and some geometric (sub-rectangular) shapes. The Lipci carvings are so far unique in the Balkan region and their date is unknown.[3]

The Mesolithic or Middle Stone Age (*c.*8000–*c.*6000 BC) continued the traditions of hunting, food-gathering and fishing which had developed in the Palaeolithic, and changes in style of living began only with the appearance of farming and settlements which distinguish the Neolithic or New Stone Age. During post-glacial times the lands east of the Adriatic began to take on the character and appearance they possess today. As the ice caps along the Adriatic–Danube watershed started to melt deciduous trees began to cover the plains and hills, while

---

[2] Crvena Stijena: Basler 1971 and Basler et al. 1975; Krapina: Alexander 1972.

[3] Adriatic region: Basler 1983; Lipci: Pušić 1971, also Brodar and Brodar 1983 (Aurignacian hunter complex in Slovenia).

open lands in the Danube basin saw the spread of grasslands where flourished cereal plants, including wheat, barley, oats and rye, later domesticated by man. In the woods and mountains there dwelt animals that are still typical of the region, deer, wild cattle, pigs and goats.[4]

Farming communities first appear in the lands between the Adriatic and the Danube in the context of the Starčevo Culture (*c*.6000–4500 BC), named after a site on the Danube a little below Belgrade. These are at present the earliest farming groups known north of the Vardar valley, and did not generally spread beyond the plains around Belgrade, that is northern Serbia, the Banat and Vojvodina. Some settlements of this culture have been found in eastern Bosnia at Gornja Tuzla, Obre north of Sarajevo, Varos, and also at Vučedol in Croatia (see figure 2). In northern Albania the Early Neolithic has been identified along the middle course of the Black Drin at Burim, farther upstream at Rajce and, in a later phase, at Kolsh near Kukës at the Drin confluence. In Central Albania the sites at Blaz in the Mat valley and in the Korcë

Figure 2 Reconstruction of Vučedol Eneolithic settlement

[4] Malez and Osole 1971.

basin are akin to the Adriatic Neolithic, identified at Smilčić near Zadar. The sites were evidently well chosen and continued in occupation sometimes for thousands of years. As occupation debris accumulated to form an artificial mound or 'tell', the many stratified layers have enabled archaeologists to construct elaborate chronologies, not only for individual sites but also relative to many others. From these has been deduced a 'spread' or 'advance' of farming methods, in the form of a slow north-ward movement towards the Middle Danube, that brought an increase in population and which either eliminated or integrated older communities of hunters and gatherers.[5]

The economy of these Neolithic farming 'tell'-sites was a mix of cereal farming, animal domestication and hunting and fishing. Crops included wheat, barley, millet and beans; livestock included cattle, pigs, sheep and goats. Implements included ground stone tools, axes and adzes, with large flaked tools as scrapers and sickle blades. Obsidian, a natural vol-canic form of glass obtained from Hungary, was also used for tools. Bone provided the material for needles, spoons and spatulas, and clay was baked for loom-weights and spindle-whorls. Human and animal figurines made of clay resemble those found in Greece and Asia Minor. They have a cylindri-cal shape, with no limbs and the head indicated only by incisions for the detail of features. The principal evidence for recognizing the successive phases and associations of these early farming communities consists of hand-made pottery of fired clay in a variety of forms, decorated with finger impressions, applied cordons and incised lines. South of the watershed farming methods had reached the southern Adri-atic coast by the middle of the sixth millenium. Pottery with incised and impressed ornament associated with ground stone implements has been found in many sites on the Dalmatian coast and islands. The large ditched enclosure at Smilčić near Zadar produced impressed pottery vessels similar to those of southern Italy, and the same pottery has been found on the

---

[5] Serbian Neolithic: Srejović 1988; Gornja Tuzla: Čović 1971a; Obre: Benac 1973; Varos: Benac 1971c; Vučedol: Schmidt 1945; also Divoštin: McPherron and Srejović 1988. Albanian sites: Korkuti 1987.

northern Adriatic islands Cres, Krk and Mali Lošinj in the Kvarner Gulf and on the mainland in caves of the Velebit mountains.[6]

The next phase of the Neolithic farming era in the Middle Danube is named from the site of Vinča, which is also on the Danube below Belgrade. The Vinča Culture (*c*.4500–4000 BC) around the southern edge of the Danube basin marks the spread of farming into the hills and valleys on the south and west towards the mountains and the Adriatic. The mixed economy based on cereals and livestock of this culture was similar to Starčevo but it is distinguished by its pottery which exhibits a greater variety of form and ornament. The shapes include carinated and straight-sided bowls with three- or four-footed pedestals, 'altars', or tables, with hollow feet and pots decorated with animal features. The decoration consists of burnishing in patterns and incised ribbon and maeander designs. For all the impression of innovation which this material conveys there is no evidence that the Vinča settlements represent any large-scale immigration into the lands west and south of the Middle Danube. Along the Adriatic coast the newer farming communities are distinguished by their painted pottery. This shows similarities with the pottery of Greece and Italy and also with the Trieste region (Vlaško Culture). It is named Danilo Culture from the long occupied hill settlement of Danilo Gornje near Šibenik, where the remains include 24 huts with floors partly paved with stone. There was an active stone-working tradition, while the pottery falls into two types, a painted ware with Italian connections and a burnished ware with spiral and maeander patterns. Danilo settlements are numerous along the coast and on the islands, in particular Hvar, but did not spread inland. There are no traces of early farming in the mountains and high valleys of Bosnia or Montenegro. In Albania the middle Neolithic has been identified at the settlements of Cakran on the lower Vijosë and at Dunarec in the Korcë basin.

---

[6] Adriatic Neolithic: Batović 1971a (Smilčić), 1976a, Mirosavljević 1971 (Cres), Rapanić 1984 (Cetina valley).

The closest ties appear to be with the Danilo Culture of the Dalmatian Adriatic and the early phase of Kakanj (Obre) in Bosnia, and also with some groups in southern Italy.[7]

Though metal objects do appear sporadically among implements of Neolithic farming communities, especially in Bosnia and on the Adriatic, the knowledge of metal-working and the use of implements of metal came late to the western Balkans. The spread of copper and bronze was a slow process: it was barely complete by around 2000 BC and even then for centuries after the use of metal was confined to a few simple forms of implement. Though it continues much debated, it seems to be still the view of some archaeologists that the spread of metal in the Danube lands was marked by a large-scale migration of new people into the area from steppes of western Asia and the Black Sea region. Moreover, many believe that this was the only major movement of population in the area, the later Aegean migrations that marked the end of the Bronze Age (1200 BC) being merely a southward shift of Balkan and lower Danube communities towards the Aegean and the Near East. The three phases of the Bronze Age in the western Balkans, Early Bronze 1900/1800–1600/1500 BC, Middle Bronze 1600/1500–*c*.1300 BC and Late Bronze to *c*.1200 BC, appear to be later and less sophisticated versions of those in the Danube basin, the eastern Balkans and the Carpathians, all of which reached full development by the end of the third millenium. Archaeologists currently believe that a gradual formation of local cultures and the ethnic groups they are judged to represent took place during the latest phase of the Stone Age (Eneolithic), and that these were consolidated rather than curtailed by the arrival of newcomers from the east. It is also suggested, though not uncontested, that these newcomers were Indo-European speakers. A symbiosis between these and the existing communities resulted in the formation of the principal tribal groups of what are now called the Palaeo-Balkan peoples. On this, it is suggested, there is warrant to base the hypothesis of an unbroken continuity in population from the Early Bronze Age

---

[7] Vlaško: Barfield 1971, 53–4; Danilo: Korošec 1958; Hvar: Novak 1955, 1971; Cakran: Korkuti and Andrea 1975; Dunavec: Korkuti 1975.

down to the first historical records of Balkan peoples. In this
equation the principal regional groups defined by characteristics
of their material culture are then identified with historical
groups thus: East Balkan Bronze Age represents Thracians, the
Balkano-Danubian the 'proto Daco-Moesians', and the West
Balkan the Illyrians.[8]

In the western Balkans there are few remains to connect with
these bronze-using 'proto-Illyrians', except in western Serbia
and eastern Bosnia. Moreover, with the notable exception of
Pod near Bugojno in the upper valley of the Vrbas, nothing is
known of their settlements. Some hill settlements have been
identified in western Serbia but the main evidence comes from
cemeteries, consisting usually of a small number of burial
mounds (tumuli). In eastern Bosnia at the cemeteries of Belotić
and Bela Crkva the rites of inhumation and cremation are
found, with skeletons in stone cists and cremations in urns.
Metal implements appear here side by side with those of stone.
Most of the remains belong to the fully developed Middle
Bronze Age. Similar burials have been discovered on the Glasinac plateau east of Sarajevo; several mounds are known to
have remained in use from the beginning of the Bronze Age.
Here inhumation is the dominant rite. The metal objects found
at these sites tend to be of Central European origin and remain
in use down to Iron Age times. It is these Bronze Age communities which have been identified as ancestors of the historical
Illyrians.[9]

Outside western Serbia and eastern Bosnia not a lot is known
of early metal-using communities. Objects of metal occur in
the established Neolithic settlements at Butmir and Lisičići and
in some of the caves on Hvar (Grabak and Zelena Pečina),
where bronze axe-picks, axe-hammers, chisels and flat axes
were in use by around 2000 BC. The impression of continuity
from the age of stone to that of metal comes also from the
cave dwelling at Hrustovača Pečina in the Sana valley and
the Debelo Brdo hill-settlement overlooking Sarajevo, which
acquired defences around this time. The pottery in use here

[8] M. Garašanin 1982a, 1988a.
[9] Pod, Bugojno: Čović 1971b, 1975b; Belotić and Bela Crkva: D. and M.
Garašanin 1971b; Glasinac: Benac and Čović 1956, Čović 1980–1.

shows similarities with that of metal-using communities in the Sava and Drava valleys (Vučedol and Slavonian cultures) and also, though in much smaller quantities, with pottery in the Hvar caves. A distinguishing feature of the Bronze Age is the practice of raising mounds of soil or stone above the burials of individuals. This was accompanied by an elaborate ritual, indicated by encircling rings of stones and the deposition of precious objects as grave goods, including battle axes and daggers. In Albania the first metal-using culture (Chalcolithic, 2600–2100 BC) is represented in the first and second levels at Maliq in the Korçë basin (see figure 3). The early houses were erected on oak piles, then later ones directly on the ground with walls of bundled reeds. Implements were of flint, polished stone, bone, horn and clay (weights for fishing nets) and included also copper axes, spearheads, needles and fish-hooks. There are links with other Balkan sites of this period, notably Bubanj in southern Serbia and Krivodol in Bulgaria, as well as some correspondences with Macedonian sites. Albanian archaeologists stress the essentially local character of this culture, where the earlier traditions have been detected as persisting even in newer phases that have been associated with a new immigrant ruling class.[10]

This rather tidy portrayal of a succession of early farming cultures using ground and flaked stone tools and then some largely imported metal implements comes to an end with the middle phase of the Bronze Age (1600/1500–*c*.1300 BC). The change is signified by the manifest ability of the people some identify as 'proto-Illyrians' to exploit the rich mineral deposits of Bosnia and Slovenia, notably copper, tin and gold. The techniques of using two- and three-piece moulds, casting-on, hammering and annealing become commonplace. The hoards of working tools and ingots testify to the specialist smith, and those of finished metal goods to the activity of the travelling merchant. Hitherto the Adriatic coast and hinterland were remote from the main centres of stone-using farmers and the first spread of metal. The balance now shifts in the sense that

[10] Butmir: Munro 1900, 189–217; Lisičići: Benac 1971a; Dalmatia: Marović 1976a, 1981; Maliq: Prendi 1977–8.

Figure 3 Remains of Neolithic pile-dwellings at Maliq, Albania

the Dalmatian coast is joined by sea routes with Italy and the
Aegean. Bronze objects reflecting contacts with the latter
include double axes, daggers, rapiers and ingots in the form of
miniature ox-hides, while links with the north are to be seen
in the trapeze-hilted dirk from the island of Osor and brooches
from Unešić near Šibenik. A few imports from the Mycenaean
Bronze Age of southern Greece, including a sword and some

Figure 4 Tumulus burial with central grave at Pazhok, Albania

pottery on Hvar, may represent seaborne trade. The middle of the second millennium may have seen the beginnings of the trade in amber objects down the Adriatic, from the south shore of the Baltic via the Vistula, Slovakia and around the eastern Alps to the head of the Adriatic. A relatively sudden expansion of external contacts may be reflected in an increased occurrence of weapons around the Adriatic.[11]

In Albania evidence for the Middle and Later Bronze Ages (*c.*2000–1200 BC) comes mainly from Maliq and from other sites in the Korcë basin and from the Mat valley in the north-west. At Maliq there is a break in continuity with earlier cultures, which some have linked with the arrival of Indo-European speakers in the Korcë basin. Their appearance is signified by pottery with corded decoration, and was followed by a process of fusion with existing communities. This period sees the beginning of the tumulus burials at Pazhok in the Devoll valley (see figure 4) and, slightly later, at Barç in the Korcë basin. The Middle Bronze Age (identified with Maliq phase IIIc) is held to represent a period of 'consolidation' and is also represented at the Nezir cave in the Mat valley. In this era the external links are predominantly with the Aegean cultures, from which imported objects include swords, daggers,

[11] Batović 1980a.

spearheads, knives and sickles. The varied and elegant forms of Late Bronze Age pottery (Maliq IIId; fifteenth-twelfth centuries BC) are decorated in red and ochre in geometric patterns, identified by Albanian archaeologists as 'Devollian ware' and believed to have remained in use unaltered until the end of the Iron Age. A wider distribution in Macedonia and Epirus is the basis for suggestions of a southward and eastward movement of Illyrian peoples. The large haul of bronze objects from burial tumuli, some of which continued in use for several centuries, include some local types, notably 'Skodran' axes found in northern Albania along with imported double axes and swords. Later these Aegean forms were to be replaced by northern types, among them socketed axes and tongue-grip swords.[12]

Just as ancient writers could discover no satisfactory general explanation for the origin of Illyrians, so most modern scholars, even though now possessed of a mass of archaeological and linguistic evidence, can assert with confidence only that Illyrians were not an homogeneous ethnic entity, though even that is today challenged with vigour by historians and archaeologists working within the perspective of modern Albania. Notions once widely canvassed of a 'proto-Illyrian' people of Indo-European origin once widespread across Europe were always at best unproven and have now been generally discarded. In the twenties and thirties of the twentieth century, belief in the existence of a European sub-stratum of now vanished Illyrians was an attractive idea to those bent on emphasizing the pure Aryan origin of the nordic peoples of Europe. In the other direction there seems now to be increasing scepticism towards theories of direct Illyrian involvement in the movement of new peoples into Greece at the end of the second millennium BC. Similarly, many have now discarded the simple identification of European Illyrians with the Urnfield Culture of Late Bronze Age Central Europe. This particular equation stemmed from the 'pan-Illyrian' theories propounded early this century by philologists who could discover traces of Illyrians scattered across the linguistic map of Europe.[13]

---

[12] Mat valley (Burrel): Kurti 1983; Pazhok: Bodinaku 1982; Barç: Andrea 1976b, 1977–8; Nezir: Andrea 1985, Prendi 1984 (axes).
[13] Illyrian ethnogenesis: Korkuti 1982, Prendi 1985b.

A more cautious reconstruction of Illyrian origins or 'ethnogenesis' has emerged from archaeologists at Sarajevo, notably A. Benac and B. Čović. Working from the relative abundance of prehistoric remains in Bosnia and adjacent areas, they suggest that during the Bronze Age there took place a progressive 'Illyrianization' of peoples dwelling in the lands between the Sava and the Adriatic. Since their homeland lay aside from the main route of migration across southeast Europe the movement of peoples at the end of the Bronze Age had relatively little impact on them. On the other hand, the beginnings of the Iron Age around 1000 BC is held to coincide with the formation of the historical Illyrian peoples. This hypothesis, based on a large mass of evidence, well excavated and fully analysed, has an internal consistency that is impressive and appears now to command the field. On the other hand, its value for Illyrian origins as a whole is limited, not least because it largely ignores the many contacts and presumed interactions between Illyrians and other cultures, notably those of the Mediterranean. Moreover, the 'Bosnia-centred' theory offers no explanation for the origins of differences between peoples historically designated as Illyrian, such as those between the Liburni in the northwest and the 'real Illyrians' of the southeast, in what is now Montenegro and northern Albania. It is, however, equally difficult to accept the view that such differences are due principally to the survival of populations with older cultures later subsumed into the family of the Indo-European-speaking Illyrians. Current theories of Illyrian ethnogenesis cannot fail to impress through their weight of archaeological evidence; but material remains alone can never tell the whole story and can mislead. Also, while it is true that Pan-Illyrian theories have been set aside, the questions which prompted their formulation still remain: there are traces of Illyrian names, and some historical tradition, for the presence of Illyrian peoples in parts of Europe beyond the limits of their historical homelands, and also in Asia Minor. What one is to make of these remains a problem. In general the linguistic evidence for Illyrians in Greece, Asia Minor and Italy is yet to be interpreted. In the case of Italy there is not only the testimony of names from literary sources and inscriptions but also indications in the archaeological evidence that there was a movement of peoples across the Adriatic

Library of
Davidson College

into Italy during the first century of the first millennium (1000–900 BC). Nonetheless the theory of an Illyrian migration across the Adriatic has been challenged by A. Benac, who argues that the Illyrian linguistic and material remains in Italy need amount to no more than the result of several centuries of commercial intercourse. In sum, the destructive impact of later research on the earlier generalizations regarding Illyrians should be regarded as a step forward. The problem remains for prehistorians how to construct a valid scheme of analysis with which to tackle the formation of Illyrians.[14]

Iron Age Illyrians[15]

The five centuries between the Late Bronze Age (1300/1200 BC) and the middle of the eighth century witnessed not only the spread of iron use and iron-working but mark for Greece and neighbouring lands the beginning of recorded history, when names and events are preserved and descriptions of peoples and places were first written down. The same period saw movements of people southwards to Macedonia, Greece and Asia Minor from the direction of the Danube and the southern Balkans. The years 1200–1050 BC, during which there took place in Greece the decline of Mycenaean fortresses and the beginning of the classical city-states, are marked among Illyrians by a rich material culture and contacts with the Aegean world. These links were then broken and were not to be re-created until around 800 BC. During the Early or Hallstatt (named from the site near Salzburg in Austria) Iron Age (mid-eighth to mid-fourth century BC), the first phase of Illyrian history, the principal external influences were the Greek Aegean and northern Italy (Bologna and Este). Though widespread from the seventh century onwards the Greeks had relatively

---

[14] Illyrian formation: Benac 1964, 1976, M. Garašanin 1988a; Illyrians in S. Italy: Benac 1988.
[15] Early Iron Age in Yugoslavia: Čović and Gabrovec 1971, M. Garašanin 1982b, Vasić 1973, Benac et al. 1987, Gabrovec 1964–5, 1966a (Slovenia), Vasić 1977 (chronology), Jevtić 1983 (pottery). In Albania: Prendi 1975a, 1985a, Hammond 1982a.

little impact on the material culture of the southern Illyrians (Bosnia, Serbia, Montenegro and Albania) until the expansion of Macedonia in the fourth century. By way of contrast the communities in Croatia, Slovenia and western Bosnia were deeply influenced by the Italic cultures, especially in parts of Slovenia (Lower Carniola). An invasion of horse-riding and cart-driving 'Thraco-Cimmerians' from the direction of the Black Sea was once thought to have influenced the western Balkans at the start of the Iron Age but this is now doubted. On the other hand, the expansion of Achaemenid Persia into the southern Balkans is believed to be the likely explanation for significant cultural influences from that direction during the late sixth and early fifth centuries.[16]

Since the first excavations at the end of the nineteenth century the Glasinac group has been the best known of the Late Bronze and Early Iron Age communities in the western Balkans. Their centre is the Glasinac plateau east of Sarajevo, but the complex of material culture now extends to include sites in western Serbia around Užice (Ražana, Kriva Reka, Godljevo, Štrpci, Pilatovići and others) and in northern Montenegro (Gotovuša and Barakovac). Linked with Glasinac are groups around Sarajevo (Debelo Brdo, Zlatište and Sobunar), in northeast Bosnia (Dvorovi near Bjelina), in Serbia (Šabač, Mramorac, Umčari, Novi Pazar and others), in northern Albania (Mat, Burrel, Çinamak, Kushi and others) and the adjacent southern Adriatic (Gubavica near Mostar, Radimlja, Plana, Kačanj, Mosko, Ljubomir, Glogovik and others). The typical Glasinac settlement is a fortified hill-top (see figure 5a), of which not one has yet been fully examined. Burials consist of skeletons beneath earth tumuli defined by stone circles of around ten metres diameter and often contain two to four graves (see figure 5b). Down to the sixth century tumuli occur in groups of around ten but later the number increases. Major tombs contain a central burial surrounded by rough stones, with secondary burials around, outside the stone enclosure and generally orientated east–west. The graves are often rich in finds but the contents vary. The presence of quantities of weapons indicate a

[16] Etruscan influences: Starè 1975.

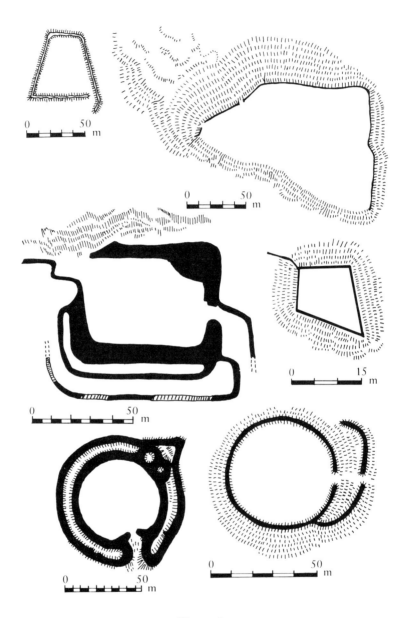

Figure 5
a) Plan of settlements on the Glasinac plateau

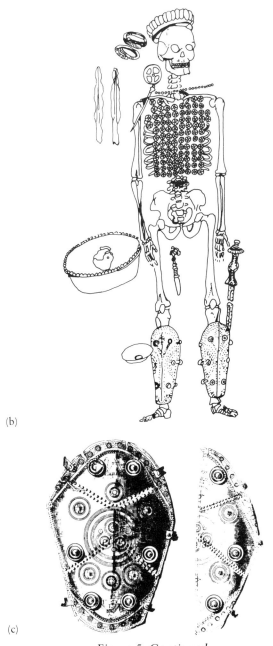

(b)

(c)

Figure 5 Continued
b) Chieftain burial at Glasinac (Ilijak, Tumulus II)
c) Bronze greaves from Glasinac burial

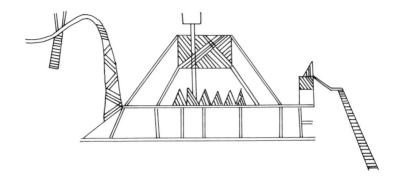

Figure 5 Continued
d) Design of ship incised on bronze greaves from Glasinac

dominant warrior class (see figures 5c and 5d). An increase in
cremation graves during the late sixth and early fifth centuries
may reflect a collapse of the tribal structure and change in
prevailing religious belief.[17]

Settlements and associated burials persisted at Glasinac until
the late fourth century, having continued without significant
interruption from the developed (Middle) Bronze Age. It has
been estimated that at the height of its prosperity from the
eighth to sixth centuries the population of the area had
increased by a factor of seven. The emergence of a local ruling
elite suggested by tombs containing prestigious imports marks
a concentration of power in eastern Bosnia comparable with
that which appeared around a century later in Slovenia. During
the sixth century the rulers of Glasinac may have been
expanding their power in several directions. Nevertheless Glasinac itself remained out of direct contact with the Greek world,
an isolation that may have accelerated a decline after the early
fifth century. The rapid falling-away in the number of burials
before the end of the fourth century seems to indicate a general
desolation, probably marked by the departure of whole groups
towards the expanding world of Greece and Macedonia.

Excavations of tumuli in northern and central Albania have

[17] Glasinac culture: Benac and Čović 1957, Čović 1979, Govedarica 1978.

furnished significant evidence for the southernmost Illyrians. The area known to the Greeks as Illyris lay between the Lakes and the Adriatic, and included the valleys of the Black and the united Drin, Mat, Shkumbin and Seman, and the coastal plain as far south as the river Vijosë. In the Zadrimë plain around the lower Fan and Mat most tombs contain single warrior-graves with numerous weapons. In the cemetery at Burrel there are 80 tumuli of this type. In character and content these graves match those of Glasinac and there can be no doubt that there was some connection between the two groups though the nature of that link remains a subject of debate between Yugoslav and Albanian archaeologists. Burials continued down to the fourth century, though in decreasing numbers. Down to the end of the sixth century an abundance of weapons, including spears, curved swords, knives, battle-axes and, in a few cases, bronze cuirasses, helmets and greaves, is testimony to the power of a warrior class. Their jewellery and bronze brooches are also similar to those found in Glasinac burials. Cemeteries of tumuli have been explored in the Drin valley between Debar and Kukës, notably at Çinamak (67 tumuli), Kënetë (see figure 6) and Kruma. Several features of their construction, including enclosing the burial within stone slabs, of ritual, such as smashing pots on the surface of the rising tumulus, and content, including a taste for amber ornaments, link these communities with those of the Mat valley to the west. The earliest tumuli date from the Late Bronze Age and some continued in use as late as the fourth century. Linked with these groups are those whose tumuli cemeteries with cremations lie across the Yugoslav border in southern Kosovo (Dibičak near Suva Reka and Romaja near Prizren), whose iron weapons, two-handled cups and poor-quality ornaments match those from graves at Kënetë and Kruma. At the same time the burials in Zadrimë and the Mat differ from those of the Drin valley, which also continued down to the fourth century, in the use of iron for weapons but bronze for ornament. In the latter iron is employed for both, while silver pins occur in burials of the late sixth century.[18]

[18] Prehistoric tumuli in N. Albania: Kurti 1985, 1987 (Burrel), 1971, 1976a (Mat), Hoti 1982 (Bardhoc), Jubani 1982 (Kruma), 1983 (Kënetë); in Kosovo: Jubani 1985, 1986a, Slavković-Djurǐ 1964 (Suva Reka), Djurić

Figure 6 Tumulus graves at Kënetë, Albania

In central Albania the cemetery of 25 tumuli at Pazhok commenced in the Late Bronze Age (*c.*1300 BC) but would appear to have gone out of use by 700 BC, though many of its tumuli have yet to be explored. Further east in the Korcë basin, which lies south of the Lakes, the great tumulus at Barç (41 m diameter) contained a primary burial of the Late Bronze Age. After a considerable interval burials began to be inserted into the mound and continued for around three centuries until around 850 BC. So far nearly 200 graves have been recovered, representing a large ruling elite rather than the succession of a single dynasty. The earlier burials contained jewellery and ornaments of gold and bronze, an early variety of the 'spectacle'-brooch, and pottery decorated with knobs and nipples, the so-called Devoll ware. The burials at Barç contain signifi-

Glišić and Todorović 1975 (Romaja); in Montenegro: Parović-Pešikan 1976 (Kotor), Pušić 1976 (Kotor), Leković 1980 (Njegoši), Srejović 1980–1 (Lisijevo polje).

cantly fewer weapons than those in the Mat and Drin valleys. As a whole they appear to relate more closely with a group of burials a few miles to the south at Kuç i Zi, also in the Korcë basin, which so far represent the most southerly extension of the Glasinac–Mat material culture. The earlier of two tumuli (29 m diameter) contained five cremations in urns and many skeleton burials in trenches, some of which were stone-lined. Many weapons were recovered, among them swords, spears, arrows, knives and choppers, while ornaments include bronze bracelets, beads and pendants, which match closely those from southern Kosovo and Glasinac. One suggestion is that these burials belong to a ruling dynasty of the eighth century that had moved to the area from somewhere in the Glasinac region to the north. Also connected with this regime may be the complexes of fortifications guarding entry to the Korcë plain, which Albanian archaeologists have dated to the ninth and eighth centuries. These include Symize and Bellovode on the west, Bilisht in the south, and the group around Tren on the east, controlling the 'Wolf's pass' (Gryke e Ujkut) leading to Little Prespa Lake. The 18 burials in the second tumulus at Kuç i Zi, beginning around the middle of the seventh century, are skeleton graves with few weapons and no 'Glasinac' jewellery. Some of the pottery is hand-made in local forms but most is wheel-made and imitates Greek forms. Greek imported pottery was also found and there were two examples of mouthpieces of sheet gold tied across the faces of the deceased. The marked differences between the burials in the two tumuli at Kuç i Zi may represent the difference in material culture between a ruling dynasty of northern (Glasinac) origins and one with southern connections that ruled until some time after the middle of the sixth century. According to one reconstruction (Hammond) we have the evidence for an Illyrian dynasty being replaced by a Chaonian regime from northern Epirus.[19]

The communities on the east and southeast borders of the Glasinac province remain little known. In southern Serbia and Kosovo the Early Iron-Age communities are represented by

[19] Sites in central Albania: Bodinaku 1975, 1982 (Pazhok); Andrea 1975 (Barç), 1976b, 1977–8 (Kuç i Zi), 1976a (Korcë basin culture); Korkuti 1971, 1973, 1976 (Tren fortifications).

cemeteries of 'flat' urn-burials dated mainly to the eighth century. Those at Donja Brnjica, Gornja Stražava, Donja Toponica
(which continues into the seventh century), Karagač, and
others, represent a distinct local group (Donja Brnjica). The
burial urns were covered with stone slabs, above which, in the
case of later burials, a mound of earth was raised. These
cemeteries appear to represent communities which had
developed from earlier local groups and exhibit few signs of
outside contacts. Further south another local group has been
identified in southern Kosovo around Suva Reka in the Topluga
basin north of Prizren, where sites include the hill-forts Belaće-
vac and Hisar and cremation graves at Široko. The settlements
and cemeteries of this group, which has similarities with those
in the Black Drin valley, were in use between the eighth and
fifth centuries.[20]

In northern Serbia the hilly country south of Belgrade has
produced several hoards and tombs of the late eighth and
seventh centuries (Rudovci, Barajevo, Rodišić, Žirovnica, Rož-
anci, Rtanj, Aljudov Manastirica, etc.). Their contents have
been compared with those from burials across the Danube
in southwest Transylvania (Bilvaneşti-Vinţ), Wallachia (Balta
Verde and Gura Padinei) and also in Bulgaria (Drzhanica). East
of the river Morava tumulus burials containing both skeletons
and cremations of the late seventh and sixth centuries have
been identified as a group from the metal-working centre at
Zlot, a cave-site in eastern Serbia (Vrtište, Vranovo, Dub,
Konopnica). The associated black-burnished pottery appears to
belong to the Basarabi tradition of southwest Romania, which
extends into northwest Serbia and Slavonia. Pins characteristic
of the Zlot group occur at several sites in northwest Bulgaria,
mainly west of the river Iskar. The presence of both burial rites
beneath tumuli has been interpreted as the result of the local
tradition (cremation) being mixed with burial customs originating from the area of Glasinac and also from the south.[21]

Large quantities of material have been recovered from burials

---

[20] Srejović 1971 (Donja Brnjica), 1973 (Karagač), Trbuhović and Trbuhović
1970 (Donja Toponica), Ercegović-Pavlović and Kostić 1988 (S. Serbia)
[21] Vasić 1972, Dumitrescu 1976 (Basarabi), Kosorić 1976 (Drina basin),
Stojić 1986 (Morava basin).

in areas bordering Illyrian lands on the southeast, the historical regions of Pelagonia around Bitola, Paeonia around Štip, along with the middle section of the Vardar (Axios) valley, north of the Demir Kapija gorge, historic Lychnitis around Ohrid and in Dardania around Skopje in the upper Vardar basin. Among the many tumuli surviving in Pelagonia only Visoi has so far been fully investigated. A central grave aligned west–east, lined and covered with stones, was surrounded by dozens of radially located skeleton burials in similar graves. There are other tumuli dated to the eighth century whose contents indicate an origin in the Glasinac province. In the fertile region of Paeonia around Štip tumulus cemeteries of the Early Iron Age (Orlovi Čuki, Gorno Pole near Star Karaorman, Radanje, Kunovi Čuki, Donje Orizare and others) have a central stone-lined grave surrounded by others in a radial formation, while the pottery forms also suggest links with the north and the northwest.[22] The appearance in Pelagonia and Paeonia of these tumuli burials apparently closely connected with the Glasinac province has been interpreted as evidence for a temporary Illyrian domination of these regions. Using a fragment from Strabo's account of Macedonia (now missing from his *Geography*), Hammond has identified the evidence for an ephemeral Illyrian domination of that country. Eighth-century burials in the great cemetery at Vergina on the river Haliacmon in the coastal plain of Macedonia which contain 'spectacle'-brooches, diadems, bronze belt-plates and, down to the mid-seventh century, numerous spears (often in pairs) and bronze pendants, are testimony for the presence of Illyrians. Marking a relative decline in material wealth these newcomers from the north may represent an abrupt change of ruling class. An Illyrian presence has also been detected in the tumuli of Pelagonia (Visoi and Prilep), in Eordaea (Pateli), along the course of the lower Vardar (Axiupolis, Gevgheli and Chauchitsa) and in Paeonia. Here the bronze pendants, beads and buttons from Radanje and Orlovi Čuki and the burial arrangements match those at Visoi, and the Illyrian presence here may have persisted

---

[22] Vasić 1976, Mikulčić 1966, 1971 (Pelagonia), Simoska and Sanev 1976 (central Pelagonia), Pašić-Vinčić 1970 (Orlova Čuka), D. Garašanin 1976 (Radanje), Kitanoski 1983 (burial rites in Pelagonia).

until the end of the seventh century. This Illyrian dominance lasting overall from around 850 to around 650 BC at various times encompassed most of the northern and western areas of ancient Macedonia.[23]

Evidence for the Early Iron Age in regions to the west of Glasinac is both small in quantity and uneven in distribution. In central and western Bosnia, Hercegovina and Central Dalmatia no major settlement of the period has yet been investigated, with the exception of Pod near Bugojno in the Vrbas valley (see figure 7). This hill-top settlement was occupied from the Middle Bronze to the Late Iron Age and has yielded exceptional evidence for a regular arrangement of streets and houses as early as the period from the tenth to the eighth century. In western Hercegovina there is sufficient in common in the material from the period of the sixth to fourth centuries from a number of sites to identify a local group (Gorica, Crvenica, Posušje, Postranje, Zagvozd, Grude, Drinovci, Petrovići-

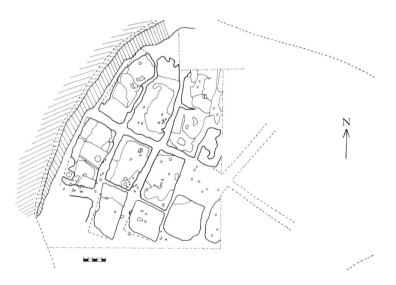

Figure 7 Plan of hill-settlement at Pod, Bugojno (later phase)

[23] Hammond 1970, 1972 ch. 14, 1982a; Georgiev 1978 (Kumanovo grave).

Rakitno) along with Ston at the base of the Pelješac peninsula and finds on the islands Brač (Vičja Luka) and Korčula (Blato). Though the area is dominated by numerous fortified hill-settlements (gradina), most of the evidence so far recovered comes from 'flat' skeleton-graves built of stone slabs. Since these often contain more than one inhumation they were evidently family tombs. Cremation occurs at Gorica (after which this group is named) near the northeastern edge of the Imotsko polje. The most distinctive feature of the Gorica group is the large number of weapons, including iron spears, curved, short swords and knives, many later versions of the 'Greco-Illyrian' helmet and several imported greaves (Ston, Zagvozd and Vičja Luka). Before the sixth century this was a group of predominantly local character which then evidently increased its power and prosperity through contacts with the Greek Adriatic and southern Italy, enabling a southward expansion towards the coast and islands.[24]

The material record in northwest Bosnia, including the middle Sava and the lower courses of its principal tributaries (Sana-Una, Vrbas and Bosna) is dominated in the Early Iron Age by the major settlements and accompanying cemeteries at Donja Dolina on the Sava near Bosanska Gradiška, and by Sanski Most amid the rich iron-ore deposits around the lower Sana. Donja Dolina began as a settlement of pile-dwellings on the river, but by the Late Iron Age the river deposits and occupation debris had raised the site above water level and the pile-dwellings were replaced. The settlement was enclosed with a wooden palisade plastered with mud. The rectangular houses generally contained three rooms, one with a hearth of fired clay (see figure 8a). The houses were linked by raised wooden walkways in a regular arrangement so as to form narrow streets. The flat cemetery alongside the pile-dwellings contained skeletons laid in wooden coffins or directly on the earth (see figure 8b).

The occupation of Donja Dolina lasted from the seventh to

---

[24] Western Bosnia: Čović 1971b (Pod, Bugojno), Benac 1971d (Zečovi, Prijedor), Čović 1961–2 (Crvenica, Duvno); Gorica group: Čović 1975c (Vitina), Marović 1961–2, 1963–5 (Brač), 1979 (Cetina valley), 1981 (Brač), Protić 1985 (Vis), Radmilli 1970 (Lastovo).

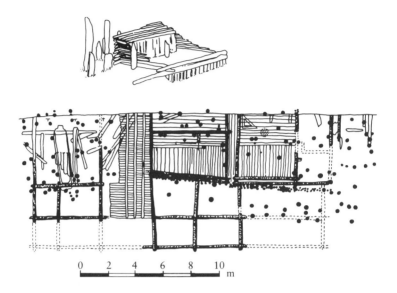

0   2   4   6   8   10
                            m

Figure 8 a) Plans and sections of houses at Donja Dolina

the first century BC, and indeed longer if it was a direct continuation of the closeby Gornja Dolina of the Pannonian Urnfield
Culture occupied from the twelfth century. Climatic change
may have caused the abandonment of this settlement and some
of the inhabitants may have moved to occupy a pile-settlement
at the river's edge. But it was only towards the end of the
seventh century that this fairly insignificant riverside settlement
was transformed into a major centre of exchange for the
northwest Balkans, signalled by the appearance of exotic
objects from cultures as remote as Greece and northern Italy.
Doubtless its position on a major navigable river contributed
to this advance but the rise to commercial prominence is probably to be explained by the emergence of greatly enriched ruling
groups on the west in Slovenia and to the east and southeast
in the Glasinac complex. Whether or not Donja Dolina was
itself the centre for one of these new powers is hard to tell, if
only because of its relative isolation. On the other hand, the
presence of well-armed warriors in its community may indicate
some degree of local independence. Though not deserted until
Roman times the commercial prominence of Donja Dolina

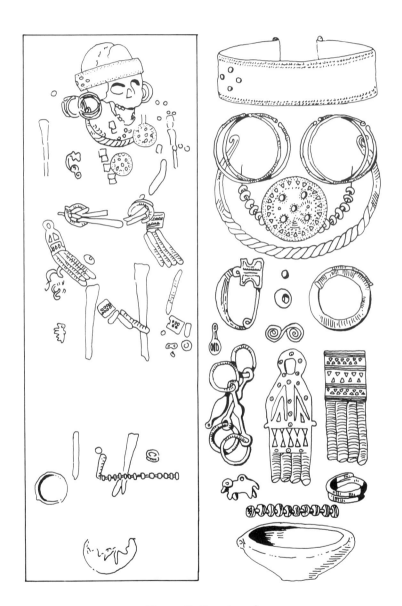

Figure 8 Continued
b) Woman's grave at Donja Dolina, with objects enlarged

appears to have vanished as rapidly as it had arrived, during the fourth century when many changes, including the Celtic migrations, disrupted long-distance trade patterns which had been established for around two centuries.[25]

At Sanski Most houses with hearths were found alongside the river Sana. There were also round forging-furnaces together with implements for smelting and forging iron, which was evidently the principal activity carried on in the settlement. Not far away a 'flat' cemetery contained skeleton burials and cremation urns, the latter probably of later date, with a few graves lined and covered with stones. Pottery similar to that of Donja Dolina includes single- or double-handled cups and bowls, but the later cremation urns, large and biconical, are similar to those in the cemeteries further to the west around Bihać in the Una valley. Jewellery in the graves at Sanski Most appears to be a mixture of Slovenian (brooches, belt-buckles and bracelets) and western Bosnian (Japodian) types (pins, bronze discs, temple bands and decorated bronze buttons). Weapons found at Sanski Most include iron spears and single-edged short swords. A double-edged Greek sword and two pairs of greaves, also imports, were recovered. Most of the graves date to the fifth and fourth centuries and, taken as a whole, the material culture appears to reflect a group of local origin, though imitating some Slovenian forms. What appears to have been a shift in burial rite from inhumation to cremation, similar to that observed at Glasinac and elsewhere has been taken as evidence for the arrival of new people from the north.[26]

In the region of Slavonia lying between the middle and lower courses of the Drava and Sava a significant discovery has been the cemetery near the hill-fort at Kaptol near Požega, in a valley enclosed by low hills. Tumuli of the Early Iron Age were found to incorporate a stone-built chamber containing up to five cremations, both with and without urns. The polished black pottery, mainly in biconical forms, has incised geometric decoration and moulded additions such as animals' heads. In addition to iron spears and battle-axes there were imported helmets, a

---

[25] Donja Dolina: Truhelka 1904 and 1909, Marić 1964a.
[26] Fiala 1899 (Sanski Most), Marić 1971b (Vis, Drventa).

Corinthian type and an early version of the 'Greco-Illyrian' helmet, and a pair of greaves that may be presumed to have reached this site via Donja Dolina, since there are close resemblances between the material from the two sites. The Kaptol burials belong to an established local warrior elite of the sixth century similar to those in the Glasinac region, although here horses were more important to judge from the presence of horse-bits and other tackle in the tombs.[27]

To the east of the Kaptol group a major community of the Early Iron Age has been identified in the region around the mouths of the Drava and Sava, including the district of Srem, northern Serbia and the Banat plain across the Danube in the region of Vojvodina. This group appears to be linked with that of Basarabi, named after a site on the Danube near Calafat in southwest Romania, whose distinctive pottery appears in many settlements within the above area. The most significant finds come from two major hill-forts which have been excavated, Bosut near the Sava west of Sremska Mitrovica, near the mouth of the river Bosut, and Gomolova, a major 'tell'-like settlement also on the left bank of the Sava, a few miles downstream from Mitrovica. Excavation here on a large scale revealed long-established settlements commencing around the middle of the eighth century with large houses containing altars of fired clay. The connection between Bosut-Gomolova and the Basarabi group may have once been close, but by the sixth century these links appear to have diminished, when local characteristics in the pottery become more evident. The material culture of these settlements was altogether different from those of the communities represented by the several large urn cemeteries around Dalj, near the mouth of the Drava, which are a later continuation of the Urnfield Culture in the transition from Bronze to Iron, although no settlement has yet been investigated. It is in this area that an apparently sudden and widespread distribution of bronze horse-harness of the late eighth and seventh centuries has been interpreted as the evidence for an invasion of horse-riding groups from the direction of the Black Sea and South Russia, the so-called Thraco-Cimmerians. There appears to be

[27] Veyvoda and Mirnik 1971, 1973 (Kaptol), Vinski-Gasparini 1978.

a growing scepticism towards the reality of this invasion, and some specialists now prefer the simpler explanation that with the spread of iron use came an increase in the use of the horse in the plains.[28]

By far the largest quantity of material evidence for the Early Iron Age in the Illyrian lands comes from the northwest, western Croatia including the northern Adriatic and the Istrian peninsula, and Slovenia in the southeastern Alps. In the 'Level Corner' (Ravni Kotari) around Zadar on the Adriatic, between the rivers Krka and Zrmanja the material culture of the historical Liburnians has been recovered in abundance from their cemeteries and their settlements. The latter include hill-top sites such as Radovin and Bribir which, like others yet to be investigated, were later fortified with walls of dressed stone and in the Roman era were formally constituted as self-governing cities. Other, low-lying sites on the coast such as Zadar and Nin were also to be developed later as Roman cities. The settlements at Radovin and Nin have furnished evidence for stone defences and stone houses, arranged in rows parallel with the ramparts and with a central open space. Inhumation appears to have been the preferred burial rite, with skeletons placed in a crouched position in graves that are sometimes lined with stone slabs. Large clay vessels were often used for the burial of children. Most graves were in 'flat' cemeteries but a few tumuli, some containing several graves, are recorded. By comparison with that of other groups the pottery of the Liburnians is relatively little known as it rarely occurs in graves. There are quantities of imported wares, including Daunian from south Italy, some Hellenistic and a small quantity of classical Greek. The main finds consist of jewellery, on the basis of which Batović has been able to suggest an elaborate chronology for Liburnian material culture. In contrast, weapons are almost unknown, save for some eighth-century bronze two-

[28] Brukner 1971, Tasić 1972 (Gomolava), Medović 1978 (chronology), Tasić 1988 (ethnic identities), Vasić 1989 (Banoštor graves).

edged swords from Nin. Over the six main phases of development there appears to be a continuity from the ninth century down to the Roman era.[29]

Behind the Velebit mountains along the coast between Liburnia and Istria the high plain of Lika has proved exceptionally rich in Iron Age finds that may be taken to represent the material culture of the historical Japodes. Several major cemeteries, notably Prozor and Kompolje, have yielded many artefacts, while several settlements (Vrebac and Mali Obljaj), including cave-sites, have been identified and partly investigated. The hill-forts were protected by ramparts of stone blocks and earth and contained rectangular houses. Both 'flat' and tumulus cemeteries occur, the former being more common with skeletons laid in stone-lined graves. Cremation was already spreading into the area in the eighth century and by the fourth had become the dominant rite, both with and without urns. As in the case of that of their Liburnian neighbours on the south, the chronology of Japodian material culture is based upon jewellery rather than pottery. Contacts of the Lika communities with the Adriatic appear to have passed via the Liburnians but when the power of the latter declined contact with northern Italy may have become closer. By this time the Lika Japodes had evidently moved across the Velebit to control the coast between the Zrmanja and Istria. In the fourth century they also evidently expanded northwards to dominate the Vinica area of Lower Carniola. To the east the Una valley around Bihać appears to have come under Japodian control by the fifth century. Some early graves of the eighth and seventh centuries are seen to exhibit closer parallels with groups further east in Bosnia and Hercegovina but by the end of the fifth century graves in the major cemeteries at Jezerine, Golubić and Ribić, in use continuously down to the Roman period, exhibit a cultural unity with the Lika. By the middle of the fourth century what can be identified with reasonable certainty as the material culture of the historical Japodes had become one of the major

---

[29] Liburnians: Batović 1965, 1976b, 1970 (Nin), 1968, 1971b (Radovin), 1980b (Bribir), 1976c (Adriatic connections), Ćus-Rukonić 1980–1 (Osor).

groups in the western Balkans, reaching from the river Zrmanja in the south to the Kupa in the north and from the Adriatic to the Una valley.[30]

An area where the material culture of the Early Iron Age has an exceptional richness and distinctive character is the valley of the Krka around Novo Mesto, the area of Slovenia known as Dolensko (formerly Lower Carniola). Later the Dolensko appear to have expanded westwards into the area of Upper Carniola around Ljubljana. A major settlement of this region, the only one so far excavated, lay at Stična in the hills between Novo Mesto and Ljubljana and was occupied continuously from the end of the eighth century to the Roman period. An area of around 800 by 400 metres is enclosed by a wall of several phases built of large undressed limestone blocks (up to 3 by 1.5 m) and with earth and small stones packed between, which was backed with an earth rampart. After the original construction the defences of Stična were remodelled in the fifth and sixth centuries. Around the time that the Stična settlement was becoming established there appear in the area tumuli burials that replace the cemeteries of the Urnfield Culture dating from the tenth to eighth centuries. What this change represents is today much debated. By the late seventh and sixth centuries large tumuli appear with skeleton burials in a radial arrangement around an unoccupied centre, enclosed by stone slabs or wooden coffins or simply laid in the earth. The similarities between these burials and those of Bosnia and Macedonia has supported a hypothesis of a migration into Carniola from the southeast that was associated with an exploitation of the minerals in which the region is rich. The skeleton burials are for the most part confined to the Dolensko area. Certainly the case for these being immigrants from Bosnia appears to be strong, but unfortunately there are too many gaps in the archaeological record of the intervening areas for there to be any certainty in the matter.[31]

[30] Japodes: Drechsler-Bižić 1975b, 1958 (Vrebac), 1961, 1966, 1971 (Kompolje), 1972–3 (Prozor), 1975a (Osik, Gospić), Marić 1971a (Una valley), 1975a (eastern frontier), Radimsky 1895 (Jezerine), Radimsky et al. 1897 (Ripač), Raunig 1971a (Golubić), 1980–1 (Ripač).
[31] Dolensko (Lower Carniola) group: Archeološka Najdišča Slovenije

The early pottery of the Dolensko group soon breaks away from the Urnfield traditions as new pedestal forms begin to appear. Next there follows a fashion of imitating metal vessels, with vertical and horizontal ribbing. Imported pottery from Venetic northeast Italy also reached the area, along with wares from Apulia and Greece (Attica). From the late seventh century the Dolensko culture is distinguished by an abundance of metal vessels, including buckets, situlae (water-buckets for the ritual of wine-drinking), cauldrons, tankards, etc. Much of this metal-work was evidently produced locally, satisfying a great demand on the part of the ruling elite. The decoration of metal vessels and other objects evolved into the remarkable collection of styles known today as Situla Art, which reached its fullest development in Dolensko only in the fifth century, when numer-ous examples of situlae with figural decoration occur in tombs. The origins of the craftsmanship and of the style of Situla Art would appear to lie further west among the Veneti, where the earliest examples are dated to the late seventh century. Possibly there was a transfer of workshops from that area to Dolensko brought about by changes underway in northeast Italy. Here the appetite for traditional fashions in metal ornament was giving way to a taste for the finer and more elegant productions of the Greeks and Etruscans. The old style may have suited the rulers in Dolensko, direct, uncomplicated and explicit in reflecting their own ways of life. If the workshops identified in such places as Vače, Magdalenska Gora and Novo Mesto were those of craftsmen trained among the Veneti then what may have been a speculative venture turned out to be a great success. On a large variety of metalware, including also belt-buckles, scabbards, brooches and pendants, the Situla style becomes the distinguishing feature of the Dolensko Culture (see figure 9). Large quantities of weapons and some armour are also a feature of the Dolensko Culture. The most common are spears and socket-axes and there are some bows and arrows. Helmets

(inventory and map of sites), Frey 1966, Gabrovec 1964–5, 1966a, Dular 1982 (pottery), 1983 (Črnomelj), Frey and Gabrovec 1969, Gabrovec, Frey and Foltiny 1970, Gabrovec 1975 (Stična), Wells 1978 (Stična), 1980 (Magdalenska gora), Knez 1978, 1980b (Novo Mesto), Puš 1982–3 (Ljubljana), Pahić 1973 (Slovenian Drava).

Figure 9a) Burial tumulus at Stična, 1964 excavations

occur in tombs over the period from the eighth to the fourth centuries. In the seventh century there appears a local variety of helmet, bowl-shaped and made of leather strengthened with bronze studs. This was replaced later by an Italic design made of bronze pieces forged together, replaced in turn by a double-crested type. In the fifth century there appears a much more durable type of Italic helmet named after the find at Negau (now Negova), on the river Mur near Gornja Radgona in north-east Slovenia, which had a long period of use over a wide area. The examples of bronze body-armour found in tombs at Stična and Novo Mesto were imported and have been dated to the late seventh century. The trappings for horse-harness are also common in Dolensko, with examples of spurs appearing in the fifth century.[32]

[32] Situla art: Knez 1976, 1980a, 1983.

Figure 9b) Scenes on Vače situla

The current chronology and analysis of the Dolensko Culture and its outliers is based largely on the work of Gabrovec. According to this scheme the first phase, which lasts from the mid-eighth to the mid-seventh century, is marked by the coincidence of iron-working and tumuli burials with pottery and jewellery made in local shapes. From the seventh to the

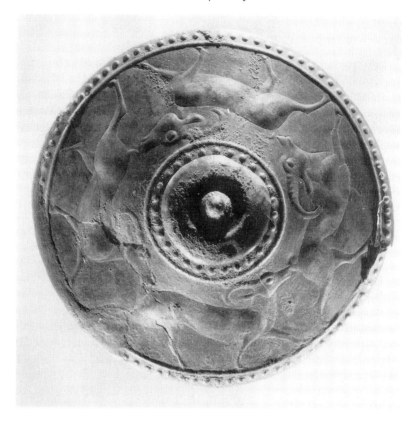

Figure 9c) Bronze situla-cover from Stična

fourth centuries Italic influences increase and the local warrior elite displays a steadily increasing material prosperity, reflecting an expansion of their power over neighbouring communities. At the height of their prosperity in the fifth century the military role becomes less prominent in favour of images of an elite taking their pleasures against the background of a stable political ascendancy. This has been inferred specifically from the changing repertoire of Situla Art, where the battle themes and warriors appear to give way to the pleasures of the hunt, and such agreeable pastimes as banqueting and musical and athletic festivals. The golden age soon passed and during the early fourth century there begin large cemeteries of warrior graves, but it has been concluded that by the end of the fourth century this area had been taken over and settled by Celts.[33]

The tract of hilly country extending southwest from Lower Carniola towards Istria, known as Notranjska (Inner Carniola), has produced several important sites of the Iron Age, notably the cave shrine of Škocjan (St Kanzian), though no single place has yet furnished evidence for a continuous occupation from Hallstatt (Early Iron Age) to La Tène (Late Iron Age) times. The metal hoard and flat cemetery at Škocjan have produced brooches, bowls, helmets and spears that in some respects resemble those from the Dolensko area and from St Lucia. Similar material has also been found in the cemeteries at Socerb and Štanjel. The hill-top settlement at Šmihel has three associated flat cemeteries, one of the eighth–seventh centuries, the others containing mainly fourth-century graves. The material from the cemetery at Križna gora of the eighth–sixth centuries is different from that in the rest of Notranjska and has similarities with the Lika group, while the fact that a third of the graves contain skeletons seems another indication of links with communities further south. It has been suggested that the interruption of cemeteries in this area after the seventh century was caused by the domination of the Dolensko group. Similarly a recovery of local independence, following decline of the latter's power, may be signified by the reappearance of major cemeteries in the fourth century.[34]

The Iron Age communities of the Istrian peninsula at the head of the Adriatic are known from several sites, where the finds suggest that a single cultural group had formed by the eighth century. Their typical fortified settlements on hill-tops had begun to be occupied already in Bronze Age times. These castellieri, as they are known in Istria, often enclose two or three crests, with single or multiple ramparts on the naturally unprotected sides. They vary greatly in situation and in physical character, from just above sea-level to around 700 metres, and from an area of a few hundred square metres to vast complexes

[33] Dolensko history: Frey and Gabrovec 1971 (chronology), Gabrovec 1973, Petru 1973, Mason 1988, Teržan 1985.
[34] Notranjska group: Guštin 1973 (chronology), Urleb 1973 (Križna gora).

of several square kilometres. They contained rectangular timber and clay houses. Burial was in flat cremation cemeteries, sometimes without but mainly with urns, in a stone-lined grave that was sometimes covered. Boundary walls of a dry-stone construction defined family burial plots. The dead were cremated wearing their clothes and their jewellery. Skeleton burials are rare. A particular feature of the Istrian material culture are the carved stones from Nesactium on the east coast. Here a princely tomb suggests that predecessors of the kings who reigned there in the third and second centuries were already wielding power in the fifth. There is much yet to be understood about the Istrian culture of the Iron Age, and publication of some of the major collections of evidence will assist in this regard. There seems little doubt that what was basically the product of local evolution over several centuries was from the sixth to fourth centuries much altered by Italic influences. The origins of some elements may lie in the impact of the Pannonian Urnfield Culture on local Bronze Age groups, from which several traits, including grave-construction, pottery ornament and the lack of brooches, continued down to the first appearance of Italic influences. As a result of these, Istria became part of a more uniform, Italic-dominated complex around the Adriatic, which included Liburnia and the Lika.[35]

In the Alpine valley of the river Soča or Isonzo several large cemeteries, including St Lucia containing more than 7000 graves, together form a distinct group. They belong to the inhabitants of hill-fort settlements of which as yet little is known. The graves were lined and covered with stone slabs and contained the cremated remains of the deceased wearing clothes and jewellery. The graves contain pottery, metal vessels and jewellery but are devoid of weapons. The Soča group seems to have consisted of a local culture, somewhat isolated in the southeast Alps, which was radically altered by Italic influences in the course of the seventh century. This development appears to have been connected with the establishment of long-distance trade routes between the Mediterranean and the Balkans. St

[35] Istria: Bačić 1970 (fortifications), Kučar 1979 (Beram cemetery), Mladin 1974 (bronze vessels and helmets).

Lucia lay at a major crossroads of these routes, and it is there that occurs by far the greatest concentration of burials. Italic wares were not only forwarded eastwards but were also very likely manufactured there. A new economy grew up with an emphasis on commerce and crafts as the population appears to have concentrated more and more in a few large centres such as St Lucia and Kobarid, while other places, such as Tolmin where rectangular houses on stone foundations have been found, were abandoned. During the late sixth and fifth centuries, the period to which the richest graves in the region belong, the role of St Lucia appears to have increased as a centre for prosperous traders. At the same time the wide range of objects found in graves of a similar period in the cemetery suggests perhaps an increasing economic stratification within the population, with a wealthy minority among a multitude of the poor. Political changes in the fourth century evidently disrupted the pattern of commerce on which the settlement had depended and its prosperity dwindled rapidly.[36]

This section has described in outline the 20 or so groups defined by material remains who occupied the Illyrian territories during the Early Iron Age (eighth to fourth centuries). From this there emerges no support for clear-cut definitions of Illyrians, either through a compact unity in the archaeological evidence or through any apparent consistency in habits of ritual or daily life across the different cultural groups. At the same time some conclusions regarding origins and development can be drawn. Several groups, notably those in Istria, Liburnia, northern and southern Serbia, central Bosnia and Dalmatia, had already been formed before the start of this period, but an Early Iron Age prosperity brought instability to their traditional pattern of social relations and a decline had already set in before the end of the seventh century. New groups emerged, notably those of Glasinac and Dolensko (Lower Carniola), through exploiting the qualities of iron to amass a wealth of cattle and create fortified settlements. Their elites are distinguished by graves that are rich in weapons and jewellery

---

[36] Soča (Isonzo) group: Gabrovec and Svolšjak 1983, Teržan, Lo Schiavo and Trampuž-Orel 1984–5 (St Lucia), Svolšjak 1976 (Most na Soči), 1973 (Tolmin), Bartosiwicz 1985 (faunal evidence).

and contain imports from Italy and Greece. The new rulers supported long-distance commerce centred on such places as Donja Dolina and St Lucia. In the burial mounds we can now recognize the increasing dominance of powerful chiefs with their armed followers, such as those at Glasinac (Ilijak and Osovo) and Dolensko (Stična and Novo Mesto). By the fifth century the power of these chiefs, based in tribal alliances, had reached a peak, but in the following century there was a decline as the tribal structures began to be challenged by new forms of central authority developing in adjacent lands.

3

Naming Illyrians

Illyrian language[1]

Though almost nothing of it survives, except for names, the Illyrian language has figured prominently in several theories regarding the spread of Indo-European languages into Europe. In the late nineteenth century the names of persons and places recorded by ancient written sources and on inscriptions convinced some scholars that Illyrian-speakers had once been widespread across Central and Eastern Europe, the Balkan peninsula, Asia Minor and southeast Italy. In the early twentieth century there was a confident identification of Illyrian as a primary sub-stratum of Indo-European from which whole families of European languages later developed.

Theories of this kind flourished in a time when there was also a greater confidence on the part of archaeologists. Most were willing to accept that the appearance of a new language was somehow connected with the movement of whole communities, best illustrated by the historically documented migrations of the Celts between the fifth and third centuries BC and also by the barbarian invasions of the Roman Empire between the third and the sixth centuries AD. Many still hold to the view that it is possible to detect traces of invasions by Indo-Europeans in the material culture of this or that region.

---

[1] On Illyrian language, names and etymology: Crossland 1982, Polomé 1982, Russu 1969, Šašel 1977a, Rendić-Miočević 1956, Katičić 1976a, 1976b, 1980, 1984.

As regards the Balkans, there has been in existence for several decades a theory that movements of new peoples into Europe from the direction of Asia around the beginning of the Bronze Age (before 2000 BC) marked the arrival and dispersal of Indo-European speakers. Serious problems arise with this and similar theories when one comes to examine the processes of evolution and fragmentation that produced the historically attested languages of the Balkans within barely a thousand years. This question has most recently been taken up in a stimulating and provocative book by Colin Renfrew (1987). While it is hard to avoid notions of invasions and migrations in a discussion of the Illyrian language and its origins, there are clear signs that the old familiar landscape of European linguistic and archaeological evolution is becoming a desolation of vanished certainties in both disciplines.

At this stage it may be useful to outline the limits of Illyrian territory as indicated in the onomastic evidence, that is, names of persons, peoples and places recorded in the Greek and Roman sources, as set out by I. I. Russu (1969). The southern limit starts on the coast of central Albania and passes inland to Yugoslavia to include the Lakeland, the Skopje basin and the Kosovo–Metohija region. Then it turns north to follow a line west of the river Morava to the vicinity of Belgrade on the Danube. On the north the Sava and Drava valleys are included along with an area north of the latter extending in the direction of Lake Balaton in western Hungary. From there the limit passes southwestwards, skirting the southeast Alps, to meet the Adriatic in Istria. Finally the ancient districts of Calabria and Apulia in southeast Italy are included. In addition to a distribution of Illyrian personal and place-names the Messapian language recorded on more than 300 inscriptions is in some respects similar to Balkan Illyrian. This link is also reflected in the material culture of both shores of the southern Adriatic. Archaeologists have concluded that there was a phase of Illyrian migration into Italy early in the first millennium BC, not only in the south but also further north from Liburnia to Picenum. A more cautious view suggests that while Messapian may have developed as a branch of Illyrian, or rather 'pre-Illyrian', a substantial difference between the two had developed by historical times. For this reason the problem of Messapian is better considered as a distinct entity within the early languages of Italy rather than as an extension of the Balkan Illyrian province.[2]

The Greeks had a word for the speaking of Illyrian (*illurizein*) and recognized a language distinct from Greek. As preserved in Strabo's *Geography* the Greek tradition identified Illyrians as a people (*ethnos*) different from Macedonians and Thracians as well as from the Greeks. On the other hand, Greek sources are far from clear over any distinction between Illyrian and the inhabitants of Epirus: 'Epirote' as a political or ethnic term was evidently not current before the fourth century BC, and the phrase 'epirote peoples' means no more than 'peoples of the mainland', that is, seen from the island of Corcyra where the Greeks first settled in the region. It cannot yet be established that there were peoples in the northwest of mainland Greece who spoke a language that was neither Illyrian nor Greek. When Strabo refers to 'bilingual' people beyond the mountains west of Macedonia, the presumption is that the languages spoken were Greek and Illyrian. Ancient writers tell us almost nothing of the Illyrian language, although there is no doubt that it continued to be spoken well into the Roman period. They furnish a handful of authentic Illyrian words, including 'rhinos' for 'fog', 'sabaius' or 'sabaia', a local variety of beer, and 'sybina' for a lance or hunting-spear. Studies of the Illyrian language must continue to depend on the large number of attributable names, tribal, personal and geographical, preserved in ancient literary and epigraphic sources.[3]

Modern study of Illyrian names began with the catalogues of geographical (1925) and personal (1929) names compiled by H. Krahe, modelled on the dictionary of Celtic names compiled by Alfred Holder (1896–1914). These were followed by studies of the Illyrian language by Krahe (1955–8), Anton Mayer (1957–59) and I. I. Russu (1969). A new era began with Jürgen Untermann's analysis of Venetic names (1961) which defined the separate linguistic identity of the Venetic peoples.

---

[2] On limits of Illyrians: Marić 1964b, Degmedžić 1967 (archeological and literary evidence), Katičić 1977a (Paeonians), Ilievski 1975 (Greece), Suić 1967a (Istria), Simone 1972, 1976 (Messapian), 1986, Pisani 1976, Marin 1977 (Illyrians in Italy).

[3] Crossland 1982.

This pioneering work of local definition has been imitated, for the most part successfully, in later studies of the names of other Illyrian groups. Géza Alföldy's catalogue and analyses of personal names from the Roman province of Dalmatia (1964, 1965 and 1969) remain fundamental and are matched by the works of Andras Mócsy on Pannonia (1959) and Moesia Superior (1970). Duje Rendić-Miočević has published several studies of names from the territory of the Delmatae, on the middle Adriatic around Split, notably from the native centre at Rider (Danilo) near Šibenik, and we owe to Fanoula Papazoglu (1978) a valuable examination of the ethnic affinities of the Dardanians from the evidence of names. Perhaps the most significant contribution has been the work of Radoslav Katičić. Following the lines of Untermann's study of Venetic names, Katičić (1962, 1963) has defined two 'onomastic provinces' among the Illyrians. The southern province includes the ancient region of Illyris in central and southern Albania, the heart of the Illyrian kingdom around the Lake of Scodra, and the Adriatic coast and hinterland up to and beyond the Neretva valley. The Middle Dalmatian-Pannonian province lies further north and is considerably greater in area. In the northwest lies the Venetic province, including the Liburni, the Istrian peninsula and the region of Ljubljana in Slovenia beyond the Julian Alps.

These two Illyrian onomastic provinces are defined by the near exclusive distribution of some personal names. Among the southern 'real' Illyrians these include Epicadus, Temus (a female name), Gentius (in Greek Genthios), Pinnes (or Pinnius), Monounios (recorded on coins), Grabaei (a tribal name), Verzo and Zanatis. The middle Dalmatian-Pannonian province exhibits a larger variety of names, of which those characteristic of the area include Andes (m.)/Andia (f.), Baezus/Baezo, Bubant-, Iettus, Paio, Panes, Panto (m.)/Pantia (f.), Pinsus, Plares, Sinus, Stataria, Stennas, Suttis and Vendo. The province defined by these includes the Adriatic coast between the rivers Titus (Krka) and Hippius (Cetina), western, central and southern Bosnia, the middle and upper Una valley and the Lika plain. On the east the district (Sanjak) of Novi Pazar and western Serbia are also included.

There is a measure of overlap between the three provinces (Venetic and the two Illyrian). Thus Bato occurs both among the southern Illyrians and also on the Dalmatian coast, in western and central Bosnia and further north in Pannonia. Verzo occurs in Salona and also in western Bosnia. An element of the Illyrian royal name Skerdilaidas appears in eastern Bosnia as Laidus and among the Delmatae at Rider as Laedicalius and L(a)edietis. Similarly the middle province includes names with a wider dispersal: the root of Aplis/Aplo occurs also in Liburnia and Istria, where it is an element in Magaplinus. The name Beusas, genitive Beusantis, which is found among the Delmatae, has been compared with the Messapic Bosat, with Buzetius among the Japodes and with the Pannonian Busio. The names Daza, Dasius and Dazomenus have been connected with Dasmenus in Pannonia and Dazos in southern Italy. The meaning of these plausible correspondences is hard to determine: neither the internal links between the three principal Illyrian onomastic provinces nor those between them and other areas indicate more than that the languages spoken by peoples in the Illyrian territories were somehow related if not altogether common. Though they are separately identified in the historical sources there was undoubtedly a close association between Liburni and Veneti, from the distribution of distinctive names with the stems *hosti* in Hostiducis (genitive), or *vols-/volt-* in Volsetis (gen.), Volso, Volsonus, Voltimesis (gen.) and Voltis(s)a.

Place-names from the Illyrian territories add little to our knowledge of the Illyrian language. The recurrent element *-ona*, for example, Aenona (Nin), Blandona (south Liburnia), Emona (Ljubljana), Narona (Vid), Scardona (Skradin near Šibenik), Salona (Solin near Split), does no more than indicate that Illyrian place names followed a basic Indo-European configuration. Indo-European characteristics in the formation of personal names include the derivation of feminines in *-on*, for example, the masculine Aplis/Aplinis with feminine Aplo/Aplonis, or the use of the prefix *epi-* in Epicadus, the different derivations in *-nt-* and *-menos* in Dasant-, Dasmenos, and the use of numbers as personal names, Tritonus/Tritano, Sestus/Sextus/Sesto. Finally the impact of Celtic on Illyrian nomenclature has been much discussed but attributions of individual names are far from certain. Among the Japodes the names Iaritus, Matera, Nonntio and Sinus, are ascribed to Celtic influence, as are Sarnus, Sinus and Vepus among the

Delmatae. Place names containing the element -*dunum*, for example, Noviodunum on the Sava, Carrodunum on the Drava and Singidunum (Belgrade) on the Danube represent evidence for Celtic penetration of the area.[4]

A notable addition to the repertory of Illyrian names has come from the cemeteries in the vicinity of the Greek colony Dyrrhachium (Durrës). Many hundreds of graves had their inscribed tombstones still in place, simple cylindrical stelai, decorated, if at all, with a simple band of laurel and inscribed, mostly in Greek, with the single name and patronymic of the deceased. The names so far reported include Andena (f.), Antis (f., two examples), Batina, Batouna, Boiken, Breigos, Brykos, Genthios, Dazaios/Dazos (two examples), Epe(n)tinus (from the place Epetium, Stobreč on the coast south of Split), Epicadus (ten examples), Epidamnos, Zaimina, Isnthena, Koreta, Lydra, Mallika, Monounios, Pladomenus, Plator (five examples), Platoura, Scodrina, Strabainos, Syrmas, Syra, Sychos, Tadus, Tata, Teutaia (four examples)/Temiteuta. New additions to the list of south-Illyrian names include Andena (Andia), Plaios/Plaianus/Plaia, and also Scodrina from the Illyrian capital Scodra, an adjectival form that appears on local coins. Known south Illyrian names include Genthios, Cillanus, Epicadus, Laidas, Laidon, and Teutaia, and those new to the list include Billena, Isnthena, Mallika and Strabainos.[5]

With such a large repertoire of Illyrian names it is possible to consider etymologies and links with other Indo-European languages of which a fuller record survives. Thus it seems generally agreed that the name of the Illyrian queen *Teuta* of the third century BC derives from *teutana*, which means 'queen'. Similarly, Gentius, the last of the Illyrian kings, defeated by the Romans in 168 BC, has been connected with a noun, in its Latin form *gens, gentis*, meaning 'class' or 'kin' and appropriate for the leader of such a group. These are exceptions and no satisfactory etymologies have yet been produced even for some of the most distinctive Illyrian names.

A more difficult question is how Illyrian fits within the family

[4] Polomé 1982.
[5] Toçi 1965, 1970, 1976, 1986, Simone 1977.

of Indo-European languages. As a whole this has been divided into a western group (Germanic, Venetic, Illyrian, Celtic, Italic and Greek) and an eastern group (Baltic, Slavic, Albanian, Thracian Phrygian, Armenian, Iranian and Indian). The distinction turns on the consonant 's' in the latter and 'ch', 'h' or 'k' in the former, and the two groups are identified by the words for the number 100, *centum* in Latin and *satem* in Old Iranian, although subsequent discoveries have led to a questioning of this tidy geographical separation. One explanation attributes the difference not to separation within some linguistic family-tree but to a mechanism of change from 'ks' to 's' in the central area while leaving the older forms untouched at the periphery. In the case of Illyrian the problems appear to be multiplying: if, as some have argued, Illyrian belongs not to the *centum* group but to the *satem*, the common etymology of Gentius and *gens* must be discarded. There is no evidence that Illyrian in fact belongs to the *satem* group, but the argument that it does is crucial to the case that modern Albanian is descended from Illyrian. So far no satisfactory scheme for the analysis of Illyrian names has been proposed. The common name Bato may derive from the same root as the Latin battuere meaning 'to strike', or is just as likely to derive from the root **bha* 'say' or 'tell', the Latin *fari*. A connection of the common Illyrian name Epicadus and the stem **kad*, meaning 'outstanding' or 'flourishing' in Sanskrit and Greek, is denied by those who argue for the *satem* attribution of Illyrian, preferring words meaning 'destruction', 'deprived of', 'quick, ardent' and 'sharp, bold'. It is hard to see any way forward in arguments of this kind. While some scholars appear entirely engaged with placing Illyrian in this or that group, there are indications that some of the divergences once regarded as definitive of the two Indo-European groups in fact arose at a much later stage of the development of language. In the end the strongest evidence for the connection between Illyrian and Albanian must be the few direct correspondences of vocabulary often cited.[6]

[6] Polomé 1982, Cimochowski 1976. For some Illyrian etymologies, Stanko 1987a–b, 1988a–b, 1989.

Illyrian names

The further refinements of Illyrian onomastic provinces proposed by Géza Alföldy for the area included in the later Roman province of Dalmatia comprise most of the historic Illyrian territories. Five principal groups are identified: (1) 'real Illyrians' south of the river Neretva and extending south of the provincial boundary with Macedonia at the river Drin to include Illyris of north and central Albania; (2) the populous Delmatae after whom the province was named, who occupied the middle Adriatic coast between 'real Illyrians' and Liburni; (3) the Venetic Liburni on the northeast Adriatic; (4) the Japodes who dwelt north of the Delmatae and behind the Liburni, where names reveal a mingling of Venetic, Celtic and Illyrian elements; and (5) the Pannonian peoples in the north of the province, in Bosnia, northern Montenegro and western Serbia. Alföldy's identifications of names with these groups, some known only from around the time of the Roman conquest, have been challenged by R. Katičić. He rejects a Pannonian onomastic province distinct from that of the Delmatae because the number of names on which it is based is too small, while there is too much that is common in the distribution of names between them. Similarly, Alföldy's identifications and interpretation of Celtic names among the Japodes and in the east of the Pannonian onomastic province have also been queried. For Katičić the occurrence of Celtic personal names in these areas is less likely to be evidence for a mixed 'Illyrian-Celtic' native population, or a Celtic element surviving from the migrations of the fourth century BC, than the consequence of movement in the Roman period associated with military service and the processes of Romanization.[7]

Typical names among the (1) 'real Illyrians' according to Alföldy are: Annaeus/Annaius, Epicadus, Epidius, Pinnes, Plare(n)s, Tatta, Temeia, Zanatis and Ziraeus. Other names less well known but which may also originate in the area include Agirrus, Blodus, Boria, Glavus, Laedio, Laiscus, Mad-

---

[7] Alföldy 1964a, Katičić 1964.

ena, Posantio, Pravaius, Scerdis, Teuda, Zorata. A smaller group found in the area appear to originate from the central Dalmatian province: Bato, Dasius, Dazas, Ditus, Messor and Verzo. A few names which occur in the upper Neretva valley around Konjic appear to be of Celtic origin: Boio, Bricussa, Iacus, Mallaius and Mascelio – a suggestion which seems to be confirmed by Celtic styles of dress on figured tombstones. Alföldy suggests that this Celtic component may derive from the impact of the migrating Celts on the Illyrian Autariatae, but it now seems that they dwelt not there but further south between the 'real Illyrians' around the Lake of Shkodër and the Dardanians of Kosovo. Throughout this area the formula of nomenclature is that of the single personal name with the father's name (patronymic) in the genitive.[8]

Between the 'real Illyrians' and the Liburni the (2) Delmatae appear to exhibit a similarly characteristic group of names. Their territory is exceptionally rich in onomastic evidence, with hundreds of native names recorded at Rider (Danilo near Šibenik) and with several smaller concentrations at several other centres. Characteristic names include Aplis/Apludus/Apurus/Aplus/Aplius, Baezo, Beusas/Beuzas, Curbania, Cursulavia, Iato, Lavincia, Ledrus, Messor, Paio/Paiio, Panes/Panias/Panius (Pantus?)/Panentius, Pant(h)ia/Panto (f.), Pinsus, Pladomenus, Platino, Samuntio, Seio/Seiio, Statanius/Staticus/Stato/Status, Sestus/Sextus/Sexto, Tito, Tizius, Tritus, Var(r)o. Other names appear among the Delmatae whose origins lie outside their territory. A Liburnian element is suggested by Acenica, Clevata, Darmocus, Germanicus (the native stem Germanus/Germus, with the charactistic Venetic ending -*icus*), Labrico, Lunnicus, Melandrica, Turus. A second group of names is common with the Pannonians and, though some are found also in the southern Illyrian province, their origins seem to lie among the former: Bardurius, Bato, Carrius, Dasantilla, Dasas/Dazas, Dasto, Plator/Platino, Scenobarus, Verzo/Verzulus. Several of these are also to be found among Illyrians settled far away in the mining area of the province Dacia at Alburnus Maior. From the southern Illyrians the names Boria, Epicadus, Laedicalius, Loiscus,

---

[8] Katičić 1963b, 1966a.

Pinnes and Tato are present, from the Japodes Diteio and
Ve(n)do, and a few names are of Celtic origin, Kabaletus, Litus,
Nantanius, Sarnus, Sinus, Sisimbrius and Vepus. The formulae
of nomenclature among the Delmatae are more varied than
among the southern Illyrians, although the single name with
patronymic is widespread. In the western districts of the Delmatae (some of which still belonged to the Liburnians until not
long before the Roman conquest) a two-name formula appears
to have spread from the Liburni, in the same areas where
Liburnian names are also found. The commonest form is personal name plus family name plus patronymic, for example,
Plator Carvius Batonis (filius) or Aplis Lunnicus Triti f(ilius).
A local variation appears to have the family name included in
the patronymic formula, Platino Platoris Tizi filia, 'Platino,
daughter of Plator Tizus'.[9]

The language of the (3) Veneti is better documented than
others in or near the Illyrian territories. The evidence includes
more than 300 inscriptions, most from the major settlements
of Ateste and Patavium (Padua), along with a shrine near
Lagole di Calalzo on the upper Piave and another at Gurina-
Alpe near Kotschach, on the far side of the Plöcken pass in
the Gail valley. Finds of individual inscriptions extend to
Istria and across the Julian Alps. The texts are brief and
follow a similar pattern of dedications to various deities and
epitaphs on tombstones and cremation urns. Enough of the
language and vocabulary survives to indicate that Venetic
was a northwest Indo-European dialect with several points of
correspondence with Latin. The distribution area of Venetic
inscriptions is concentrated in the western part of that area
where Venetic names occur on inscriptions of the Roman
period. This includes Istria, the Emona (Ljubljana) region
and the Liburnian coast and islands down to the river Titus
(Krka). The repertoire of Venetic personal names include
several Roman family (*gens*) names ending in -*icus*, -*ocus*,
-*inus*, -*iacus*, -*arius*, -*anius* and -*anus*, also family and personal names ending with -*avus*. Individual names include
Accius/Axius, Cantius, Carminius, Appuleius, Avitus, Tutor,

[9] Rendić-Miočević 1948, 1956, 1976a.

Barbius, Boniatus, Cervius, Cusonius, Dasimius, Dasant-, Firmius, Laetus, Lucanus, Lucillus, Muttius, Mulvius, Oaetus, Oppius, Plaetorius, Regius, Veitor, Titius, Turus, Voltiomnos and Volumnius.[10]

Across the passes of the eastern Alps the names on inscriptions in the Norican region of the Roman period are predominantly Celtic, and it seems that this state of affairs came about with the Celtic movements into the area after 400 BC. The identity of the pre-Celtic inhabitants of this large area, which includes most of the Danube basin above the Danube bend, remains a problem. What little evidence there is indicates that they may, in the southern area at least, have been Veneti and Illyrians of the Pannonian-Dalmatian group. Venetic inscriptions have been discovered carved on rock faces and on portable bronze dedications, probably dating to the second century BC. Latin inscriptions of the Roman period indicate the survival of a Venetic element in the upper Drau, the lower Isel and upper Möll valleys. Moreover some tribal and geographical names in the same region, Laianci, Aguntum, Saevates and Sebatum, are patently not of Celtic origin. The material evidence is not conclusive but does not conflict with the notion of a Venetic survival. They may indeed be the Carni, in Roman times a people confined to northeast Italy, but who in earlier times extended far into the eastern Alps. In the Roman period the Venetic component was still strong in the area of Ljubljana (Ig) where, in addition to some names of Celtic origin, the following Venetic-Istrian names occur: Ampo, Fronto, Lucius, Pletor, Plotius, Plunco, Rega and names formed from the root Volt-. Possibly a people named by the elder Pliny as Catali somewhere in this area may be connected with the Istrian Catari of the Tergeste (Trieste) region and may represent a survival of Veneti around Ljubljana. The name of the Carni has survived in Carniola, a later name for part of what is now Slovenia, the Austrian province Carinthia (Kärnten), Mons Carantanus (Ulrichsberg near Virunum) and the early medieval centre Car-

[10] Untermann 1961.

antum (Karnburg), and possibly in the name of the Norican settlement and later Roman fortress Carnuntum on the middle Danube below Vienna.[11]

The names of the (3) Liburni demonstrate their Venetic character, with such roots as *Vols-/Volt-* and the endings *-icus* and *-ocus*, and set them apart from the rest of the Adriatic Illyrians: Acaica, Aetor, Boninus, Cliticus, Colatina, Curticus, Darmo, Dumma, Hosp(olis), Hostiducis (gen.), Hostiices, Lambicus, Malavicus, Marica, Menda, Moicus, Oclatinus, Oeplus, Opia, Opiavus, Oplica, Oplus, Plaetor, Patalius, Recus, Suioca, Tarnis, Toruca, Trosius, Vadica, Velsounus, Verica, Viniocus, Volaesa, Volscus, Volsetis, Volso, Volsonus, Volsounus, Volsus, Voltimesis, Vol(l)tis(s)a, Zupricus. Also the name Turus, common among the Liburni but found as well among the Delmatae and the Japodes, is of Liburnian Venetic origin. The majority of these names are unknown among the eastern and southern neighbours of the Liburni, except in a few border districts. In addition a smaller group of names appear to be of exclusively Liburnian rather than general Venetic origin, since they do not occur in other Venetic or Illyrian districts: Aeia, Barcinus, Buzetius, Caminis (gen.), Ceunus, Clausus, Granp(. . .), Iaefus, Lastimeis, Mamaester, Pasinus, Picusus, Tetenus, Vesclevesis (gen.) and Virno. The separate identity of the Liburnians is also indicated by formulae of nomenclature. The single name plus patronymic common among Illyrians is rare. In a region where the Roman three-name formula (*praenomen, nomen gentile* and *cognomen*, for example, Caius Julius Caesar) spread at an early date, a native two-name formula appears in several variants. That with personal name plus family name is found in southern Liburnia (Ravni Kotari), while that with personal name plus family name plus patronymic is found throughout the Liburnian area, for example, Avita Suioca Vesclevesis, Velsouna Suioca Vesclevesis f(ilia), Avita Aquillia L(uci) f(ilia), Volsouna Oplica Pl(a)etoris f(ilia) and Vendo Verica Triti f(ilius).[12]

The (4) Japodes dwelt behind the Liburnians in the hills

---

[11] Alföldy 1974 (Venetic in Noricum).
[12] Untermann 1970.

and forests of southern Croatia and western Bosnia. Their onomastic evidence appears to be a mixture, with some names typically Illyrian: Ditius, Ditueio, Ditus, Pantadienus, Plator, Platurius, Sestenius, Sestus, Tatonia, Teuda, Tritus and Vendes. Most occur in the eastern parts of their territory, notably around Bihać in the Una valley. Names of likely Liburnian origin include Turranius, Turrinius and Turus, which may indicate, along with the evidence of name formulae, a Venetic element among the Japodes. A group of names identified by Alföldy as of Celtic origin: Ammida, Andes, Iaritus, Matera, Maxa, Mellito, Muntanus, Nantia, Nonntio, Parmanicus, Poia, Sarius, Seneca, Sicu, Silus and Sinus are distributed throughout Japodian territory. A smaller group confined to their territory are to be regarded as typically Japodian: Anadrus, Deidmu, Dennaia, Loantius, Rufantius, Stennas/Stennato and Vandano. Alföldy's list of Celtic names has been queried by Katičić, with eight of the 16 (Andes, Iaritus, Maxa, Muntanus, Parmanicus, Sarius, Sinus and Silus) being discarded. Four names are accepted as definitely Celtic: Nantia, Nonntio, Poia and Sicu. Mellito has a Greek and Celtic element, while the Celtic associations of Ammida, Matera and Seneca remain questionable. Rather than constituting evidence for the surviving Celtic element in the ethnically mixed Japodians described by ancient writers, Katačić argues that the Celtic names are the result of outside contacts and the immigration of Romanized Celts during the first two centuries AD. The formulae of Japodian names are the single name or single name plus patronymic. A two-name native formula of Venetic type is found where the first of the names appears to serve as a praenomen in the Roman fashion, occurring mainly around Bihać and in the Lika, for example, Secundus Turrinius Muntani filius, Sestus Platorius Triti f(ilius).[13]

The (5) Pannonian peoples occupied a large tract of territory north of the Delmatae, extending across the Roman provinces of Dalmatia and Pannonia, comprising the Bosnian valleys, parts of the Sava and Drava (Drau) valleys, and from the Japodes in the northwest to Macedonia in the southeast. Names

[13] Katičić 1965, Rendić-Miočević 1975a.

typical of the Pannonian Illyrians according to Alföldy are common also among the Delmatae: Bato, Dasas, Liccaius and Scenobarbus. Names originating from the Delmatae or southern Illyrians include Carvus, Laidus, Plator, Temans, Teuta, Varro and Verzo. A smaller group is confined to the northeast Pannonians: Arbo, Arsa (possibly Thracian), Callo, Daetor, Iauletis (gen.), Proradus and Vietis (gen.). Alföldy's Pannonian onomastic province has been challenged by Katičić on the grounds that the evidence of four distinguishing names is insufficient. Bato is not confined significantly to the Pannonians and seems to be no less attached to the Delmatae and to the southern Illyrians. Similarly Dasas/Dasius and Scenobarbus also occur among the Delmatae, and only the confined distribution of Liccaius indicates a distinctive Pannonian-Illyrian name. In arguing for the unity of the Dalmatian-Pannonian onomastic province, Katičić observes that Alföldy lists four Pannonian names, seven of the Delmatae and five south Illyrian. But only one of these is fairly certainly Pannonian, two of the Delmatae and three south Illyrian, indicating that that the proposed division between Delmatae and Pannonian is not valid. The two-name formula is found among Pannonians, and the few known examples around Pljevlja in northern Montenegro may not be of local origin (see below). Most are styled with the single name plus patronymic, for example, Teuta Vietis and Bato Liccai f(ilius). Among the Pannonians within Roman Dalmatia the western groups, including the Maezaei and Daesitiates, exhibit few outside connections, and those are with Delmatae immediately to the south, though in Alföldy's view the two groups are quite distinct, with many of the latter's names unknown among Pannonians. This is in marked contrast to the more varied picture among the southeast Pannonians, notably the territory of the Pirustae, where in addition to Pannonian names, including the ethnic Pirusta and Scirto, a significant group of names of external origin is on record.[14]

The presence of Illyrians in the Celtic province of Noricum-Pannonia is for the most part marginal. There is no base for the

[14] Mócsy 1967.

simple equation, once widely entertained, that the population of the pre-Celtic Hallstatt Iron Age in and north of the eastern Alps were Illyrian-speakers, a refinement of earlier 'pan-Illyrian' theories now discarded. It is doubtful if the small number of Illyrian personal names in the south and southeast of the Celtic province represents any kind of ethnic survival from before the latter's migration in the fourth century BC. At the same time, it has been observed that it is in the same areas that the traditions of the material culture of the earlier Hallstatt Iron Age persisted with the least change down to the Roman period. Most of the Illyrian personal names and the few place-names occur on the sparsely populated margins of Carinthia. They may represent remnants of an Illyrian population expelled from this fertile region southwards into the Pannonian-Dalmatian region, with which the Illyrian names of Noricum are connected. On the other hand, movements of people during the Roman era can account for a dispersal of Pannonians and Delmatae, especially in such a productive mining region as the eastern Alps.[15]

In Roman Pannonia the Latobici and Varciani who dwelt east of the Venetic Catari in the upper Sava valley were Celtic but the Colapiani of the Colapis (Kulpa) valley were Illyrians (north Pannonian), exhibiting names such as Liccaius, Bato, Cralus, Lirus and Plassarus. The few names on record for other groups in the Sava valley belong to a more southerly Pannonian-Dalmatian group, the Illyrian Jasi with Scenus, the Breuci with Scilus Bato, Blaedarus, Dasmenus, Dasius, Surco, Sassaius, Liccaius and Lensus, and the Amantini and Scordisci around Sirmium with Terco and Precio, Dases and Dasmenus. It seems that at the time of the Roman conquest Illyrian peoples were not to be found north of the river Drava. Most of the people in northern Pannonia have Celtic names, except for a group of Pannonian Illyrians, Bato, Breucus, Dases, Dasmenus, Licco, Liccaius, etc., in the northeast around Brigetio. These are likely to represent a people called the Azali, Illyrians transported there from southern Pannonia during the wars of conquest

---

[15] Alföldy 1974 (Illyrian in Noricum).

under Augustus and settled near the Danube between two Celtic groups, Boii in the west and Eravisci in the east.[16]

Around the middle Drina and the western Morava the onomastic evidence suggests a significant Celtic element among the population, confirmed also by tombstones with Celtic symbols and fashions of dress. Alföldy has detected descendants of the Celtic Scordisci once dominant in the central Balkans. The number of Illyrian names in that area, Genthena, Tatta, Dasius and Thana is small compared with the Celtic: Aioia, Andetia, Baeta, Bidna, Catta, Dussona, Enena, Iaca, Madusa, Matisa, Nindia, Sarnus, Seius, Totia and perhaps Pinenta. If the Scordisci did retain their Celtic character into the Roman era the Illyrian element may represent an assimilation of groups from the existing native population. Alföldy's inventory of 15 Celtic names among the Scordisci has been severely pruned by Katičić. Only three, Catta, Iaca and Totia are judged to be certainly Celtic, with another four, Aioia, Bidna, Matisa and Nindia, possible. Six, Andetia, Baeta, Dussona, Enena, Madusa and Pinenta, are not, while Sarnus and Seius are either Celtic or north Illyrian. This Celtic presence around the middle Drina and Morava does not, in the view of Katičić, represent a Celtic survival of the Scordisci but was rather a consequence of contacts with the Celtic world following the Roman conquest. Whether the Scordisci were a Celtic or an Illyrian people has been considered by Fanoula Papazoglu (1978). The enquiry is at the outset confronted with confusion among the ancient writers. A tradition preserved by Strabo calls them Celtic, referring to their invasion of Greece and the southern Balkans in the third century BC. Others describe them as Illyrians and one has them as Thracians. Appian includes the Scordisci in what must be a late version of the Greek myth of Illyrian genesis. Moreover, to make the matter more uncertain, there seems to be real doubt as to whether the Scordisci, whose name appears to be of Illyrian origin, were ever really a separate people rather than a mixed group of Celts and Illyrians formed during and after the third-century migrations. This would explain their frequent and sudden changes of territory during

---

[16] Katičić 1966b (Celtic in Slovenia).

the three centuries of their history, the result of fluctuations in
their political relations with neighbouring peoples of the central
Balkans. Certainly attempts to reconstruct a coherent history
or identity for this people through combining and reconciling
the written sources have rarely seemed to repay the effort.[17]

The application of onomastic evidence to this matter seems
to give rise to further problems. As we have seen, Katičić
has questioned Alföldy's identification of Celtic names, mainly
female, from the western Drina, the western Morava and
Mount Kosmaj south of Belgrade, and also the same scholar's
suggestion that male children received Roman names, with
Illyrian and Celtic traditional names being reserved for females.
In the opinion of Papazoglu the material evidence is decisive
for the existence of a pre-Roman Celtic population along the
south bank of the Danube between the mouth of the Drava at
Mursa and that of the Timok in eastern Serbia, and this represents the historical Scordisci. Also there are a number of
Celtic place names in this area: Cornacum, Cuccium, Bononia,
Malata, Cusum, Acumincum, Rittium, Burgenae, Taurunum,
Singidunum, Tricornium, Vinceia, Viminacium, Lederata, Pincum, Taliatae and Egeta. Even here the picture is far from
clear: for example the name Pincum (Velika Gradište near the
entrance to the Danube gorge) is claimed as a Celtic, Illyrian
or Thracian name in each of the principal works of reference
for these languages, and several others on the list have been
claimed for more than one language. We may perhaps leave
the difficult problem of Scordiscan identity with a summary of
Papazoglu's reconstruction based on the historical, linguistic
and material evidence. The Scordisci were a warrior-dominated
Celtic group whose numerical strength did not increase even
in the period when they dominated the central Balkans. Their
heartland was the Danube bank between the Drava and the
Danube gorge, an area they continued to inhabit after major
defeats at the hands of Romans and Dacians. Even here they
were intermixed with older strata of Illyrians, Dacians and
Thracians, and the only part of their territory where a settled
Celtic population was probably in the majority was the lower

[17] Alföldy 1964b, Katičić 1965, Papazoglu 1978.

valley of the Morava. The survival of Celtic Scordisci away from the river Danube is impossible to gauge from any variety of evidence currently available, though immigration in the Roman era is a more likely explanation for the few Celtic names on record.

The evidence of personal names indicates an intrusive element in the population among the Pannonian Illyrians of northern Montenegro around Pljevlja and Prijepolje. Apart from some names of Thracian origin, Bessus and Teres, and some Celtic names, Arvus, Belzeius, Cambrius, Iaritus, Lautus, Madussa and Argurianus (either Thracian or Celtic), the only name of south Illyrian origin is Plares. On the other hand, there are many that are characteristic of the Delmatae, for example, Carvanius, Germanus, Lavianus, Panto, Pinsus, Pladomenus, Stataria, Testo, Tritto, Vendo and Verzaiius. The link with the Delmatae appears to be confirmed by the presence of the two-name formula, adopted by some western groups of the Delmatae from the Liburnians, for example, Cato Stataria, Tu(r)i f(ilia). This formula survived into the Roman era when some enfranchised natives exhibit two cognomina: P. Ael(ius) Pladome[nus] Carvanius, Aurelia Titulla Arguriana, Aurelia Titulla Cambria and Titus Aurelius Severus Celsianus. The area is remote from the homeland of the Delmatae and their presence may be explained as the result of mass eviction from near the Adriatic in order to accommodate new Roman settlers. The areas to which they were transported may well have been chosen because of the severe depopulation that had occurred during the final stages of the Roman conquest.[18]

Along the eastern margins of the Illyrians there is a broad area of intermingling or 'contact zone' between names of Illyrian and Thracian origin, running from the Danube below Belgrade down the west of the Morava valley to the Vardar and the northern border of Macedonia. The number of recorded native names in this area is not large. Those of Illyrian and Thracian origins occur together in the mining area of Mount Kosmaj south of Belgrade and there is another group of names from the Metohija area of Dardania. Native names of Roman

---

[18] Alföldy 1964a (Delmatae in northern Montenegro).

soldiers recruited in the second century AD from Scupi (Skopje) in the south and Ratiaria (Archar) on the Danube include a few names of Pannonian Illyrian origin, for example, Dassius and Andio, but familiar Thracian names, Bitus, Sinna, Dolens, Drigissa, Mucco, Auluzon, Mucatral and Daizo, are in the majority. The Illyrian component is markedly stronger in Dardania, including Das(s)ius, Scerviaedus and Andia, but Thracian names are also found, Sita and Nanea. Whether the Dardanians were an Illyrian or a Thracian people has been much debated and one view suggests that the area was originally populated with Thracians who were then exposed to direct contact with Illyrians over a long period.[19]

The ethnic affinities of the Dardanians, from whose name is said to derive the modern Albanian word for 'pear' (dardhë), as revealed in the evidence of names from their territory have been examined by Papazoglu. Literary sources record Dardanian names for three medicinal plants. From the *Materia Medica* of Pedanius Dioscurides, a Roman military doctor from Anazarbus in Cilicia who lived in the time of Nero, we learn that *gentiana* was called *aloitis* and *aristolocheia makra* or *klematitis* (wormwood or birthwort, a herb promoting childbirth) was called *sopitis*. From another writer we learn that *cacalia* was the Dardanian name for *Mercurialis tomentosa* ('hairy' Mercury); this also occurs as a personal name on an imperial rescript issued at Viminacium on the Danube in AD 294. The recorded names of Dardanian leaders during the Macedonian and Roman wars, Longarus, Bato and Monunius, whose daughter Etuta was married to the Illyrian king Gentius, are all Illyrian. Native names on Roman tombstones of the second to third centuries are unevenly distributed in Dardanian territory, with several areas entirely devoid of evidence. Illyrian names in Dardanian territory include Andio, Andinus, Annus, Anna, Catulla (?), Cinna, Citto, Dasius (four examples)/Dassius (seven examples), Dicco, Epicadus, Epicaris, Messius/Messa, Plannius, Scerviaedus, Tata/Tatta, Times (three examples), Turranis, Turelius (two examples), Vanno (two examples), Varanus

---

[19] Dardanian names: Mócsy 1974, Papazoglu 1978. Also Mirdita 1981, Petrova 1983–4.

(two examples), Varanilla and Varidius. The Thracian names include: Auluporis, Auluzon, Bithus (three examples), Celsus (two examples), Celsinus, Cocaius, Daizo, Delus, Dida, Dinentilla, Dizas, Dizo (two examples), Dolens, Eptaikenthos, Ettela, Mania, Murco (three examples)/Moca, Mucatralis, Mucatus, Teres (three examples), Torcula and Tzitzis.

In the matter of distribution the Thracian names are found mainly in eastern Dardania, from Scupi to Naissus (Niš) and Remesiana, although some Illyrian names do occur. The latter are entirely dominant in the western areas, Priština–Mitrovica (Kosovo) and Prizren–Peč, while Thracian names are absent. The meaning of this state of affairs has been variously interpreted, ranging from notions of 'Thracianization' (in part) of an existing Illyrian population to the precise opposite. In favour of the latter may be the close correspondence of Illyrian names in Dardania with those of the southern 'real' Illyrians to their west, including the names of Dardanian rulers, Longarus, Bato, Monunius and Etuta, and those on later epitaphs, Epicadus, Scerviaedus, Tuta, Times and Cinna. Other Dardanian names are linked with the central Dalmatian group as defined by R. Katičić, for example, Andius/Andia, Andinus, Annus/Anna, Dasius and Plannius. Yet this leaves a number of Dardanian names with no parallel outside the area, including Ambia, Blicities, Bubita, Cocaius, Ettela, Maema, Mescena, Mesta, Momonia, Nanea (four examples), Ninis, Pasades, Pitta, Romma, Sausa and Utinadius. These make any neat apportioning of the Dardanian onomastic material less plausible and suggests that the Dardanians are better regarded as a separate onomastic province. The problems are no less in regard to the place-names in the region, where claims of Illyrian or Thracian origins have been similarly advanced. Out of a total of 20, only four, Naissus, Remesiana, Scupi and Margus, are definitely Thracian and eight Illyrian, Anausaro, Arribantion, Draudacum, Gabuleum, Creveni, Scardus, Sarnuntum and Ulcinium (?). The two groups are distributed in a pattern similar to the personal names, Thracian only in the east and Illyrian mainly, but not entirely, in the west.

As modern scholarship becomes more sceptical of simple theories of how change occurred in the remote past, so the homogeneities of prehistoric and historic formations have been revealed as false or illusory. The idea of major undifferentiated peoples such as Celts, Dacians, Thracians and Illyrians still remains useful as a general concept but attempts to define more precisely such groups lead to confusion and disintegration. This state of affairs has become more marked as new methods and techniques enable archaeologists to pay greater attention to locally definable groups within the increasing mass of material evidence. In the case of the Illyrians the tendency of modern historical and linguistic researches has been to define Illyrians as a name applied by Greeks to a group of Indo-European-speaking peoples in Albania and Montenegro. To the north of these were other peoples, dwelling between the Adriatic and the Drava valley, who spoke a language akin to that of these 'real' Illyrians, to whom the Illyrian name was applied, along with the Roman geographical term Illyricum in the years pre-ceding the conquest, but who were generally identified as Delmatae and Pannonii. Beyond these the Venetic peoples of northeast Italy, Istria, the northern Adriatic and the eastern Alps, sometimes included by ancient writers with Illyrians, are set apart by their language from these two principal Illyrian groups.

Part II

Greek Illyrians

4

Neighbours of the Greeks

Adriatic Illyrians

During the reign of the emperor Antoninus Pius (AD 138–161), that high summer of the Roman Empire, a senior administrator, retired from the imperial service, devoted his leisure to composing an account in Greek of Rome's rise to world empire. The work was arranged according to the different nations and peoples Rome had defeated and incorporated, and one chapter, titled *Illyrike*, dealt with Illyrians. Appianus of Alexandria was an admirer of the Roman Empire and he was most at ease when recounting the wars and victories which led to its creation. Social and political themes he found generally less congenial or more difficult to record and his short section on Illyrians bears this out. Nevertheless, the works of Appian are a valuable source for the formative years of the Roman Empire, though this status is due in part to their survival nearly intact while the works of better informed historians have perished.

The *Illyrike* opens with an account of the lands and the origins of Illyrians:

The Greeks call those people Illyrian who dwell beyond Macedonia and Thrace, from Chaonia and Thesprotia to the river Danube. That is the length of the country, while its breadth is from Macedonia and the mountains of Thrace to Pannonia and the Adriatic and the foothills of the Alps. It is five days' journey in breadth and thirty across, say the Greeks. The Romans measured the country as above six thousand stades in length (750 Roman miles) and about twelve hundred stades (150 Roman miles) in width. (*Illyrike* 1)

They say that the country was named after Illyrius, son of Polyphemus; for the Cyclops Polyphemus and his wife Galatea had three
sons, Celtus, Illyrius and Galas, who all migrated from Sicily and
ruled over peoples named after them, Celts, Illyrians and Galatians.
This seems to me to be the most acceptable of the numerous myth-
ologies among the many peoples. Illyrius had six sons, Encheleus,
Autarieus, Dardanus, Maedus, Taulas and Perrhaebus, also daught-
ers, Partho, Daortho, Dassaro, and others. From these sprang the
Taulantii, the Perrhaebi, Enchelees, Autaries, Dardani, Partheni, Dassaretii and the Daorsii. Autarieus had a son Pannonius, or Paeon,
and the latter had sons, Scordiscus and Triballus, from whom also
nations bearing similar names originated. But these matters I shall
set on one side for those who study the distant past. (*Illyrike* 2)

How the name Illyrian came to be applied to many different
peoples, as indicated here by Appian and also by similar
accounts in the works of other writers, is still debated. A widely
accepted explanation is that Illyrii was once no more than the
name of a single people known to have occupied a small and
well defined part of the south Adriatic coast, around the Lake
of Shkodër astride the modern frontier between Albania and
Yugoslav Montenegro. Appian's mythological genealogy of
Illyrians reflects the use of the name as a generic term for
different peoples within a reasonably well defined but much
greater area, the western Balkans between the Middle Danube
and the Adriatic. The key evidence for Illyrians as the name of
an individual people in the south comes in the *Natural History*
of the Elder Pliny, composed in the middle decades of the first
century AD. This names 'Illyrians properly so-called' (*Illyrii
proprie dicti*) among the native communities in Roman Dalmatia (*NH* 3.144). Evidently these were the first people of this
area to become known to the Greeks, causing their name to
be applied to other peoples with similar language and customs.[1]

Appian's description of the Illyrian territories records a southern boundary with Chaonia and Thesprotia, where ancient
Epirus began south of the river Aous (Vijosë). The country

---

[1] Pajakowski 1980.

immediately to the north, between the coast and the high mountains, was known to the classical Greeks as Illyris and was inhabited by several peoples whose eponymous ancestors appear in Appian's Illyrian genealogy quoted above. The Taulantii descended from Taulas dwelt in the Mat valley and in the hinterland of the Greek colony Epidamnus, the later Dyrrhachium (modern Durrës). Behind these dwelt the Encheleae around the upper Drin and Lake Ohrid, while in the middle and upper valley of the river Genusus (Shkumbin) dwelt the Parthini, descended from Partho, daughter of Illyrius. From this it has been inferred that if the first Greek contacts with a people called Illyrians took place when the latter dwelt around the Lake of Scodra, that is, north of the Taulantii and Parthini, there must have occurred later a southward movement of Illyrian people into an area once inhabited by Greek speakers. There may be some coincidence between this notional Illyrian expansion with a southward movement of iron-using peoples early in the first millenium BC.[2]

In the southern Balkans the territorial definition of ancient peoples is no less difficult than has proved to be the case with modern nation states formed out of the Ottoman Empire, and for similar reasons. In areas where a large proportion of the population was accustomed to seasonal movement innovation in their material culture derived mainly from their contact with itinerants, and notions of a frontier can often have little meaning, either in political or material terms. This state of affairs is evident not only in the vague descriptions of Illyrian peoples by Greek writers but even in the frontiers between Greeks and non-Greeks in that direction. Thus Herodotus (4.49), writing in Athens around the middle of the fifth century, seems to imply a greater Illyria, extending from Epirus to the Veneti and inland to the Serbian Morava (his Angros in the land of the Autariatae). This account fits fairly well with the onomastic evidence and may have been based on the evidence of traders familiar with Illyrian territory. Yet the Greek world

---

[2] Hammond 1982a.

as a whole knew little of these more remote Illyrians and from around the middle of the fourth century BC a much narrower definition appears to have prevailed.[3]

The earliest surviving account of the Illyrian peoples is to be found in the *Periplus* or *Coastal Passage*, a clockwise account of the sailor's route around the Adriatic composed probably around the middle of the fourth century BC. The name and origin of its author are not known, although a mistaken tradition has attributed the work to Scylax of Caryanda, a famous mariner who navigated the Indian Ocean and the river Indus on behalf of the Persian king Darius at the end of the sixth century. The Adriatic voyage is described in 14 chapters, starting from southern Italy:

14   After Lucania the people of the Japyges extend as far as mount Orion, which lies in the Adriatic. The voyage along the coast of Japygia lasts six days and six nights. There are in fact Greeks dwelling in Japygia and their cities are Heraclea, Metapontum, Tarentum and the port Hydruntum on the coast within the Ionian or Adriatic sea.

15   Next after mount Orion and the Japyges comes the people of the Samnites, who extend from the Tyrrhenian sea to the Adriatic. The voyage along the Samnite country lasts two days and one night.

16   After the Samnites comes the people of the Umbri, where lies the city of Ancona. This people worships Diomede, as a result of the benefits received from him, and they maintain a shrine of Diomede. The voyage along Umbria lasts two days and one night.

17   After the Umbrian people come the Tyrrheni: they extend from the Tyrrhenian sea on the far side to the Adriatic. In their country lies the Greek city Spina and the river Spines, and the voyage upstream to the city is around twenty stades. The journey from the city of Pisa to that same place lasts three days.

18   Next after the Tyrrheni is the Celtic people, who were left behind from the Celtic expedition and who occupy a small territory extending to the Adriatic. At this point comes the innermost recess of the Adriatic.

19   After the Celts come the people of the Veneti, in whose land is the river Eridanus. Here the passage lasts one day.

---

[3] Cabanes 1988a.

20   After the Veneti the river Ister. This river flows also into the Pontus Euxinus, facing in the direction of Egypt. The coastal voyage along the Istrian region lasts a day and a night.

21   After the Istri is the people of the Liburni. In the territory of that people are the following coastal cities: Lias, Idassa, Attienites, Dyyrta, Ampsi, Osi, Pedetae, Hemioni [= Alos, Tarsatica, Senites, Dyyrta, Lopsi, Ortopeletae, Hegini]. These people are ruled by women, who are the wives of freeborn men, but they cohabit with their own slaves and with the men of the neighbouring regions. Before the coast lie islands, of which I can record the following names (for there are many others which have no name): the island Istris 310 stades long and 120 stades wide, the Elektrides, and the Mentorides are the large islands. Then comes the (river) Catarbates. The voyage along the coast of the Liburni lasts two days.

22   After the Liburni there come the Illyrian people. The Illyrii dwell by the sea as far as Chaonia, which lies opposite Corcyra, the island of Alcinous. There is situated the Greek city called Heraclea, with a harbour. There dwell the Lotus-eaters, barbarian peoples with the names Hierastamnae, Bulini, and Hylli who are neighbours of the Bulini. This people tell that Hyllus the son of Hercules had his dwelling among them. They are a barbarian people occupying a peninsula a little smaller than the Peloponnese. The Bulini are also an Illyrian people. The voyage along the land of the Bulini as far as the river Nestus takes one day.

23   The Nesti. After the river Nestus the voyage follows a course around a bay which is called the Manius bay and which takes one day. Within the bay lie the islands Proterius, Cratiae and Olynta. The distance between them is [?8 or 12] stades or less and they lie in the direction of Pharos and Issa. The former is now Pharos the Greek island and the latter Issa, on both of which there are Greek cities.

Before one reaches the river Naron a broad strip of land extends far into the sea.

There is an island close to the coastal region named Melite, and another close to it is named Black Corcyra, where the land extends out from the coast in a second promontory but the other faces in the direction of the river Naron. Corcyra lies twenty stades from Melite and eight from the mainland coast.

24   Manii. After the Nesti is the river Naron. The passage into the narrows of the river is unimpeded. Indeed triremes and cargo vessels sail as far as the trading settlement which lies upwards of eighty stades from the sea. The people living there are the Manii, who are by race Illyrians.

Beyond, there is a huge lake, extending from the inland side of the trading settlement as far as the Autariatae, an Illyrian people. In the lake is an island of one hundred and twenty stades, that is especially favourable for agriculture. The river Naro flows on out of this lake. From the Naron to the river Arion is a day's voyage.

Then from the river Arion (to the river Rhizon) the voyage is a half-day. There are the rocks of Cadmus and Harmonia and a shrine not far from the river Rhizon. From the river Rhizon to Bouthoe is (a half-day voyage, as it is also to the Rhizon) trading settlement.

25 Enchelei. The Enchelei are an Illyrian people, who inhabit the land after Rhizon. From Bouthoe to Epidamnus, a Greek city, the voyage takes a day and a night, by land three days.

26 Taulantii. The Taulantii are an Illyrian people, in whose land is the city Epidamnus. A river flows by the city, by name the Palamnus. Then from Epidamnus to Apollonia, a Greek city, the journey on foot takes two days. Apollonia lies fifty stades from the sea and the river Aias flows by the city. From Apollonia to Amantia the distance is 320 stades. From Amantia more within the Ionian Gulf is the city Oricus.

The journey to the sea of Oricus is eighty stades, of Amantia sixty. Bounding all these on the south are the Atintanes, below Oricus and Chaonia as far as Dodona.

Around this area are the Ceraunian mountains in Epirus, and nearby is a small island, named Sason. From there to Oricus the voyage is one third of a day.

27 These are the Illyrian peoples, extending from the Bulini up to this point. The opening of the Ionian gulf extends between the Ceraunian mountains and the Japygian peninsula. And to the city of Hydruntum from the Ceraunian mountains the crossing is around five hundred stades. This is the entrance to the gulf, and that which lies within is called the Ionian gulf. There are many harbours in the Adriatic: the Adriatic and Ionian gulf are one and the same.[4]

In this surviving version the *Coastal Passage* attributed to Scylax contains confusions, later interpolations and plain errors. Yet this first authentic account of the Adriatic lists the names of several Illyrian peoples on the east coast down as far as the river Aous (Vijosë). Their northern limit was the river Catarbates, beyond which dwelt the Liburni, Istri and (V)eneti who are not included among the Illyrian peoples. From the

[4] *Scylacis Caryandensis Periplus maris ad litora habitata Europae et Asiae et Libyae*, GGM vol. 1, pp. 15–96 (Greek text with Latin version).

basis of this document, along with information from other writers, it is possible to reconstruct a political geography of the eastern Adriatic as it was known to the Greek world around the middle of the fourth century BC. In a later work of the same character, the *Coastal Voyage* (*Periegesis*) attributed to Scymnus and compiled at the end of the second century BC, a narrower definition of Illyrians excludes the Bulini and Hylli to make Illyrian territory commence on the coast around Šibenik, north of Split. In the previous century the geographer Eratosthenes had moved the limit of the Illyrians northwards to the Neretva but excluded the Nestoi who dwelt around the river Nestos (Cetina). These definitions of Illyrians may have been academic until around 200 BC when Illyria meant the kingdom on the south Adriatic. The later extension of Illyria/Illyricum to all the lands between Adriatic and Danube came only in the Roman era.[5]

Beginning in the south the first Illyrians near the coast were the Bylliones beyond the river Aous in the hinterland of Apollonia. Their hill-settlement developed later into the town of Byllis, at Gradisht on the right bank of the Aous. The identity and location of the Atintani/Antintanes remain a problem. One recent solution is that there were in fact two groups of this name, the Atintanes in Epirus and the Illyrian Atintani in the region Çermenikë north of Elbasan. Another view locates Atintanes among the hills on the right bank of the Aous in the Mallakastra north of Tepelen and perhaps as far as the area of Skrapar. This places them in a key strategic situation on the route between the Adriatic and Thessaly via the Metsovo pass or to Macedonia via the Korcë basin. Whether or not the commonwealth (*koinon*) of the Illyrian Bylliones attested after 232 BC belonged to these Atintanes, who according to Thucydides were connected with the Molossians, is not clear. Their chief settlement at Gradisht had acquired an urban character by the middle of the third century.[6]

The Taulantii were a group who at various times dominated

---

[5] Anonymi [Scymni Chii ut fertur] Orbis Descriptio, *GGM* vol. 1 pp. 196–237 (on Adriatic, lines 369–443).

[6] Atintani/es: Hammond 1967b, 1989 (two peoples), Papazoglu 1970c (against division); Bylliones: N. Ceka 1984, 1987a, 1987b.

much of the plain between the Aous and the Drin. It was
Illyrian Taulantii from Epidamnus who occupied the site of
Apollonia before the arrival of the Greek colonists around 600
BC. Once they were called in by the Greek settlers to seize
Epidamnus, after they had been ejected by the Liburni. Among
groups who may have belonged to the Taulantii, known to
Greeks for their method of preparing mead from honey, were
the Abri, named by the sixth-century writer Hecataeus as neigh-
bours of the Chelidones, the 'snail-men', who may have lived
on their northern borders towards the Mat or Drin valleys.[7]

Behind the coast Illyrians bordered the Chaones, the Epirote
people of whom the Dexari or Dassaretae were the most northerly and bordered the Illyrian Enchelei, the 'eel-men', whose
name points to a location near Lake Ohrid. According to
Polybius (5.108), the Dassaretae possessed several towns,
though none has yet been definitely located, including Pelion,
Antipatreia (probably Berat), Chrysondym, Gertous or Gerous
and Creonion. Livy's reference to 'Pirustae of the Dassareti'
(45.26) in the second century BC may be an error of the
manuscript: Pirustae dwelt some way to the north in Bosnia
and northern Montenegro and were among the last of the
Illyrians to surrender to the Romans. North of Dassaretis in
the middle and upper valley of the Genusus was the territory
of the Illyrian Parthini, likely to have been part of the Taulantii
until they first appear as Roman allies late in the third century
BC.[8]

The region of Lake Lychnitis (Ohrid), which abounds in fish,
lies at a narrow point of the Adriatic–Aegean watershed and
through it passes not only the main east–west route but also
one between north and south. This was the territory of the
Enchelei, whose rulers claimed descent from the hero Cadmus.
Said to have come from Phoenicia, he arrived in Greece and,
after many adventures, founded and ruled over Thebes along
with his wife Harmonia. Later they moved to the Enchelei,
then at war with Illyrians, but who had received an oracle that

[7] Hammond 1966. Abri and Chelidones: Hecataeus, *FGrHist* vol. 1,
F100–1; Taulantian honey: Aristotle, *On Marvellous Things Heard* 22 (LCL
vol. 14, p. 246).
[8] Hammond 1966, 1967b, 606–7.

victory would be theirs if they received Cadmus as king. After this had come about as foretold, Cadmus and Harmonia ruled over them and founded the towns of Bouthoe (Budva) and Lychnidus (Ohrid). In the end king and queen were transformed by Zeus into dragons and removed to Elysium, while his son Illyrius or Polydorus succeeded to his throne. The *Periplus* places the Enchelei on the coast north of the Taulantii and attributes to them Bouthoe, on the coast near the Gulf of Kotor, which also figures in the Cadmus legend. If the Taulantii extended north to the Mat valley the Enchelei may have controlled the lower Drin and the plain around Shkodër. At this point the *Periplus*, as we have it, is muddled over the river Naron, the modern Neretva, and the Arion, which must be the ancient Drilon, the Albanian Drin. It seems best in this matter to follow the solution of M. Suić that the lake is in fact the Lake of Shkodër, into and out of which the Drin has flowed at various times in its history. Accepting this makes it possible to place the Autariatae beyond the lake and north of the lower Drin, which makes better sense than much further north in the mountains around the upper Neretva.[9]

With the Enchelei on the lower Drin and the Black Drin up to the source at Ohrid, their northern neighbours will have been the Autariatae, dwelling beyond the mountains which now divide northern Albania from Yugoslavia. What Greek sources tell of this remote people amounts to hardly more than anecdote. Whether or not the Ardaei already occupied the coast between the Lake of Shkodër and the Neretva remains in doubt. The rise to power on the Adriatic during the third century of these neighbours of the Autariatae will have involved the absorption of several smaller groups recorded for that area, including the Labeates, who appear to have retained their separate identity into the early Roman period.

The Illyrian Manii dwelt on the lower Neretva on the long narrow bay formed by the northwards-projecting peninsula Pelješac, and named Manius Bay after them. To their north the Nesti occupied the coast and hinterland around the Nestus (Cetina). This region was later occupied by the Delmatae but

[9] Katičić 1977b, Suić 1953, Papazoglu 1963, 1978, Martinović 1966.

their name does not appear until the second century BC. Opposite the Nesti on the mainland were the larger Dalmatian islands, Melite (Mljet), Black Corcyra (Korčula), which lies close to the tip of Pelješac, and then Pharos (Hvar) and Issa (Vis). In Crateia we may discern the name Brattia (Brač) and in Olunta that of Solentia (Šolta), which lie nearer to the mainland opposite Split. If the river Catarbates which marks the southern boundary of the Liburni is the Krka, the ancient Titus, which flows into the Adriatic through Lake Prokljan near Šibenik, then on the short stretch of coast between that and the Nestus (Cetina) are to be located some lesser Illyrian groups, the Bulini, Hierastamnae and Hylli. There seems to be no connection between these and the Delmatae later so dominant in this region, nor is there yet any reference to Salona at the head of its great bay or to Tragurium (Trogir) and Epetium (Stobreč) which were once possessions of the Greek colony on Issa. The Hylli take their name from Hyllus, a mythical son of Heracles, and the name persisted into Roman times as that of the headland on the coast south of Šibenik, the peninsula Hyllica, a place connected also with the cult of the hero Diomede. The name of the Bulini may be recalled by Bulinia, a place somewhere in this area on the Peutinger Map, a late Roman road map which survives in a medieval copy discovered in the sixteenth century by Conrad Peutinger. There seems little doubt that these smaller Illyrian communities known individually in the fourth century were later absorbed by the Delmatae. This is the case with the Caulici, Mentores, Syopii and Hythmitae listed in the region by Hecataeus of Miletus of the sixth century and with the Ismeni and Mentores named in the second century BC by the *Periegesis*.[10]

The Liburni are placed by Hecataeus on the innermost part of the Adriatic gulf. In the Periplus they dwell on the northeast Adriatic between Illyrians and Istri, where much of the coast is closed off from the interior by the Velebit mountains and screened by the islands of the Dalmatian archipelago. The Liburnian name seems to have passed into general use from the time when they dominated not only the entire Dalmatian

---

[10] Suić 1955. Hecataeus, *FGrHist* vol. 1, p. 20, F93–6.

coast but even for a time held Corcyra (Corfu) from which they were ejected by Corinthian settlers in the eighth century. A Liburnian maritime supremacy, or thalassocracy, recalls a historical tradition from a time when peoples were possibly moving across the Adriatic from east to west, from Liburnia into Picenum and from Illyria into Messapia and Japygia. The garbled list of places on the Liburnian coast in the *Periplus* has been reconstructed to name Tarsatica (Trsat near Rijeka), Lopsica (Sv Juraj), Senia (Senj) and Ortopula (Stinica), all in the northern part of historical Liburnia. The difficulty here is that this interpretation necessitates the identification of the river Catarbates with the Zrmanja (the ancient Tedanius) north of Zadar, placing the southern limit of the Liburni farther to the north than was ever later the case. Another, and more plausible, reconstruction lists Apsyrtae, the modern islands Cres and Mali Lošinj in the Kvarner, Alypsoi of the later Lopsica among the northern Liburni, and some of the major settlements on the plain behind Zadar, including Nedinum (Nadin), Aenona (Nin) and Jader (Zadar). In that case the Catarbates, literally the 'steeply-falling', is the Krka, which marked the boundary between Liburnians and Dalmatians in Hellenistic and Roman times. Finally, a long-standing association between the head of the Adriatic and the amber trade explains the name Elektrides (from *elektron*, the Greek word for amber) for some islands of the Kvarner gulf, including Cres, Krk and Mali Lošinj. The Mentores named by Hecataeus and other writers may denote other islands, such as Rab (ancient Arba) or Pag (Gissa). The reference to the Istrian peninsula as an island of around 40 by 15 miles is a not uncharacteristic error of the *Periplus*.[11]

For all its confusions the *Periplus* leaves no doubt that the inland peoples between the Adriatic and Sava were, if not altogether unknown, at least not in regular contact with the Greek world of the fourth century BC. A possible reference by Hecataeus to the Japodes, who occupied the Lika plain behind the Velebit, – 'Japygia a town in Italy and in Illyria' – does not alter this picture. Aside from amber there may have been

---

[11] Suić 1955.

little to attract Greeks towards the Liburnian shore of the upper
Adriatic, even if we treat as exaggeration the remark of a citizen
of classical Athens that sending a ship into the Adriatic at all
was an act of madness. An unfamiliarity with the upper Adriatic
is implied by the wide currency of the story that a branch of
the Danube flowed into it, by which it was possible to sail
between the Black Sea and the Adriatic. The fable was somehow
bound up with a similarity in name between the Adriatic Istri
and Ister, the Greek name for the (lower) Danube, as they came
to know it from the direction of the Black Sea. Also connected
with this was a belief that there existed an isthmus between
the head of the Adriatic and the Black Sea, repeated by Theopompus, a historian of the fourth-century BC, from whom it
was copied by the *Coastal Voyage* attributed to Scymnus of
Chios, by which time the story had become embedded in myths
of the heroes. This version actually has a branch of the Danube
entering the Adriatic. This is the background to one version of
the return voyage of the Argonauts, up the Danube and Sava
to enter the Adriatic by the Po, which appears in the poem of
the third-century Apollonius of Rhodes. Absyrtus, the slaugh-
tered half-brother of Medea, was commemorated by an island
in the northern Adriatic, while another story has it that Olcinium (Ulcinj) on the coast of Montenegro near the Lake of
Shkodër was a foundation of the pursuing Colchians.[12]

The fantastic story of the return voyage of the Argo may
echo voyages by Greeks in the remote past, venturing far
beyond the known limits of their world. That they should
return via the distant Adriatic may derive from the route of a
known trade link with Central Europe. A similar basis may
be suggested for Herodotus' story (4.32) of the Hyperborean
offerings: 'According to the Delians, certain sacred offerings
wrapped up in wheat-straw come from the Hyperboreans into
Scythia, whence they are taken over by the neighbouring
peoples in succession until they get as far west as the Adriatic;
from there they are sent south, and the first Greeks to receive

---

[12] Beaumont 1936, Katičić 1970, 1976c, Hecataeus, *FGrHist* vol. 1, p. 20,
F97 (Japygia).

them are the Dodonaeans' (of Dodona, the famous oracle of Zeus in Epirus). Something of the mechanics of prehistoric trade is revealed by the manner in which these gifts, which may have been pieces of amber destined for the Apollo of Delos, were passed from one group to another on their journey. Another voyage on this scale may lie behind the story of the treacherous Trojan Antenor who travelled to the Adriatic after the fall of Troy, where he is said to have founded several towns. One tradition connects him with Black Corcyra (Korčula). Another, already current in the time of the fifth-century dramatist Sophocles, tells of a descent of the (V)eneti from the (H)eneti of Asia Minor which was the background to yet another tale that Antenor, who had led them to Thrace, then journeyed to the head of the Adriatic and founded the town of Patavium (Padua).[13]

The classical Greeks had only to travel a short distance to the north or the northwest to find themselves in a land that was remote and strange. Soon after the sailor turned north out of the Gulf of Corinth a short voyage brought him to the river Achelous, where the Greek world ended. Beyond this the Greek communities of Acarnania and around the Ambracian gulf were outposts in a barbarian world. Futher north again Thesprotia was a remote land at the end of the world, and even the famous oracle of Zeus at Dodona among the Molossians was not easily accessible. Greek writers such as Thucydides viewed the 'mainland' (*epeiros*) from the perspective of Corcyra with its Corinthian colony facing across the strait. For the educated Athenian, people of this land lived in the old primitive ways, though this view was also taken of the Aetolians who, though Greek, had not yet advanced to the civilized urban life. Beyond Corcyra there were no city-states (*poleis*) but only tribes (*ethne*), such as the belligerent Chaonians. Few comprehended their languages, they dwelt in unfortified villages, ate their food uncooked and knew little of the vine. Though more accurate information must have become available over the centuries

[13] Katičić 1988 (Antenor), 1989 (Diomedes).

many later writers seemed content to pass on this portrayal by Thucydides. For Ephorus, writing in the fourth century BC, Acarnania was the end of Greece in that direction.[14]

As we have already seen, the *Periplus* sets the southern limit of Illyrians around Apollonia, where Chaonia began, but offers no ethnic definition for several groups between Illyrians and Greeks, including Chaonians, Thesprotians, Cassopaeans and Molossians. Though Polybius' doubts as to whether the Aetolians were really Greeks (18.1, 5) may be discarded as the partial view of an upper-class Achaean towards a rival power, there does appear to have been a consistent tradition from the time of Homer that Greeks ended with Acarnanians and barbarians began with Thesprotians. To Plutarch, who came from Chaeronea in Boeotia, Greeks living north of Acroceraunia (Cape Linguetta/Kep i Gjuhëzës) were exiles. Nevertheless there does seem to be evidence that these peoples of Epirus between Acharnania and Illyria spoke a language akin to Greek, though this is contested by Albanians who would have them to be Illyrians. From this point of view the use of Greek by these peoples by the middle of the fourth century must be reckoned as an alien official language, employed by a king (370–368 BC) of the Molossians for two decrees at Dodona. Perhaps more telling in favour of their non-Illyrian character is that well-born Molossians were admitted to the major athletic festivals of Greeks, an invitation never extended to Illyrians.[15]

Greeks among Illyrians

The full development of an iron-using material culture among Illyrian peoples by the eighth century BC coincides with the start of lasting contacts with the Aegean civilizations of archaic and classical Greece. The intensive use of iron ore and the mastery of iron-working techniques led to economic and social change. The exchange of commodities between different groups increased in volume and was a catalyst in the formation of

[14] Cabanes 1988a.
[15] Cabanes 1988a, 31 (Molossian decrees).

tribal groups, with an increasing consciousness of collective identity under individual rulers. The later stages of this culture are marked by princely burials with rich grave goods. In addition to the Italian connections it has been suggested that traces of archaic Greek influence can be seen in some of the ornament, notably in the warrior frieze on the famous situla from Vače. In the western and central Balkans the developed Iron Age among the Illyrians is still viewed principally through the contents of tumuli burials on the Glasinac plateau, where the persisting conservatism of Illyrian burial traditions has long been recognized.

The distinguishing objects of this culture are double-arched fibulae, bracelets and iron weapons, notably swords, axes, shields, etc. A love of amber, for beads, necklaces and charms, was evidently common among the Illyrians and is often cited as a distinguishing feature of their burial groups. The climax of this culture is evident in rich burials of the sixth and fifth centuries, when the princes and princesses of the warrior elites were buried clad in all their finery, with gold and silver belts and girdles, bracelets, spears, varieties of pottery, jewellery, hairpins and pendants. A feature of some of these burials is the presence of high-quality pottery, metalware and jewellery of Greek origin. In addition there are other objects of similar character which may be the work of Greek craftsmen but whose design and ornament suggest that they were created specifically for Illyrian and other 'barbarian' tastes. This group of objects has been much discussed over the years. Some scholars have argued that they are the work of Illyrian craftsmen imitating Greek fashions and from this notion has stemmed the concept of a 'Greco-Illyrian' material culture of the sixth to fifth centuries BC.[16]

The principal finds-spots of Greek imports in the Illyrian territories include the following: Atenica (princely tombs of the late sixth/early fifth centuries BC with Ionian glass, glass-paste and amber beads and an Attic plaque depicting a wild boar); Glasinac (South Italian archaic objects, bronze vessels, Ionian pottery, classical (probably Attic) metalwork, armour and

[16] Mano-Zissi 1973, Popović 1975, Parović-Pešikan 1985, 1986.

ornaments); Novi Pazar (large cache of regalia, gold and silver jewellery, beads, and Attic pottery); Kačanj (warrior graves of the late sixth to early fifth century with Attic pottery, Greco-Illyrian helmets and silver jewellery); Ljubomir (warrior burials with fifth century Attic pottery, pins and brooches); Mramorac (burials with silver belts and bracelets with ornament in a Greek style, possibly late sixth century); Umčari (burials with silver belts, pins, brooches, etc. with Greek ornament); Ražana (cemetery of around 500 BC containing Greco-Illyrian helmet); Bela Crkva (burial with miniature pots imitating Greek forms of the late fifth century); Sremska Mitrovica ('boat'-earrings and gold necklace, possibly Ionian of around 500 BC); Široko (settlement remains with Greek pottery and jewellery); Batinci (silver belts with Greek-style ornament); Tuzla (tombs with 'Greco-Illyrian' objects, glass-paste beads and pins); Josainička Banja (Hellenistic pottery, including Megarian bowls, in settlement). Among the southernmost Illyrian communities several cemeteries have produced some of the best-known evidence for this Greco-Illyrian culture. Easily the most famous are the burials at Trebenište near Lake Ohrid, where the contents of princely burials have been much discussed since the first finds were made during the First World War, particularly the gold face-masks and sandals. Greek imports in the tombs, which consist of relatively modest burials of around the mid-sixth century, princely burials of the early fifth century and some later burials, include Ionian and other bronze tripods, bronze crater, hydria, a candelabrum base, lekythoi, kylices, filigree jewellery, silver brooches, glass amphorae and miniatures. Other sites in the same area include Saraj, Brod near Bitolj (Greek pottery or local imitations in possible seventh century Corinthian form), Visoi near Bitolj (two groups of burials, Visoi I with Greek pottery and jewellery, Visoi II later cremations with finds similar to Trebenište); Radolište near Lake Ohrid (tombs with Greek imports of late sixth or early fifth century, pins, brooches, bronze vessels, earrings and Greco-Illyrian helmet dated to the second half of the sixth century); Karaorman in Paeonia near Štip (six tombs with Greek painted pottery and jewellery, with a Greek coin of around 480 BC); Trebeniško Kale (tombs dated to the fourth to second centuries with pottery in Hellenistic forms and jewellery); and Demir Kapija, a long established settlement on the Vardar south of Stobi in Paeonia at the entrance to the gorge (Greek pottery of fifth to fourth century in settlement of Macedonians and Greeks).[17]

By what means and by what routes these Greek objects came to lie among the treasuries of Illyrian tombs remains largely a matter of speculation. It may be that for a period an overland transit existed from the direction of Asia Minor and the Black Sea, and it has been suggested that Herodotus' account of the Danube basin may have been based on information of Ionian traders starting inland from Istros near the Danube delta. Another matter of debate has been the extent of commercial iclinks before the end of the fifth century from the direction of the Adriatic and southern Italy. Certainly the reception of Greek prestige goods by the Illyrian elite appears confined to the sixth and fifth centuries, mainly from the second half of the former and from the early years of the latter. After the middle of the fifth century Greek imports are, with a few exceptions, absent from Illyrian tombs, and only the Glasinac tumuli furnish evidence for a continuing reception of Greek imports. Hellenistic products of the fourth to second centuries are confined mainly to regions bordering Macedonia, and there is almost nothing from areas further north. The brief duration of this Greco-Illyrian connection may be explained by two factors, a collapse of the power of native rulers among the Illyrians and the shifting balance of political power in Greece. The fact that a significant proportion of the imports have an Attic or Ionian origin suggests that the cessation of commerce with the Illyrians was linked with a decline in Athenian power after the middle of the fifth century and the later outbreak of the Peloponnesian War with Sparta and her allies. In a later period the main direction of Greek penetration was from the direction of the Adriatic and southern Italy.[18]

---

[17] Parović-Pešikan 1964; Trebenište: Filow 1927, Vulić 1933, Popović 1956, Lahtov 1955; Novi Pazar: Mano-Zissi and Popović 1969.
[18] Lisičar 1973, Batović 1984 (Corinthian pottery), Petrić 1980 (Apulian imports), Glogović 1979 (S. Italian in Istria), Mano 1976b, 1986 (trade

If one may accept this reconstruction there remains the problem of what is termed the 'Greco-Illyrian culture'. Several types of object which occur in similar contexts to those of the Greek imports listed above have been classified either as Greek products created specifically for an Illyrian taste or as the products of Illyrian workshops working in close imitation of Greek models. Perhaps the most discussed example is the open-faced bronze 'Greco-Illyrian' helmet. Dated to the late sixth and fifth centuries, these have been found down the Adriatic coast as far as Albania and in the Ohrid region. Their origin has been sought in an early Peloponnesian, probably Corinthian, type recorded at Olympia and dated to 700–640 BC. A helmet from Canosa in southern Italy has suggested to some that the traffic in these helmets may have been linked with this area. It seems unlikely this very distinctive helmet was a local product of scattered workshops but, as seems to be indicated by its distribution, was a type produced specifically for the northern warriors and possibly may be related to some form of mercenary service by Illyrians. The same uncertainty persists regarding the few isolated finds of early Greek objects from the western Balkans, such as bronze running figures from Prizren and from Albania, a maenad from Tetovo on the upper Vardar and the fine bronze-working smith, probably Peloponnesian work, from Vranište near Bela Palanka in Serbia, all of which are dated to the same era of prestigious imports, the late sixth and early fifth centuries.[19]

Several other varieties of jewellery and ornament are thought likely to be local production in imitation of Greek models, notably double 'omega'-pins, arched brooches and silver bracelets with snake's head terminals. These were placed alongside Greek imports in princely burials and are generally identified from an inferiority in production technique, notably in the large variety of objects at Trebenište; but they are also found

routes in S. Illyria), Parović-Pešikan 1985–6 (pottery imports in Bosnia), Vučković-Todorović 1973 (E. Yugoslavia), Bousquet 1974 (Tetovo epitaph), Parović-Pešikan 1978 (sixth century inscription at Lipljan).

[19] Greco-Illyrian helmets: Marović 1976b, Vasić 1982–3, Andreou 1985, Osmani 1988; weapons: Vasić 1982a, Parović-Pešikan 1982 (Greek machaira), Vasić 1983 (bronze vessels), Vasiliev 1983 (transport of bronzes).

later in the large cemetery at Budva on the Adriatic and among the Japodes at Kompolje in the Lika. It may well be that the gold masks, gauntlet and sandals in Trebenište, and the gold and silver and silver belt appliqués with repoussé ornament including Greek motifs such as palmettes, are local, if Greek-inspired creations for Illyrian taste. What appears to have been a successful symbiosis in material culture between Greeks and the Illyrian rulers can be compared with a similar relationship already identified for the same period in other areas of Europe, notably the Celtic northwest, which bordered the highly productive Mediterranean cultures of Greece and south Italy. Display of exotic ornament and gorgeous apparel will have served to underwrite the status of a native elite, who controlled the sources of wealth, exportable raw materials including metal ores, timber, hides and cereals along with slaves and mercenaries, that brought such prestigious goods to a chief's stronghold and in due course to his family burials in remote Illyria. The precious imports included fine dress ornaments and the utensils for banquets and wine-drinking in the grand manner, many of which were destined for the oblivion of the tomb. How much the Illyrian princes had in common with their contemporaries in western Europe is hard to judge but their common taste for objects garishly ornamented in the Greek style appears beyond doubt.[20]

Greeks were generally reluctant to risk life among Illyrians and, with two notable exceptions, their settlements came late and never amounted to much. North of the Gulf of Corinth they appear to have made little impact on territories west of the Pindus. As one travels westwards across the mountainous spine of mainland Greece there are marked changes in climate and vegetation: temperatures are generally lower and the winter rainfall is heavy and prolonged, forming real rivers with a permanent flow. Forests are more widespread and there is excellent pasturage. The movement of flocks revolves around the great seasonal festivals of St George (23 April) and St. Demetrius (23 October). In this world meat and milk are

[20] Parović-Pešikan 1983 (Apulian and Etruscan imports to Adriatic hinterland).

important for the diet. Women have a more significant role
than in the world of the classical *polis* further east, and the
extended family remains the basic unit of society. At the political level there is nothing to compare with the closed and
integrated *polis* but a looser and more dispersed federation of
groups belonging to a single tribe. Confronted with this society
and its different ways Greek writers soon resort to labels such
as 'brigands' or 'pirates'. Even after centuries of relatively stable
contact the Greeks took little account of changes which had
occurred among these peoples, where even the urban settlements that had grown up under their influence still retained
the character of mountain strongholds.[21]

If we omit such tales as the settlement of Oricus on the
Bay of Valona by Euboeans following the Trojan War, the
first recorded advance by Greeks in the direction of the
Illyrians was made by Corinthians. In 733 BC Chersicrates,
a member of the Bacchiad clan ruling at Corinth, established
a settlement on Corcyra (Corfu) that served as the principal
staging-point on the voyage between Greece and the west.
Having ejected some Eretrians from Euboea and some Liburnians from the northern Adriatic, the Corinthians soon prospered. The next expansion of the Corinthian empire came
around a century later when a joint expedition from Corinth
and Corcyra founded on the Illyrian mainland the colony
Epidamnus on the headland Dyrrhachium, the name by which
the city was later known.[22] Along with Apollonia further
south, the new settlement brought the short sea crossing to
southern Italy under Greek control and was for centuries a
terminus of the principal highway across the southern Balkans, later engineered by the Romans as the Via Egnatia.
These settlements will also have secured control of that route
to the interior and access to the silver deposits of the region.
The foundation myth of the colony is offered by the historian
Appian as a digression from the Roman civil war between
Pompey and Caesar in 48 BC:

[21] Cabanes 1988a.
[22] Hammond 1982b, Myrto 1986, N. Ceka 1972, 1976, Petrova 1980
(currency).

Dyrrhachium some believe to be the same as Epidamnus, on account of the following error. A barbarian king of the region, by name Epidamnus, built a city on the coast and named it after himself. Dyrrhachus, the son of his daughter and, as it was believed, of Poseidon, added a harbour to the city which he named Dyrrhachium. When Dyrrhachus was attacked by his brothers, Heracles, returning from Erythrae (whence he had carried off the oxen of king Geryon) made an alliance with him in return for a share of his territory. From this the citizens of Dyrrhachium claim Heracles as one of their founders because he had a share of their land, not dishonouring Dyrrhachus but because they took even greater pride in Heracles as being a god. They say that in a battle Heracles mistakenly killed Ionius, the son of Dyrrhachus, and, having raised a burial mound, threw the body into the sea so that it would be named after him. In a later period the Bryges, returning from Phrygia, seized the city and surrounding territory, then the Taulantii, an Illyrian people, took it from them and the Liburni, another Illyrian people, took it from the Taulantii. They were in the habit of making plundering expeditions against their neighbours in very fast ships. And because these were the first the Romans came up against they bestow the name Liburnae on very fast ships. Those expelled from Dyrrhachium by the Liburnians obtained help from the Corcyraeans then masters of the sea and drove out the Liburni. The Corcyraeans mixed in their own settlers with them and for this reason it came to be regarded as a Greek port. But believing its name to be ill-starred, the Corcyraeans changed the name and called it Epidamnus from the upper city, and Thucydides also calls it by that name, but in the end the old name triumphed and it is now called Dyrrhachium. (*Civil War* 2.39)

The Illyrian element in the Greek colony appears to be borne out by the contents of early cemeteries, in which Corinthian grave-pottery of the seventh and sixth centuries is found alongside cremation urns of the local type. The successive rule of Taulantii and Liburni in the historical tradition may represent the southward movement of Illyrian peoples during the early Iron Age from around 1000 BC into the area known as Illyris. The presence of Bryges at Epidamnus in the account of Appian seems to be confirmed by other sources, including the *Coastal Voyage* attributed to Scymnus of Chios and Strabo's *Geography*. No later record of their presence in the area survives and nor can any link be established with the Bryges of Thrace, supposedly descended from the soldiers of Xerxes' army, who

appear four centuries later in the army of M. Brutus during
the Philippi campaign. The settlement at Epidamnus became a
flourishing centre for commerce and remains today the principal port (Durrës) for the region. We learn that its constitution
was oligarchic and that many of the inhabitants were not
citizens. By the sixth century the city had erected its own
treasury for dedications at Olympia. Thucydides' account of
the internal conflicts (*stasis*) during the 430s BC makes clear
that this was not the first trouble of this kind in the colony. In
the struggle for power between democrats and aristocrats, the
latter supported by Corcyra, the Taulantii continued to play a
major role in the affairs of the city. When the democrats gained
the upper hand their opponents turned for help to the Illyrians.
They appeared in strength to besiege the city in 435, in the
process causing much damage to the city's economy through
their occupation of the surrounding country.[23]

The second Greek settlement on the Illyrian mainland was
Apollonia, traditionally founded in 588 BC on a headland overlooking the mouth of the river Aous (Vijosë), ten stades from
the river and 50 from the sea. It lay close to the frontier
between Illyris and Epirus and may have been established to
make secure the former's control of that area. Around 600 BC
Corinth is said to have responded to an Illyrian invitation and
contributed 200 settlers to an already existing trading post.
Others, especially from Corcyra, followed these. The colony
was said to have been named Gylaceia after its founder the
Corinthian Gylax, but later took the name from Apollo. For
several centuries Greek and Illyrian communities appear to
have maintained a separate existence. That is the impression
from cemeteries with contents that are quite different, one with
imported pottery, the other exhibiting the older tradition of
burial mounds and the rite of inhumation. Apollonia's prosperity during the sixth and fifth centuries BC was based on
herds, well nourished in the surrounding pastures. The excep-

---

[23] Anamali 1970, Bakhuizen 1986; cemeteries: Dhima 1985a, Myrto 1984,
Tatari 1987, Hidri 1983; pottery production: Hidri 1986, 1988, Tatari
1977–8 (local), D'Andrea 1986 (export); also Tatari 1985 (building
construction), 1988 (Hellenistic house), Zeqo 1986 (stone and terracotta
figures).

tional richness of Apollonian territory sustained a notably narrow oligarchic regime, described by Aristotle, who could discover no trace of democracy in a city where a minority of freemen controlled a majority that were not freeborn. The privileged were evidently descendants of the original colonists while their subjects were not captured or purchased slaves but rather the native population of the area with the status of serfs integrated into the highly successful economy of the city.[24]

Epidamnus and Apollonia were for centuries the principal ports for traffic between Greece, the western Balkans and the middle Danube. In the Hellenistic period they were first strategic bases for the military ambitions of kings of Epirus and Macedonia and then, especially Apollonia, the principal ports of disembarkation for Roman armies. Apollonia also acquired among Romans the reputation of a centre of higher learning, and may have been the original terminus of the Via Egnatia. By the second and early first centuries BC the coins of the two cities were circulating widely in the middle Danube basin, evidently serving as a convenient silver currency for merchants and slave-traders. Most of the remains of Epidamnus/Dyrrhachium lie beneath the modern city Durrës, Albania's principal port, testifying to its continued prosperity. Apollonia, by way of contrast, had lost its harbour as the course of the river altered, and the ruins of the Hellenistic and Roman city stand forlorn on the hill of Pojani.

No Greek settlements are known to have been established on the mainland north of Epidamnus/Dyrrhachium. North of the river Drin neither coast nor hinterland invited permanent settlement and, although Greeks undoubtedly lived and traded in several places, the three formally constituted colonies were all on islands, Black Corcyra (Korčula), Issa (Vis) and Pharos (Hvar). On the opposite coast the Po valley settlements of Spina and Adria, which flourished during the fifth and fourth centuries as the destinations of long-distance sea trade from Phocaea and Aegina, acquired something of the character of

---

[24] Beaumont 1952, Blavatsky 1966 (foundation), 1971, Anamali 1970, Bakhuizen 1986; cemeteries: Mano 1976a, 1977–8, Korkuti 1981 (pre-colonial tumuli), Nemeskeri and Dhima 1988 (racial mixture in cemetery), Bereti 1977–8, 1988 (Triport occupation), Vreka 1988 (Hellenistic black-glaze).

colonial settlements. In material terms the commerce between
Greece and the upper Adriatic was the procurement of salt,
corn and cattle, for which the Greeks offered wine, pottery and
metal wares.[25]

Early in the sixth century settlers from Cnidus in Asia Minor
settled on the Dalmatian island Black Corcyra (Korčula), so
named from its dense vegetation to distinguish it from its larger
namesake further south. The citizens of the latter assisted the
venture after the Cnidians had rescued 300 boys from the
hostile Periander, tyrant of Corinth. The settlers named their
colony after the land of their benefactors. The site of the
settlement has not been located but lay either in the west or in
the northeast at the narrow passage with the peninsula Pelješac,
where the modern city Korčula enjoys two excellent harbours.
Some coins with a Corcyraean legend may belong to the settlement but the venture appears to have failed, and the island is
known to have received at least one other new settlement,
probably in the third century BC. Native Illyrians do not figure
in the story of the colony on Black Corcyra but they are
certainly prominent in the early history of the colony settled in
385 BC on the island Pharos (Hvar) from the Aegean island
Paros, famed for its marble. In traditional fashion they accepted
the guidance of an oracle, but the settlers received more tangible
assistance from Dionysius, the ambitious ruler of Syracuse, who
had around the same time engineered an Illyrian attack on the
Molossians in Epirus. The account of Diodorus says that he
had already sent a colony to the Adriatic and founded 'the city
named Lissus'. The Parians on Pharos were soon in difficulties
with the natives and needed help from the tyrant.

This year the Parians who had settled on Pharos allowed the previous
barbarian inhabitants to remain unharmed in a well fortified place,
while they themselves built their city by the sea and enclosed it with
a wall. Later the earlier inhabitants took offence at the presence of
the Greeks and called in the Illyrians dwelling on the mainland
opposite. These crossed to Pharos in a large number of small boats
and, more than ten thousand strong, killed many Greeks and did

---

[25] Nikolanci 1976a, Braccesi 1977, Bakhuizen 1987, Woodhead 1970
(Dionysius of Syracuse).

much damage. However Dionysius' commander at Lissus sailed up with a large number of triremes against the Illyrian light craft and, having sunk some and captured others, killed more than five thousand of the barbarians and took around two thousand prisoner. (*Diodorus* 15.14)

The third Greek colony known in this central sector of the Dalmatian coast was Issa on the north side of the island Vis. Nothing is recorded of its foundation, but coins and internal organization (recorded on inscriptions) suggest that it was a Syracusan settlement. It has been proposed that it was this place and not Lissus far to the south at the mouth of the Drin from which help came to the Greeks on Pharos, since Issa lies only 25 miles away. The voyage from Lissus was more than ten times as long, but a garrison at the latter would fit better with Dionysius' schemes involving Illyrians and Molossians. A more stable relationship with native Illyrians is implied by the decree recording the details of a settlement from Issa on Black Corcyra. On the document, which has been dated to the third century BC, are named the Illyrians Pullus and Dazus, while most of the text specifies the allotment of lands to individual families, both within and without the walls of the settlement, grouped by the traditional Dorian 'tribes' of Dymanes, Hylleis and Pamphyloi.[26]

A handful of inscriptions and some locally struck coins with a limited circulation testify to a survival of the Greek settlements on Pharos and Issa, though only the latter appears to have maintained its independence until the Romans appeared in 229 BC. Pharos was subject to the Illyrian dynasty of Agron, albeit under the rule of the native Demetrius of Pharos. The site of the colony was Starigrad, a sheltered harbour in the northeast of the island. The near square enclosure of the walls lies beneath the modern town, close to the fertile plain of Jelsa.

---

[26] D. Rendić-Miočević 1980 (Corcyra Nigra), Cambi, Kirigin and Marin 1981, Kirigin and Marin 1985 (Issa necropolis), Zaninović 1978, 1984b (hill-forts on Hvar), 1980–1 (land division on Hvar), Slapšak 1988, Stančić and Slapšak 1988, Bintliff and Gaffney 1988 (land division and survey on Hvar), Kirigin and Popović 1988 (Greek watchtower), Migotti 1986 (Hellenistic pottery in Hvar), Margetić 1971, D. Rendić-Miočević 1970a (colony of Issa on Korčula).

This had been occupied divided into a rectangular grid of roads and paths at the time of the original colonization, and it may have been this which caused the initial accommodation with the Illyrians to decline into hostility. The near rectangular walled area of Issa contained a planned city with parallel streets. Recent discoveries here include a remarkable series of burials dating to the Hellenistic period, containing Greek pottery and with some of the inscribed tombstones still in their original positions. Around this period, the first half of the second century BC, Issa appears to have prospered under Roman influence and possessed at least two settlements on the nearby mainland, at Tragurium (Trogir) and Epetium (Stobreč), both of which have produced Greek remains. When these places were threatened by the local Delmatae it was Issa's appeal to Rome which brought the first confrontation between the latter and this powerful people. The survival of Issa and Pharos was owed to their own resources. Perhaps Issa may have gained some profit from long-distance commerce, though more as a port of call than as a centre for trading with the natives of the mainland.[27] Though far from their Greek origins the two colonies maintained links with their homeland, Pharos on one occasion appealing to its metropolis for 'repair and support'. Nevertheless, an impression of isolation and gradual decline is suggested by Pliny's reference to 'the fading memory of many Greek towns and strong cities' (*NH* 3.144) in Illyria.

[27] Nikolanci 1968–9 (Corinthian pottery on Issa), 1976a, 1976b (Asia Minor imports), 1980 (inscription), D. Rendić-Miočević 1970b, 1976b (coinage).

5

Enemies of Macedonia

Conquering kings: Philip, Alexander and Pyrrhus[1]

Illyrians first appear in the record of Greek affairs not long before the Peace of Nicias ended the first phase of the Peloponnesian War in 421 BC. Before Athens suffered defeat at Delium in 424 BC, Sparta had sent an expedition under Brasidas to assist King Perdiccas of Macedonia and other opponents of Athens. At first the Spartans avoided involvement in Macedon's war with Arrhabaeus the son of Bromerus, ruler of Lyncus (Lyncestis), but in 423 they joined an expedition which ended with ignominious retreat by the Macedonians and a brilliantly contrived escape of the Spartans. After an initial success against Arrhabaeus, Perdiccas persuaded his allies to await the arrival of Illyrian mercenaries. The latter opted instead to join the army of Arrhabaeus and, as the historian Thucydides observes, 'the fear inspired by their warlike character made both parties now think it best to retreat.' When the Spartans finally reached safety they proceeded to loot supplies from the Macedonian army, causing a rupture of the pact between the king and the Spartans. The historian attributes to the Spartan commander a morale-raising harangue to his men, clearly shaken by the fearsome appearance of a new enemy:

[1] For accounts of the fourth and third centuries, Cabanes 1988a, Hammond 1966, Hammond and Griffith 1979, Hammond and Walbank 1988.

they may terrify those with an active imagination, they are formidable in outward bulk, their loud yelling is unbearable and the brandishing of their weapons in the air has a threatening appearance. But when it comes to real fighting with an opponent who stands his ground they are not what they seemed; they have no regular order that would make them ashamed of deserting their positions when hard pressed; with them flight and attack are equally honourable, and afford no test of courage; their independent mode of fighting never leaving anyone who wants to run away without a fair excuse for so doing. (4.126)[2]

In the troubled reign of Amyntas III (393–370/369 BC), father of Philip II, a powerful and apparently stable regime among the southern Illyrians first emerges. This marks the beginning of a succession of wars which were to end only with Roman intervention and the end of the Macedonian monarchy two centuries later. The surviving accounts are both incomplete and in places contradictory, although the general course of events seems clear. Diodorus the Sicilian (*c*.30 BC), who probably followed the fourth-century Greek writer Ephorus, describes a catastrophic attack by Illyrians in 393/2 BC:

Amyntas the father of Philip was driven from his country by Illyrians who attacked Macedonia. Giving up hope for his crown, he made a present to the people of Olynthus of his territory which bordered on theirs. For a time he lost his kingdom but he was soon restored by the Thessalians, regaining his crown and ruling for twenty-four years. Some say that after the expulsion of Amyntas the Macedonians were ruled for two years by Argaeus and that it was after this interval that Amyntas recovered the kingship. (14.92, 3)

Diodorus' account of a near identical Illyrian raid ten years later is generally taken to be an erroneous duplication but this is far from definite. Certainly it would not have been at all untypical of the Illyrians to repeat a raid and exploit their victory in the same manner after an interval of a few years. Between the two invasions of Macedonia, Illyrians are said to have launched an attack on Epirus in 384/5 BC. The instigator is said to have been Dionysius of Syracuse, eager to interfere

---

[2] Hammond 1972, 104–7.

in the Adriatic, on this occasion in support of Alcetias the exiled king of the Molossians. The Sicilian tyrant contributed 2000 troops and 500 sets of armour, in which the Illyrians set about the Molossians in battle and, it is claimed, killed more than 15,000, withdrawing only when a Spartan army came to the rescue of the Epirotes. The episode made plain the rise of Illyrian power on the northwest fringes of the Greek world, though when they launched a similar attack 25 years later the Molossian king Harrybas evacuated his non-combatant population to Aetolia and gave the Illyrians to understand that his lands were open to them. The strategy worked and the Molossians fell upon the Illyrians laden with booty, and robbed and expelled them.[3]

In 370 BC the worthy Amyntas died full of years, having restored the fortunes of his kingdom after Illyrian disasters. His marriage to Eurydice of the Lyncestae had produced three sons and a daughter. His eldest son succeeded through election but the reign of Alexander, who was said to have bought off the Illyrians and delivered his brother Philip to them as a hostage, was brief. During a campaign in 368 or 367 he was murdered by his kinsman Ptolemy who was himself suppressed in 365 by the king's younger brother Perdiccas. The latter died early in 359 in a shattering defeat at the hands of the Illyrians, not the first occasion he had fought against them. More than 4000 Macedonians were killed 'and the remainder, panic-stricken, having become exceedingly afraid of Illyrian armies, had lost heart for continuing the war' (Diodorus 16.2, 8–9). The scale of this disaster may later have been exaggerated in order to magnify the achievement of Philip, but it seems that once again Illyrians had brought Macedonia close to collapse, when the kingdom was also threatened by Paeonians, Thracians, Chalcidians and Athenians.[4]

The Illyrian victory of Philip early in his reign was to prove decisive for the security of Macedonia in that quarter. Having struck a treaty with Athens late in 359 and dealt with the

[3] Hammond and Griffith 1979, 172–5 (no duplication), Diodorus Siculus 14.92 (393/2 BC), 15.2 (383/2 BC), 16.2 (360/359 BC).
[4] Justinus 7.5 (Alexander), Diodorus Siculus 16.2, Hammond and Griffith 1979, 188.

Paeonians early in the following year the new king concentrated all his power against the Illyrians. With 600 cavalry and 10,000 infantry he advanced into their territory and rejected an offer by the Illyrian ruler Bardylis of a treaty on the basis of the status quo, demanding instead surrender of all the Macedonian towns they held. Bardylis gave battle with a force which matched that of Philip. The Illyrians formed a defensive square and there was a long fight with heavy casualties until the Macedonian cavalry broke through, and Illyrian losses were said to be 7,000. Macedonia now controlled all the territory as far as Lake Lychnitis (Ohrid) and was now as well placed to attack the Illyrians as they had once been to raid Macedonia. It was a famous victory. Though some information about Bardylis is provided by the contemporary historian Theopompus and by other writers, none identifies his regime with any people or tribe other than Illyrians. In the great battle with Philip he is said to have fought on horseback at the age of 90, and there is no suggestion that he did not survive the encounter. He was, it is said, by origin a charcoal-burner who amassed a fortune and founded a dynasty by sharing out the booty gained in raids he had directed. Nothing stands on the record to locate the centre of his power, save for the fact that Philip's victory in 358 BC gained control of Lyncestis. A later victory by Philip over Cleitus the son of Bardylis apparently reduced the latter to the status of a client, and this may have been achieved by operations against Dardanians. In that case the power of Bardylis may have been centred among the southern Dardanians of Kosovo and Metohija, from which it expanded to the southwest as far as the Molossians, south to Lyncestis and, for short periods, southeast to include Macedonia.[5]

Philip II was soon again at war with Illyrians, though evidently not those ruled by Bardylis. Diodorus informs us that in 356 BC kings of the Thracians, Paeonians and Illyrians combined to resist the rising power of Macedonia, by whom each had already been defeated. Philip moved before the allies

[5] Papazoglu 1961 (Heraclea Lyncestis), Diodorus Siculus 16.4, Hammond and Griffith 1979, 213–14.

could unite their forces, and 'struck terror into them and compelled them to join their forces with the Macedonians'. The
coalition had evidently been contrived by the Athenians, and
the names of the rulers involved, Grabus of the Illyrians, Lyppe-
ius of the Paeonians and Cetriporis of Thrace, are preserved in
an Athenian decree ratifying the alliance. The victory over the
Illyrians in 356 BC, achieved by Parmenio in a major battle,
along with the victory of the royal chariot at the Olympic
Games, were later recalled as propitious coincidences with the
day on which Alexander the Great was born. The Illyrians of
Grabus are unlikely to have been the subjects of Bardylis
defeated only two years earlier, though some have suggested
Grabus was his son and successor. His name suggests some
connection with the Grabaei, a minor people of the Illyrians
who lived on the southern Adriatic near the Lake of Shkodër.

In 344/3 BC, according to Diodorus: 'Philip had inherited
from his father a quarrel with the Illyrians and found no means
of reconciling his disagreement. He therefore invaded Illyria
with a large force, devastated the countryside, captured many
towns and returned to Macedonia laden with booty' (16.69,
7). Some detail is furnished by Didymus, an Alexandrian com-
mentator on the Philippics of Demosthenes of the first century
BC, who records that among the many wounds sustained by
Philip, one came from the Triballi (in 339 BC) and another
during an earlier campaign against Illyrians. On this occasion
the king was pursuing the Illyrian Pleuratus, when Hippostratus
the son of Amyntas and 150 of the elite corps of the Companions were casualties. Next the historian Justinus compresses
into a single sentence the reference to an Illyrian war which he
places between 346 and the end of 343 BC. The enemy are
named as 'the Dardani and other neighbouring peoples', whom
Philip defeated and took prisoner 'by a deceit'. Finally, under
the year 336/5 BC, in the context of incidents leading up to the
murder of Philip by Pausanias, Diodorus records that, 'as Philip
was engaged in battle with Pleurias, king of the Illyrians, Pausanias, one of the royal bodyguard, stepped in front of him and,
receiving on his body all the blows directed at the king, so met
his death' (16.93, 6). From these scraps of evidence one may
reconstruct a series of calculated forays intended to secure the

Illyrian rear of Macedonia, prior to the planned expedition
against the Persian king that would remove the best of the
army to Asia.[6]

The first demonstration of the exceptional military talent
of Alexander, son of Philip II, took the form of a spectacular
sweep through the Balkans, in which the strength and versatility
of the army he had inherited from his father were fully tested.
In the spring of 335 BC, the year following Philip's death, an
expedition moved north from Amphipolis and, having brushed
aside any Thracian resistance, crossed the Haemus (Stara
Planina) to attack the Triballi on the right bank of the lower
Danube. After a battle in which 300 of the Triballi were killed,
Alexander crossed the river and defeated the Getae. The Triballi
now formally surrendered, and among others who came to pay
their respects were 'Celts from the Ionian gulf' who dwelt 'in
a distant country that was hard to penetrate', presumably the
lands between the head of the Adriatic and the middle Danube.
Expressions of friendship were reciprocated, though the Celts
made it clear they were far from being in awe of the Macedonians.

Next came trouble with the Illyrians. When the returning
army had reached Paeonia, Alexander received news that Cleitus the son of Bardylis had taken up arms and that he was
supported by Glaucias of the Taulantii over towards the Adriatic, and also that the Autariatae were planning to ambush his
army on the march. Alexander knew little or nothing of this
people but he was assured by his ally king Langarus of the
Agrianes that there was little to fear from them. With Alexander's approval he attacked them and inflicted severe damage but
died before he could enjoy the promised reward. At this point
the Illyrians decided to launch an attack on Macedonia, before
Alexander and his army returned from the Danube. It was the

[6] Diodorus Siculus 16.22 (356 BC), Plutarch, *Alexander* 3, Justinus 12.16
(birth of Alexander), Isocrates, *Philipp.* 21, Demosthenes *Philippic.* 1.48 (350
BC), *Olynthiac* 1.13 (349 BC) Diodorus Siculus 16.69, 3 (344/3 BC), Didymus
Comm. on Demosthenes Philippic. col. 12, 64, Justinus 8.6, Diodorus Siculus
16.93 (336/5 BC). Hammond 1966, 245–6, Hammond and Griffith 1979,
469–74, Hammond 1981, Hatzopoulos 1987, Tronson 1984 (marriage of
Philip II with Illyrian Audata).

Figure 10 Rock-cut tomb at Selcë e Poshtme, Albania

news of Philip's death which had stirred the northern peoples
to action: 'Illyrians, Thracians, Dardanians and other barbarian
tribes of dubious and untrustworthy nature, who could never
be held in check by any means if they were all to revolt at the
same time' (Justinus 11.1, 6). Alexander advanced his forces
up the river Erigon (Crna Reka) to Pelion, where Cleitus had
moved to await Glaucias and the Taulantii. The site was well
protected and was ringed by commanding heights, held by the
troops of Cleitus. One possible location is the isolated hill-
settlement at Goricë in the plain of Poloskë near the river
Devoll, which has Hellenistic and later fortifications, and was
clearly a central place in this part of Dassaretis, the Korcë basin
south of Ohrid. More recently Albanian archaeologists have
identified Pelion with the remains at Selcë e Poshtme on the
upper course of the Shkumbin. Here the most notable remains
are a group of tombs, with chambers and architectural façades
carved out of a rock face (see figure 10). Their princely character has suggested a comparison with the famous royal tombs
at Vergina in Macedonia, and this has been partly borne out
by the contents of one of them. Alexander's Illyrian campaign
is described by Arrian. The Macedonians arrived before Glaucias and the Taulantii but the Illyrians, having sacrificed three
boys, three girls and three black rams, made as if to attack.

When the Macedonians also began to move they abandoned
their defensive positions and fled into Pelion, leaving the sacrificial victims where they had fallen. The day after Alexander
began his blockade Glaucias and his large army arrived, probably from the west via the Tsangon pass. Alexander now
extricated his outnumbered forces from a dangerous position
and, using fully the discipline and training imposed by his
father on the Macedonian army, succeeded in defeating both
Cleitus and Glaucias. Alexander's campaign was fought not in
Illyris but in Dassaretis, the plains south of Lake Ohrid, though
the area had long been under Illyrian control, being open to
attack both from the north and from the west. The whole
episode is recounted by Arrian as a demonstration of Alexander's brilliance as a general, in which the Illyrians were overawed,
outwitted and humiliated by a trained army, a combination of
the wedge of armoured infantry (the phalanx) and heavy cavalry whose charge, given the right ground, was unstoppable.
Yet against the highly mobile light infantry and cavalry of the
Illyrians a commander who lost his nerve could easily lose his
whole army. The escape and victory of Alexander and his army
brought home to the Illyrians, or at least some of them, how
much had changed since they had brought Macedonia to its
knees barely 50 years before.[7]

Glaucias of the Taulantii, though defeated by Alexander in
335 BC, survived for more than a generation and was still ruling
in 302 BC. In 317 BC, six years after the death of Alexander
and with power in Macedonia in the hands of the ruthless
Cassander, Glaucias offered asylum to the infant Pyrrhus after
the expulsion of his father Aeacides from his kingdom among
the Molossians. The infant prince was placed in the care of
Glaucias' wife Beroea, who was herself a Molossian princess.
Cassander, eager to gain Epirus, took offence at this action
and offered to pay 200 talents for Pyrrhus but the offer was
declined. Three years later Cassander came west, defeated Glaucias and seized Dyrrhachium and Apollonia on the borders of
his territory. After another three years, in 312 BC, Corcyra

---

[7] Arrian Anabasis 1.1–6. Hammond 1974a, 1977, Bosworth 1981
(disputing location of Pe(l)lion), Hammond and Walbank 1988, 39–49. Selcë
e Poshtme: N. Ceka 1976, Manastirli 1976.

recovered the two cities and handed Dyrrhachium over to Glaucias, even though he was now bound by treaty not to attack allies of Macedonia. Pyrrhus grew to manhood safe among the Taulantii and around five years later, on the death of Alcetas the king of Epirus, Glaucias marched south and established on the throne the 12-year-old Pyrrhus. In 303/2 BC Pyrrhus came to the court of Glaucias, presumably by now his adoptive father, to attend the marriage of one of his sons.[8]

For the first 20 years of his reign the restless and energetic young ruler of Epirus was much involved in the struggles of Alexander's successors. In 301 BC he fought with distinction in the great battle at Ipsus in Asia Minor on the side of Antigonus, when the cause of a central power in the empire of Alexander was finally defeated by a coalition of rivals. Later he tried to seize control of Macedonia itself, where many of the soldiers saw in him a new Alexander. Once he fought his brother-in-law Demetrius, the son of Antigonus, in single combat. When he finally gained Macedonia his regime is said to have lasted only seven months (287 BC), as the Macedonians preferred their old general Lysimachus. Back in Epirus he turned his ambitions to the west, which was to bring him into a memorable conflict with the rising power of Rome in the Italian peninsula. The reign of Pyrrhus, who died in 272 BC, for all his adventures elsewhere, saw his kingdom in Epirus rise to a position of power on the west of Greece and Macedonia. Links with his neighbours were strengthened by marriage alliances. One of his wives was Birkenna, daughter of Bardylis, son of the Cleitus (of the Dardani?) defeated by Alexander. This alliance may have secured the inland Dardani to the north, while his links with the Taulantii may have assisted his enterprises. It seems clear that at some time Pyrrhus was able to annexe the lands of the Taulantii in the northern coastal plain of Albania, as well as the key port of Dyrrhachium; and the advance may even have continued farther north to include the area around the Lake of Shkodër, heart of the later Illyrian kingdom.[9]

More than a century of warfare with Macedonia and Epirus

---

[8] Diodorus Siculus 19.67, Polyaenus 4.11 (314 BC), Diodorus Siculus 19.74 and 78 (313 BC), Hammond and Walbank 1988, 154–5.
[9] Cabanes 1976, Franke 1955, Hammond 1966.

had brought the Adriatic Illyrians between Epirus and the river Neretva into direct and lasting contact with the Greek world. They were to lead to major changes in the social and economic life of this region, some of which can now be more clearly observed thanks to the material evidence gathered by Yugoslav and Albanian archaeologists. Changes in the pastoral economy of a population dwelling in villages brought an increase in population and more settlements based on a land economy, aiding the growth of central authority, at first that of the king. The growth of towns will also have engendered a demand for greater political autonomy that placed strains on the traditional tribal structures. To some the evidence suggests a spiritual and mental acculturation to an urban life on the Hellenistic pattern. At the same time there is little sign, even when Roman conquest brought an end to this era of Illyrian development, that genuine urban societes had developed: Illyrian loyalties lay with the traditional figures of chief and tribe (*ethnos*).

There is a general impression from the historical sources that this was a period of growth in the Illyrian population. Attacks by them came frequently and in great strength. The pressure of such growth on a pastoral economy will have seen a move to agriculture as a means of increasing the sources of subsistence. In the case of upper Macedonia, where conditions were similar, Philip forced whole communities to leave the hills for the plain, thus increasing his own authority as well as the economic base of his kingdom. In some Illyrian areas it is possible to trace the growth of certain villages into major local centres for defence, markets and religion, in fact a small local town. The spread of agriculture among the southern Illyrians, inevitably confined to the small areas of cultivable land, is hard to measure. Perhaps the ability of Illyrians to fight as hoplite infantry, as against the Molossians in 385/4 BC, indicates an increase of Illyrian peasantry.[10]

We know little of Illyrian society in the fourth and third centuries BC. They appeared in war as free warriors under their chiefs or some overlord such as Bardylis or Glaucias. At home there is no sign of chattel slavery on the classical model. Refer-

[10] Cabanes 1988a, 185–90.

ences to slaves of the Dardanians or 'helots' of the Ardiaei have been much discussed. These were not prisoners exported for sale in the slave markets of the Hellenistic world but rather dependent communities, who from time to time even participated in expeditions. The subject population at Apollonia were evidently native communities who worked the fields belonging to the colony's oligarchy. An authentic traffic in slaves may have developed later through the colonies of Apollonia and Epidamnus and may be the explanation for the spread of their coins across the Balkans in the second and first centuries BC. During the third century records of the freeing (manumission) of slaves began to be inscribed on stone at Apollonia, Klos, Byllis and Buthrotum. As in other societies the status of a leader was determined by the number of warriors who followed. Obedience to a higher authority such as a king was channelled through the collective loyalty of a tribe to the chief. In return he acknowledged the source of his power by offering security and protection when needed. Polybius presents us with an image of society in the Illyrian kingdom as peasant infantry fighting under aristocratic proprietors (*polydynastae*), each one of whom controlled a town within the kingdom. The persistence of the old tribal ties appears to be reflected by the use of traditional tumulus burial as late as the Christian era. Here the chief still lay at the centre with his companions at rest around him. We can imagine this order of society being based on the many hill-settlements which had acquired defences by the end of the fourth century BC. At Gajtan near Shkodër an area of nearly five hectares was enclosed by a rampart of unworked stones but the structures within were merely shacks of timber and clay. Such a place was evidently created by a local ruler mainly as a place of refuge, and there seems little warrant to suggest that it was the first stage of a genuine urbanization, cut short later by foreign conquest.[11]

Livestock remained the principal product of Illyrians. Their mutton soon gained a reputation among the Romans, while King Pyrrhus had already gained a place in the reference books for his methods of cattle-breeding. Quantities of cereal were

[11] Cabanes 1988a, 190–7.

produced, though there is no means of measurement except for requisitions in time of war, notably the Dyrrhachium campaign during the civil war between Caesar and Pompey. Illyrian vineyards enjoyed no great reputation among Greeks and Romans, though there is an intriguing possibility that the viticulture of the Bordeaux region derived from Illyrian Dyrrhachium. The background to Roman intervention in Illyria in 229 BC was in part commercial. Italian traders were active along the Illyrian coast at the time, while the foundation of a Roman colony at Brindisi in 244 BC indicates an interest in the short crossing of the Adriatic. Timber from the Illyrian hinterland was valued down to medieval and modern times, notably for ships but also as a source of fuel. Except for such basic items as cloth or Alpine cheese, both valued abroad, little or nothing was made among the southern Illyrians until the growth of towns stimulated the introduction of new techniques, masonry construction, brick, tile and pottery manufacture and metal-working. Nothing is so far known of the extraction of silver, and the location of Damastion, with its remarkable silver coinage, remains a mystery. Somewhere to the north or northeast of Ohrid seems likely. Nor is there yet any evidence for working of the copper deposits in the Shkumbin valley. The deposits of asphalt (*Ad Picarias* on ancient road maps) inland from Apollonia were exploited during the Greek and Roman periods though remains of the working are yet to be found.

Specialized production of pottery in Illyria commences with imitation of south Italian forms at Dyrrhachium, where in the second century BC 'Megarian' bowls with moulded decoration were also produced. There local production and stamping of tiles in kilns spreads as far north as the Shkumbin. The chief centre of production was Apollonia but other centres include Gurezezë, Dimale (Krotinë), Klos, Byllis and Margëlliç, but the names on stamps are Greek rather than Illyrian. In the Korcë basin and on the island St Achilleus in Lake Little Prespa stamped storage jars have been discovered. Stamped amphorae of Rhodian origin (220–180 BC) may be significant evidence for long-distance commerce but who were the consumers at this period remains unclear.[12]

---

[12] Cabanes 1988a, 197–204, Dibra 1981 (hoard of axes, hoes and scythes near Shkodër).

No Illyrian production of coins is known before King Monunius struck his coins at Dyrrhachium (see figure 11), followed by Mytilus around ten years later. An early dating of the first Scodra coins, generally linked with the Macedonian occupation around 213 BC, to the middle of the third century is better discarded, mainly because no coins are known to have been issued by Illyrian rulers of a later period such as Agron, Teuta, Scerdilaidas, etc. By around 230 BC, when Epirote domination had waned, coins were circulating around the lower Aous valley, from Byllis, Amantia, Olympe and other places, though never in quantities to match those from the two coastal colonies. The early Scodra coins are small bronze issues intended for local circulation, but the main local currency was based on silver issues from the major centres, Dyrrhachium, Apollonia and Epirus. In the kingdom of Illyria an authentic local coinage appears only in the second century BC under King Gentius.[13]

The 'Illyrian town' has been a major theme of research in modern Albania, involving study of the origins, growth, political and social organization and relations with the surrounding territory, including the establishment of outlying satellite fortifications in the border districts of Illyris and Epirus. The first construction of fortifications is dated now to the fifth century

Figure 11 Silver coin of 'King Monunius' minted at Dyrrhachium: diameter 21 mm

[13] Cabanes 1988a, 204–7. Coin circulation: Gjoncegaj 1984a (Corcyra), 1984b (Epirus), 1986 (others), 1976b (Byllis circulation).

BC, and designated as a 'pre-' or 'proto-' urban phase defined through investigations at Gajtan around three miles southeast of Shkodër. An area of around four to five hectares was enclosed by a stone rampart about 3.5 metres wide of unworked blocks but with two faces of closely fitting stones enclosing a core of smaller stones. There were no towers in this phase and at the most one or two gates (see figures 12a and 12b). More than two dozen sites with defences erected in this manner have been identified, including simple refuges such as Tren and Ventrok in the Korcë basin, Ganjolle near Gajtan, and elaborate defensive complexes such as Gajtan, Shkodër, Marshej, Lissus phases I and II, Zgërdhesh phase I and Ošanići I and II.[14]

The formation of proper urban centres takes place in the southernmost districts of Illyris, adjoining Chaonia and the Aous (Vijosë) valley, before the end of the fifth century BC but that stage is not reached in the north, that is, in the Mat valley and the Shkodër basin, until around a century later. After 350 BC Illyrian towns are believed to have become established at Lissus (Lezha) and Shkodër and in the interior at Antipatreia (Berat) and also at Selcë e Poshtme in the Shkumbin valley, a suggested location for Pelion. Perhaps the most remarkable development took place at Byllis of the Bylliones (see figures 13a and 13b), where the earlier settlement at Klos on its confined hill-top was replaced by a new settlement on the adjoining hill that developed the imposing character of a Hellenistic and later Roman city. The defended area of some of the new Illyrian towns reached 30–40 hectares, with perimeter walls fortified with straight-sided or sometimes round towers, such as survive at Lissus (see below). The gates were likewise well protected in a fashion appropriate to resisting Hellenistic techniques in siege warfare employing artillery. This era of

---

[14] Early fortifications: Prendi 1976a, N. Ceka 1977–8, 1983, 1985a, 1986, Karaiskaj 1976, 1977, 1977–8b (Marshej near Shkodër); typology: Zheku 1977–8, 1980, Korkuti 1973, 1976, Islami 1976b, 1984, Jubani 1972b (Gajtani)m Jubani and N. Ceka 1971 (Rosuje), 1986b (Kodra e Pazarit), Fistani 1983 (Kratue near Shkodër), Lera 1975 (Symize near Korcë). Montenegro: Mijović and Kovačević 1975 (challenging Albanian chronology), Parović-Pešikan 1980 (Risan hinterland), 1977–8 (Gulf of Kotor). On Adriatic settlements, Suić 1975.

Figure 12 a) Plan of Gajtan fortress, Albania
b) Gate of Gajtan fortress

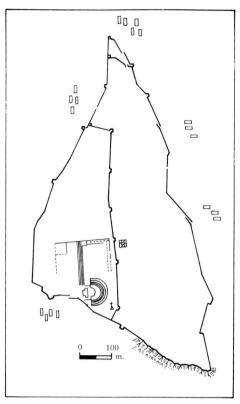

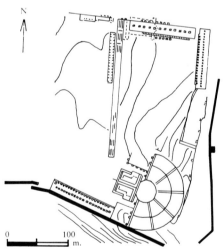

Figure 13 a) Plan of Byllis, Gradesht, Albania
b) Plan of Byllis, central area

urban development is marked by the first construction of public buildings, which at Byllis were eventually to include a theatre, stadium and double portico, all executed in coursed blocks of dressed stone.

Buildings of a distinctly urban character have recently been revealed in several major settlements. The urban character of Byllis is evident by the middle of the third century BC, surrounded by a cordon of strongholds protecting the territories of the commonwealth (*koinon*) of the Bylliones, at Gurzezë, Margelliç, Rabie, Matohasanaj. These are constructed in regular dressed masonry, with defences dated to the late fourth or early third century BC similar to those further south in Epirus. Further north the massive defences at Berat (Antipatreia or Bargulium) may belong to the era of direct Epirote rule before 230 BC. The location of Dimale (or Dimallum), a settlement in the territory of the Parthini, at Krotinë west of Berat, depends on tiles stamped DIMALLITAN (in Greek). Though the enclosed area is less than 15 hectares, there was at least one building of a public character – a portico over 30 metres long with seven niches which appears to imitate similar buildings at Apollonia. At Zgërdhesh (see figures 14a and 14b), southwest of Kruja, there are defences similar to those at Gajtan, dated locally to the sixth to fifth century BC. Imported Apulian pottery appears at the end of the fourth century but the walls of coursed masonry belong to a later period. Except for a semicircular structure in the lower part of the town no public buildings are known in the ten-hectare settlement, which has been identified as the Albanopolis of Ptolemy's *Geography*. Studies of the well-preserved fortifications at Acrolissus and Lissus suggest that the former came first and was built in the late fourth century. There was a major reconstruction of the latter in the first century BC, when the more roughly dressed blocks were replaced by smooth, close-fitting masonry. No interior structures have yet been located. The function of Lissus (see figures 15a, 15b and 15c) near the mouth of the Drin was to guard the route inland and to furnish a secure anchorage for Illyrian shipping. Little is known of Illyrian Scodra, mainly because the Rozafat fortress has remained in use until modern times. Similarly few traces are now to be seen of Illyrian defences at Meteon (Medun), Olcinium (Ulcinj) and Rhizon

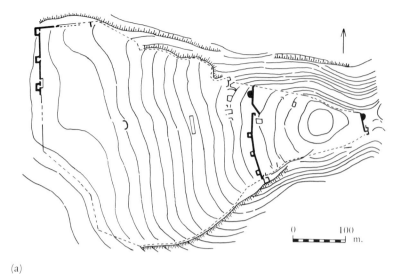

(a)

Figure 14 a) Plan of Zgërdhesh fortress, Albania
b) Zgërdhesh west perimeter wall and towers

(b)

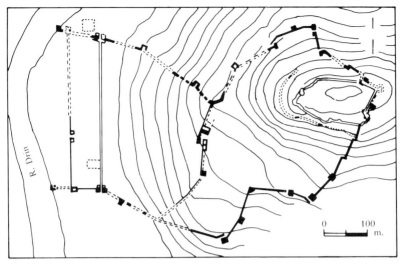

(a)

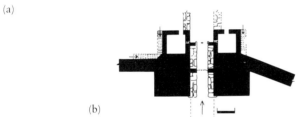

(b)

(c)

Figure 15 a) Plan of Lissus, Lezha, Albania
b) Plan of southwest gate at Lissus
c) Main gate in wall of middle town, Lissus

(Risan). In the second century AD a native of Roman Risinium, who had risen to command the army of Africa, recalled the 'Aeacian walls' of his Illyrian home, perhaps alluding to Aeacus of Aegina who assisted Apollo and Poseidon in building the walls of Troy. Nothing has yet been reported on the settlement at Selcë e Poshtme, a candidate for the location of Pelion, and there is so far no certain location for Uscana, the strategically placed chief settlement of the Illyrian Penestae.[15]

The rapid move to a form of urbanization among the southern Illyrians, during the late fourth and early third centuries BC, matches the rather better observed developments to the south in Epirus. For the Illyrians a question remains as to the extent that this development was a direct consequence of external stimulus, notably Molossian Epirus in the time of Pyrrhus, and whether there is any genuine evolution from the earlier period that warrants the use of such descriptions as 'pre-' or 'proto-' urban. The matter will be resolved only by systematic excavation in the interior of these settlements, which so far has not been attempted. What evidence there is at present tends towards a negative conclusion, and it seems likely that many of the roughly fortified hill-sites were more likely refuges for herdsmen and flocks on the move or for the inhabitants of local villages in level country, and therefore are unlikely to produce evidence for permanent occupation.

[15] Urban development: N. Ceka 1985b, Cabanes 1988b, Anamali 1976b. Lissus: Prendi and Zheku 1971, 1972, 1986, Zheku 1974, 1976, Prendi 1981 (inscriptions); Shkodër: Hoxha 1987 (Bronze Age remains); Berat: Baçe 1971, Spahiu 1975, 1983; Selcë: N. Ceka 1972; Byllis/Klos: Papajani 1976a, 1979 (theatre), Vreka 1987 (Gurzezë near Cakran); Dimale: Hammond 1968, Dautaj 1972 (brick stamps), 1976a, 1976b (economy), 1984a (coins), 1984b (stoas), 1986 (political organization); Zgerdhesh: Islami 1972b, 1975, Papajani 1977. Also Lahi 1988 (Beltoje near Shkodër), N. Ceka 1975b (fortifications of Amantini), Anamali 1972, Prendi and Budina 1972 (Irmaj, Gramsh), Islami 1970 (Xibri, Mat district), Anamali 1975 (Podgradec), Budina 1985 (Antigoneia). Baçe 1974 (Kanine), 1975 (Gulf of Vlora), 1979, Bereti 1985 (Triport), N. Ceka 1987c (Margelliç), Jubani and N. Ceka 1971 (Rosuje).

Celts, Autariatae and Dardanians

The 'coming of the Celts' has long been an acceptable hypothesis for archaeologists grappling with the huge quantities of material from this era, and its wide application in Central and Southeast Europe has had a direct bearing on defining the limits and identities of the Illyrian peoples, notably in the region of the middle Danube and its major tributaries. That in parts of this area, including the eastern Alps, Middle Danube and Sava and Drava valley, the majority of the settled population were Celtic-speaking is generally accepted from historical and onomastic evidence. Yet how they came to be there and what, if anything, happened to an 'existing population' are questions awaiting answers. One central and long-lasting hypothesis among archaeologists is that the arrival of Celtic-speakers in several areas north of the Alps coincides with, and indeed is, the point of transition from the earlier to the later phase of the European Iron Age. That named after Hallstatt in the eastern Alps not far from Salzburg came to an end around 400 BC and was replaced by that of La Tène, after a lakeside settlement in Switzerland, famous for its elegant style of curvilinear non-figural ornament often referred to as 'Celtic' art. By the late second and early first centuries BC the two cultures had fused into a uniform version of La Tène across most of Europe north of the Alps.[16]

Ptolemy's history of Alexander's campaigns recorded that, following his brilliant victory on the Danube in 335 BC, an embassy came from the Celts to seek the alliance and friendship of the young king. The point of the anecdote, as retold by Arrian and the geographer Strabo, was to show how this people 'who lived a long way off in a country not easy to penetrate' told Alexander that their greatest fear was not him but the sky falling upon their heads. Alexander, though not a little insulted, granted the alliance and sent the envoys home. They had come from the far west, 'around the Adriatic' in the version of

---

[16] Guštin 1984, Jovanović and Popović 1981, Todorović 1968 (bibliography), Majnarić-Pandžić 1978 (N. Croatia), P. Popović 1978 (coin use), Knez 1983 (Novo Mesto), Bolta 1966 (Celje).

Ptolemy preserved by Strabo (7.3, 8) or 'dwelling on the Ionian gulf' in Arrian (1.4, 6). Though it is true that the Periplus locates some Celts on the north Adriatic coast of Italy, it is more likely that these came from the northwest Balkans or even the eastern Alps and the middle Danube. The arrival of Celts in this area by the early fourth century is indicated by the account of Justinus, based on Celtic tradition in the work of Pompeius Trogus (Book 24). Around the end of the fifth century some of the 300,000 migrating Celts crossed the Alps and sacked Rome but the rest, by a progress which caused great devastation, reached the Illyrian coast and made their homes in Pannonia. They mastered the Pannonians and for many years continued warring with neighbouring peoples.[17]

The fourth-century historian Theopompus may be the source of an account of fighting between Celts and Illyrians, both equally detested by the average Greek, where the one achieved victory by inflicting on the other the agonies of severe diarrhoea:

When the Celts attacked, with a knowledge of (Illyrian) intemperance, they ordered their soldiers to prepare food in their tents as sumptuous as possible, and then to add to it a type of medicinal herb which had the effect of emptying and purging the bowels. When this took effect many were caught by the Celts and killed, while others cast themselves into the river from the unbearable pain. (Theopompus, quoted by Athenaeus 10.60)

In a version of the story included by Polyaenus in a collection of Stratagems (7.42), the Illyrians involved were the Autariatae, whom the Celts lured by feigned flight to consume the doctored food left in their tents. Yet the story is a commonplace and may have been judged by Theopompus as appropriate to the Illyrians, famed for their love of food and drink, perhaps as background material to his account of Philip II's Illyrian victory in 359/8 BC. If it ever happened, the likely date for the episode is early in the fourth century.[18]

The Autariatae were the most remote of the Illyrian peoples

[17] M. Garašanin 1970, Gavela 1975a.
[18] Papazoglu 1978.

known to the Greek world in the era of Philip and Alexander, and a good deal of what is recorded of them is near fantasy. Perhaps the only reliable evidence is the report in Arrian (from the eye-witness Ptolemy) that the Autariatae had planned an attack on Alexander's army during their homeward march in 335 BC. This would also tally with the tradition repeated by Strabo that they were 'once the greatest and most powerful of the Illyrians'. Another anecdote, which probably also originated in Greece in the fourth century BC, describes a long-running feud between the Autariatae and the Ardiaei over the possession of a salt-source near their common border. Water which flowed out each spring from the foot of a great mountain produced excellent salt through evaporation within five days, which was then fed to livestock. The site, not named in the sources and now not easily located (possibly at Orahovica in the upper Neretva valley), was far inland and enabled the Ardiaei to avoid having to import salt and thus to have few contacts with other peoples. There was an arrangement between the two peoples to extract the salt in alternate years but when this broke down war ensued. The picture of the Ardiaei remote from the sea and from other people does not match their later reputation for seaborne activity and may relate to a period before they had moved to occupy at least part of the coast between the Neretva and the Drin. Even so, Appian observes that though powerful on the sea, the Ardiaei were destroyed in the end by the Autariatae 'who were best on land', though they too sustained heavy losses.[19]

Taken together, the intelligible sources locate the Autariatae inland from the Ardiaei and the Lake of Shkodër, extending east to the Dardani and north, or rather northeast, to the Triballi. In modern terms their territory will have included the valleys of the Lim and the Tara (perhaps somehow connected with their name) beyond the mountains of northern Albania, and also the western Morava, an area of the Balkans barely known to the ancient geographers. It is tempting to identify

---

[19] Aristotle, *On Marvellous Things Heard* 138 (LCL 14. 308–10), Strabo 7.5, 11, Appian, *Illyrike* 3. Perhaps the salt source was 'Stane Vode' (salt water) near Orahovica, a few miles north of Konjic in the upper Neretva valley, Patsch 1922, 43 note 4.

these Autariatae, probably a general name for a whole group of smaller peoples known later by their individual names, with the people of the Glasinac culture in eastern Bosnia, where a tradition of tumulus burial had continued almost without interruption from Bronze Age times. In the early (Hallstatt) phase of the Iron Age a similar local tumulus culture between the Drina and the Morava appears to have spread east into Serbia by the end of the fifth century BC. This may represent the expansion of the Autariatae at the expense of the Triballi until, as Strabo remarks, they in their turn were overcome by the Celtic Scordisci in the early third century BC. Similarly the decline or fragmentation of the Autariatae is matched by a rise to prominence of the Ardiaei on the coast and of the Dardani inland.

In the matter of material remains the princely burials of the early fifth century BC contained in two tumuli (35 and around 70 metres in diameter) at Atenica near Čačak in western Serbia might well belong to the Illyrian Autariatae in a time of prosperity before the Celtic migrations (see figures 16a and 16b). The smaller mound contained a central burial beneath a truncated cone of chopped stones and a secondary interment near the perimeter beneath a similar construction of stones. The larger mound contained only a central burial in a tomb constructed of rectangular slabs. All three bodies had been cremated outside the tumulus before burial, and the remains dispersed in the grave. Before the burial platform of the larger tumulus was constructed a sacrifice of young animals including a dog, a wild boar and a wild sow and three oxen (see figure 16c). That the smaller tumulus contained a female burial is inferred from the many beads and pendants of glass and amber, with birds' and rams' heads, gold and silver appliqués, buttons and a silver brooch. The burial contained the iron tyres of a chariot or burial cart, which had been consumed along with the corpse. The contents of the second burial were similar but included also weapons, a spear, bronze arrows and an Attic gold plaque decorated with the figure of a boar, and undoubtedly was that of a male child. Both burials included pottery and metalwork of Greek (probably Ionian) origin. The larger tumulus contained a male burial with similar contents but included also a sword, bronze arrows, harness and the remains of a chariot. Among Greek imports were an Ionian wine jug and several bronze dress plaques of similar origin and a bone dagger handle. This isolated burial of what was probably a single family placed prominently in the broad valley of the western Morava implies an established authority that felt able to consign high-value prestige goods into their burial mounds.[20]

In 1957, the year before the Atenica burials were discovered, a spectacular find of objects dating to the same period was made beneath a medieval church near the town of Novi Pazar, which lies on a tributary of the Ibar on the borders of Bosnia and Serbia. An iron-bound oak chest (1.85 m by 0.85 m) concealed in a pit more than two metres deep contained a fine collection of jewellery and dress ornaments. No trace of a cremation or skeletal remains were found and it is possible that this is an example of hidden treasure rather than deposited grave goods, although on balance a context of burial appears the more probable. In addition to imported Greek pottery, bronze vessels and jewellery described above, the contents of the chest included what some archaeologists regard as typical local productions, among them a gold belt, earrings, gold, silver and bronze brooches and carved pieces of amber. Objects that tend to be labelled 'Greco-Illyrian' included a bronze wine-strainer, gold pectorals, aprons and plaques (*pteryges*) and more than 1000 attachments of sheet gold in various shapes. The character of the ornaments and the absence of weapons suggests the robes and regalia of several Illyrian princesses, but the belts, pectorals and some of the brooches were worn by males. What the Novi Pazar hoard represents remains a puzzle but most likely it was the family treasure of an Illyrian ruler with a marked taste for Greek imports of the highest quality.[21]

The Autariatae had the misfortune to be driven from their homelands by a plague of frogs which fell half-formed from the sky, a story which attracted the curiosity of several ancient writers. This is the version of Heraclides, an Egyptian civil servant of around 170 BC:

---

[20] Djuknić and Jovanović 1966a, 1966b (Atenica), Zotović 1972 (Kremni, Illyrian cemetery near Užice), 1984 (Pilatovići near Požega), 1987 (burial near Priboj in Lim valley).
[21] Mano-Zissi and Popović 1969 (Novi Pazar).

Somewhere in Paeonia and Dardania frogs fell from the sky like rain
and there were so many that the houses and streets were full of them.
During the first days the people somehow bore it by destroying them
and shutting up the houses. But as this achieved nothing, and their
very cooking pots got filled with frogs which got boiled and baked
with the food, and neither could the water be drunk, nor could men
put foot to the ground for the multitude of them, and as the stink
from the dead creatures was odious, the people abandoned their
homeland. (Heraclides, frag. 3, *FHG* vol. 3 p. 168)

No sense can be made of this horror story but it is reliably
reported that the people were migrating from their homeland
late in the fourth century BC. In 310 BC they were in Paeonia,
where they were on the point of achieving a victory over king

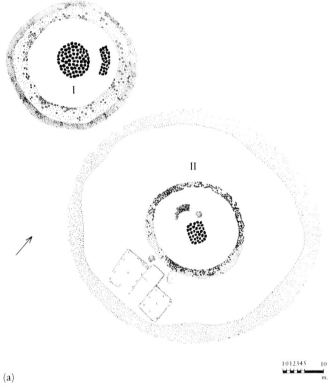

(a)

Figure 16 a) Plan of burial tumuli at Atenica, Serbia

(b)

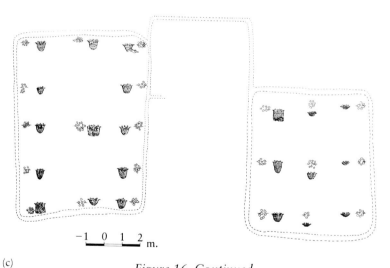

(c)

Figure 16 Continued
b) Stone tomb in Tumulus I at Atenica
c) Plan of sacrificial areas in Tumulus II at Atenica

Audoleon when Cassander came to the rescue and the Illyrians, along with their families totalling in all 20,000, were settled on Mount Orbelus in eastern Paeonia on the frontier of Macedonia and Thrace. Their migration was attributed to the plague of frogs (along with mice or rats) but they were treated realistically by the sinister Cassander, who in typical Macedonian fashion sought to exploit them as an ally against the northern neighbours of his territory. Behind the threat of the frogs and other creatures may have been the real threat from the Celts now pressing into the southern Balkans. It is reported that Cassander did fight with Celts in Thrace, perhaps to drive off an attempted raid on Macedonia. The story that the sufferings of the Illyrian Autariatae was retribution by the divine Apollo of Delphi for their having joined in the attack on his sanctuary in 279 BC is undoubtedly a fiction by those eager to claim the credit for any misfortune suffered by the Illyrians during that period. Celtic pressure may have been the reason for the dispersal of other groups of Autariatae, such as the 2,000 serving in the army of Lysimachus during the winter of 302/1 BC who went over to 'One-eyed' Antigonus. Perhaps their mercenary service commenced when Lysimachus made expeditions against the Getae on the lower Danube. Whatever the background to these incidents it is around the end of the fourth century that the name of the Autariatae vanishes from the historical record, although there is nothing in the material evidence from their homeland that indicates any sudden or dramatic change.[22]

We are indebted to the geographer Stbo for a singularly ambiguous portrayal of the Dardanians: 'they are so utterly wild that they dig caves beneath their dung-hills and live there; but still they have a taste for music and are always playing musical instruments, both flutes and strings' (7.5, 7). Though their territory and ethnic associations remain in doubt, the Dardani were for several centuries an enduring presence among the peoples of the central Balkans, 'the most stable and conservative ethnic element in an area where everything was exposed to constant change' as the Yugoslav scholar Fanoula

[22] Papazoglu 1970a, 1978. Cassander and the Autariatae: Diodorus Siculus 20.19; Justinus 15.2; Orosius, *Historia* 3.23, 26; Delphi: Appian, *Illyrike* 4; Antigonus: Diodorus Siculus 20.113.

Papazoglu puts it. While the once formidable Autariatae had vanished long before the Roman conquest, and the Triballi, Scordisci and Moesi all declined to insignificant remnants, the Dardani endured. In the Greek and Roman worlds the humble music-loving Dardani in their remote valleys beyond Macedonia came to be linked with a people of the same name who dwelt in northwest Asia Minor, and who gave their name to the district of Dardania from which the modern name Dardanelles is derived. Other coincidences of ethnic names supported notions of a connection between the Balkans and Asia Minor, the Mysians in the latter matching the Balkan Moesians and the Phrygians corresponding to the Bryges. A current explanation cites as a likely context the large-scale movement of peoples at the end of the Bronze Age (around 1200 BC), when some of the established powers around the eastern Mediterranean were afflicted by the attacks of 'sea-peoples'. By Roman times the nature of the connection between Balkan and Asian Dardani had become altogether a more delicate matter. Then the connection was explained by a movement in the opposite direction: a certain Dardanus who ruled over many tribes in Asia Minor was responsible for settling the Dardani west of the Thracians. Tradition had it that this Dardanus was founder of the Trojan ruling house, a matter of some importance when the rulers of some of the great powers of antiquity, including Epirus, Macedonia and Rome, claimed a Trojan ancestry. But if Dardanus and his people were descended from the Balkan people the latter's notoriously uncouth ways will have been an embarrassment. The accepted version was that the Dardani were a kindred people of the Trojans who had degenerated in their new home to a state of barbarism.[23]

Though for a time probably subordinate to the power of Epirus, the Dardani maintained an independence that was later eroded by Macedonia and finally extinguished by the Romans. It seems likely that the Illyrian Cleitus defeated by Alexander was probably a ruler of the Dardani. After 335 BC nothing is reported of them, not even when the neighbouring Paeonians

[23] On Dardanians: Papazoglu 1978, 131 ff., Srejović 1973 (formation); settlements: Mikulčić 1973, Mirdita 1975, M. Garašanin 1975a.

rebelled in 322 BC after the death of Alexander, until 284 BC
when Lysimachus seized control of Macedonia and Paeonia,
where a deceit caused Ariston, the son of king Audoleon, to
take refuge among the Dardani. Not long after the death of
Lysimachus in 281 BC a large force of Celts moved south
through the central Balkans and, late in 280 or early in 279,
overwhelmed the army of Macedonia under Ptolemy Ceraunus.
During his brief reign the latter had faced opposition from
Ptolemy the son of Lysimachus, who was aided by Monunius
king of the Illyrians. An inscribed bronze helmet found near
Ohrid may have belonged to a soldier of this ruler (see figure
17). He may have belonged to the Dardani since a later ruler
of that people bore the same name, though it also occurs in
the old Thracian territories of Lysimachus. It is not certain that
he is the same Monunius who offered help against the Celts to
Ptolemy Ceraunus. The gesture was rejected with contempt, as
if the sons of Alexander's all-conquering soldiers needed help
from the likes of Dardanians, even when they came as 20,000
men in arms. The Dardanian king's response was to forecast
the downfall of Macedonia. A coin of Macedonian type bearing
the name of Monunius may be evidence for the aspirations of
the Dardanian ruler in the kingdom, perhaps in the time of
confusion following the Celtic invasion. Nor is it certain if this
was the same ruler who gained power over the Taulantii
and struck a coin of Dyrrhachium with the legend King
Monunius.[24]

The rapid decline of Epirus following the death of Pyrrhus in
272 BC may have been hastened by attacks from once obedient
northern neighbours. Alexander II is known to have fought an
Illyrian war against Mytilus whose Dyrrhachium coins bear the
royal title. Conceivably the latter was a successor to Monunius
and ruler of the increasingly powerful Dardani, rather than
merely a local dynast. While Dardanians may have taken control of the Taulantii, it seems that the principal directions of
their expansion were now towards the east and north, against
Paeonia and into the Morava and Nišava valleys against the

---

[24] Polyaenus 4. 12, 3 (Audoleon); Justinus 24. 9–11, Pompeius Trogus Prol.
24 (Monunius).

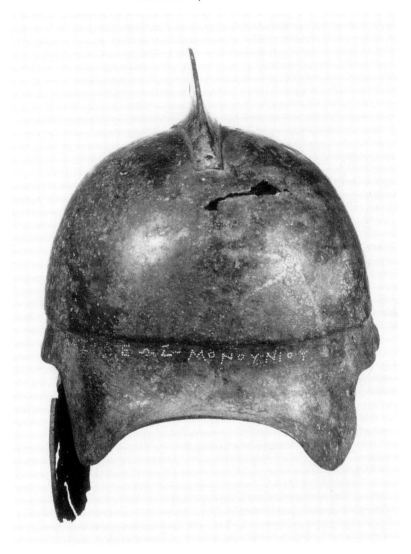

Figure 17 Bronze helmet inscribed 'Of King Monunios'

Triballi. Unlike Macedonia, the Dardanians had apparently suffered little from the passage of the Celts through their lands, though it was in their territory that Lonovius and Lutarius detached themselves from the main force to move against

Thrace, while the rest continued south under Brennus to Macedonia and Greece. The Dardanians were not slow to attack
when they returned north after defeat, wandering about the
countryside exhausted with hunger and cold.[25]

Save for a doubtful episode early in the long reign of Antigonus Gonatas, there is no record of action by the Dardani or
any other northerners in the direction of Macedonia for nearly
a generation. From later evidence it seems that this was a period
of recovery and consolidation on the northern frontiers of
Macedonia, including the construction of new fortifications,
watch-towers and other means of defence that rarely attract
the attention of historians. Dardanians were again a threat in
the reign of Demetrius II (240/39–229 BC), when they invaded
Paeonia and won a victory over the Macedonian king not long
before his death. Longarus, the first to be named ruler of the
Dardanians, directed the attack. Events in this area now become
more prominent in the affairs of Greece and Macedonia, since
a threat from the north was likely to cause the Antigonids
to abandon any enterprise under way in Greece and hasten
home.[26]

Antigonus Doson, regent for the first decade of Demetrius'
son Philip V, claimed a victory over the Dardanians 'exultant
after the death of Demetrius'. Part of Paeonia was annexed to
Macedonia and Antigoneia was founded on the river Axius,
the main invasion route from the north. In 222 BC Doson won
a famous victory over the Spartans at Sellasia, but hastened
back home within a few days when news came that the Illyrians
had invaded and were looting his kingdom. According to Polybius he found them still in the country and forced them to a
battle which he won but he so over-exerted himself in shouting
encouragement to his troops that he burst a blood-vessel and
fell fatally ill. It seems likely that these Illyrians came from
Dardania, since it was the Dardani who were again prominent
in attacks on Macedonia in the first years of Philip V's sole
reign. During the Social War against the Aetolians and Spartans
(220–217 BC), 'the Dardanians and all the neighbouring peoples

[25] Passage of Celts: Livy 38.16, Pausanias 10.19, 7; retreat: Justinus 24.8,
Diodorus Siculus 22.9.
[26] Pompeius Trogus 28, Livy 31.28, Justinus 28.3, 4.

who cherished everlasting hatred of the Macedonian despised the youth of Philip and constantly provoked him' (Justinus 29.1). Polybius describes what must have been a typical episode in these years. In 219 Philip was in Acarnania in northwest Greece when news came that the Dardanians, assuming that he was on his way to the Peloponnese, collected their forces for a raid. When Philip reached his capital Pella he found that the Dardani had learned of his return and called off the attack, enabling Philip to send his men home early for the autumn fruit-picking. Two years later Philip decided to strike first and seized Bylazora, 'the largest city in Paeonia, very conveniently situated on the pass from Dardania to Macedonia' (Polybius 5.97). The situation, probably the modern Titov Veles on the river Vardar, commands the upstream entrance to a long defile and, no less important, a route southwestwards into Pelagonia via the Babuna valley and over the Babuna pass or along the Raec valley and over the Pletvar pass to Prilep. The capture and, one assumes, the garrisoning of Bylazora appears to have brought a swift end to Dardanian raids, and may be compared with the capture and occupation of Lychnitis a century and a half before by Philip II following his defeat of Bardylis. As Macedonia was finally gaining what passed for peace on its northern border, Philip, the Illyrians and the Greeks were concentrating their attention westwards on the great struggle being fought in Italy between the Romans and the Carthaginians under Hannibal.[27]

Even the Roman allies who had felt abandoned when the Romans agreed a peace with Philip in 205 BC will have been surprised at the speed with which they returned to the area once the war with Hannibal and Carthage was over. Philip had profited from the armistice and his ambitious schemes in the direction of Asia Minor were evidently no longer hindered by troubles on his northern borders. When the Romans returned to Illyria in 200 BC under the experienced commander P. Sulpicius Galba, they expected support from their former allies. These began to appear at the Roman headquarters in Dassaretis.

[27] Philip V and Dardanians: Hammond and Walbank 1988. Polybius 2.70 (Doson), 4.66 (219 BC), 5.97, Mikulčić 1976 (Bylazora).

From the Dardani came Bato, son of the Longarus who had once fought against Philip's father Demetrius II. The Roman commander told them he would call on their help when his army had entered Macedonia.[28]

The king anticipated that the Roman line of advance would be into the Erigon valley and he was determined to protect his flanks from raids by Roman allies, the Aetolians in the south and the Dardanians in the north. He ordered his son Perseus to block the pass (probably the Debреšte pass via the Treska valley) leading into Pelagonia. When the Romans made their move Philip recalled the troops under Perseus, and his cavalry defeat at Ottolobus on the river Erigon, though not a major reverse, was the outcome of a gamble after learning that Illyrians and Dardanians had crossed the passes in strength and were already in Macedonia. Though the invasions were concerted, it was the Dardanians who did the most damage. When Philip's commander Athenagoras tried to ambush them on the homeward march they recovered from the effects of the surprise attack to form up in regular order and fight a battle in which neither side was able to claim victory. Later some of the Dardanians were killed or wounded by the Macedonian cavalry, but no prisoners were taken 'because these troops do not leave their ranks impulsively but keep close order both in combat and in withdrawal' (Livy 31.43). The episode shows how much the Dardanians had been influenced by the military traditions of the Hellenistic world. Two years later a Roman general addressing his troops on the eve of their victory over Philip at Cynoscephalae reminded them that they were not up against the Macedonians of Alexander but merely those who not long before had been a prey of the Dardanians. News of the Roman victory drew the Dardanians once again down the Vardar valley, but Philip caught and defeated them near the Paeonian capital Stobi with an army he had hastily conscripted from the cities of his kingdom. The Macedonians continued to hold

---

[28] Livy 31.28 (Bato, son of Longarus).

Bylazora and through that Paeonia, whose return the Dardanians were still demanding 30 years later after another major
Roman victory.[29]

In the later years of his reign Philip V launched an offensive
against his northern neighbours, above all against the Dardanians. The Roman version implies that behind it there lay a plan
for revenge on the Romans, even to the extent of planning
an incredible overland expedition across the Balkans to Italy.
Though most of the stories regarding the aims of Philip were
likely fictions emanating from his enemies in Greece, it seems
possible that Philip had grasped how Rome might be threatened
in the area where Italy was weakest, from across the Julian
Alps in the northeast. Against a background of rising distrust
and suspicion, both states may have become aware of the long
but not impossible route across the Balkans, down the Morava
to the area of Belgrade, then west up the Sava valley. It may
have been during these years, between the second and third
wars of Rome and Macedonia, that the eastern and northern
approaches to the Illyrian lands first became known to the
Greek and Roman world, although more than one and a half
centuries would elapse before, in the principate of Augustus, a
Roman army would cross the Danube basin.

While on campaign in Thrace in 184 BC Philip sent agents
to 'stir up the barbarians along the river Danube, that they
might invade Italy' (Livy 39.35). Two years later Philip was
pleased to learn that the Bastarnae had accepted his alliance
and were offering a princess in marriage for one of his sons –
Perseus as it turned out. This formidable people, evidently of
German origin, dwelt beyond the lower Danube but were often
willing to join in expeditions far from their homelands. In the
following year we find Philip founding a new city on the river
Erigon, which was named Perseis in honour of his eldest son,
and at the same time ordering mass deportations from Paeonia,
where he then filled the towns with 'Thracians and other
barbarians, as being likely to remain more securely loyal to
him in the coming hour of danger' (Polybius 23.10), that is,
war with Rome. Three years later, it is reported, after he had

[29] Livy 31.38–41; 33.19 (after Cynoscephalae).

assembled his army at Stobi and moved against the Thracian
Maedi, he headed for the Haemus mountains because he
believed the story that from the top one could see the Black
Sea, the Adriatic, the Danube and the Alps: 'to have these
spread out before his eyes would have, he thought, no small
weight in determining his strategy in a war with Rome' (Livy
40.21).[30]

In fact Philip's purpose for the Bastarnae was more specific
to the security of Macedonia: they were to eject the Dardanians
and take over their country. It was a typically ruthless yet
realistic scheme, and was later imitated in the Danube lands
on more than one occasion by the Romans. The Romans, or
rather some of them, may have been receptive to stories that
the Bastarnae were on their way to Italy accompanied, it was
predicted, by the kindred Scordisci through whose lands their
route lay. To get the Bastarnae to Dardania the king had gone
to great trouble and expense to arrange safe passage through
the Thracians. They left home after a good deal of hesitation
but had got as far as Amphipolis when, in the summer of 179
BC, news arrived that King Philip was dead. Soon there was
trouble with the Thracians and the Bastarnae retreated to
Donuca (perhaps Rila), a high mountain in western Thrace.
After further skirmishes some decided to return home and set
off for Apollonia and Mesembria on the Black Sea coast of
Thrace, but the rest, under the leadership of Clondicus, pressed
on to Dardania and set about ejecting the population in accordance with their arrangement with the late king. A full-scale war
now ensued. The Dardanians, faced at first not only with
attacks by the Bastarnae but also the Scordisci and Thracians,
blamed the attack on the new King Perseus and asked the
Romans for help. The king denied any responsibility and the
Romans were inclined to believe him, well aware that there
was anyway little that they could do in the matter. The Dardani
were at first penned up in their strongholds but held out until
the allies of the Bastarnae had left and then attacked. The
details are not recorded but the Dardanians evidently threw

[30] Philip and Bastarnae: Hammond and Walbank 1988, 469–70. Livy 39.35
(184 BC), 40.5 (182 BC), 39.53 (Perseis).

out the invaders, from the story that in 175 BC the Bastarnae lost many men and horses while crossing the frozen Danube and that among the survivors was Clondicus who had led the people into Dardania four years earlier and who would appear again six years later with his people in Macedonia as a potential ally of Perseus against the Romans.[31]

Accepting the possibility that Macedonia could mount an invasion of Italy by the overland route through the Illyrians, it seems that some believed Rome in its turn could get at Macedonia from the direction of northern Italy. This is the only reasonable explanation for the behaviour of G. Cassius Longinus, the Roman consul of 171 BC sent to oversee Roman interests in northeast Italy. The Senate received a request from the recently founded colony Aquileia for help with its defences against the hostile Histrians and Illyrians. When they suggested that this might be a suitable matter for the consul Cassius the senators were astonished to hear that some time before he had asembled his army at Aquileia and, with 30 days' rations and guides who knew the way, had set off for Macedonia through the land of the Illyrians. The senators were indignant that the consul had abandoned his province, was intending to trespass on another's, was leading his army by a dangerous route through foreign peoples and had left Italy exposed to attack from all directions. The troubles of Aquileia were forgotten as three senators were sent to tell the consul that he was not to engage any people unless the Senate had already declared war on them. Next year we find the Senate receiving furious complaints against Cassius, from the Gauls, Carni, Histri and Japodes. Apparently the consul and his army had set out for Macedonia peacably enough but then came back killing, burning and looting in all directions. The Senate disclaimed any responsibility for this conduct and announced that had they known they would never have approved the enterprise. But the former consul was now a military tribune with the army in

---

[31] Livy 40.57–8, 41.19 (176 BC), Polybius 25.6 (177/6 BC). A Macedonian settlement at Isar-Marvinci (? = Idomene) may have been devastated in this war, Sokolovska 1979–82, Sokolovska and Mikulčić 1985. An overland assault on Italy from the direction of the Balkans was later contemplated by Mithridates of Pontus and, reputedly, by the Dacian king Burebista in 49 BC.

Macedonia and, since he could not be charged with these
complaints in his absence, the Senate could do no more than
promise a fair hearing if they wished to prosecute him on return
from active service. In the meantime the Senate pacified the
aggrieved peoples with suitable presents, including 2000 asses
in cash for each of the envoys and for Cincibilis, the prince of
the Gauls, and his brother who had come as an envoy, two
five-pound necklaces of twisted gold, five 20-pound silver vessels, two horses with harness trappings for head and chest,
along with their grooms, cavalry weapons and military cloaks,
and clothing for the prince's attendants, both free and slave.
The Gauls molested by Cassius are described as dwelling 'across
the Alps', and they are likely to have been Celtic people across
the Julian Alps, beyond the Carni and Histri and north of the
Japodes. From this area also may have come the Gallic chief
Balanus who came to Rome in the following year to offer help
against Macedonia. He too received presents, a two-pound
gold necklace, a horse with ornamental trappings and cavalry
weapons.[32]

During the long reign of Philip V there are signs that the
Macedonians were creating a scheme of defence to keep out
the Dardanians and other 'eternal enemies'. It was based on
well-chosen fortified strongholds manned with permanent garrisons: Bylazora on the Vardar/Axius, Sintia probably somewhere to the west (perhaps around Kičevo or Gostivar) and
Perseis on the river Erigon (Crna Reka). Beyond these places
whole areas were cleared of population and systematically
devastated in order to make invasion and retreat even more
hazardous. In the third war between Rome and Macedonia we
hear of an embassy from Perseus to the Illyrian Gentius early
in 169 BC leaving Stuberra on the upper Erigon for Scodra
and 'crossing Mount Scardus, journeying through the so-called
desert of Illyria, which, some years before, had been de-
populated by the Macedonians to make it more difficult for
the Dardanians to raid Illyria and Macedonia. Their journey
through this region was accompanied by great hardship'
(Polybius 28.8). Along with these strongholds and cordons of

[32] Livy 41.1–7, 43.1 and 5.

devastation it seems clear that the depopulation of Paeonia and the settling there of Thracians had nothing to do with any impending war against Rome but was yet another element in the defence of Macedonia. When war began in 171 BC, Perseus still judged it worthwhile to make a pre-emptive strike against the Dardanians, 'by the way, in contempt of the Roman power and as a diversion' (Plutarch, *Aemilius Paullus* 9), it was claimed. He reportedly killed many of them and brought back a great amount of booty. Because of this, and because of the now well-established cordon of defence, the Dardanians appear to have taken no part in a war which was to bring to an end the rule of kings in Macedonia.[33]

[33] Hammond and Walbank 1988, Sokolovska 1978 (Demir Kapija), Mikulčić 1985 (Stobi). Papazoglu 1970b, Hatzopoulos 1987 (inscription from Oleveni near Bitolj, recording Macedonian victory over Dardanians by Philip II or V).

6

Kingdom of Illyrians

A new power on the Adriatic[1]

From the end of the fifth century we have seen how it was possible for regimes among the southern Illyrians to exploit periods of weakness in Macedonia and Epirus, notably Bardylis of the Dardani and Glaucias of the Taulantii. Under a Philip, Alexander or Pyrrhus the tide was reversed and the Illyrians were not only held off but even reduced to subject status. The dynasty of the Antigonids in third-century BC Macedonia was far from weak but was more than once distracted from its effort to retain power in Greece by trouble on the northern frontier. There is now an impression, although it can be no more than that, of a new and more lasting political order emerging among the Illyrians, not only among the Dardanians. The most notable example of this was the rise of a new power based on the Ardiaei, an Illyrian people on the south Adriatic coast well placed to profit from the decline of Epirus after the death of Pyrrhus. Agron, son of Pleuratus, belonged to the ruling house of the Ardiaei: 'Agron was king of that part of Illyria which borders the Adriatic sea, over which sea Pyrrhus and his successors had held sway. In turn he captured part of Epirus and also Corcyra, Epidamnus and Pharos in succession, and established garrisons in them' (Appian *Illyrike* 7). The new

---

[1] Hammond and Walbank 1988, Hammond 1968 (229–205 BC), Wilkes 1969, May 1946 (217–167 BC), Islami 1974, 1976a, Cabanes 1986.

power disposed of 'the most powerful force, both by land and sea, of any of the kings who had reigned in Illyria before him', we are informed by Polybius (2.2). The Illyrians used the lembus, a small and fast warship with a single bank of oars which could carry 50 soldiers in addition to the rowers. Raids by sea from the Adriatic were probably a familiar threat to the northwestern Greeks. What was new was the use of a land army to follow up and profit from victories gained by the navy.[2]

In 234 BC the royal succession in Epirus came to an end and a federal republic was instituted. In the south, the western part of Acarnania seceded from this arrangment. Their independence was soon threatened by the Aetolians who began to occupy territory around the Gulf of Ambracia, including Pyrrhus' old capital Ambracia, which forced the Epirotes to establish a new centre at Phoenice. Besieged at Medion, the Acarnanians sought assistance from Demetrius II of Macedonia, who for most of his reign had been at war with the Aetolian and Achaean Leagues. In response to the request the king brought Agron and his Illyrians on the scene. The Illyrian attack mounted in either 232 or 231 BC is described by Polybius.

One hundred lembi with 500 men on board sailed up to land at Medion. Dropping anchor at daybreak, they disembarked speedily and in secret. They then formed up in the order that was usual in their own country, and advanced in their several companies against the Aetolian lines. The latter were overwhelmed with atonishment at the unexpected nature and boldness of the move; but they had long been inspired with overweening self-confidence, and having full reliance on their own forces were far from being dismayed. They drew up the greater part of their hoplites and cavalry in front of their own lines on the level ground, and with a portion of their cavalry and their light infantry they hastened to occupy some rising ground in front of their camp, which nature had made easily defensible. A single charge, however, of the Illyrians, whose numbers and close order gave them irresistible weight, served to dislodge the light-armed troops, and forced the cavalry who were on the ground with them to retire to the hoplites. But the Illyrians, being on higher ground, and charging down from it upon the Aetolian troops formed up on

[2] Hammond 1968 (kingdom of Agron).

the plain, routed them without difficulty. The Medionians joined the action by sallying out of the town and charging the Aetolians. Thus, after killing a great number, and taking a still greater number prisoners, and becoming masters also of their arms and baggage, the Illyrians, having carried out the orders of their king, conveyed their baggage and the rest of their booty to their boats and immediately set sail for their own country. (Polybius 2.3)

This defeat of the Aetolians, famed for their victory over the invading Gauls a generation before, caused a sensation in Greece. Agron was beside himself with delight when his ships returned and he learned of the victory from his commanders. The king then drank so much by way of celebration, it was reported, that this, and 'other similar indulgences', brought on an attack of pleurisy which killed him within a few days.[3]

Illyrian success continued when command passed to Agron's widow Teuta, who granted individual ships a licence to universal plunder. In 231 BC the fleet and army attacked Elis and Messenia in the Peloponnese. On the way home they called for supplies at Phoenice in Epirus, which, for a consideration, the garrison of 800 Gaulish mercenaries handed over to them. The Epirotes, who had evidently not been involved in recent events, quickly assembled an army to relieve the town. News that the Illyrian Scerdilaidas was marching south through the pass at Antigoneia caused the Epirotes to send part of their forces north to secure that town. At Phoenice the Epirotes became careless and during the night the Illyrians were able to leave the town, cross the river – after replacing the wooden bridge which the besiegers had partly dismantled – and take up a good position to offer battle, which they proceeded to win the next day. The scale of the fighting now began to increase. The Epirotes had already begged assistance from the Greek Leagues, while the Illyrians, having joined up with the force under Scerdilaidas, marched inland to Halicranum (in the plain of modern Ioannina). Here they were preparing to do battle with the Leagues, and were choosing a good site, when orders to withdraw arrived from Queen Teuta, on the grounds that some of the Illyrians had gone over to the Dardani. A truce was

---

[3] Hammond 1967b, 591 and 595 f.

agreed, Phoenice was returned for a price, along with freeborn prisoners. Slaves and the loot were put on the ships while the army under Scerdilaidas marched north by the pass at Antigoneia. The continued Illyrian success was another shock for the Greeks: 'For seeing the most securely placed and powerful city of Epirus thus unexpectedly reduced to slavery, they one and all began to feel anxious, not merely as in former times for their property in open country, but for the safety of their own persons and cities' (Polybius 2.6). The Epirotes signified their acceptance of the Illyrian victory by sending envoys to Teuta promising cooperation with them and hostility towards the Leagues. Teuta was delighted with the profits of the expedition. Phoenice was the most prosperous place in Epirus, and centre for the growing commerce with Italy. It was Illyrian interference with that commerce which brought Roman forces across the Adriatic for the first time.[4]

Even before the first war against Carthage (264–241 BC), from which they gained control of Sicily, the Romans had been aware of the danger to the Adriatic coast of Italy from seaborne attack. In 246 a colony of Roman citizens was settled at Brundisium to keep a watch on the Ionian gulf. 'From time immemorial Illyrians had attacked and robbed ships sailing from Italy' (Polybius 2.8, 1). During their occupation of Phoenice a number of the Illyrian ships had engaged in privateering against Italian merchants. So many were now robbed, murdered or captured that the Roman Senate, after ignoring earlier complaints, realized that something had to be done. Polybius (2.8) furnishes a suspiciously vivid account of a Roman embassy to Queen Teuta, a version of events that was intended to justify the Roman invasion of Illyria. It was led by the brothers L. and Gn. Coruncanius. On arrival they found Teuta celebrating the end of a rebellion in Illyria and engaged in laying siege to the Greek island city Issa (Vis), 'the last town which held out'. When the ambassadors complained of injuries to Romans, Teuta promised that no royal forces would harm them but said she was unable to put an end to the tradition of private enterprise. One of the ambassadors lost his temper and prom-

---

[4] Dell 1967b (Illyrian motives in 230 BC).

ised 'to improve relations between sovereign and subject in
Illyria'. The queen heard this 'with womanish passion and
unreasoning anger' and arranged for the insolent envoy to be
murdered on his homeward voyage. News of this caused the
Romans to prepare for war: legions were enlisted and the fleet
assembled, and there was general indignation at 'the queen's
violation of the law of nations'.[5]

The Roman invasion of Illyria in 229 BC appears to have
caught Teuta and the Illyrians completely off guard. As soon
as the weather permitted, the queen had ordered south a naval
expedition even larger than those of previous years, with most
of the ships heading for an attack on Corcyra. Some landed at
Epidamnus, entered the city to procure food and water with
weapons concealed and almost captured it; but they were
thrown out after a fight and the careless citizens thus 'received
a useful lesson for the future' (Polybius 2.9, 6). These ships
now joined the main Illyrian force in the siege of Corcyra. The
Corcyraeans, along with Apollonia and Epidamnus, sought
assistance from the Leagues of Greece. Ten Achaean ships were
engaged by the Illyrians, reinforced by seven warships of the
Acarnanians, off the island Paxos south of Corcyra. By superior
tactics the Illyrians took four triremes and sank a quinquereme,
while the rest of the Greeks managed to escape. Corcyra was
surrendered and was occupied by a garrison under the command of Demetrius from the island of Pharos (Hvar). The main
Illyrian force sailed north for another attack on Epidamnus.
The Illyrians were now on the point of controlling all the
coastline north of the Gulf of Corinth, including the sea routes
to Sicily and Italy via Corcyra.[6]

The Roman consul Gn. Fulvius had planned to sail his 200
ships to Corcyra to raise the siege. Even when he learned the
island had surrendered he still sailed there, having already
entered secret negotiations with Demetrius, who had fallen out
of favour with Teuta. Thus Corcyra welcomed the Romans
and, with the compliance of Demetrius, surrendered the garrison. The city became a 'friend of Rome' and would hencefor-
ward rely on Roman protection from the Illyrians. Demetrius

---

[5] There are discrepancies between the pro-Roman versions of Appian and
Polybius, Hammond 1968, 5–6.
[6] Polybius 2.9–10.

now served as adviser to the Roman commanders for the rest of the war. Meanwhile the consul A. Postumius brought an army of 20,000 infantry and 2000 cavalry across from Brundisium to Apollonia, which now joined the Roman alliance. The fleet under Fulvius reached Apollonia and the two forces advanced in the direction of Epidamnus, causing the Illyrians to abandon the siege and disperse their forces. The city was received into Roman protection and the army now moved inland among the Illyrian peoples of the hinterland. Here the Romans received delegations from many peoples, including the Atintani and Parthini, from whom a formal surrender was accepted. At sea the blockade of Issa was raised and the city also was received into Roman protection. As the Romans approached the Illyrian heartlands there was more resolute opposition. The fleet moved northwards and attacked Illyrian coastal towns, at one of which, the unidentified Noutria, Roman losses included a magistrate of the Republic (*quaestor*) and some military tribunes, although 20 ships laden with plunder were intercepted. The besiegers of Issa fled to Arbo (not identified), and the queen herself retreated to Rhizon (Risan), in the Gulf of Kotor. The Romans decided that enough had been achieved and hostilities ceased. The consuls handed over Illyria to Demetrius and withdrew the fleet and army to Epidamnus, from which the greater part returned to Italy under Fulvius. Having assembled 40 ships and some troops from allies in the area the other consul remained across the Adriatic to keep a watch on the Illyrian Ardiaei and the peoples under Roman protection. Before the end of winter, envoys of Teuta appeared in Rome and a treaty was concluded. According to its terms the queen would abandon Illyris, except for a few places, and promised not to sail south of Lissus at the mouth of the Drin with more than two ships, even then unarmed vessels. The terms of the settlement were conveyed to the Leagues in Greece, where they were well received since 'the Illyrians were not the enemies of this or that people, but the common enemies of all alike' (Polybius 2.12). So ended the first Roman action against Illyrians.[7]

---

[7] Polybius 2.11–12, Appian, *Illyrike* 8, Cassius Dio 12 frg. 49. N. Ceka 1970 (Parthini).

The Illyrians had been forced to give up all their recent conquests south of the Drin. The Romans had gained control of the strategic ports Epidamnus, Apollonia and Corcyra. In the hinterland several of the Illyrian peoples had now the status of Rome clients, as was certainly the case with the Parthini in the Genusus (Shkumbin) valley and the Atintani further south. Moreover not only were the Ardiaei prevented from moving at will by land and sea into Epirus and western Greece – as in 230 BC when Scerdilaidas appeared on the scene to profit from the lucky capture of Phoenice – but they were now cut off from the inland route to Macedonia, their patron and ally against the Greek Leagues. To what extent, if at all, the Romans had Macedonia in mind when they made their dispositions after the first Illyrian war has been much debated. They may well not have taken much account of recent events involving Macedonia, Illyrians and the Greeks. For their part the Macedonians will have been aware that the Romans now controlled the main route to the Adriatic and that they had ended Illyrian control of Dassaretis. Macedonia took no part in the events of 229 BC. Hitherto the Antigonids had shown little interest towards the Adriatic, and when they might have moved to support their Illyrian ally the kingdom was recovering from the aftermath of a Dardanian raid.[8]

The decade after 229 BC witnessed a revival of Illyrian power under Demetrius of Pharos, who had succeeded Teuta and married Triteuta, mother of the infant King Pinnes. The alliance with Macedonia was also revived, as the latter's fortunes recovered under the regent Antigonus Doson. In 222 BC an Illyrian corps of 1600 fought with distinction under the command of Demetrius at Sellasia, where the Macedonians won a conclusive victory over the Spartans. Before then, when Rome was preoccupied with a war against the Celtic peoples of the Po valley in northern Italy (225–222 BC), Demetrius was said to have detached the Atintani from their Roman alliance and, in contravention of the settlement of 228 BC, to have sailed south of Lissus and engaged in piracy. The Romans also sus-

[8] Hammond 1968 (geography of Roman settlement); Roman motives: Dell 1967a, 1970b, Levi 1973.

pected that Demetrius had some sort of understanding with the Histri at the head of the Adriatic, who were interfering with Roman supply ships. These were evidently the 'pirates' attacked by a Roman fleet in 221 BC (Appian, *Illyrike* 8). Early in the summer of that year, when tension was rising in Greece as Macedonia made an alliance with the Achaean League against the Aetolian League, the Illyrians attacked in their traditional manner. Demetrius and Scerdilaidas (presumably the same who commanded a land army ten years earlier) sailed south of Lissus with 90 Illyrian warships (lembi). After an assault on Pylos in the western Peloponnese had failed they separated their forces, Demetrius taking his chances in plundering the Cyclades while his colleague returned north. On putting in at Naupactus with 40 ships Scerdilaidas was encouraged by his brother-in-law Amynas, king of the Athamanes, to join the Aetolians in their planned invasion of Achaea. Meanwhile, back in Illyria, Demetrius continued operations during the following winter, it is said, attacking and seizing Roman allied cities in Illyris. The Romans, who had hitherto ignored the activities of their former ally, decided that the harbours on the coast of Illyris had now to be made secure, in view of the threat of another war with Carthage.[9]

Unlike Teuta in 229 BC, Demetrius was prepared for the Roman invasion. He placed a garrison in Dimale (Dimallum), a fortress inland from Apollonia, eliminated his opponents in other places and stationed 6000 of his best forces on his home island Pharos. As before, both consuls of the year accompanied the Roman expedition, but the leading role was played by Aemilius Paullus, who was to be killed in the great Roman disaster at Cannae three years later. Having decided that Dimale was crucial to Demetrius' power in the region, the consul prepared to besiege it but was able to take the place by assault within seven days. As a result all the towns of the area submitted to Roman protection, each receiving the appropriate terms and conditions. Next the Romans moved against Demetrius on his island of Pharos, who awaited the attack with good troops, ample provisions and war materials behind strong fortifi-

[9] Dell 1967b, 1970a, Hammond 1968.

cations. In order to avoid a long siege Aemilius decided to risk another frontal attack. The army was moved from the mainland to a wooded area of the island, while a small force of ships was sent out to tempt Demetrius from behind his fortifications. The strategy worked, and when the main Roman army appeared from another direction on the island the Illyrians were forced to give battle cut off from their city. Demetrius deserted his forces (who soon surrendered) and fled to Macedonia, in whose service he died later fighting bravely. The Romans destroyed the fortifications of Pharos and before the summer was over Aemilius was back in Rome receiving congratulations for a job well done. Any threat to the Roman hold on Illyris had been eliminated, all the gains of the first war had been secured, and the old restrictions of movement imposed on the rulers of Illyria.[10]

The career of Demetrius drew Rome and Macedonia closer to conflict. He may indeed have returned to Illyria and have been attacked by another Roman force, although the regime of Pinnes, now confirmed as king, was left intact. In contrast, Scerdilaidas who was also an ally of Philip of Macedonia, managed to avoid any entanglement with the Romans, although his support for Macedonia against the Aetolians in 218 BC was curtailed by 'plots and conflicts' caused by the rulers of various cities. In 217 BC Hannibal defeated the Romans at Lake Trasimene and his army later moved across to the Adriatic coast of Italy, first to Picenum and later to Apulia. This renewed Roman concern regarding the state of affairs in the Adriatic. In their first direct communication with Macedonia they demanded the surrender of Demetrius, while Pinnes was ordered to pay the arrears of 'tribute', presumably some sort of reparations imposed after the recent war. The former demand was refused and no response from the latter is recorded. At this point Scerdilaidas ceased his support of Philip, maintaining that the promised subsidy was in arrears. He dispatched 15 ships, ostensibly to collect and escort the payment, but at Leucas south of Corcyra his forces killed two of Philip's Corinthian friends and seized their four ships. They then sailed south and began to

[10] Polybius 3.18–19, Appian, *Illyrike* 8, Cassius Dio 12 frg. 53.

plunder shipping around Cape Malea in the southern Peloponnese. In response Philip prepared a strong naval force, 12 decked-ships, eight open vessels and 30 light craft called 'hemioliae', which headed south at full speed to deal with the Illyrians. Now Scerdilaidas attacked Macedonia overland: seizing strongholds in Dassaretis, he looted Pissaeum in Macedonian Pelagonia and overran some frontier districts of Philip's kingdom. Before the winter Philip had occupied the area of Lychnitis, cutting off the direct route from Illyria, and extended his power to Dassaretis, which brought him into direct contact with the Roman clients in Illyris. It is reported that Philip was already contemplating an advance to the Adriatic and possibly an invasion of Italy, urged on by his counsellor Demetrius. In order to do this he had to secure a base on the Adriatic, a port such as Epidamnus or Apollonia, and this was not possible unless he committed a fleet to the Adriatic. There he would face not only the lembi of Scerdilaidas but also the heavier warships of the Roman navy.[11]

In 216 BC Philip sailed towards the Adriatic with 100 of his own lembi, built in Macedonia by Illyrian shipwrights during the previous winter. On learning that the Roman fleet was off western Sicily he passed Corcyra, apparently heading for Apollonia. Near the mouth of the Aous he learned that a Roman fleet was heading for Apollonia to support Scerdilaidas. In the event Philip's hasty retreat, sailing non-stop two days and nights to reach Cephallonia, proved a serious blunder since there were in fact only ten Roman ships, dispatched to bolster up Scerdilaidas after he had reported Philip's naval preparations and pleaded for Roman assistance. 'If Philip had not fled from these [ships] in such a panic he would have had the best chance to attain his ambition in Illyria' (Polybius 5.110), was a contemporary verdict on this incident. In 215 BC Philip concluded a formal treaty with Hannibal: if Carthage made peace with Rome there would be no war against Macedonia; Rome would surrender control of Corcyra, Apollonia, Epidamnus, Pharos, Dimale, the Parthini and the Atintani; Demetrius and his allies would be restored to power in Pharos and in other

[11] Polybius 595, 101 and 108, Hammond 1968.

territories then under Roman control. The Roman response
was to station a fleet at Tarentum to guard the coast and keep
watch on the Macedonians. In 214 BC, aware that his new ally
was engaging the Romans at Tarentum, Philip moved with
rather more determination that he had shown two years before.
His fleet of 120 lembi tried to seize Apollonia but when they
failed to make a quick capture moved south to seize Oricus,
though this lacked both fortifications and supporting manpower. The Roman commander M. Valerius Laevinus, having
placed a garrison of 2000 men at Apollonia, headed south with
his warships, and some legionaries embarked on transports and
recaptured Oricus, Philip's weak garrison offering only token
resistance. Now Laevinus learned that Apollonia was close to
capitulation to a Macedonian siege and sent 2000 men on
warships to the mouth of the river Aous. Under the prefect
Naevius Crista they made a detour and managed to enter the
city at night by a route unknown to the besiegers. The next
night the Roman troops and the citizens, having realized the
general state of slackness in the Macedonian army, marched
into the enemy camp and would have reached the king's tent
if the slaughter of men near the gate had not raised the alarm.
It is reported that 3000 were captured or killed. The camp was
looted and the siege equipment taken over by the citizens for
their own use in any future attack. Anything else of value was
handed over to the Romans. Laevinus moved his ships to the
mouth of the Aous to block Philip's escape by sea. The king
beached and set fire to his ships and marched home 'with an
army for the most part robbed of its arms and possessions'
(Livy 24.40, 17), while Valerius and the fleet wintered at
Oricus. Illyria had witnessed the first direct clash between
Rome and Macedonia, which had ended in a total humiliation
for the latter.[12]

In spite of this setback Philip persisted with his efforts in the
northwest and during the next two years was able to detach
the Parthini and Atintani from the Roman alliance. In 213 or
212 BC he moved into the heart of Illyria and captured the
strongholds of Lissus and Acrolissus on the lower Drin. This

---

[12] Polybius 5.109–10, Livy 24.40. Budina 1976 (Oricus).

success attracted more support from among the Illyrians. The troublesome regime of Scerdilaidas would now appear to have been eliminated while Philip had acquired a naval base on the Adriatic from which he could not only threaten Roman Italy but also maintain direct contact with Hannibal in Italy. The Roman response was an alliance with the Aetolian League against Philip which others, including Scerdilaidas and his son Pleuratus, were invited to join. Rome promised 25 quinque-remes to support the land operations of their allies: as far north as Corcyra all the moveable loot should be the Roman share. By this extension of the war into Greece the history of Illyris and the Illyrians became dominated by conflicts between Rome and Macedonia. For the moment, however, all these matters were for the Romans merely a distraction from the effort against Hannibal and Carthage.[13]

For around a century the kingdom of the Illyrians was a minor but stable power on the margin of the Hellenistic world. No Greek writer is known to have made a serious study of Illyrians in their homeland and what has been transmitted about them is often little more than nonsense, such as the Hellenistic historian Alexander's tale of the Illyrian Dando who lived to be 500 without becoming senile. Greek writers – notably the contemporary historian Polybius – depict Illyrian rulers, especially Queen Teuta, as victims of their irrational conduct and murderous instincts. In the light of such prejudice it is difficult to make any valid comparison between institutions of the Illyrian kingdom and those of the more established powers around the eastern Mediterranean, Macedonia, Perga-mum, Syria, etc. The monarchy was hereditary, indicated by the succession of the infant Pinnes to Agron (*c.*230 BC). Control was in the hands of Agron's widow Teuta, though not the mother of Pinnes, and subsequently of Demetrius of Pharos, who married Triteuta, mother of the infant king. Military command was in the hands of Scerdilaidas, possibly Agron's brother, but the prominent role of women, even in a polyga-mous society, may be compared with that among other

---

[13] Philip's conquests in Illyria: Polybius 8.14–14b (Lissus, Dassaretae, Uscana), Livy 29.12 (Dimale, Parthini and Atintanes). H. Ceka 1971 (coin hoard of *c.*213 BC). Lissus: Prendi 1975b, 1981.

Hellenistic dynasties. Like the kings of Macedonia and Epirus, Illyrian rulers contracted a succession of marriages as a means of sealing alliances with other powers.[14]

The power of the Ardiaean dynasty was centred on fortresses around the Lake of Shkodër, notably Lissus, Scodra, Meteon (Medun) and others on the coast including Bouthoe (Budva), Olcinium (Ulcinj) and Rhizon (Risan) in the Gulf of Kotor. It seems doubtful whether, except for temporary success in time of war, the Illyrian kings ever exercised effective control south of Lissus, where the coastal plains, productive of cereals and pasture, remained under the control of Dyrrachium and Apollonia. It was seafaring which brought Illyrians to the notice of the Greek world, notably their piratical raids in lembi which, though of no use for the bulk cargoes of merchantmen, were well able to bear away loot and prisoners. Piracy had long been a familiar and largely accepted hazard in the Greek world. With their forces combined pirates – notably those of Crete – could prove effective allies and some established powers did not hesitate to employ them. As we have seen, the Illyrians became accustomed to assisting the kings of Macedonia, providing the terms were right. The actual responsibility of the Illyrians for what appears to have been the chronic menace of piracy in the Adriatic was grossly exaggerated in a Roman version of history formed at this period. On land the Hellenistic powers made extensive use of mercenaries. Like Thracians to the east the Illyrians were also an important source of military manpower, and often served as separate contingents under their own leaders. Individuals may have been recruited to the armies of Macedon and Pergamum but none is recorded in any commanding role during this period.[15]

Something of the material culture of the subjects of the Illyrian kings has been revealed by the contents of a cemetery of the late third and second centuries BC excavated in 1956–8 at Vele Ledine, Gostilj, in hilly country bordering the Lake of

---

[14] Papazoglu 1967, 1986 (Illyrian 'politarchs' in 229–205 BC), Walbank 1976.
[15] Torr 1895, 115–16 (lembus).

Shkodër (see figure 18). The 131 tombs contained 136 burials, most of individual adults, along with another 19 burials of those whose origins differed from the rest. The burials were not symmetrically arranged and nor were there any external indications of the existence of the graves, save for two into which spears had been driven upright after burial had taken place. Grave goods alongside the extended corpses included offerings of food and drink and small jars which probably contained perfume. The vessels have Greek forms and most are of south Italian type, while the many bronze and silver brooches belong to the middle La Tène type. Male burials contained only double-pin brooches, female burials single-pin. Among several coins were issues of Scodra, preceding and during the reign of Gentius, along with some from the period after his

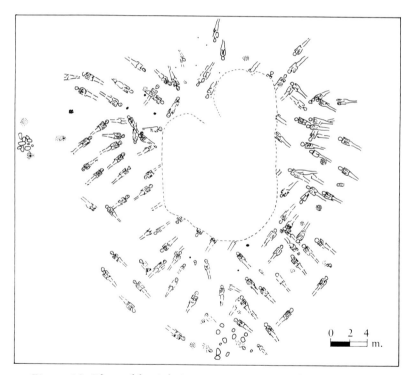

Figure 18 Plan of burials in cemetery at Gostilj, Montenegro

deposition in 168 BC. Three silver belt-plates and one of bronze
of the well-known 'Greco-Illyrian' type were decorated with
figures of warriors and magical symbols.[16]

Roman alliance and conquest

Roman alliance with the Aetolians against Macedonia will have
encouraged the latter's enemies to seek an immediate profit
while forcing its allies to reflect on the depth of their loyalty
to the king. In 210 BC Philip raided some of the most southerly
Illyrian communities in the hinterland of Apollonia. In 208 BC
Philip's garrison at Lychnidus was betrayed by its commander
to a local leader Aeropus, who proceeded to invite the Dardani
into the area. When they reached the plain of Macedonia the
king was forced to abandon operations in Greece. A similar
pattern of events occurred in the following year and the Dardanians now became such a threat to the Macedonian war effort
in Greece that their actions may have been instigated by the
Romans, employing their allies in Illyria as intermediaries. Then
all changed when the king made a separate peace in 206 with
the Aetolians and in the following year with the Romans, after
the latter had invaded Illyris from a base at Apollonia. For a few
years at least Philip could turn his forces against his perpetual
enemies in the north, Illyrians, Dardanians and Thracians.[17]

Both Scerdilaidas and his son Pleuratus are listed among the
parties to the peace of 205 BC, but by 200 BC the latter was
ruling alone in Illyria, when he appeared at the Roman headquarters in Dassaretis offering to assist the expedition against
Macedonia. The Roman consul Galba declined the offer but
promised to seek Illyrian help when his army was in Macedonia.
Although Pleuratus is reported to have invaded the territories
of Philip V at least once, his contribution to Roman victory in
197 BC would appear to have been minimal. Nonetheless the
king was rewarded with possession of the strategic region
Lychnitis, which had been in Macedonian hands for nearly two

---

[16] Basler 1972, also Ylli 1976 (Leshnje, Skrapar), Korkuti 1972 (Gajtan near
Shkodër).
[17] Livy 29.12, Hammond 1968.

centuries, and also control over the Parthini, former Roman allies in the Shkumbin valley. This placed under Illyrian control the route to Macedonia from the west, but the Roman intention was rather to deny control to Macedonia than to signal their regard for Pleuratus. Be this as it may, the Illyrian king became famous for what he had gained from loyalty to the Romans: 'in return for doing nothing he was made the greatest of the rulers of Illyris' (Polybius 21.23). Pleuratus was permitted to plunder the coast of Aetolia with 60 lembi during the next round of warfare in 189 BC, but received no gains of territory at the conclusion of hostilities. Nevertheless, for around 20 years a king of Illyria profited from the hostility between Rome and Macedonia, but matters were to turn out very differently for his successor.[18]

By 181 BC the loyal Pleuratus had been succeeded by his son Gentius. The coast and hinterland south of the Drin remained under Roman control, and nothing is known of how the Illyrian kingdom exploited, if it really ever did, the territories awarded to it in 197 BC, notably the area of Lychnitis around Ohrid. Instead the Illyrians moved to increase their power over kindred peoples living to the north and west. Among the islands the Greek city of Issa had retained some form of independence under Roman protection but Pharos remained an Illyrian possession. On the mainland the Delmatae and the Daorsi were at one time subjects, but the former were reported to have defected soon after the accession of Gentius. Illyrian strength lay in their ships and it was their interference with Adriatic shipping which once more aroused Roman interest in the area. In 180 BC a Roman praetor responsible for coastal protection arrived in Brundisium with some ships of Gentius said to have been caught in the act of piracy. An embassy to Illyria failed to locate the king; but the praetor discovered that Romans and Italians were being held for ransom at Corcyra (Korčula in Dalmatia rather than Corfu). No outcome of the affair is reported and it may well be that the Senate accepted a claim by Gentius' envoys that the charges were false. Ten years later,

---

[18] Pleuratus and Rome: Livy 31.28, 33.34, 38.7; Polybius 17.47, 21.11 and 21. Dell 1977 (Roman–Illyrian relations 200–168 BC).

when Rome was gripped with war-fever against Perseus of Macedonia, Issa accused Gentius of plotting war with the king and now the Illyrian envoys were denied a hearing before the Senate. Instead the Romans seized 54 Illyrian lembi at anchor in the harbour of Epidamnus. On the eve of war a Roman senator was sent to Illyria to remind the king of his formal friendship with the Roman Republic. Nothing is recorded of relations at this time between the Illyrians of Gentius and the Dardanians, both Roman allies in the previous war against Macedonia. In 169 BC there was a report that Gentius had his brother Plator killed because his plan to marry Etuta, daughter of the Dardanian chief Monunius, would have made him too powerful and that he then married the princess himself.[19]

In 170 BC a Roman army failed twice to enter Macedonia from the direction of Thessaly, and Perseus used the respite to raid Illyrians from a base at Stuberra, in the hope, it is reported, of tempting Gentius to become his ally. In midwinter 170/169 BC Perseus launched a successful raid on the Illyrian Penestae and captured their chief town Uscana (perhaps Debar on the Drin or Kičevo on a tributary of the Vardar). This people are not otherwise recorded but there seems no reason to connect them with a subject class of the population in Thessaly known by the same name. During the previous summer Roman forces based at Lychnidus had, after an initial failure, captured Uscana with the help of Illyrian allies and expelled a Macedonian garrison of Cretan mercenaries. Perseus recaptured the place with little difficulty along with several other Roman posts in the area, including Oaneum on a river Aratus, which controlled the route leading west to the kingdom of Gentius among the Labeates around Scodra. At this point Perseus sent his first embassy to Gentius, consisting of the Illyrian exile Pleuratus for his command of the Illyrian language and the Macedonian Adaeus from Beroea. They found Gentius at Lissus and informed him of Perseus' successes against the Romans and Dardanians and his recent winter victory among the Penestae. The Illyrian replied that he lacked not the will to fight the Romans

---

[19] Livy 40.42 (180 BC), 42.26 (172 BC) and 48; Polybius 29.13, cf. Livy 44.30 (fratricide).

but only the money. No promises were made on this point either by this embassy or another sent from Stuberra shortly afterwards. Meanwhile, the Roman commander failed to recapture Uscana but took hostages from those among the Penestae who professed loyalty, and also from the Parthini further west, among whom his troops were stationed in winter quarters. Perseus continued his efforts to involve Gentius in the war, preferably, it was said, at no cost to his treasury. The Illyrian exile Pleuratus raised 1000 infantry and 200 cavalry from the Penestae that in 169 BC fought for Macedonia with distinction in the defence of Cassandrea.[20]

The Roman invasion of Macedonia in 168 BC forced the king to promise a subsidy to Gentius, whose ships might be employed to attack the Romans. A sum of 300 talents was mentioned and Perseus sent his companion Pantauchus to make the arrangements. At Meteon hostages were agreed and Gentius accepted the oath of the king. He sent Olympio with a delegation to Perseus to collect the money, and the treaty was concluded with some ceremony at Dium on the Thermaic gulf. The 300 talents were counted out of the royal treasury at Pella and the Illyrians were permitted to mark it with their own stamp. An advance of ten talents was forwarded to Illyria and when this was passed over by Pantauchus the king was urged to commence hostilities against the Romans. When Gentius imprisoned two Roman envoys sent by Appius Claudius at Lychnidus, Perseus recalled the rest of the subsidy in the belief that Gentius was now his ally, come what may.[21]

Appius Claudius was succeeded at Lychnidus by the praetor L. Anicius Gallus, who was assigned responsibility for operations against Gentius. It appears that the Illyrians planned one of their usual expeditions with army and navy in the direction of Epidamnus, and an army of 15,000 was assembled at Lissus. After detaching 1000 infantry and 50 horsemen under his half-brother Caravantius to deal with the Cavi, otherwise unknown, Gentius advanced south for five miles and proceeded to attack

[20] Livy 43.18–19 (Uscana and Oaneum), Hammond 1966 and 1972, 43 f. (= Kičevo), Frashëri 1975 (Uscana = Debar/Dibra), Kaca 1981 (Dibra region), Polybius 28.8–9 (embassy to Gentius).
[21] Livy 44.23 (treaty at Dium), Polybius 29.2.

Bassania, a town under Roman control. Anicius was based at
Apollonia where, in addition to Roman forces, there were 2000
infantry and 200 cavalry from the Parthini, commanded by the
chiefs Epicadus and Algalsus. What happened next is missing
from the record but it seems that the Romans defeated the
Illyrian navy sent to attack supply-routes, and the story resumes
with Gentius trapped in Scodra and hoping for relief from
Caravantius. When the king finally surrendered to the praetor
the Roman army marched to the north end of the lake, where
at Meteon they captured Gentius' queen Etleva, his brother
Caravantius and his sons Scerdilaidas and Pleuratus, and
released the imprisoned Roman envoys. Gentius was placed in
custody and sent to Rome. Anicius, leaving Gabinius in charge
at Scodra and G. Licinius to control Rhizon and Olcinium,
moved his army south to attack Macedonian possessions in
Epirus. The whole campaign had lasted only 30 days.[22]

At the end of the season, after settling his army in winter
quarters, Anicius returned to Illyria, where the five com-
missioners from Rome had reached Scodra. All the chiefs from
the areas affected by his operations were summoned to hear
what the Senate and Roman people had decided. The Illyrians
were to receive their freedom, and Anicius undertook to remove
garrisons from all cities, citadels and strongholds. Not only
freedom but also exemption from tribute was conferred on
Issa, the Taulantii, the Pirustae of the Dassaretii, and also on
the people of Rhizon and Olcinium because they had all joined
the Roman side while Gentius was yet undefeated. Similarly
the Daorsi were granted freedom from tribute because they had
deserted Caravantius and gone over with their arms to the
Romans. Half the tax which they had previously paid to the
king was imposed on the Scodrenses, the Dassarenses, the
Selepitani and the rest of the Illyrians. Finally, following the
example of Rome's organization of the defeated Macedonians,
Illyria was divided into three regions. The location of the first
is not clear but was probably in the south around Lissus, the
second was Labeatis, around the lake, and the third lay on the

---

[22] Livy 44.30–2.

coast around Rhizon, Acruvium and Olcinium.[23] Bronze coins with similar types issued by Lissus (figure 19a) and the Labeates (figure 19c) may belong to the first and second of these regions, while those of the Daorsi struck apparently at Ošanići possibly to the third.

The celebration of the praetor's triumph 'over king Gentius and the Illyrians' took place in February 167 BC, but suffered somewhat from comparison with the awesome spectacle of the triumph of Aemilius Paullus over Macedonia which the Romans had witnessed the previous December. As many observed, everything was on a smaller scale, but still well-earned for a total victory by land and sea over the Illyrians, an enemy confident in their terrain and their fortifications. In the triumphal procession were paraded military standards of the Illyrians, the royal furniture, 27 pounds of gold, 19 of silver, 13,000 denarii and 120,000 Illyrian silver pieces. In front of Anicius' chariot were led Gentius, his brother, his wife and children and several leading Illyrians. Generous rewards were paid to the allies and the fleet, the same 45 denarii as had been granted to Roman citizens who had served in the campaign. The soldiers were in high spirits during the triumph and their commander was the subject of many songs. Besides the gold and silver, the booty realised 20 million sesterces for the treasury. The Senate ordered Gentius and his household to be confined at Spoleto but when its citizens objected they were tranferred to Iguvium in Umbria. The 220 captured Illyrian lembi were presented to the peoples of Corcyra, Apollonia and Dyrrhachium (Epidamnus).[24]

A significant indication of Hellenistic influence on the Illyrians is furnished by the locally produced coinages of the third and second centuries BC. They are similar in character to those issued from the fourth century BC onwards by Greek settlements on the Adriatic coast. Their limited circulation suggested that they were intended for trade with the native Illyrians rather than with the rest of the Greek world. The 'Greco-Illyrian' coins tend to be small, roughly produced

[23] Livy 45.26, H. Ceka 1984, Hammond and Walbank 1988.
[24] Triumph of Anicius: *Inscriptiones Italiae* XIII pt. 1, pp. 81 and 566, Livy 45.43.

bronzes (silver is scarce, especially towards the north). The obverse has generally the head of a deity or sometimes that of a ruler, with divine attributes – such as the club, bow and arrow of Herakles – on the reverse. Other reverse types include the familiar themes of produce, corn, the vine and pottery vessels, of animals, including goats, stags and does, and images of seafaring, including merchantmen. The silver and bronze coins of Dyrrhachium and Apollonia occur in large numbers not only along the coast but also far inland, especially from the late fifth century BC until production ceased around 100 BC. The circulation of the coins of Damastion included Dardania (Metohija and the Morava valley) and beyond, and to the west the southern Adriatic coast from Scodra to Split. This dispersal suggests a pattern of commerce among the southern Illyrians less directed towards the south (where the coins are rare) than towards the central Balkans. This complements the archaeological evidence for a rupture in the trading connections between the Illyrians and the Greek world after the middle of the fifth century BC.[25]

One of the first coin issues by the Adriatic Greeks remains something of a mystery. A city named Herakleia struck bronze coins to a Syracusan standard which circulated locally in the fourth century BC, but the location of the city remains to be identified, the area of Split and the island of Korčula being among current suggestions. Similarly, coins with the legend DIM or DI, many overstruck issues of other cities, would appear to have been produced somewhere on the island of Hvar. Something approaching a local dominance was achieved by coins of the colony Pharos on the same island and Issa on the island Vis. Silver and bronze issues of the former are known in whole and fractional (half, quarter and sixth) denominations. The 16 or so types of Issaean coinage begin in the mid-fourth century with the 'Ionio' series, the name of either a local hero or contemporary ruler,

---

[25] Dukat and Mirnik 1976, H. Ceka 1972a, 1972b (Bakёrr hoard of *c.* 200 BC).

if not a reference to the figure after whom the Ionian Gulf was named.[26]

The first Illyrian rulers known to have issued coins were king Monunius and his successor Mytilus in the early third century BC. The most productive was Gentius, whose treasury of 120,000 pieces of silver we have seen conveyed to Rome after his defeat in 168 BC. Two of his mints were located at Scodra and Lissus, and his coins were also struck at Dyrrhachium. Here the royal title is absent from a silver coin, and the name Gentius, not uncommon at Dyrrhachium, may belong not to the king but to a local magistrate, although around 30 to 40 examples of bronze have been recorded with the legend 'king Genthios'. The coins of Lissus, with the Greek legend 'LISSI-TAN' (see figure 19a), begin with autonomous issues under Macedonian influence (*c.* 211–197 BC), followed by the issues of Gentius with a galley on the reverse (see figure 19b) and a third series from the period after the king's removal. The Scodra coins fall into three similar groups, the first and third with the legend 'SKODRI-NON' (see figure 19c) and the second with 'of king Genthios'. Coins of Gentius are relatively scarce compared with those of the otherwise unknown 'Ballaios' or 'king Ballaios' (see figure 19d), who appears to have ruled after 168 BC at Queen Teuta's old stronghold Rhizon (Risan). His silver issues are rare, but bronze coins, without the royal title, occur on Hvar, both in single finds and in hoards, and at Rhizon in a different series bearing the royal title. The coins of Ballaios were widely imitated in the region, sometimes so crudely as to be unintelligible. Rhizon also produced silver and bronze coins, some bearing a Macedonian shield type which have been dated to around 211–197 BC. Two other coinages of Illyrian peoples are dated to the period following 168 BC. Those with the legend DAORSON with a galley on the reverse were produced by the Daorsi. They dwelt around Stolac near the Neretva valley in Hercegovina, and their fortress at Ošanići shows signs of Greek influence. Finally coins with the legend 'LABIATAN' were

---

[26] D. Rendić-Miočević 1970a (Ionio), 1976b, Bonačić-Mandić 1987 (Pharos).

(a)

(b)

*Figure 19 a) Bronze coin of Lissus: head of Artemis (obv.), thunder-
bolt and legend LISSI-TAN (rev.), 2nd century BC; diameter 12 mm
b) Bronze coin of Illyrian king Genthios (Gentius): Illyrian deity
wearing broad hat (obv.), Illyrian ship and legend GENTH (rev.),
180–168 BC; diameter 20 mm*

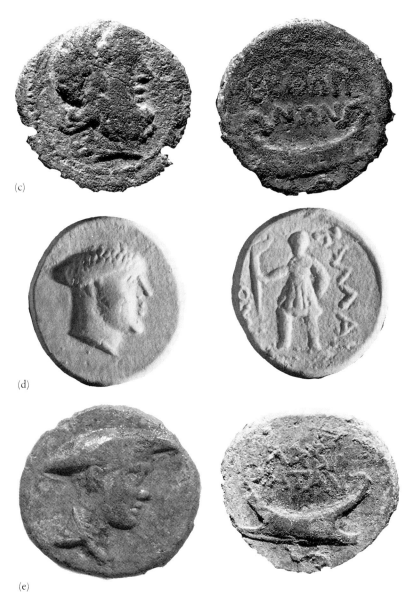

Figure 19 Continued
c) *Bronze coins of Scodra: head of Zeus (obv.), Illyrian ship with legend SKODRI-NON (rev.), 2nd century* BC; *diameter 17 mm*
d) *Bronze coin of King Ballaios; diameter 16 mm*
e) *Bronze coin of Labeates: Illyrian deity wearing broad hat (obv.), Illyrian ship with dolphin and legend LABIATAN (rev.), 2nd century* BC; *diameter 20 mm*

produced by the Labeatae of the Lacus Labeatis (Lake of Shkodër) (see figure 19e) and, like the earlier pieces of Scodra, bear on the reverse a galley, that traditional image of Hellenistic Illyria.[27]

[27] Monunius: D. Rendić-Miočević 1981, Picard 1986; Gentius: Islami 1972c, H. Ceka 1976b (portrait), D. Rendić-Miočević 1972–3; Lissitan: Jubani 1972c, H. Ceka 1976b, also a 'Redon' legend on Lissus coins, Papazoglu 1974 (personal name), D. Rendić-Miočević 1985 (Illyrian hero); Labiatan: H. Ceka 1984, Franke 1976 (coin production); Ballaios: Dukat and Mirnik 1976, Visona 1985 (in Italy); Daorsi: Marić 1979c.

Part III

Roman Illyrians

7

Illyricum

Dalmatian and Pannonian Illyrians

By the middle of the second century BC the Romans knew enough of the Illyrians and their country not to risk large armies in search of glory. Control over the Adriatic coast may have been attained by the end of the century but the interior was yet to be penetrated. Not until Augustus decided to station the legions around the perimeter of the Empire was the effort made to make secure the overland route through the Pannonian Illyrians between Italy and the East. That could only be done at a great cost and not before a rebellion of Illyricum brought the regime of Augustus to the brink of disaster.

We may begin with the Venetic peoples, Veneti, Carni, Histri and Liburni, whose language set them apart from the rest of the Illyrians. The Veneti, from whom were named Venetia and Venice, were known to the Greek poet Alkman in the late seventh century for their love of horses. They inhabited the plain between the Alps and the mouth of the Padus (Po), defined on the west by the Athesis (Adige) and on the east by the Piavis (Piave) or Tilaventus (Tagliamento), where they bordered the Carni. According to Polybius (2.17) the Veneti were an ancient people, but how they were connected, if at all, with the Veneti of southern Brittany or with the Slavonic Venedi or Veneti (Wends) located by Tacitus on the southern Baltic is not known. Their name had linked them in myth with the Heneti or Eneti of Paphlagonia in northern Asia Minor, notably in the story of how the Trojan hero Antenor fled to Venetia, where he founded the city of Patavium (Padua), birthplace of the historian Livy. There is no record of any conflict between the Romans and the Veneti. From the outset the interests of the two seem to have coincided, as the Romans came into hostile contact with neighbours of the Veneti during the decade before the Second Punic War. The Veneti give the impression of being a stable lowland people, with established settlements at Opitergium (Oderzo), Tarvisium (Treviso), Montebelluna, Acelum (Asolo) and Altinum, in addition to the major settlements at Ateste (Este) and Patavium (Padua). Their material remains are known to archaeologists as the Este culture, from the discoveries made at the site of Ateste. At Padua, which like Este was an undefended settlement, remains of huts buried beneath a depth of up to five metres of silt have been located, some protected by a dam of tree-trunks. The walls were of clay daub, the floors and hearths were also made of clay, above which were set clay or metal fire-dogs. Their cemeteries, where the rite of burial was in an urn within a stone cist or large jar, have yielded many objects. In the fifth century and later some graves were marked with tombstones inscribed in the Venetic script. The contents of the graves offer little indication of social differences: most appear to have had an adequate provision of personal implements and accoutrements along with a selection of pottery vessels.[1]

The Carni dwelt in a great arc of the eastern Alps (Alpes Carnicae, later Juliae) between Raetia and Histria and, according to Ptolemy, also extended into the plain of Venetia. On the coast the later Roman colonies at Aquileia, Concordia and Tergeste (Trieste) and, towards the interior, Forum Julii (Cividale di Friuli) were all settled in their territory. Inscriptions in the Venetic script, dated to the second century BC, and personal names on Latin inscriptions attest the presence of a Venetic population in the eastern Alps and Carinthia which retained its identity well into Roman times. The Carni are not prominent in the record of Roman wars, and their name is barely mentioned in the record of assaults on the colony settled

---

[1] Barfield 1971, 116–26, Untermann 1978, Karouškova-Soper 1983 (castellieri).

at Aquileia in 181 BC. Half a century later the Carni are among the peoples 'forced to come down from the mountains' named on the monument erected near Aquileia to the consul of 129 BC, C. Sempronius Tuditanus, though the main enemy on this occasion were not the Carni but rather the Japodes, their neighbours on the southeast.[2]

The Histri, as they were generally known, inhabited the Istrian peninsula. Strabo (7.5, 3) and Appian (*Illyrike* 8) describe them as Illyrians, but their language was akin to that of the Veneti and Carni and distinct from the rest of the Illyrians. On the west the limit of their territory may have been the river Formio, south of Tergeste (Trieste), or the Timavus further west. On the east they may have extended to the Kvarner (Quarnero) gulf. As a whole Istria is not fertile, but its rocky soil produces fine olives and the quality of its oil was reckoned close to the best. The best harbour was Pola (Pula) on the west coast near the southern tip of the peninsula. Between there and Tergeste lay Parentium (Poreč), which like Pula was later the site of a Roman colony, and A(e)gida (Koper). On the east side, between the Arsia (Raša) and the southern tip of 'Cape Pola' (*promunturium Polaticum*), was Nesactium and the smaller Istrian settlements Mutila and Faveria. Off the southwest coast the islets Pullaria (Brioni) have been secluded residences for the mighty since Roman times.[3]

Along with Illyrii and Liburni, the Histri appear in Livy's history (10.2) as notorious pirates, but the first recorded action against them took place in 221 BC. They were accused of attacking Roman supply-ships and were also said to have been acting in concert with Demetrius of Pharos, then ruling in Illyria. An expedition under both consuls of the year was victorious but nothing is reported of the outcome. By 186 BC the Romans were in contact with Gauls beyond the Julian Alps. Though these exchanges were for the most part friendly the

---

[2] Gabrovec 1966a (ethnic groups in Slovenia), 1966b (settlements), Guštin 1978 (fortifications), Valič 1983 (Carnium/Kranj); Carni and Taurisci: Alföldy 1966, Petru 1968, Frey and Gabrovec 1969 (Stična), *Inscriptiones Italiae* XIII pt. 3, p. 73, no. 90 (Sempronius Tuditanus).

[3] Suić 1967a (boundary on Timavus); pre-Roman settlement: Gnirs 1925, Bačić 1970, Mihovilić 1979 (Medolino).

Romans suspected that the Celts had designs on northeast Italy, where some had already begun to construct a fortified settlement (*oppidum*). In 183 BC the Romans were able to demolish this and even claimed to have disarmed 12,000 Celtic warriors without conflict. When the Gauls complained they were told that their property would be returned to them if they agreed to go home. An embassy of senior senators crossed the Alps and a peace was made. This left the Romans free to secure the area by placing a colony at Aquileia among the Carni and, when that was done in 181 BC, dispatch the expedition against the Histri which the consul Claudius Marcellus had intended two years before. In 178 BC the consul Manlius Vulso marched into Istria and lost a legion at Tergeste, but in the next year, with the fleet stationed at the mouth of the Timavus, king Aepulo was defeated at Nesactium. The town was captured and destroyed, as were also Mutila and Faveria: 'all Histria was pacified and all the surrounding peoples formally surrendered and furnished hostages' (Livy 41.10–11). In spite of these victories the position of the colony was far from being secure, and in 171 BC Aquileia was seeking Roman assistance to complete its defences in the face of attacks by Carni and Histri. The latter were also involved in the operations of C. Sempronius Tuditanus, the consul of 129 BC, against the Japodes.[4]

The fourth of the Venetic-speaking peoples around the head of the Adriatic were the Liburni, who occupied the coast and islands between Istria and the river Titus (Krka) and had been known to the Greeks since at least the eighth century BC. While they were regarded by the Romans as pirates in earlier times some Greeks had found them hospitable to travellers. The fertility of their flocks was a subject of comment, though we learn from a Roman source that their wool could not make garments with a soft texture. The combination of seafaring and pastoralism seems likely to have accounted for some features of Liburnian society which attracted the attention of ancient writers, notably in the first century BC the learned Roman Varro, who had first-hand knowledge of the area. There was

---

[4] Roman expeditions: Appian *Illyrike* 8, Livy 39.55 (181 BC); 40.18 and 26; 41.1–5 and 8–13 (178 BC). Sempronius Tuditanus (note 2 above).

an unusual licence for Liburnian women and one Greek writer reports that the society was dominated by women. These were the wives of free men who would cohabit with their own slaves and with men of neighbouring districts. Varro reports the sexual freedom permitted to unmarried women and a contemporary describes a communistic system of child-rearing. Liburnians possessed their women in common, it was said, and children were reared together until the age of five. When eight years old, each male was allotted to a father according to physical resemblance. This unusual social order appears to have lasted into Roman times, when a kinship group (*cognatio*) descended through the female line appears in a Latin epitaph.[5]

Liburni figure among the peoples with piratical habits named by Livy under 301 BC, but it seems to have been a long time before the Romans chose to interfere with their activities. Their own design of warship, the *liburna*, with its low freeboard, had already been adopted by the Romans during the wars against Carthage, in preference to the high-bulwarked galleys. The Liburni were affected by the activities of Sempronius Tuditanus in 129 BC, as we learn from Pliny (*NH* 3.129) that, on a monument erected to the general, there was recorded the distance 'from Aquileia to the river Titus, 2000 stades' (around 250 miles). The end of their sea-power, and with that their independence, came nearly a century later, when Octavian's admiral Agrippa seized their ships in 35 BC. Four years later Liburnian ships may have played a major part in the defeat of Cleopatra's navy at the decisive battle off Actium in northwest Greece.[6]

The principal settlements of the Liburni lay in the south of their territory, in the coastal plain around Jader (Zadar), between the rivers Tedanius (Zrmanja) and Titus (Krka). It seems that the Liburnian name was only later extended to include the smaller settlements along the coast northwards to Istria after the fourth century BC. Liburnian possessions also

[5] Pseudo-Scymnus 422 (hospitable), 371 (fertile sheep), Pliny *NH* 8.191 (wool), Varro *De Re Rustica* 2.10, 9 (freedom of women), Pseudo-Scylax chap. 21 (dominated by women), Nicolaus of Damascus *FGrHist* vol. 2A p. 384 F103d (rearing of children), Alföldy 1961, 1963 (cognatio).
[6] Panciera 1956 (liburna).

from this time included the islands of the Kvarner, Curictae (Krk), Arba (Rab), Apsyrtides (Cres-Lošinj) and Gissa (Pag). By the middle of the first century BC they were losing territory to their neighbours on the south, the Delmatae. Over the centuries it would appear that the Liburnians, having once controlled the Adriatic down to Corfu, were being steadily pushed northwards, probably the result of pressure from new Illyrian groups, including the Ardiaei and Delmatae, moving towards the Adriatic. The most fully investigated pre-Roman settlement is the Beretina gradina at Radovin, 15 miles northeast of Zadar. The area of the hill-top (205 by 185 m) was inhabited more or less continuously through the Iron Age and Roman period, being finally abandoned in the sixth century AD. In pre-Roman times there were ten rectangular houses arranged in a circle around the perimeter. Later these acquired tile roofs and other improvements but the overall plan was not altered. A large occupation deposit included Greek storage jars, some black-glazed ware and some fine pottery from Apulia. The ramparts of the settlement were kept in repair throughout, with the earlier perimeter of dry-stone walls being mortared in Roman times. No trace was found of any monumental or public architecture.[7]

The coast and hinterland of central Dalmatia up to and beyond the Dinaric mountains was inhabited by the Delmatae, after whom the Roman province Dalmatia was named, their own name being derived from their principal settlement Delminium near Duvno. Beyond the Dinara, Delmatae occupied the plains of Livno, Glamoč, and Duvno, and, between the high mountains and the coast, the plains of Sinj and Imotski and the Čikola and Cetina valleys. Strabo (7.5, 5) describes how that mountain, the Adrion, divides their land into two parts, one facing towards the sea, the other away from it. Their presence on the Adriatic coast may have been the result of a southward migration, perhaps caused indirectly by the impact of the Celtic migrations on the Pannonian Illyrians.

---

[7] Liburnian settlements: Batović 1968 (Radovin), 1974 (Jagodnja), 1978 (Bribir), Mendjusić 1985 (Bribir cemetery), Matejčić 1968 (Rab cemetery), Brušić 1976, 1978 (Šibenik area), Čače 1988 (oppidum on island Murter), Chapman and Shiel 1988 (settlement pattern).

The evidence of names suggests that they were more closely linked with the latter than with the Venetic Illyrians or the southern Illyrians.[8]

The first record of the Delmatae informs us that they had once been subject to the Illyrian king Pleuratus but had broken away on the accession of Gentius in 181 BC, when they proceeded to attack neighbouring communities, forcing them to pay tribute in cattle and corn. In 158 BC the Greek city of Issa complained to her Roman ally that the Delmatae were molesting their mainland settlements at Tragurium (Trogir) and Epetium (Stobreč); similar complaints were received from the Daorsi, neighbours of the Delmatae on the south, who had been rewarded in the settlement of Illyria ten years before. A Roman ex-consul, C. Fannius Strabo, was sent to investigate and report on affairs in Illyria and in particular on the activities of the Delmatae. According to Polybius (32.13) the embassy reported that the latter had not only refused them a hearing but made no provision for their accommodation and even stole the horses they had borrowed for the journey. In fear for their safety they had departed as discreetly as possible. The Senate was indignant, but, observes the historian, the decision to send an expedition across the Adriatic was a matter of considered policy. Illyria had been neglected since the defeat of Demetrius in 219 BC and it was high time Illyrians were reminded of Roman authority. Moreover, the Senate felt that as 12 years of peace had elapsed since the war against Perseus of Macedon it was time to rekindle the military ardour of the Romans. These were the true causes for the war, but for public consumption it was the insult to Roman ambassadors. This was not to be the only occasion a Roman army was sent across the Adriatic for battle practice. The expedition in 156 BC led by the consul C. Marcius Figulus was caught off guard while pitching camp and driven back to the river Narenta, having perhaps advanced from the territory of the Daorsi. Next the Romans evidently marched via the Trebižat valley to Delminium, but failed to catch their enemy unawares and could only set up a blockade before winter set in, though some lesser strongholds were taken.

---

[8] Zaninović 1966, 1967.

In the following year the consul P. Cornelius Scipio forced a surrender. The fortifications were destroyed, the place was turned into a sheep-pasture and the consul returned home to celebrate his triumph over 'the Delmatae'.[9]

The Delmatae were famous for their hill-forts, many of which were occupied from prehistoric to late medieval times. A riverside settlement of the Delmatae on the Cetina near Sinj similar to the Japodian and Pannonian examples may be exceptional. Their hill-forts, or gradina, tend to be located on ridges overlooking the plains not on the heights but on projecting spurs. The neck of the spur was usually well defended but often the rest of the perimeter relied on steep slopes and ravines. Some figure prominently in accounts of Roman campaigns and tend to be described as *castella* or *oppida*, including Andetrium (Muć), Bariduum (in the upper Cetina valley), Burnum (on the river Krka), Synodium, Ninia (Knin), Osinium (Sinj), Salvia, Setovia (in the Čikola valley), Tilurium (Gardun), Neraste, Pituntium, Promona (Teplju), Rider (Danilo), Oneum (Omiš) and Salona.[10]

Something of the nature and distribution of these places has been learned from recent fieldwork in the plain of Duvno, which lies at an altitude of 890 to 900 metres and is an oval of around 20 by 9 kilometres. The subterranean river Šuica crosses the plain, of which the central area is marshy except in summer, and the fringes are suitable for cultivation. Most settlements still follow an ancient pattern of distribution at the margins of the plain. The later Roman city, the municipium Delminium, lay near Duvno, which remains the modern administrative centre. Around the edges of the plain a ring of fortifications occupied the lower hills and promontories (see figure 20). Most were enclosed with a rampart of heaped-up stones surmounted with a wooden palisade. Out of a total of 37, the majority lie along the southwest and northeast sides of the plain, and combine an easily defended location with a good

---

[9] Appian *Illyrike* 11, Strabo 7.5, 5 (Delminium), Zaninović 1961–2.
[10] Hill-forts of Delmatae: Čače and Jurić (Metković area), Marović 1975 (Salona), Oreč 1987 (Posušje), Petrić 1978 (Pelješac), Zaninović 1968 (Burnum), 1982 (hill-forts on islands), 1971 (continuing occupation in Roman period).

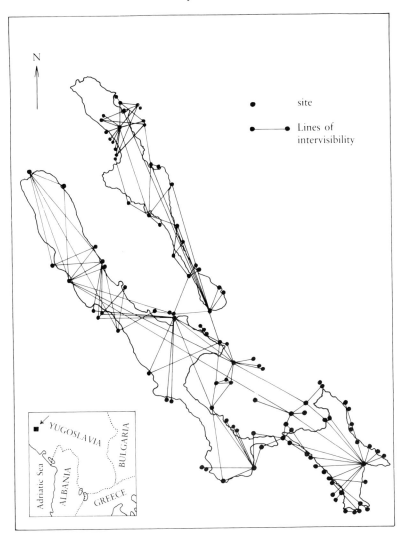

Figure 20 Fortified places around the poljes of Duvno, Livno and Glamoč with lines of intervisibility

view over the surrounding terrain. A few have yielded evidence for occupation in the Bronze Age but the finds tend to be concentrated in the third and second centuries BC. By this period there had been created a scheme of defence for the communities

in the Duvno area that included at least eight fortified observation posts beyond the immediate vicinity of the plain. The
main points of entry were guarded by pairs of fortifications
which can never have functioned as independent strongholds.
The fortress on the Lib hill nine kilometres from Duvno was
exceptional in serving as an acropolis for the larger settlement
on the terraces below. Here was evidently the central place that
had reached a stage of proto-urban development and which
remains the most likely location for Delminium. In some hill-
forts mounds of stones similar to burial tumuli were raised at
a point on the defensive perimeter often, though not always,
most exposed to attack. Whatever their defensive function, the
discovery of human bones suggests that their primary purpose
may have been to serve as burial mounds. The perimeter
defences of the Duvno plain ceased to function after the Roman
conquest, although some were occupied piecemeal as refuges
in late Roman times.[11]

While the Romans were launching their first attacks on the
Delmatae, we hear little of the southern Illyrians following the
defeat of Gentius. In 135 BC Ardiaei and Pleraei are reported
to have made an attack on 'Roman Illyria' and, on refusing to
make amends, were the target of an expedition by the consul
Servius Fulvius Flaccus (Appian *Illyrike* 10). Something is
known of the Daorsi, once subject to Gentius but whose timely
desertion was rewarded by the Romans. They dwelt on the left
(south) bank of the Neretva and their principal settlement was
Ošanići, on a steep hill above Stolac in the Bregava valley,
where coins bearing the Greek legend DAORS have been found.
Excavations from the 1960s have revealed a complex succession
of defensive constructions and associated buildings. The earliest
was a straight wall across the most exposed side of the hill
around 60 metres long and built of coursed masonry with
blocks around 2 by 1 metre (see figure 21a). Later this was
strengthened by two square towers (*c*.10 m), involving demo-
lition of part of the wall and the construction of a covered
entrance passage 4.5 metres wide (see figure 21b). The main

---

[11] Benac 1975a, 1985, Govedarica 1980–1 (Veliki Gradac), 1982, Bojanovski 1975 (Delminium), Marijan 1985–6 (communal grave near Livno), Milošević 1986 (2nd century BC hoards of iron tools from Delmatae).

(a)

(b)

Figure 21 a) Wall masonry at Ošanići, Hercegovina
b) Gate at Ošanići

path leading to the inner acropolis ran along the south side of the hill and was terraced and stepped into the rock at several places. Inside there was a cistern 11 by 7 metres cut 2.70 metres into the rock and lined with fine plaster. The final elaboration consisted of an outer defence on the east in the form of a 'zig-zag' wall and several short lengths of curved wall in a similar 'zig-zag' arrangement. The central area is dominated by a mound of stones, in which traces of retaining walls have been dated to the fifth century BC and may represent the earliest phase construction on the site. The wall, towers and entrance on the east are assigned to the fourth century BC, partly from a comparison with fortifications in Albania. The settlement appears to have been destroyed in the first century BC and was not reoccupied.[12]

The finds from Ošanići, which include imported pottery, are dated from the fourth to second centuries BC. In spite of extensive investigation almost no trace was discovered of internal arrangements or domestic buildings. Some evidence for the economy of the settlement came to light in 1977 with the discovery of a remarkable hoard of 245 metal objects of bronze and iron weighing in all 345 kilograms, hidden in the crevice of a nearby cliff. The inventory includes moulds for bronze ornaments, for metal relief plates and for reliefs in silvered tin; there are also moulds for making bronze pails and dishes, an iron anvil, cutters, chisels, hammers and punches, compasses and some unused bronze plates (see figure 22). For making fine jewellery there are silver wire for soldering, a small anvil, a soldering tool and jewellery scales, along with several unworked or half-finished pieces of glass. The blacksmith's tools include tongs, hammers, wide metal cutters, clamps, adzes and pick-axes. For wire-making there are iron plates with holes of different diameter for drawing wire along and clamps for use in the process. Carpentry is represented by chisels, knives and calipers. This cache of tools, which must have come from workshops in or near Ošanići, indicates the range of specialist skills carried on at the chief settlement of the Daorsi. The deposit has been dated to the second century BC and was likely made in the face of some danger, although a few objects date from an earlier period, notably the bronze moulds of around 300 and 200 BC, a jewel box of around 300 BC and a bronze pail of the fourth or third century. The key evidence for the date of deposition are the silver-wire brooches that match those in the warrior burials at Gostilj near the Lake of Shkodër of the first half of the second century BC.[13]

Nearly 40 years passed before the next Roman attack on the Delmatae, but the motives, according to Appian, were no less

[12] Ošanići: Marić 1976, 1979a–c, Marijanović 1984, Marić 1975b (fortified settlements).
[13] Marić 1978, 1979d (belt-plates), 1979e (bronze moulds).

Figure 22 Bronze-casting mould from Ošanići

dubious. In 118 BC the consul of the previous year, L. Caecilius Metellus, led an expedition against them for which he was awarded a triumph and the title Delmaticus. War was declared, we learn, not because the Delmatae had done anything wrong but merely in order to procure another triumph for the Metelli family. In the event 'they received him as a friend and he wintered among them in the town of Salona, following which he returned to Rome and was awarded a triumph' (Appian *Illyrike* 7), although other versions suggest that this may not be the whole story. The next reported campaign was altogether a more serious business, although little is known of it except that the proconsul C. Cosconius, probably in the years 78 to 76 BC, overcame most of the Delmatae in a two-year campaign which concluded with the capture of Salona. From 58 to 50 BC the Delmatae were in the charge of Julius Caesar, proconsul of Gaul and also of Illyricum, though the commander was able to give little attention to his Adriatic responsibilities. During the subsequent civil war between Caesar and Pompey the Delmatae supported the latter, in opposition to the communities of Roman settlers at Salona, Narona and elsewhere, who remained loyal to the party of Caesar. Late in 48 BC the Delmatae ambushed a Caesarian army of 15 infantry cohorts and 3000 cavalry under the ex-consul A. Gabinius at Synodion, probably somewhere in the Čikola valley. Five cohorts were overwhelmed and their standards captured. Gabinius reached Salona but was so short of supplies that he had to plunder them from the Delmatae, leading to further losses. Roman proconsuls continued to engage the Delmatae after Caesar's victory over Pompey. In 45–44 BC P. Vatinius wrote from Narona more than once to Cicero pleading the great man's help in securing his triumph. He complains that there were not merely 20 oppida as was generally believed but nearer 60. In the end Vatinius obtained his triumph, celebrated on 31 July 42 BC. The Delmatae were still proving troublesome and it may be that C. Asinius Pollio, leading politician and patron of the poet Virgil, achieved some success against them when, during his consulship in 40 BC, he moved his forces down the Adriatic from northern Italy to Macedonia.[14]

After eliminating the disruptive power of Sex. Pompeius in Sicily in 36 BC, Caesar's heir Octavian devoted the following years to operations across the Adriatic, first in 35 BC against the Japodes and Pannonians then, in 34–33 BC, against the Delmatae. Not only had they remained in arms since the departure of Vatinius ten years before, but they still held the five Roman standards seized from Gabinius' army in 48 BC. We can follow the course of the campaign from the commander's own report, preserved by Appian. First the army moved against

[14] Morgan 1971 (Metellus), Wilkes 1969.

Promona, where the war-leader Verzo had stationed most of his army of 12,000 men. After some fighting the citadel was taken, Verzo killed and the Delmatae ordered to disperse by his successor Testimus, while the Romans attacked against strongholds. The army advanced up the Čikola valley, where Gabinius had lost the standards at Synodion. In a battle at Setovia (probably the Sutina gorge) Octavian was wounded and left the scene, handing over command to Statilius Taurus, who organized a winter blockade that brought some of the Delmatae to capitulate. Early in 33 BC Octavian returned to receive their surrender, along with the standards of Gabinius, some booty and a promise to pay the arrears of tribute unpaid since Caesar's time. Though other peoples of the region were involved in the surrender it was the victory over the Delmatae that justified one of the three triumphs celebrated by Octavian, on 13 August 29 BC, followed on successive days by those granted for the Actium campaign of 31 BC and the Egyptian campaign of 30 BC. This happens to be the last explicit record of Delmatae at war with the Romans, though the victory of Octavian in 33 BC is unlikely to have embraced the whole people. In what became known as the Dalmatian war of AD 9 Bato, leader of the Pannonian Illyrians, was trapped in the fortress of Andetrium (Muć) barely 20 miles inland from Split. By then, however, the name of the Delmatae had begun to be applied to the area between the Adriatic and the Sava valley, as the Roman province Dalmatia was established.[15]

The Japodes, who dwelt north of the Delmatae and behind the Liburni, are generally described as Illyrians. Hecataeus in the sixth century BC knew of them and they retained a separate identity into Roman times. On the north and west they bordered the Carni and Histri and on the north the Celtic Taurisci beyond the upper Sava. In the west they were later confined by the Velebit range, and their southern boundary was the river Tedanius (Zrmanja), where they bordered the Liburni. Within these limits the Japodes inhabited the Lika plain and the Una valley around Bihać in western Bosnia. Before the second cen-

---

[15] Schmitthenner 1958, Wilkes 1969, Mirković 1969.

tury BC they may also have held the coast between Istria and
the Tedanius, later occupied by the Liburni. Strabo has some
interesting observations on the Japodes:

> Next in order comes the voyage of one thousand stades [c. 125 miles]
> along the coast of the land of the Japodes. They are situated on
> Mount Albion [probably the Velebit range], the last mountain of the
> Alps, which is very high and reaches down to the interior on one
> side and to the Adriatic on the other. They are indeed a war-crazy
> people but have been utterly worn down by Augustus. Their cities
> are Metulum, Arupium, Monetium and [A]vendo. Their lands are
> poor, the people living for the most part on spelt and millet. Their
> armour is Celtic but they are tattooed like the rest of the Illyrians
> and Thracians. (7.5, 4)

Strabo's 'Celtic element' has proved hard to detect in the rich
material culture of the Japodes, while Celtic names on inscriptions need not, it appears, be connected with their 'Celtic-
Illyrian' character. Some major settlements and associated cemeteries of the Japodes have been examined in the northern Lika,
at Crkvina, Kompolje near Otočac and Vital near Prozor, which
have been identified respectively as Avendo of the Avendeatae
and Arupium of the Arupini, both of which were attacked by
Octavian in 35 BC. Across the Kapela mountains the Japodes
are known from riverside settlements and cemeteries in the Una
valley around Bihać, but not those in the Sana valley, which
belonged to the Pannonian Maezaei.[16]

The most intriguing relics of the Japodes are the 15 or so
engraved stone cremation chests whose figured decoration and
date are still a matter of debate. The first to be found was the
fragment from Jesenice in 1890, on which the engraving of a
helmeted warrior holding a drinking horn in his right hand
and a spear in the other was dated to the period of transition
from the Early to Late Iron Ages (c.450–400 BC). Later finds
of Japodian burial urns, as they are generally known, include
several intact examples with engraved scenes on the inner and

---

[16] Rapanić 1975 (Lika in general), Drechsler-Bižić 1966, 1971 (Kompolje),
1970 (Trošmarija), 1975c (fortified settlements), 1986 (houses), 1988 (Prozor
cemetery), Kurz 1967a (economy), 1967b (ethnic identity).

outer surfaces (see figure 23). The repertoire of figured scenes relates to funeral ritual and the cult of the deceased and includes processions, some of mounted warriors, and dances. The departed souls are represented by serpents in scenes where libations are poured to the memory of the departed, some of whom are portrayed in the manner of a classical hero. Some

Figure 23 Incised scenes of warriors drinking and funeral dancers on a Japodian burial-chest from Ribić, Bosnia

have observed a correspondence between the imagery of the
Japodian urns and that of the 'Situla Culture' in the northwest,
for example, the scene of a bird perched on the back of a
bullock. Most are agreed that the decoration of the urns belongs
to a time when the Japodes of the Una valley were in close
contact with the cultures of northeast Italy, and the majority
should thus be dated to the fifth or fourth century BC. Compli-
cations arose when the Sarajevo archaeologist Dimitri Sergejev-
ski suggested that one of the urns (from Ribić) belonged to the
Roman period, while another (from Jeserine) had a second-
century Latin epitaph inscribed on one surface. The Ribić
example can be explained as a secondary use and a Roman
date for the collection as a whole must be ruled out, if only
because of the generally Greek – and at that tending to archaic
Greek – rendering of the scenes. There have been attempts to
distinguish an early group of urns, whose ornament echoes
Situla art, from a second, slightly later group, in which Greek
influence is stronger. A third group believed to exhibit minimal
influence from either of the above sources is viewed as a later
degeneration of Japodian art. In this group are those with Latin
epitaphs of the Roman period (first to second century AD).
Continuity in a local tradition of engraved ornament is to be
seen on other monuments of the Roman period, including altars
dedicated by chiefs of the Japodes at the shrine of Bindus
Neptunus at a spring near Bihać (see figure 30).[17]

The first reported contact between Japodes and Romans
occurred in 171 BC, when the Senate apologized to them and
other peoples for the scandalous conduct of the consul Cassius
Longinus. In 129 BC they were attacked by the consul G.
Sempronius Tuditanus who, in the course of a hastily prepared
campaign, was saved from disaster only by the experienced
general D. Junius Brutus; however, he was safely back in Rome
to celebrate a triumph over the Japodes on 1 October. Situated
south of the main route between Italy and the Danube, the
Japodes figure little in the Roman conquest of Illyricum. There
was an attack on them in the seventies BC by a certain P.

[17] Raunig 1971b, 1972, 1975, Vasić 1967, 1977–8 (Japodian urns), Rendić-
Miočević 1982, Šarić 1975b, 1983–4 (Lika urns).

Licinius, an incident recalled for his being deceived by their pretence of a retreat. The best reported episode is the march of Octavian through their country in 35 BC. Starting probably from Senia (Senj) on the coast, the army crossed the Velebit by the Vratnik pass and attacked the 'Cisalpine' Japodes of the Lika plain. The inhabitants of Monetium (Brinje) and Avendo (near Otočac) surrendered at their approach, but the Arupini of Arupium (on the Vital hill near Prozor) held out for a while, then scattered into the forests. After surrender they were allowed to retain their strongholds intact. Next a crossing of the Albius (Kapela) brought the invaders up against the 'Transalpine' Japodes. The fortress of Terponus (Gornje Modruš) was soon captured, but Metulum (perhaps Vinčica near Ogulin) was a different proposition. Here the defenders made effective use of Roman siege equipment captured from a Roman army which had attempted an impossible overland march from Italy to Macedonia during the civil war in 43 BC. When eventually captured, Metulum, the greatest settlement of the area, was destroyed by fire. This was the first occasion when these Japodes surrendered to the Romans: it is also the end of the recorded history of the Japodes.[18]

By the second century BC the eastern Alps and the plains between the river Drava and the Danube were populated by Celtic-speaking peoples, represented by names on epitaphs of the Roman era. South of the river Drava, in the Sava valley and its Bosnian tributaries as far south as the Ardiaei and Delmatae, dwelt the Pannonians, Strabo tells us (7.5, 3). Their names have much in common with the southern Illyrians, the Delmatae and the Japodes to their south and west. East of the Pannonians the Scordisci have an Illyrian name perhaps connected with the mons Scordus or Scardus (Šar planina west of Skopje). Their recorded history begins in 279 BC when, according to Appian (*Illyrike* 5), the survivors from the Celtic bands defeated at Delphi returned north to settle around the lower Sava and Drava and adopted the name Scordisci. Nothing further is reported of them until 179 BC, when they are cited

---

[18] Livy *Epitome* 59 (Junius Brutus), Julius Frontinus, *Strategemata* 2.5, 28 (Licinius), Appian *Illyrike* 16–20 (Octavianus), Schmitthenner 1958.

as potential allies of the Bastarnae in a projected invasion of Italy. By the middle of the second century the Scordisci posed a serious threat to Roman Macedonia, culminating in their invasion of Greece and sack of Delphi shortly before 80 BC. Their power appears to have ended after defeat by a Roman army sent to punish their sacrilege, and later they were subject to the Dacians.[19]

Strabo tells us that there were really two groups of the Scordisci, a 'Greater' dwelling on the Danube between the confluence of the river Noarus (?Drava or Sava) and the Margus (Morava), and a 'Lesser' between the Margus and the Triballi and Mysi, who inhabited the Timok valley (7.5, 12). The material culture and ethnic affinities of these people are still much debated. Several well-fortified oppida and some open settlements along the Serbian Danube below Belgrade have been connected with the Scordisci. Yet the matter is further complicated by a 'Geto-Dacian' element in the 'Celtic' material culture, and there is continuing debate whether the oppidum at Židovar across the Danube from the mouth of the Morava was a Celtic or Dacian settlement. In later phases stone defences strengthened with cross-timbers enclosed small huts with sunken floors, thatched roofs and doors with lock and key. A circular enclosure containing small pits has been identified as a form of shrine. The wheel-made pottery has both grooved and painted decoration and metalwork includes bronze and silver bracelets with serpent-head terminals. Singidunum on the Kalmegdan hill, Belgrade, overlooks the confluence of Danube and Sava and was later the base of a Roman legion; it may have been a settlement of the Scordisci, to whom belonged a nearby pre-Roman cremation cemetery at Rospi Ćuprija.[20]

The Romans first came into contact with Pannonians from

---

[19] Papazoglu 1978.
[20] Todorović 1966 (material culture); Židovar: Gavela 1952, 1969, 1975; Belgrade: Božić 1981a, M. Popović 1982, Todorović 1963, 1967 (Rospi Ćuprija), 1971 (Karaburma), Ercegović 1961 (Zemun), Todorović 1973–4 (Ritopek warrior-grave); Gomolava: Petrović 1984, Jovanović 1977–8 (Dacian pottery), Jovanović and Jovanović 1988 (settlement); coinage: Črnobrnja 1983 (minimi), P. Popović 1987, Jovanović 1973–4 (art), Božić 1981b (astragalus belts).

the west rather than from the direction of Macedonia, although when and under what circumstances this took place remains far from clear. One reconstruction of the sources deduces an attack by the consul of 156 BC on the Pannonian settlement Segestica, the later Siscia (Sisak), in the same year that the Romans first attacked the Delmatae. The general scarcity of references to Pannonians may be a reflection of their subjection to the Scordisci. Pannonians do not figure in the migration of the German Cimbri in 113 BC across the middle Danube basin as far as the Scordisci and then west to the Taurisci of the eastern Alps, where, at Noreia in Carinthia, they repulsed a treacherous attack by the Roman consul Cn. Papirius Carbo. Strabo (7.5, 3) identifies the Pannonian peoples as Breuci, Andizetes, Ditiones, Pirustae, Maezaei and Daesitiates. This is significant for a correct identification of the Pannonians before the Roman provinces Dalmatia and Pannonia began to cause confusion, since among the peoples named by Strabo only the Breuci and Andizetes were included in Pannonia.[21]

The Pannonians of Bosnia and western Serbia exhibit no homogeneous or distinctive material culture. The general impression is of long-established communities gradually adopting new ways of life from more advanced societies of the plains to the north and east, but receiving few imports from Greece via the Neretva or from Italy via the Sava valley. Their lands were prolific in timber and rich in mineral deposits, especially along the main river valleys, the Sana, Vrbas, Bosna and Drina, although how much the deposits of gold, silver and iron were worked in pre-Roman times remains uncertain. On the west the Pannonian neighbours of the Japodes were the Maezaei, whose cemetery at Sanski Most in the Sana valley contained some imported objects from Greece and Italy of the fourth and third centuries BC, along with traditional ornaments such as spectacle-brooches. Few Pannonian settlements have been examined, although one notable exception is the riverside settlement at Donja Dolina on the river Sava.

Away from the broad valleys the typical Pannonian settlement appears to have been the hill-top fortress enclosed by a

[21] Mócsy 1974.

stone wall and wooden palisade, many first occupied and fortified in the Bronze Age. A settlement of this type has been partly
excavated at Pod near Bugojno, in southwest Bosnia, on a
terrace around 40 metres above a tributary of the Vrbas. The
plateau was first occupied in the Bronze Age but was then
deserted for around four centuries until the early Iron Age (*c.*
700 BC). The plateau of around 150 by 100 metres was enclosed
by an earth rampart to which a stone wall was added in the
second half of the fourth century. At least 16 levels indicate a
continuous occupation down to the end of the first millenium
BC. The interior was traversed by two principal streets at right
angles. Excavation in the northwest and southwest quarters
revealed a regular arrangement of rectangular houses within a
grid of streets or alleys. This remained unaltered throughout
the life of the settlement, the only noteworthy alteration (sixth
century BC) being the removal of part of a house adjoining the
main intersection to leave an open area around six metres
square. Each house contained up to three hearths and several
ovens or furnaces. Large amounts of iron slag and of bronze
and iron waste, along with clay moulds and crucibles, indicate
the manufacture of weapons, domestic implements, vessels and
jewellery in bronze and iron, including also implements for
cloth-making. Much of the local metalwork seems to have been
influenced in form and ornament by imports from southern
and central Italy. Commerce with those areas was indicated by
the presence of bronze and pottery vessels. The settlement at
Pod was no ordinary hill-fort. In spite of its small area the
place had a distinctly urban character, while the evidence for
metal-working suggests a central place in the economy of Pannonians along the Vrbas valley. South of the hill a suburban
settlement grew up to cover more than 1000 square metres.
When the hill-fort came to be abandoned in the Roman period
this became the principal settlement; it flourished into late
Roman and medieval times, with an early Christian basilica
and associated cemetery being succeeded by an even larger
medieval burial ground. A similar fortified settlement, with a
long occupation continuing into Roman times, existed on the
Debelo brdo hill near Sarajevo.[22]

[22] Čović 1975b (Bugojno).

In eastern Bosnia the use of the Glasinac plateau for burials throughout most of the first millenium BC suggests a continuity of population, possibly the Autariatae, who may have been ancestors of the historical Daesitiates and Pirustae. In the Glasinac area, that is between the Romanija hills and the middle Drina, a total of 47 fortified places has been identified. Twenty-seven of these lie on the Glasinac plateau itself, one for each 10 square kilometres of the 270 square kilometre area. For most of these places no dating evidence is available, although they are likely to belong to the pre-Roman Iron Age with some being occupied already in the Bronze Age. An early deduction that the regular disposition of fortified places on Glasinac reflects a concerted scheme of defence implies that most of them were in use at the same period. What remains uncertain is whether or not they were fortified settlements or merely strongholds for use in times of danger. In the matter of size, 38 have dimensions ranging between 30 and 90 metres (most 50 to 60 m), four are between 90 and 150 metres diameter and two no more than 20 to 30 metres across, hardly more than fortified blockhouses. Two exceptionally large enclosures (Komina near Parizevići and Ilijak near Konovići) were major strongholds more than 200 metres across with areas of 15 to 17,000 square metres. Only a few of the enclosures are not round (18) or oval (9) in plan. Most are enclosed with a single stone or stone-and-earth wall, 2.5 to 5 metres thick and reaching heights of 2 to 4 metres. One or two have traces of double ramparts and some have one or more towers protecting single entrances.[23]

As we have seen, Pannonians do not figure prominently in the historical record of the second and first centuries BC. Unlike Celts or Dacians, they seem to have lacked any instinct for cohesion or obedience to a common authority. As Appian (borrowing from Caesar Octavianus) puts it:

Pannonia is a wooded country extending from the Japodes to the Dardani. They do not live in cities but in the countryside or in villages related by kinship. They do not assemble together for any common council nor are there any with authority over all of them. In time of

[23] Čović 1975a (Glasinac hill-forts).

battle their combined strength amounts to one hundred thousand; but they never join up together on account of a lack of any central authority. (*Illyrike* 22)

This first account of Pannonians is derived from Octavian's report of his expedition in 35 BC. Having already overcome the Japodes the army entered the Colapis (Kulpa) valley and marched through Pannonian territory for eight days to Segesta at the confluence with the Sava. When the natives showed no disposition to surrender, orders were given to devastate villages and fields. The town stood in the angle of the rivers and was further protected by fortifications, where a Roman army later excavated a canal so that it was protected by water on all sides. The capture of Segesta is described at length. Octavian asserted that the ships he had ordered to be built were not for the purpose of attacking the place but for use against Dacians and Bastarnae. He requested that he might use the place in order to further this project, but though the rulers agreed the common people shut the gates and he was compelled to storm it. Another version has it that, though the people had caused no offence, Octavian wanted to give his soldiers battle practice against a foreign people. In the event, Octavian's ships, which had been obtained from unnamed 'allies in the vicinity', were seen off by the Segestani in an action which cost the life of the experienced admiral Menodorus (Menas). The Romans captured the place after 30 days and, leaving a garrison of 25 cohorts in a walled-off part of the town, Octavian and his army returned to Italy. After the taking of Segesta, the later Siscia, nothing is reported of the Pannonians for 20 years. By then the Romans had fought another civil war and Octavian ruled the world as the emperor Augustus.[24]

The emperor recorded his conquest of the Pannonians in his *Res Gestae* or *Summary of Achievements* (chapter 30): 'Through Tiberius Nero, then my stepson and legate, I brought under Roman authority Pannonian peoples which no Roman army had approached before I became princeps and advanced the boundaries of Illyricum to the bank of the Danube.' This

[24] Schmitthenner 1958, Dukat and Mirnik 1983–4 (Roman gold coin of 42 BC from near Siscia).

claim was based not on the expedition of 35 BC but the Pannonian War, which lasted altogether from 14 to 8 BC. In the first two seasons Roman armies advanced eastwards down the Sava and Drava valleys. In 12 BC Tiberius, the later emperor, overcame the Breuci with help from the Scordisci, recently acquired allies of the Romans. Three further years of fighting probably brought the submission of the rest of the Pannonians. The war was a savage affair and the main resistance to the Romans came from the Breuci and Amantini in the Sava valley. The young males were rounded up and sold as slaves in Italy, a quite exceptional action even for the Romans. Fifteen years later a new generation of Pannonians rebelled against the injustice of Roman rule and brought on the worst crisis faced by the Romans since the war against Hannibal. The rising began among the Daesitiates of central Bosnia under their leader Bato but they were soon joined by the Breuci. The four-year war which lasted from AD 6 to 9 saw huge concentrations of Roman forces in the area (on one occasion ten legions and their auxiliaries in a single camp), with whole armies operating across the western Balkans and fighting on more than one front. On 3 August AD 8 the Pannonians of the Sava valley surrendered, but it took another winter blockade and a season of fighting before the surrender of the Daesitiates came in AD 9, 'after the loss of many men and immense wealth; for ever so many legions were maintained for this campaign but very little booty was taken' (Cassius Dio 56.16). All Illyrians were now subject to Roman rule. In the reign of Nero (AD 54–68) the ancient city of Aphrodisias in Asia Minor celebrated the victories of the Caesars with a monument incorporating figured reliefs depicting the imperial triumphs over individual peoples. Among the several Illyrian groups singled out were Japodes, Dardanians, Pannonian Andizetes and Pirustae.[25]

Pax Romana

No Illyrian resistance is known to Roman rule after AD 9, less an indication of native compliance than of the state of human

[25] Mócsy 1974, Anamali 1987, Smith 1988 (Aphrodisias).

exhaustion to which the Illyrian lands had been reduced. Until
the collapse of the northern frontiers four centuries later Illyrians remained part of the Roman Empire. Many years passed
before any signs appear of an Illyrian participation in the
Roman state to match those of the Celtic and Iberian peoples
in the west. Roman organization of the Illyrians for a long time
reflected the strategic priority of keeping control of the overland
routes between Italy and the east, at first the Via Egnatia and
later the great Balkan highway along the Sava valley.[26]

Roman treatment of the Illyrians south of the Drin had
reached a brutal climax following the victory over Macedonia
in 168 BC. In attacks by the Roman army on Macedonian allies
in northern Epirus (Molossians) and Illyris, 70 communities
were destroyed, 150,000 of the population enslaved and the
countryside devastated. The effects of this lasted well into the
Roman period and are reflected in the meagre remains from
the region of that era. A century and a half later Strabo records
the state of the region: 'Now although in those earlier times,
as I have described, all Epirus and Illyris were rugged and full
of mountains, such as Tomarus and Polyanus and several
others, they had an abundance of population; but at the present
time desolation prevails in most parts, while in the areas still
inhabited they survive only in villages and among the ruins'
(7.7, 9). As we have seen, similar atrocities accompanied the
imposition of Roman rule on other Illyrians in the course of
the century that followed.[27]

By the middle of the first century the Romans were using
the name Illyricum for their Adriatic territories north of the
Drin, south of which the province Macedonia began. When the
command of Gaul and Illyricum was assigned to Julius Caesar
in 59 BC some form of administration for the area appears to
have been based on Narona (Vid) near the mouth of the
Neretva, the starting point for campaigns against the Delmatae.
More recently the Romans had gained possession of Salona,
near modern Split, which may have finally secured Roman
control of the coast between Istria and Macedonia. By this time

---

[26] Wilkes 1969.
[27] Livy 45.33, Hammond and Walbank 1988, 567 (suggesting Penestae).

numbers of Roman settlers were becoming established along the Dalmatian coast, as traders and farmers, though contacts with the native peoples, in particular the Delmatae, were often not friendly. We learn in the time of Caesar that Narona had become a flourishing centre of commerce: Cicero had traced one of his runaway slaves to the place, but his friend the Roman governor could only report (11 July 45 BC) the fugitive's escape to the Illyrian Ardiaei (Cicero, *Letters to Friends* 5.9). The existence of Illyricum as a separate command is confirmed by the succession of proconsuls during the decade following Caesar's administration, but the northern Adriatic, including the Liburni, seems to have been regarded as an extension of Cisalpine Gaul (Po valley). The attraction of Illyricum north of the Drina to the west, while the most southerly of the Illyrians, in the province of Macedonia, adhered to the east, is revealed in the division of the Roman world made by Octavian and Antony at Brundisium in 40 BC. When the latter received the east and the former the west the point of division was fixed at Scodra. Almost immediately the architect of this pact, the consul Asinius Pollio, was ordered by Antony to attack the Illyrian Parthini in the Shkumbin valley.[28]

Following the conquest of the Pannonians in 14–8 BC, Illyricum was put in the charge of Caesar Augustus. The boundary with Italy was fixed at the river Arsia (Raša) in eastern Istria, thus placing the Liburnians in the new province but leaving the Veneti and Histri in the Tenth Region of Italy. The loss of privileges by some native communities in the northern Adriatic as the result of this demotion to provincial status may have been offset by grants of 'Italian status' to selected groups among the Liburnians. When the Pannonians finally surrendered in AD 9 the huge command of Illyricum which under Tiberius Caesar had contained two consular Roman armies was divided along the southern confines of the Sava valley between Dalmatia and Pannonia, an arrangement that was to remain unaltered for the next three centuries. As far as we can tell the eastern boundary of Illyricum ran from somewhere on the lower Sava west of Belgrade down to the Scardus mons (Šar planina) west of

[28] Wilkes 1969, Deniaux 1988 (Cicero's connections in Illyris).

Skopje. Though its line is far from certain there seems little
doubt that most of the Dardanians were excluded from Illyricum and were to become a part of the province of Moesia
organized in the reign of Claudius (AD 41–54). After the defeat
of the Scordisci early in the first century BC the Dardanians
appear as troublesome neighbours of Roman Macedonia, and
in the seventies the Roman army waged war against them with
exceptional cruelty. Their final submission to the Romans may
have occurred when Macedonia was in the charge of Antony
(40–31 BC), though any record of that achievement is likely to
have been suppressed by his rival Octavian. When established
under Claudius, the province of Moesia extended from the
Skopje basin in the upper Vardar on the south to the Danube
above and below the Iron Gate in the north.[29]

Although Illyricum continued to be employed as a geographical and later a political regional expression, it did not reappear
as an administrative term until Diocletian's reorganization at
the end of the third century AD. Then the Illyrian areas of
Pannonia were included in the new provinces of Savia, in the
southwest, and Pannonia Secunda, in the southeast. Dalmatia
was unaltered, except for the interesting separation of the area
around the Lake of Shkodër – corresponding to the old Illyrian
kingdom – to form the new province Praevalitana based on the
Illyrian towns of Scodra, Lissus and Doclea. While Dalmatia
and the Pannonian provinces were grouped in a Diocese of
the Pannonias, later Illyricum, Praevalitana was placed in the
Diocese of the Moesias on the east. Here the old name of
Dardania appears as a new province formed out of Moesia,
along with Moesia Prima, Dacia (not Trajan's old province but
a new formation by Aurelian), Epirus Nova, Epirus Vetus,
Macedonia, Thessalia and Achaea. The 'New Epirus', formed
out of the earlier Macedonia, corresponded to the old Illyris,
centered on Dyrrhachium and Apollonia. One may even see in
these arrangements something of the lasting ties of places and
peoples which had once held together the monarchies of Macedonia and Illyria being understood in the changes made by that

[29] Cassius Dio 54.34, Pliny *NH* 3.139 (Italian status), Mócsy 1974 (Illyricum
and Moesia).

most perceptive of Roman emperors. Once put back on the map Illyricum becomes a familiar name in the history of the fourth century AD. The great field armies which emerged in the long reign of Constantine I (AD 306–337) were soon established as regional forces commanded by counts (*comites*) and marshals (*magistri*). The Praetorian Prefects, now the permanent secretaries of the imperial administration, were similarly identified. Under Constantine the Dioceses of the the Pannonias, the Moesias and Dacias were united under the Prefecture of Illyricum, an arrangement which continued with few changes until the division of the Empire between the sons of Theodosius I in AD 395.[30]

By the end of the first century AD the attention of Roman armies in Illyricum had turned away from the Pannonians to watch the free peoples beyond the river Danube, now defined as the northern frontier of the Empire. Until this change came about the ex-consuls appointed to administer the Illyrian provinces were experienced commanders who were often retained in their posts for several years. Taxation was always one of the harshest features of Roman rule and was the responsibility of an imperial agent (*procurator Augusti*) who, until the Flavian period, remained responsible for Dalmatia and Pannonia together. Indirect taxes, customs, sales, slave-manumissions, etc., were the responsibility of various tax bureaux staffed by imperial slaves and freedmen. Most of the Danube lands belonged to the tax district of Illyricum (*Publicum portorii Illyrici*) controlled from Poetovio (Ptuj on the Drava) in Pannonia.[31]

The legions that conquered the Illyrians belonged to a new professional Roman army created by Augustus during the years following Actium, each recruit serving for a fixed term later standardized at 25 years with an assured reward on completion of service. Each legion consisted of more than 5000 infantrymen, all heavily armed and highly trained Roman citizens. Seven were based in the Illyrian provinces, three in Pannonia and two each in Dalmatia and Moesia. These formidable troops

[30] V. Popović 1984 (Praevalitana and Epirus Nova).
[31] Šašel 1989.

were accompanied by auxiliary cavalry and infantry, originally ethnic units from various provinces of the Empire, for whom a similar term of service was rewarded with the Roman citizenship. These were more mobile and flexible than the legions and were often deployed at major road junctions with the job of keeping watch on natives in the area.[32]

Effective control over Illyrians in their forests and glens was achieved by that most distinctive of Roman devices, the great military road. The first was the famous Via Egnatia constructed across the new province of Macedonia from Dyrrhachium to Thessalonica in the late 140s BC under the proconsul Gn. Egnatius. This was marked with milestones for a distance of 535 miles as far as the border between Macedonia and Thrace at the river Hebrus (Maritza). Until the more northerly route across Illyricum was opened under Augustus the Via Egnatia was Rome's principal link with her empire in the east, and along it were fought the civil wars which destroyed the Republic and brought the rule of emperors. After the defeat of the Pannonians in AD 9 several roads were constructed across the Dinaric ranges, an enormous achievement of engineering, not yet matched in modern times, though doubtless carried through with the labour of enslaved natives. Five were completed, two in AD 17 and three in AD 20, and all commencing at Salona, from which the new province Dalmatia was administered. At the same time the Pannonian legions were at work on the Pannonian highway between Italy and the middle Danube, although under conditions which caused them to mutiny in AD 14. The second instrument used by the Romans for consolidating their conquered territories was the colonial settlement of Romans on lands confiscated from the natives. Refined in the Italian peninsula, the institution was soon being employed successfully in overseas territories such as Gaul, Spain and Africa. In the late Republic, colonies, in Italy and overseas, became a device used by leading commanders to reward their veterans, a system later perfected by Augustus and his successors. In Illyrian Macedonia, colonies were settled at Byllis

---

[32] Mócsy 1974 (Pannonia and Moesia), Wilkes 1969 (Dalmatia).

and Dyrrhachium (see figures 24a and 24b)during the civil wars. On the Dalmatian coast several existing Roman settlements appear to have been strengthened and organized as colonies, including Salona, Narona and Epidaurum, Jader and Senia. On the coast of Istria colonies were settled at Pola, Tergeste and Parentium. The list of Roman settlements includes some of the old centres of the Illyrian kingdom, Risinium (Rhizon), Acruvium, Butua (Bouthoe), Olcinium, Scodra and Lissus. At first most of these places were dominated by families of settler origin, but within two or three generations there are signs of native Illyrians among the municipal aristocracies. A later generation of Roman colonies, often established at or near the sites of vacated legionary bases, were intended to accommodate the veterans discharged from legionary service. Such new cities included Emona, Savaria and Poetovio on the Pannonian highroad, Siscia and Sirmium at either end of the Sava valley, Aequum among the Delmatae in Dalmatia and Scupi (Skopje) among the Dardani in Moesia.[33]

Though its beginnings were marked by atrocity, Roman rule in the longer term turned out to be no more harsh than that experienced by other communities of a similar character elsewhere in the Empire. There was no deep source of spiritual resistance such as that which led to the defeat and subsequent dispersal of the Jews two generations later. Yet there was little prospect of the Romans being able to welcome a reconciled native aristocracy into the ruling order of their empire, as appeared to be the case in Gaul and Spain. Here, when some of the tribal leaders had been seduced into joining an abortive rising, a Roman commander put before them the case for Roman rule: 'Stability between nations cannot be maintained without armies, nor armies without pay, nor pay without taxation. Everything is shared equally between us. You often command our legions in person, and in person govern these and other provinces. There is no question of segregation or

---

[33] Šašel 1977c (military roads); Via Egnatia: Hammond 1972, 1974b, Walbank 1977, Ceka and Papajani 1971 (Shkumbin valley), Janakievski 1976 (west of Heraclea), Bojanovski 1974, 1978 (Dalmatia), Nikić 1983 (Livno, Glamoč, Duvno); colonies: Wilkes 1969 (Dalmatia), Mócsy 1974 (Pannonia and Moesia).

(a)

(b)

Figure 24 Figured tombstones in the Roman colony at Dyrrhachium, 1st century AD: a) Ex-slave Caecilius Laetus (Happy) b) Domitius Sarcinator (Clothes-mender) and his wife Titia

exclusion' (Tacitus, *Histories* 4.74). That must be set alongside another analysis of Roman rule. When asked by Tiberius why his people had rebelled, Bato, leader of the Pannonians, is said to have responded: 'You Romans are to blame for this; for you send as guardians of your flocks, not dogs or shepherds, but wolves' (Cassius Dio 56.16).[34]

The Romans were prepared to allow the maximum possible degree of autonomy to harmless ex-enemies. In preparing the constitution of a new province the Romans would usually dismantle any existing political association, federation, league or alliance which existed above the basic unit of city or tribe. In the case of the former, institutions would be left intact with suitable safeguards against mob rule, as these were best suited for collecting taxes and for maintaining order at the local level. Except in Liburnia there were no existing Illyrian city-states to which this policy could be applied, and the native Illyrian communities (*civitates*) were grouped into judicial assizes (*conventus*) based on some of the major coastal towns, where they would be required to attend for official and legal business. Such an organization had already existed in the time of Caesar, when 89 civitates were required to attend at Narona. The Roman organization of Illyricum brought many changes among the native communities: some were combined to form larger units more suitable for administration, while others, including some well-known Pannonian peoples, were divided. The Elder Pliny's *Natural History* (3.142–3), completed in the 70s AD, furnishes lists of the peoples in Dalmatia based on the official registers, as they were grouped into three conventus and with a numerical total of decuriae for each civitas as an indication of size. This Roman term may have been equated by the Roman officials with some subdivision within a people, either kinship group or village community. The two conventus centred on Salona and Narona included the names of several well-known peoples, but many are quite new, deriving from amalgamations or divisions determined by agents, most likely army officers, of the provincial governor.[35]

---

[34] Though some Pannonians knew Roman 'discipline, language and writing', Velleius Paterculus, *Compendium of Roman History* 2.110, Mócsy 1983.
[35] Mócsy 1974, 69–70 (military administration).

The Scardona conventus, smallest of the three, included the Japodes and 14 civitates of the Liburni. In the Salona conventus the largest group were Delmatae, with 342 decuriae. In the Narona conventus the 13 civitates include several groups formed by amalgamation of the much larger total in the earlier Narona conventus. The Ardiaei, or Vardaei as they were known to the Romans, 'once the ravagers of Italy' and now reduced to a mere 20 decuriae, and the Daorsi or Daversi, with 17 decuriae, still retained their identities south of the Neretva. On the other hand, the Deraemestae (30) were formed from several smaller groups in the vicinity of the new Roman colony established at Epidaurum (Cavtat near Dubrovnik). Several peoples who had formed the nucleus of the Illyrian kingdom, including, as Pliny (*NH* 3.144) makes a point of observing, the Illyrii 'properly so-called' (*proprie dicti*), were joined to form the civitas of the Docleatae with 33 decuriae, whose central place at the confluence of the rivers Zeta and Morača became a Roman city in Flavian times.

Beyond the Dinaric mountains the Pannonians of the Bosnian valleys were treated in similar fashion. Here the civitates were larger than those near the coast. In the Salona conventus were the Ditiones (239 decuriae) of southwest Bosnia, the Maezaei (269) of the Sana and Vrbas valleys, and the Sardeates (52) around Jajce and the Deuri (25) around Bugojno, both in the Vrbas valley. Further east the formidable Daesitiates of central Bosnia retained their name. The great rebellion of AD 6 had been led by their chief Bato, and their relatively low total of 103 decuriae likely reflects their heavy losses at that time. One of their fortresses, the castellum Hedum, was the destination of one of the military roads constructed from Salona after the end of the war in AD 9. The Narensi (102) of the same conventus are likely to be named from the river Naron/Narenta (Neretva) and were perhaps a grouping of communities along its middle and upper course. The reason why the Pirustae do not appear among the lists of Pliny seems to be explained by a comment of Velleius Paterculus, officer in the Roman army and an eyewitness of the Pannonian uprising: 'for the Perustae and the Desidiates, Dalmatian tribes who were almost unconquerable on account of the position of their strongholds in the mountains, their warlike temper, their wonderful knowledge of fighting, and, above all, the narrow passes in which they lived, were then at last pacified, not now under the mere generalship but by the strength in arms of (Tiberius) Caesar himself, and then only when they were all but exterminated' (2.115). The Pirustae, who inhabited the high valleys of southeast Bosnia and northern Montenegro, seem to have been divided between the Ceraunii (24 decuriae), whose name deriving from the Greek for 'thunderbolt' links them with high mountains, Siculotae (24), Glintidiones (44) and Scirtari, who dwelt along the border with Macedonia. In northeast Bosnia the Dindari are located by the record of one of their chiefs (*principes*) in the Drina valley. Whether or not they, along with the Celegeri of Moesia, were created from the once-powerful Scordisci remains uncertain.[36]

Less is known of the Illyrians in the province of Pannonia, and Pliny does not furnish any details of conventus organization or of relative strength according to numbers of decuriae. He names the following civitates: along the river Sava, downstream, the Catari, Latobici, Varciani, Colapiani, Osseriates, Breuci, Amantini and Scordisci; down the Drava, the Serretes, Serapilli, Jasi and Andizetes; and down the Danube, the Boii, Azali, Eravisci, Hercuniates, Andizetes, Cornacates, Amantini and Scordisci. Between the Serapilli and Boii dwelt the Arabiates. Some of these names belong to peoples known before the conquest, including Boii, Breuci, Andizetes, Amantini, Scordisci and Latobici. Others are derived from place names, Cornacates from Cornacum (Šotin on the Danube above Belgrade), Varciani from Varceia and Osseriates from somewhere on the middle Sava, or from rivers, Colapiani from Colapis (Kulpa) and Arabiates from the Arabo (Raab). In the Sava valley the strength of the once-belligerent Breuci and Amantini was broken up into smaller groups such as the Cornacates on the lower Sava and the Osseriates and Colapiani west of the Breuci. The Illyrian Azali may have been deported northwards from the Sava valley to dwell between the Celtic Boii and Eravisci on the Danube. Given these locations the evidence of personal names helps to identify the Illyrian communities in southern Pannonia. The

---

[36] Wilkes 1969.

Catari around Emona have names of Venetic origin and may
be a group of the Carni. Except for the Latobici and Varciani,
whose names are Celtic, the civitates of Colapiani, Jasi, Breuci,
Amantini and Scordisci were Illyrian. There is little known of
the civitates in Moesia. In the south the Dardani remained a
single group, while the civitas of the Celegeri in the northwest
may be newly formed out of the Scordisci.[37]

Thus the Illyrians disappeared into the Roman Empire. When
we next hear of them they are Roman Illyrians, army commanders and emperors repelling invaders and reconstructing
the Empire. Before we come to those remarkable events we
may pause to take a closer look at Illyrians during the period
when they were assimilating the richer and more varied material
culture of the Greco-Roman world. The more durable remains
from Roman times tell us much about the way of life among
Illyrians and, taken along with evidence from the pre-Roman
era, provide our clearest view of Illyrians at a period when they
were beginning to lose much of their own identity within that
of Universal Rome.

---

[37] Mócsy 1974, Dušanić 1977a (Amantini), Mirdita 1976 (Dardani).

8

Life and Death among Illyrians

Ways of life[1]

During a scene in the Roman comedy 'Threepenny piece' (*Trinummus*) a stranger is introduced: 'Indeed this man is the mushroom type; he covers the whole of himself with his head. The man's look appears Illyrian; he comes here with that dress' (lines 851–3). It is relevant to note that the dramatist Plautus came from Sarsina in Umbria on the eastern side of Italy and is likely to have been familiar with what he terms the 'Illyrian look' (*Hilurica facies*) of persons wearing a broad hat (*causea*) in the Macedonian style. More than four centuries later the historian Herodian strikes a condescending note: 'Pannonians are tall and strong, always ready for a fight and to face danger but slow-witted' (2.9). That appears to have been the common Roman view of their Danubian provincials, good fellows but best kept at arm's length, at a time when they were an uncomfortable presence in and around the capital following the victory of Septimius Severus in the civil wars at the end of the second century AD.

In the matter of physical character skeletal evidence from prehistoric cemeteries suggests no more than average height (male 1.65 m, female 1.53). Not much reliance should perhaps be placed on attempts to identify an Illyrian anthropological type as short and dark-skinned similar to modern Albanians.

---

[1] Stipčević 1977a.

Nor should one be less cautious towards the authenticity of the vivid portrayals of defeated Illyrians by Roman sculptors, such as the trophy from Tilurium or the fragment of an imperial statue from Pola. One might seem entitled to assume that the portrait on tombstones conveys an authentic likeness of the deceased. Yet while undoubtedly likely to be correct in dress, hairstyle and jewellery, the facial image was subject to fashions and stereotypes emanating from the centre of the Empire. Some Illyrians were apparently clean-shaven, and their razors have been found in their tombs. Strabo tells us that Illyrians tattooed their bodies, and needles with wooden handles suitable for this purpose are known from Glasinac and Donja Dolina. Leaving aside Strabo's comment on the dirty habits of the Dardanians, there is little on which to judge the general health of the Illyrian population. Estimates of life-expectancy, males 39 and females 36, from the remains at St Lucia can be valid only for that settlement, while deductions from the age of death given on tombstones are now judged to be unreliable. Life has always been hard in the Illyrian lands and countless wars of resistance against invaders are testimony to the durability of their populations. In the first century BC the learned Roman Terentius Varro, who knew Illyria at first-hand, describes how Illyrian women gave birth with the minimum of interruption to their toil in the fields, 'holding the new-born in their laps as if they had found it rather than given birth to it' (*De Re Rustica* 1.10).[2]

For many Illyrians agriculture was less important than live-stock, hunting and fishing. Agriculture was successful in the broader valleys where the riverside settlements have yielded a quantity of organic remains. Crops attested in places such as Ripač and Donja Dolina include bread wheat, oats (used for brewing an ale), millet and vegetables (peas, beans and lentils). The extent of viticulture among the Adriatic Illyrians before the arrival of the Greeks remains uncertain. Ancient writers imply that Illyrians had not learned to cultivate the vine,

---

[2] Skeletal evidence: Stipčević 1977a, 262 note 5; Albanian evidence: Poul-ianos 1976, Neméskeri 1986, Dhima 1982, 1983, 1985b, 1987, also Živoji-nović 1984 (Trebenište)., Mikić 1978 (Glasinac), 1981. Sculpture: Abramić 1937.

although grape seeds have been found in the two settlements named above and also at Otok on the upper Cetina. In agriculture the basic implement appears to have been the mattock, at first in bone but later of iron. The use of the coulter plough for the heavier soils is believed to be an import, either from the Celts to the north or from the Greeks to the south. The fully developed plough was evidently not used before Roman times or even the Middle Ages. The spread of iron brought into use a wide range of farming implements, including the spade, rake, shovel, balanced sickle, scythe and bill-hook, but in most cases the Roman period brought a marked increase in the efficiency of such equipment. Though not highly regarded for their agriculture or viticulture, Illyrians were certainly knowledgeable concerning the medicinal qualities of flora in their native lands. Several writers refer to the properties of the Illyrian iris (*iris Illyrica*), the stem of which can heal boils, relieve headaches and, mixed with honey, even induce abortion. The plant was used in several perfume recipes, while Roman ladies used the extract as an antiperspirant. A dried iris was also believed to relieve the misery of teething among small children. Although well known beyond the confines of Illyria, the yellow gentian (*gentiana lutea*), employed for the treatment of boils, was said to be named by king Gentius, who was the first to recognize its qualities (Pliny, *NH* 25.71).[3]

By the Roman period both the vine and olive were cultivated by the Adriatic Illyrians, but the Pannonians long continued to import wine in casks through Aquileia (Strabo 5.1, 8). Istrian wines were highly regarded, but the planting of vines on the hills north of Sirmium was a famous initiative of the late third-century emperor Probus, a native of the area. To the Greek world the Illyrians appeared heavy drinkers, from the drinking bouts of the Ardiaei from which intoxicated men were conveyed home by their women, who had also participated, to the over-indulgence of their kings Agron and Gentius. As an alternative to wine the Greeks learned of an excellent recipe for mead made from honey and water from the Taulantii near Dyrrhach-

---

[3] Beck Managetta, 1897 (Ripač), Maly (Donja Dolina), Benac 1951 (prehistoric diet), Grmek 1949 (Illyrian iris).

ium, still consumed by the Pannonian Illyrians in the age of
Attila the Hun. St Jerome, whose home lay among the northwestern Illyrians on the border of Dalmatia and Pannonia, tells
about the ordinary man's beer called *sabaium*, made from
barley. Late in the fourth century the emperor Valens (AD
364–378), who came from a Pannonian family of peasant
origin, was so fond of his native brew that he gained the
nickname 'sabaiarius'.[4]

Sheep and goats were the commonest livestock among Illyrians. Some of the riverside sites (Donja Dolina, etc.) have yielded
significant quantities of pig bones, but these seem to diminish
towards the Adriatic. It is hard to assess the importance of
hunting in the economy of settled communities. In the few large
deposits so far recorded the quantities of bones from wild
animals are no more than a small fraction, and some of these
were deer antlers that were useful as implements. The wild
boar was hunted with the spear but many smaller animals were
hunted for their skins with bow and arrow. We learn from the
late Greek medical writer Paul of Aegina (*De Re Medica* 6.88)
that some of the inhabitants of Roman Dalmatia applied to
their arrows a poison called *ninum*. This was a non-botanical
variety which, though lethal to animals, did not contaminate
the flesh and was obtained from snake-venom. Fishing was no
doubt practised by those who had the opportunity but there is
no evidence for fish tanks (*vivaria*) before the Roman period.
In riverside settlements such as Donja Dolina fishing was a
major activity, indicated by the huge dumps of fish-bones and
discarded tackle, including hooks, tridents, harpoons, wooden
floats and weights, along with remains of dugout canoes from
which the nets were cast. In the small Liburnian coastal town
of Argyruntum (Starigrad Paklenica) a cemetery of the early
Roman period yielded a variety of fish hooks deposited in the
graves. The salt that was essential for communities dependent
on their livestock was obtained mainly from the coast but also
from a few sources inland. Salt produced by evaporation along
the coast was conveyed inland over the many 'salt roads' which

---

[4] Mead: Priscus *FHG* 4, 83, Jerome *Commentary on Isaiah* 7.19, Illyrian
drink: Grmek 1950, Zaninović 1976a (wine among Adriatic Illyrians), Dautova-Ruševljan 1975 (wine amphorae in wreck near Rab).

continued in use down to modern times. The salt source that was a cause of conflict between the Illyrian Ardiaei and Autariatae may be that at Orahovica in the upper Neretva valley near Konjic. Apparently when the salt solution was drawn five days sufficed for the evaporation. For a period the two peoples had agreed to extract it in alternate years.[5]

Although there is evidence for glass manufacture among the Japodes, metal-working was the foremost industry practised by Illyrians. Some have linked its spread with the arrival of Celts in the fourth century BC. Until then most weapons, implements, utensils and ornaments were produced in bronze, a tradition which continued into the Roman period. During the late Iron Age most Illyrian communities had acquired the techniques for working the abundant and varied mineral deposits in their lands. Many Illyrian sites have produced metal-working implements, including picks and mallets for extracting and crushing the ore. Smelting-furnaces, sometimes resembling bread-ovens, occur within hill-forts. Stone and clay moulds for bronze-casting are common in Bosnia, while ingots suggest the existence of itinerant craftsmen. Burials of metal-workers at Sanski Most in northwest Bosnia have yielded a pouring scoop and the remains of a bellows.[6]

The appearance of silver objects in graves of the Late Iron Age indicates the working of local silver deposits. Among the southern Illyrians the deposits which provided Damastion (Strabo 7.7, 8), somewhere in the Ohrid region, with a silver coinage may be the same ones that attracted Corinthian interest in the area. In the Roman period the main centre of silver-mining was the aptly named Argentaria district in eastern Bosnia on the middle Drina. The large settlement under imperial control at Domavia (Gradina) was later an important source of silver for the imperial mint. Though poets refer to the gold of Dalmatia, and an exceptional strike of 50 pounds in the course of one day was reported in the reign of Nero (AD 54–68), the location of workings remains a mystery (Pliny, *NH* 33.67).

[5] Animal bones: Woldrich 1897 (Ripač), 1904 (Donja Dolina), Boessneck and Stork 1972 (Duvno area), Abramić and Colnago 1909 (Argyruntum).
[6] Fiala 1899, 302 (Sanski Most). spread of metal-working: Čović 1980b, 1984a, also Stipčević 1977a, 271–2 note 24 (furnaces in gradinas).

We are informed that the first governor of Dalmatia forced the natives to wash out the gold, though they were too ignorant to appreciate its value, and there was an imperial bureau for the Dalmatian gold mines based in Salona (Florus, *Epitome* 2.25). The most likely source seems to be river gold in central Bosnia, where remains of working from different periods have been identified.[7]

Though Roman mines and quarries were worked with the labour of condemned criminals among the Illyrians, mining remained a traditional skill that was highly valued by the Romans. Early in the second century AD there was a new organization for the silver, copper, lead and iron workings in the central Balkans, controlled by imperial agents (procurators). The names of some mining settlements appear on a local bronze coinage introduced early in the second century, including Metalla Ulpiana (around Priština) and Dardanica (Kopaonik mountains east of the Ibar). Around the same period whole communities of Illyrians moved to work the rich gold deposits of western Transylvania, in the recently conquered Dacia. Several communities are recorded, including 'castella' of the Delmatae and a village (*vicus*) of the Pirustae, who may well have been willing participants in the Dacian 'gold-rush' of the early second century AD.[8]

The archaeological evidence for Illyrian commerce consists exclusively of imports of manufactures from Greece and Italy. Illyrian exports will have consisted of natural products such as cereals and skins, and, in some regions, slaves. The Greeks as a whole appear to have distrusted the Adriatic. The Athenians kept out of it (Lysias 32.25, Athenaeus 13.612d), although a fourth-century inscription from Piraeus describes a project to found a settlement somewhere in the Adriatic area for the purpose of importing wheat. Most likely commerce in this quarter was in the hands of local Greeks from southern Italy and Sicily. One exceptional import to the Illyrian lands was

[7] Hammond 1972, 93 f. (locating Damastion near working of argentiferous lead at Resen, north of Ohrid), Wilkes 1969 (Argentaria, Domavia), Pašalić 1967 (mining in Bosnia).

[8] Dušanić 1977b, Čović 1984a, Jovanović 1982 (Rudna Glava copper mine), Daicoviciu 1958 (Dalmatians in Dacia).

amber, the fossilized orange resin from the south shore of the
Baltic conveyed south by a famous route along the Vistula
across the Carpathians to the head of the Adriatic. Illyrians
had a special liking for amber and large amounts of it have
been found in their tombs, mainly as beads and pendants of
all shapes and sizes but sometimes as inset decoration on metal
brooches. The Illyrians believed in its magical and protective
qualities and almost everyone seems to have worn it as an
amulet. Some attempted to procure a local substitute from the
resin of conifers but nothing could replace the genuine article,
and laboratory analysis has revealed that Illyrian amber came
from the Baltic, rather than from inferior sources in Hungary
or Sicily. The arrival of the Celts in the Danube basin appears
to have disturbed the amber trade and other long-distance
commerce of the Illyrians. They may be responsible for the
increased production of metal objects among some Illyrians,
but their silver coinages, modelled on the fourth-century issues
of Macedonia, do not appear among the Illyrians.[9]

Most of the pre-Roman coins produced in the Illyrian lands
were initially imitations of issues by Dyrrhachium and Apollonia which began in the fifth century BC. Greek colonies in
the Adriatic coined for local use and their currency did not
circulate among peoples on the mainland, who, we are told,
had no use for coined money. Similarly the coinages of the
Illyrian kingdom and later native issues following the Roman
conquest are of no more than local economic importance.
Roman coins appear for the first time among a few large hoards
in the northwest of the second century BC, which contain a
curious mixture of Mediterranean issues and are interpreted as
the result either of long-distance trade or piracy. The stereotype
of the Illyrian pirate became widespread in the Greek and
Roman world and acquired a notoriety that far exceeded any
actual misdeeds. The Dalmatian shore, with its many islands
and inlets, was ideal for quick raids by seaborne robbers, while

[9] Stipčević 1977a, Šašel 1977b (prehistoric trade across the Julian Alps),
Mano 1975 (trade in S. Illyria); amber: Malinowsky 1971, Teržan 1984a,
Todd, Eichel, Beck and Macchiarulo 1976 (analysis of amber), Orlić 1986
(shipwreck near Cres), Radić 1988 (terracotta ship-altars), Archaeological
Museum Pula 1986b (Istrian shipping).

shipping in the Adriatic tended to prefer the security of the east shore to that of Italy, harbourless between Brindisi and Ancona. The Dalmatians have throughout the ages been formidable sailors. In antiquity their distinctive craft was the lembus. Highly manoeuvrable and with a low freeboard, these could be devastating in concerted attacks on the average Mediterranean transport or war galley. It has been well argued that Illyrian piracy was a gross exaggeration by Greeks and Romans of the third and second centuries BC.[10]

The history of the Illyrian lands down to the present day demonstrates how a rugged terrain produces a recurring tendency to political fragmentation. In the matter of settlements there were no great concentrations of population among the pre-Roman Illyrians to compare with some of the great oppida among the Celtic peoples. The most distinctive feature of the typical Illyrian settlement, the fortified hill-top (see figure 25) is the large number that appear to have existed at the same time often in barren and isolated situations. Most of the surviv-

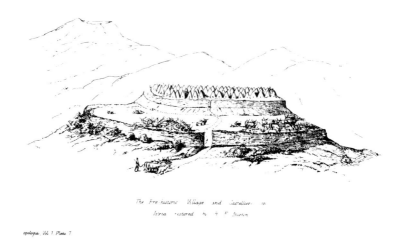

The prehistoric Village and Castelliere in Istria restored by R. F. Burton

opologia, Vol. 1 Plate 7

Figure 25 The prehistoric village and castelliere in Istria as reconstructed by R.F. Burton

[10] Kos 1986 (coin circulation in southeast Alps), Mirnik 1982, 1989 (North African), Kozličič 1980–1 (ships on coins of Daorsi), Dell 1967b (Adriatic piracy).

ing remains occur near the Adriatic in the limestone areas, but there is no reason to doubt that similar numbers existed in Bosnia or around the Sava and Drava valleys. Little is known of internal arrangements. In Istria several places had a 'spider's-web' arrangement of streets similar to that which survived in the Roman colony at Pola. In other areas houses were constructed against the perimeter walls and then extended towards the interior. The nature of larger Illyrian settlements, specifically the question of developing urbanism, has been much debated, notably in Albania. In many places Roman conquest led to the abandonment of the fortified hill-settlement and the emergence of a central place on lower ground, later organized as a city on which the local population became dependent for trade, religion and the law. Few of these places became impressive urban centres, although several major settlements in Istria and Liburnia seem to have been easily endowed with public buildings in the Roman fashion. Few Illyrian settlements have been extensively examined, except for a small number of riverside villages with pile-dwellings where organic remains have been preserved in the river silt. These include Donja Dolina on the Sava, Ripač near Bihać on the Una and Otok near Sinj on the Cetina. There is no evidence for a distinctive Illyrian dwelling. Stone houses or huts are known, sometimes in larger blocks with party walls, many of rough stones with thatch roofs. Roman rule had little impact on Illyrian houses even in some larger settlements such as the Radovin gradina in Liburnia, where the roofs of limestone slabs are identical with those in use today. These were residences of the leaders, and the majority were content with a much more humble structure such as the cone-shaped bunje, still the typical shepherd's hut of the Illyrian lands.[11]

The common garment worn by the Illyrian male was a tunic or long shirt, over which the heavy cloak was worn, as depicted on a Japodian cremation urn from Ribić near Bihać. On Roman reliefs the familiar style of the Illyrian tunic has broader sleeves

---

[11] Stipčević 1977a, 95–105, Benac 1975a (general surveys), Truhlar 1981 (Slovenia), Faber 1976 (Adriatic coast), Kurti 1979 (Mat region), Ceka 1975c (Illyrian urban culture), Baçe and Bushati 1989 (domestic dwelling in Albania), Suić 1976a, ch. 2 (physical evolution of Illyrian settlements).

and a belted waist, as on the remarkable relief from Zenica in
which the sculptor has attempted to imitate wood-carving (see
figure 26). This version of the Illyrian tunic may be the origin
of the dalmatic, the favoured garment of late Roman secular
and church dignitaries and which survives today as a church
vestment. Illyrians also wore the heavy cloak, the Roman *sagum*
similar to the earlier Greek *chlamys*, fastened at the shoulder
by a metal clasp. Breeches were a Roman stereotype of barbarian dress and may have been widespread among Illyrians.
They are depicted on a Japodian cremation urn and on a grave

*Figure 26 Four male figures on a tombstone from Zenica, Bosnia,
4th century* AD

relief from Livno among the Delmatae. Among a variety of close-fitting caps the familar Balkan skull-cap (Albanian qeleshe) appears on a relief from Zenica. The conical fur or leather cap (the Slav *šubara*) is also represented. The remarkable headgear worn by the Japodes of the Lika has no parallel elsewhere, except for some helmets in the Dolensko district of Slovenia. The leather moccasin was an Illyrian footwear adopted widely by the Slavs (*opanci*). Versions of it appear on a Japodian urn possibly of the fifth century BC and on the Roman monument from Tilurium. They were made from a single sheet of leather with the point turned back towards the leg and held with a leather strap around the ankle.[12]

The dress of Illyrian women, which is better represented on monuments of the Hellenistic and Roman eras, comprised three elements: an undergarment that reached usually to the feet, an upper garment and a cloak. The first had long sleeves but otherwise was not much different from the male tunic. In some cases women are depicted wearing only this garment and a sleeveless garment fastened at the shoulders by clasps and belted at the waist. Another over-garment was close-fitting in the upper part but fully pleated and bell-shaped in the lower. This dress is common on grave reliefs of the Roman era and is also the garb of female deities, such as Diana and the Nymphs, although it is also worn by dancers on the early Japodian urns (fifth to fourth centuries BC). A version of this Illyrian dress survives in northern Albania and in the Kosovo region. Illyrian women are also shown wearing a form of hooded cloak, on reliefs from northern Albania (Krotinë near Berat) and Livno among the Delmatae. Some ancient sources refer to a Liburnian hooded cloak (*cucullus Liburnicus*). Illyrian women are also shown wearing a variety of the Balkan headscarf, with the ends

---

[12] Stipčević 1977a, 86–90, Čremošnik 1963, 1964 (native dress on Roman relief sculpture in Bosnia-Hercegovina), Isidore of Seville, *Etymologies* 19.22, 9 (dalmatic), Teržan 1984b (dress and society), Gjergji 1971 (Albanian continuity of Illyrian dress), Jubani 1970.

tied or untied. More common are the shawls which covered both head and shoulders, already depicted on situlae of the Early Iron Age from Dolensko.[13]

Among the objects of domestic life there do not appear to have been distinctive types or forms of Illyrian pottery. The potter's best products were the burial urn, often richly decorated with paint, mouldings or incisions. Illyrians continued to make their pottery by hand down to the Roman period, except in the northwest and the south where contacts with Italy and Greece led to the use of the potter's wheel. There were no centres of large-scale production and the few kilns known suggest that they produced only for the needs of the local settlement. The production and use of metal utensils remained for the most part confined to the northwestern communities, where Italic influence brought the manufacture of buckets (*situlae*) and cauldrons. Otherwise metal vessels, like those in tombs at Glasinac, the Mat valley and Trebenište, were Greek imports. Just as with pottery, so there was no distinctive Illyrian version of the axe, probably the most common working tool found in their settlements, made in stone, bronze and iron. A distinctive type known in Istria and Slovenia, a single-edged bronze long axe sometimes decorated where the handle was inserted, was intended for combat rather than domestic use. Another common tool was the chisel, from the heavy stone- or timber-splitter used with a hammer to the handled variety for wood-carving.[14]

Illyrians used the traditional saddle quern for grinding their corn, where the grain was spread on a concave stone and then crushed by a smaller oval stone laid above. Some communities still used this quern in the Roman period, but by then most had adopted the more efficient rotary quern (*mola versatilis*), likely to have been first introduced by the Greeks. The mill

---

[13] Čremošnik 1963, 1964, Teržan 1984b, Drechsler-Bižić 1968 (Japodian headgear), Komata 1984 (Dyrrhachium relief of Illyrian Kleitia with head shawl).

[14] Komata 1971a (pottery kilns near Kuç i Zi near Korcë), Anamali 1988 (lamp manufacture at Byllis), Vinski-Gasparini 1968 (manufacture of bronze pails among northern Illyrians), Puš 1976 (impregnation of pottery with birch-bark resin), Stipčević 1960–1 (Illyrian tools).

consisted of a larger lower round stone with a convex top (*meta*) fixed in a wooden stand, on which was placed the concave upper stone (*catillus*). The latter had an opening at the top into which the grain was fed and the milled wheat came out at the sides. This implement remained in use among many Balkan communities until modern times. There is no trace of Illyrians using the donkey-powered capstan mill found in some Roman settlements. Many of the known Illyrian houses contained ovens or hearths for baking bread, for example, at Donja Dolina. A Slav method of baking bread using a heavy clay lid (*pekva*) that was heated and placed above the dough in the fireplace was inherited from the Illyrians, from the evidence of a complete example found at Ripač near Bihać.[15]

Among basic implements of the livestock economy the Illyrians employed the simple spring form of cutting shears, still used today for shearing sheep. Almost every excavated settlement has yielded numbers of loomweights of fired clay, sometimes decorated with patterns and symbols. Their deposition in graves has suggested that these designs have some inner meaning, perhaps representing the souls of ancestors as guardians of the hearth. Most Illyrian households will have had a weaving loom, while the domestic debris from several sites includes spinning-wheels in several materials, bone needles, shuttles and spindles.[16]

Illyrians loved ornaments, and on festive occasions their womenfolk would appear heavily draped with all manner of jewellery, while the men bore their highly decorated weapons (see figures 27a and 27b). The brooch (*fibula*) used for fastening clothing was worn by both sexes. Several varieties appear to have had a distinctive evolution in the Illyrian lands, notably the 'spectacle'-brooch of two concentrically wound spirals attached to the pin. The Glasinac fibula was a variant of the simple bow-fibula which is common among many Illyrian groups. Other forms which appear in the Early Iron Age include those with bosses on the arch, animal-shaped brooches, serpent-shaped and plate-brooches, the last being distinctively Liburn-

---

[15] Čović 1962, Truhelka 1904 and 1909 (Donja Dolina), Stipčević 1977a, 269 note 42 (pekvas).
[16] Stipčević 1977a, 131–2.

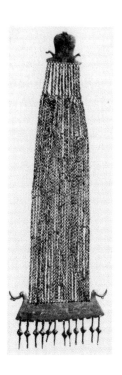

(a)

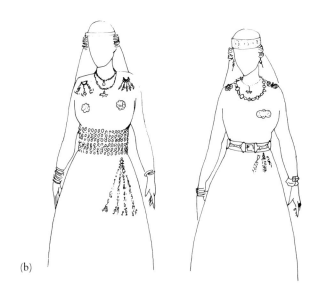

(b)

Figure 27 a) Bronze pectoral from Zaton, near Nin, Liburnia
b) Jewellery and ornaments worn by Illyrian women

ian. A significant later import was the heavy brooch with large arch and long arm named from the site of Certosa near Bologna. Another distinctive brooch, often made in silver and with a wide arch in the form of open petals, is named from the fine examples found at Štrpci on the Drina near Goražde. This type seems to have been popular among the southern Illyrians and is believed to be modelled on Greek forms.[17]

The most remarkable Illyrian headgear must be that worn by the women of the Japodes in the Lika plain, which included diadems and elaborate pendants (see figures 28a–e). The diadem was also worn by other Illyrians, including the Liburnians, where they were made of sheet bronze with geometric decoration. Illyrians could have been found wearing almost every conceivable size, shape and design of pendant. Among the Japodes and Liburnians the human face was a common image, while the bird was preferred among the southern Illyrians, including those buried at Trebenište. The triangle, often representing the human figure, was the most common geometric ornament. The Illyrians wore bracelets with terminals in the form of animals, in particular serpents' heads. The finest examples of this type are the gold Mramorac bracelets from near Belgrade dated to the fifth or fourth centuries BC. Other examples are known in silver, while their general distribution towards the south in the direction of Macedonia suggests they may have come from Greek workshops. In addition to their necklaces of amber, Illyrian chiefs wore heavy bronze torques around the neck. One can only wonder at the way their robes with rich metal ornaments and fastenings were often taken to the funeral pyre or the grave. The chest ornament (pectoral) must often have presented an intimidating aspect of shining metal. Some of the most elaborate come from Liburnian tombs, consisting of decorated bronze plates from which a variety of pendants and other ornaments were suspended. The Illyrians liked decorated belt-buckles or clasps (see figure 29). Some of

[17] Alexander 1965 (spectacle-brooches), Gabrovec 1970 (double-loop Glasinac), Bodinaku 1984, Čović 1975d, Vasić 1985, 1987, Vinski-Gasparini 1974 (bow-brooches), Vasić 1975 (spear-form), Starè 1976 (boat-shaped), Teržan 1977, Težak-Gregel 1981 (Certosa brooches), Batović 1958 (plate-brooches), Drechsler-Bižić 1951 (brooches in Bosnia-Hercegovina).

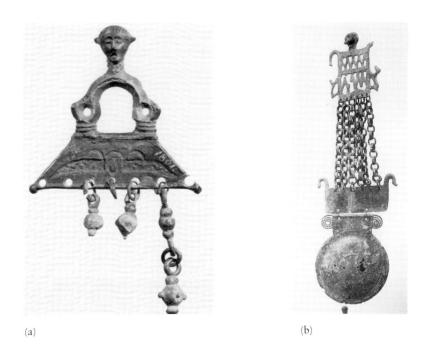

(a)   (b)

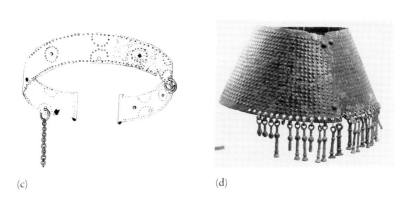

(c)   (d)

Figure 28 a) Anthropomorphic bronze pendant from Loz, Slovenia,
5th century BC
b) Bronze pendant from Kompolje, Lika, 25 cm long
c) Bronze temple-band from Gorica, Slovenia
d) Japodian metal headgear from Kompolje, Lika

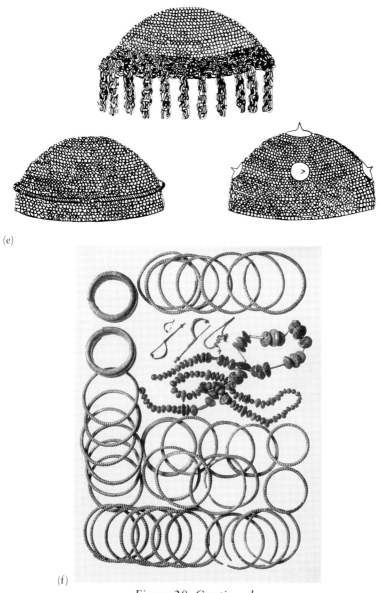

(e)

(f)

Figure 28 Continued
e) Japodian leather helmets with metal studs and mail from Kompolje,
Lika
f) Bronze and amber jewellery from burial tumulus at Stična, 6th
century BC

Figure 29 Silvered bronze belt-plate with scene of combat between warriors and horsemen, from Selcë e Poshtme, Albania, 3rd century BC

gold and silver, with openwork designs of stylized birds, have a similar distribution to the Mramorac bracelets and may also have been produced under Greek influence.[18]

For Illyrian social organization the available picture is not only incomplete but often distorted by statements of Greek and Roman writers. There was little in the Illyrian way of life that they found appealing. No writer produced a balanced account of Illyrians: the promised description of the Pannonians and Dalmatians by Velleius Paterculus (2.114), based on his experiences in the war of AD 6–9, evidently did not materialize. Most of what we have comes from second-, third- or even fourth-hand, sometimes with an interval of centuries. We have no Illyrian words for political or social organization. The material evidence, while abundant, is often hard to decipher. Some have argued that already in the Bronze Age there was a class possessing special functions and expertise whose subsistence was produced by others. Yet what this amounted to in regard

---

[18] Stipčević 1977a, 111–24, Kilian 1975; pins: Kilian-Dirlmeier 1984 (N. Albania), Veyvoda 1961 (Japodian double-pins), Vasić 1982b, 1974a (decorated buckles), Drechsler-Bižić 1968, Kastelić 1960 (diadem), Marković 1984 (ornaments in princely tomb, Lisijevo polje, Ivangrad, Montenegro), Teržan 1978 (dress-fittings from Križna Gora), Starè 1970 (Japodian pectoral), Puš 1978 (anthropomorphic pendants from Ljubljana), Jubani 1967 (significance of pendant forms in Mat region).

to such groups as priests, craftsmen or warriors is hard to tell. By the eighth century BC and the developed Iron Age a clearly defined class of warrior elite had come into existence, at least in some areas, whose status we can judge from the quantities of weapons, armour and other precious things deposited in their tombs. The formation of tribal units will have engendered warfare and given the specialist fighter a high status. There is no way of judging the extent to which outside influences contributed to these developments. The import of some high quality goods from the Greek world does not represent any direct influence over the Illyrian social order, although controlling the supply of material supplied in exchange for such items must have remained a significant concern on the part of the ruling elite.[19]

The growth of urban centres among some of the southern Illyrians can be linked to direct contacts with the Greek world in the Hellenistic era. Similarly, what is known of the internal organization of the Illyrian kingdom points to imitation of neighbouring Epirus and Macedonia. Accounts of the regime imposed on Illyrians following the Roman conquest convey little or nothing of native tribal institutions. There seems little to be gained from matching the 342 decuriae attributed by Pliny to the Delmatae with Strabo's estimate of 50 settlements or the claim of Vatinius that they exceeded 60. Some inscribed boundary stones from their territory record smaller groups, probably the inhabitants of single places, the Narestini of Nareste (Jesenice), the Pituntini of Pituntium (Podstrana) and the Onastini of Oneum (Omiš), along the coast south of Salona. Similarly there were the Barizaniates of Bariduum and the Lizaviates in the Vrlika region of the upper Cetina valley. Strabo's much discussed comment (7.5, 5) that among the Delmatae land was redistributed every eighth year may relate to the peculiar conditions of the seasonally flooded polje, where collective ownership of the land may have lasted into the Roman era.[20]

The Illyrian tribal aristocracy under Roman rule appears

---

[19] Suić 1967b (ancient references to Illyrian 'ethnology').
[20] Gabričević 1953 (communities of Delmatae in Vrlika area), Wilkes 1969.

before the end of the first century AD with the title chief
(*princeps*) and even commander (*praepositus*). At least one of
the leading families of the Delmatae based at Rider received
Roman citizenship from the emperor Claudius (AD 41–54).
Further south in the old Illyrian kingdom we meet a chief
(*princeps*) of the Docleatae and a relative who was chief of the
local fortress Salthua (probably Riječani near Nikšić), though
neither of these was yet a Roman citizen. The title of princeps
still persisted after some of the large native settlements had
been organized as Roman cities. Among the Japodes around
Bihać, altars were dedicated by leaders of the tribe to Bindus
Neptunus, deity of the local spring (see figure 30). In addition
to the (presumably) hereditary title of chief (*princeps*) one has
the title commander (*praepositus*) and a reference to his receiving Roman citizenship from Vespasian (AD 69–79). This appears
to imply that by the Flavian era the native chiefs were replacing
the senior centurions and regimental commanders appointed to
control the civitates after the conquest. Little is known of the
status of women among the Illyrians save for two interesting
comments by ancient writers. The *Coastal Passage* (*Periplus*)
attributed to Scylax of Caryanda reports that the Liburnians
were subject to the rule of women, who were free to have
sexual relations with slaves or foreigners. On a similar note
the Roman Varro, writing in the first century BC, observes that
Liburnian women could, if they chose, cohabit before marriage
with anyone they pleased. These passages have been used to
support the belief that the Liburnians represent some survival
of non-Indo-Europeans among the Illyrians, although the role
of Queen Teuta among the southern Illyrians suggests that, in
politics at least, women played a leading role among other
Illyrians.[21]

The prominence of warfare in ancient accounts of the Illyrians is matched by the large and various quantities of arms
recovered from their graves. Their principal offensive weapon
was the single-edged curved sword, similar to the Greek
machaira, a form of weapon that can be traced back to Bronze
Age times. Although a short curved sword was used by several

[21] Wilkes 1969.

Figure 30 Altars with Latin text dedicated by chief of the Japodes at Privilica spring, near Bihać, Bosnia, 1st century AD

peoples around the Mediterranean the Romans regarded the *sica* as a distinctive Illyrian weapon, used by the stealthy assassin (*sicarius*). Equally well represented in the material evidence is the long heavy spear (*sibyna*) which is described as an Illyrian weapon by the Roman poet Ennius (*Annals* 5.540). Apart from these distinctive types Illyrian graves contain a variety of knives, battle-axes, swords and bows and arrows. What is remarkable is that so many weapons were placed intact in the grave. For defence Illyrians used a light round shield of wood or leather with a bronze boss. Body armour, breastplates (see figure 31), greaves and helmets were the privilege of a minority, with a few examples of full body protection being known only in the Dolensko region of Slovenia. At Glasinac there are some chest-protectors covered with bronze studs, dated to the seventh century BC. Bronze greaves of the same period include a pair from a princely tomb at Ilijak, on which there is repoussée and engraved decoration of exceptional interest, including the Illyrian (Liburnian) warships rendered in a striking geometric style. Metal helmets are the most common protective armour in the early graves (see figure 32). More than 30 examples from the Dolensko region furnish a series of designs evolved in local workshops. Helmets at Glasinac were imported, including one prototype of the so-called Greco-Illyrian helmet, whose origin and manufacture has been much debated. An Albanian view insists that this represents a wholly

Figure 31 (above left) Bronze cuirass from Novo Mesto, Slovenia
Figure 32 (above right) Bronze helmet from a warrior-burial, Kaptol, Slovenia

indigenous Illyrian type, in use from the seventh to the second centuries BC, although the majority view is that that type had gone out of use by the fourth century.[22]

Burial and belief

We know Illyrians mainly through their burials, into which they put a great deal, both spiritually and physically. The general lack of uniformity in burial practice has tended to be cited as evidence for the mixed origins of the Illyrians, including both Indo-European and non-Indo-European elements. One distinctive feature of the Illyrian burial rite was the mound of stones and earth heaped over the grave. Though such tumulus burials are found in several areas of Europe during the Bronze Age, the Illyrians stand out for their continuation of the practice even, in some regions, well into the Roman period. The size of the mound, perhaps also the location, as well as the quality of the contents were intended to make an explicit statement of status in the community on the part of the family or kinship group. The burials of chiefs or princes were also marked out by the large number of secondary burials inserted within the mound, often in a regular arrangement, of companion warriors or others of the kin group. Apart from these features there appears to have been no means by which the identity of the deceased was indicated to the casual onlooker; in the absence of skeletal remains, only the interred objects can distinguish between a male and female burial, as is the case with the princely burials at Atenica near Čačak.[23]

There is not a great deal of informative evidence for religious or cult practices associated with the Illyrian dead. Coffin-burials

---

[22] Stipčević 1977a, 171–3 (swords), Frey 1973 (hoplite panoply in southeast Alps), Islami 1981, Stamati 1981 (cuirasses), Kilian 1973 (greaves from Ilijak, Glasinac).

[23] Stipčević 1977a, 229–36, Faber 1984 (tumulus construction), Palavestra 1984 (princely tombs), D. Garašanin 1976 (Balkan tumuli graves), Lazić 1989 (tumuli in Serbia and Montenegro), Ceka 1975a (chamber tombs in cities), Manastirli 1976 (rock-cut tombs), Cambi 1975, Šarić 1975a (sarcophagi and cremation chests in Lika).

beneath the floorboards of houses at Donja Dolina suggest that a few individuals (most people were buried in the nearby cemetery) had a special role as guardians or protectors of the hearth. The excavator of that settlement believed that the clay hearths, decorated with meanders and swastikas, in the houses may have served also as shrines related to the cult of the dead (see figure 33). The practice of burying the corpse in the crouch position, common in Bronze Age Europe, persisted among the Liburnians, and this is cited as further evidence for the survival of non-Indo-European elements among that people. The gradual shift from the rite of cremation to that of inhumation during the Roman era is generally interpreted as sign of a greater concern with the afterlife. In the Early Iron Age an older tradition of inhumation among Illyrians began to be replaced by cremation, and this is seen as evidence for a spiritual change or even 'crisis'. In regional terms cremation was more common among northern Illyrians, while the other persisted as the dominant rite in the south. It is hard to assess such changes, dimly seen over a long period of time. In the Vrlika region of

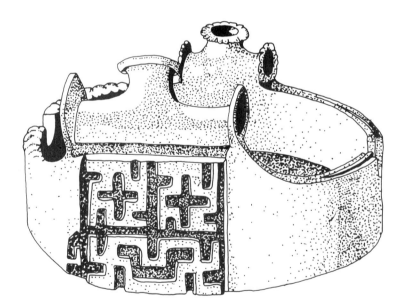

Figure 33 Decorated clay hearth from Donja Dolina, Bosnia

the upper Cetina valley, hardly 50 miles from the sea but still a remote area, Illyrian tumulus burials carried on the traditions of the Bronze Age at least down to the second century AD. In the rite of cremation the old ritual of raking the charred bones and ashes of the pyre together as filling for the grave was gradually given up in preference for the small stone cremation chest, usually decorated and inscribed, that became widespread during the Roman era. Perhaps the most distinctive form of Illyrian grave monument rendered in stone was the circular Liburnian tombstone, representing a round house or hut with conical roof of tiles or stone slabs. Most of these appear to belong to the early Roman period (first to early second centuries AD). Another form of the Roman era reflecting native traditions occurs around the Gulf of Kotor, where some tombstones are surmounted by small pyramids, representing the roof of a dwelling.[24]

There is no evidence for religious practice or observance among Illyrians to compare with that for the ritual of burial. We have no means of setting in context the reference to human sacrifice carried out by some Illyrians in the face of the expedition by Alexander of Macedon in 335 BC. The blood-thirsty ways of Illyrians are mentioned with disgust by Greek writers, notably the custom of using the skull of an enemy as a drinking tankard. The practice of mutilating prisoners may be the reason why the Autariatae killed their own weak and wounded, so that they did not fall into the hands of the enemy live and edible (Nicolaus of Damascus, *Collection of Customs*, Frag. 115, ed. Jacoby, *FGrHist* IIA). At the more spiritual level Illyrians were certainly much taken with the force of spells or the evil eye. Pliny's story that there were among Illyrians those 'who could gaze with the evil eye, cast a spell and even kill someone' (*NH*7.16) is repeated in the following century by Aulus Gellius (9.4, 8) in his compendium of table-talk among

---

[24] Stipčević 1984b, Benac 1984b, M. Garašanin 1984 (anthropomorphic tombstones), Gabričević 1983 (Sinj tombstones), Fadić 1988 (Liburnian tombstone), Zotović 1974 (Pilatovići), 1984 (Sase burials), Dobruna-Salihu 1982, 1987, Mirdita 1982 (Kosovo).

Roman intellectuals. The force of the evil eye remains wide-spread in the Balkans, but there is no reason to believe that it has a specifically Illyrian origin.

Unlike Celts, Dacians, Thracians or Scythians, there is no indication that Illyrians developed a uniform cosmology on which their religious practice was centred. An etymology of the Illyrian name linked with serpent would, if it is true, fit with the many representations of that species in the southern Balkans. Names of individual peoples may have been formed in a similar fashion, Taulantii from 'swallow' (cf. the Albanian *tallandushe*) or Enchelei the 'eel-men' and Chelidoni the 'snail-men'. The name of the Delmatae appears connected with the Albanian word for 'sheep' (*delmë*) and the Dardanians with that for 'pear' (*dardhë*). Some place-names appear to have similar derivations, including Olcinium (Ulcinj) from 'wolf' (*ukas*), although the ancients preferred a connection with Colchis. There is no question but that Illyrians acknowledged supernatural forces and identified deities whose power was expressed in the vicissitudes of daily life, health and sickness, natural abundance and disaster. Symbolic forms appear in every variety of ornament. Most common of all is that of the sun, to which were related birds, serpents, horses and the swastika, which is seen to represent the solar movement. Among the Liburnians and their Venetic neighbours the image of the sun-boat depicts the sun-disc being borne across the firmament. In Slovenia models of a horse-drawn cart may represent Phaethon's chariot, a Greek myth centred around the head of the Adriatic. Among the northern Illyrians symbols associated with sun-worship include those of water-fowl and horses along with several geometric motifs, but in the south the serpent is more prominent. The cult of the sun among the Paeonians, who dwelt between the Macedonians and Dardanians, is described by a writer of the second century AD as focused on a small disc at the top of a long pole (Maximus of Tyre, *Philosophoumena* 2.8, 6).[25]

---

[25] Benac 1984a (spiritual culture), Stipčević 1981 (cult symbols), Vasić 1974b (Paeonian sun-worship), Marović 1970 (Liburnian sun-worship), Medini 1975 (Japodian religion), Oreč 1987 (hill-top sanctuaries near Posušje and Ljubuški), Starè 1973 (sceptre in Šmarjeta burial), Čremošnik 1968 ('orans'

The image of the serpent was a potent symbol, especially among the southern Illyrians. Even in the Roman period altars were dedicated in Dardania (near Skopje) to the serpentine pair Dracon and Dracaena. It was the common terminal ornament for pins, bracelets, necklaces, pendants, etc. The symbol of fertility and potency, the serpent was later seen to represent a challenge to the hold of Christianity on the spiritual life of the Illyrians. This emerges from the account of St Jerome (a native of Illyria) of the life of St Hilarion, who came to Epidaurum in AD 365 to free its people from the scourge of the giant serpent Boas, reputed to devour cattle and people. The saint killed the serpent, and the Christians long remembered the victory (*Life of St Hilarion* 9). In that region the image of the serpent evoked not only the legend of Cadmus but also the connection between Illyrian Epidaurum and the cult of the healing divinity Aesculapius from Epidaurus in Greece, in which the reptile was also prominent. The slaying of the serpent by St Hilarion must have had a symbolic impact on the people of that region. A list of the figures and devices which appear to have had some spiritual meaning for Illyrians would include more than 60 items from the pre-Roman and Roman periods. Some came from elsewhere, from the plains to the north the swastika with horses' heads, from the Celts the use of red enamel, from the Bronze Age Aegean the double-axe, doves, lions and funeral masks, and from further east the sphinx and the cat. The protective and beneficial force of amulets is evident in the many examples of such forms as the phallus, the hand, the leg and animals' teeth.[26]

Illyrian deities are named on monuments of the Roman era, some in equation with gods of the classical pantheon (see figure 34). There seems to have been no single or dominant Illyrian deity and some were evidently worshipped only in particular regions. Thus several deities occur only in Istria, including Eia, Malesocus, Boria and Iria. Anzotica was the Liburnian Venus and appears in the traditional image of the classical goddess. Other local deities were Latra, Sentona and the nymph Ica,

praying in relief sculpture), Knez 1974 (ritual vessel), Baçe 1984 (temple architecture in Illyrian Albania).
[26] Stipčević 1981, Glogović 1988 (snake brooches).

Figure 34 Relief of Diana and other deities at Opačići, near Glamoč, Bosnia

worshipped in eastern Istria at a spring still known by that name today. Among the Japodes altars were dedicated by the tribal leaders at the Privilica spring near Bihać to the local deity Bindus, identified with Neptune, the classical god of springs and seas. North of the Japodes, the altars to Vidasus and Thana dedicated at the hot springs of Topuško reveal the local identities of Silvanus and Diana, a familiar combination on many dedications in the territory of the Delmatae. Sometimes the name of a local deity is recorded only in the Latin form, for example, Armatus at Delminium (Duvno) who was evidently a war god of the Delmatae, and the Latin Liber who appears with the attributes of Silvanus and Terminus, the protector of boundaries. The identity of Tadenus, an identity or epithet of Apollo at the Roman spa near the source of the Bosna, at Ilidža, the ancient Aquae S., is not known and the name may be of Thracian origin. From the same quarter of the Balkans the cult of the Thracian horseman spread into the Illyrian lands during the Roman period, appearing in the familiar image of the galloping rider with the short cloak streaming out behind. The Illyrian town Rhizon (Risinium) on the Gulf of Kotor had its protective deity Medaurus, named on dedications to Aesculapius at the legionary fortress Lambaesis in Africa by the legate, a Roman senator and native of Risinium, in the reign of Marcus Aurelius (161–169). The god, who is also commemorated at Risinium, is described in the verses of the text as riding on horseback and carrying a lance.[27]

Illyrian taste in artistic ornament was non-representational and geometric, with combinations of triangles, diamonds and diagonal lines incised on metal objects and pottery. The absence of figured ornament may reflect the apparent lack of mythology or anthropomorphic cults. This seems to be the only consistent feature in the art of the Illyrians that appears with the developed Iron Age of the eighth century BC. Later developments may be attributed to outside influences, notably archaic Greece and Etruscan Italy. By the sixth century a new warrior elite at Glasinac and in Dolensko shows a taste for imported objects with figured decoration. From this may have developed some technical skill in producing figured ornament. The remarkable Situla art with its great variety of figured decoration appears to have been a transplant from northern Italy. Even if Illyrian chiefs were patrons of the local craftsmen making the situlae, along with decorated belt-plates, the objects and the scenes

[27] Stipčević 1977a, 193–6, Wilkes, 1969, 255 (Medaurus), Degrassi 1970 (Istrian cults), Cambi 1980 (Anzotica), Medini 1984 (Latra), Zaninović 1984a (Liber), Patsch 1900 (Japodes).

they depict do not appear to be matched in the local material culture. Hence the current theory that they were the work of immigrant craftsmen using a repertoire of exotic scenes and motifs. The origin of the ornament on Japodian funeral urns is less clear. Some of the carving, which seems to imitate the

Figure 35 a) Tombstone of mother and daughter in native style with Greek epitaph, from near Apollonia

Figure 35 Continued
b) Family tombstone with relief portraits, from Kolovrat, near Pri-
jepolje, Serbia, late 2nd century AD

Figure 35 Continued
c) Portrait reliefs on family tombstones from near Glamoč, Bosnia,
2nd century AD

Figure 35 Continued
d) Tombstone with Latin epitaph, with depictions of jewellery (above)
and textile motifs (below), from near Sinj, Dalmatia

incised ornament of metal, may derive from the situlae, but production appears to have been the work of native craftsmen working in the more austere Illyrian geometric tradition. There seems to be little in common between the exceptional situlae and Japodian urns and the many locally produced pendants in human and animal forms found in the Japodian cemeteries of around the same period. These portrayals of animals – horse, cock, fish, etc. – in bronze pendants and glass beads, some with human features, may have been produced among the Japodes but hardly amount to a distinctive Japodian style, while the much discussed items of carved amber with human features from the grave at Kompolje are likely to be imports.[28]

The stone sculptures from Nesactium in Istria have no parallel in the Illyrian lands but are comparable with other finds from Adriatic Italy. The carvings appear to have been near life-size statues of domestic deities, probably erected at a shrine in the Early Iron Age. The most striking piece depicts a naked woman cradling a child in her arms, carved in high relief from a single block. Another fragment, perhaps belonging to the same piece, depicts a male rider and horse. There are also several naked male figures, a female head and a horse's head, while some other fragments are decorated with spiralform ornament, meanders and swastikas. Since they were discovered at the beginning of the twentieth century, estimates of their date and significance have varied greatly: one opinion linked them with the art of Mycenaean Greece, but now a local origin and a somewhat later date for the ornament is preferred. On the other hand, the double-headed fragment of sculpture, now in Pula but perhaps also from Nesactium, has a distinctly Greek appearance in the 'barbaric' style. An obvious connection with the Greek world is Spina, a trading post near the mouth of the

[28] Stipčević 1963, Grbić 1971, Čović 1984b, Gabrovec 1984, (northwest Illyrians), Vasić 1986 (metal ornament), Knez 1984 (Situla ornament), Vasić 1969 (Japodian pendants), Foltiny 1970, Dular 1978 (animal ornament in Slovenia), Rendić-Miočević 1984 (art among Illyrian Riditae), Stipčević 1976 (Illyrian and Albanian symbolism), A. Jovanović 1989 (iconography of Illyrian belt-plates).

Po established under Greek hegemony in the sixth century BC, the date which is also widely accepted for the Nesactium sculptures.[29]

It is hard to detect any impact on Illyrian art from the arrival of Celts in the Danube basin, but the reverse is the case when Illyrians came under Roman rule. Thanks to the rapid spread of stone carving, the early Roman period offers an unprecedented range of authentic Illyrian images, both figured and abstract, which vividly portray local identities and traditions even among the more remote communities (see figures 35a–d). Liburnian 'house' tombstones and the cremation chests of Delmatae and Japodes have already been noted, but there are also the anthropomorphic stelae from Sinj and the tombstones, some still in situ, from a cemetery of the early Roman period at Pljevlja in northern Montenegro, where the human features rendered in low relief have eerie unrealistic proportions, with elongated faces and pointed chins. Some local craftsmen appear to have been so conditioned by the long traditions of wood-carving that they reproduced in stone the latter's familiar texture and longitudinal graining. This may be the explanation for the remarkable late Roman funeral relief from Zenica in central Bosnia depicting four figures in traditional Illyrian dress (figure 26). Illyrian figurative art dissolves in a local Roman provincial art, though its concluding phase proved to be its richest and most varied. One can, it is true, discover in later eras the survival of Illyrian forms and ornament, but the artistic evolution that began with the developed Iron Age of the eighth century BC finally vanished with the Slav settlements of the sixth and seventh centuries AD.[30]

[29] Mladin 1966, 1980, Stipčević 1977a, 217–18 (Spina connection).
[30] Rendić-Miočević 1984, Gabričević 1980, 1983, Čremošnik 1957 (Bosnia), Cermanović-Kuzmanović 1973, 1978, 1980 (Pljevlja), Srejović and Cermanović-Kuzmanović 1987 (Serbia).

9

Imperial Illyrians

Emperors from Illyricum

Until around the time of Hadrian (AD 117–138) the Roman Empire was in the charge of a ruling minority, mainly of Italian origin, that was easily distinguishable from the subject peoples in the provinces. The latter's tribute provided most of the pay for the professional army. They were ruled by Roman senators with near absolute authority, either as legates of the emperor, commander-in-chief of the armies and chief citizen (*princeps*) of the Roman state, or, in the case of the more civilized areas, as an acting magistrate (proconsul) appointed by the Roman Senate. Unlike some of the native aristocracies in Gaul, Spain or North Africa, the Illyrian native elite made little headway within this imperial hierarchy. As a whole the Illyrian contribution to the Empire during the two centuries following the conquest consisted mainly of military service, conscripted or voluntary, in the auxiliary regiments of the army, which after service brought the reward of Roman citizenship, and in the imperial fleets. On the civil side the incorporation of native Illyrian communities as Roman cities (*municipia*) spread the citizenship among local families, whose social status and liabilities to civic office would, in theory at least, be defined by the periodic census of Roman citizens and their property.

Except among the Liburnians, no existing Illyrian communities were organized into Roman cities before the Flavian era (AD 69–96). When the limit of Italy at the head of the Adriatic was fixed in eastern Istria, the relegation of the Liburnians to provincial status may have been offset by grants of city status, and in a few cases of Italian status, to many small communities in that area. Few Liburnian natives are recorded without the Roman citizenship and many have the family names of early Roman emperors, Julius or Claudius. In southern Liburnia some of the larger pre-Roman settlements appear to have been rapidly converted into urban centres in the Roman style, with public buildings and other amenities being inserted within the perimeter of earlier walls, notably at Asseria (near Benkovac), but similar conversions took place elsewhere. In this area only the colonial settlement at Jader (Zadar) remained under the domination of settlers. During the Julio-Claudian period the coastal towns established by settlers from Italy appear to have remained estranged from the native population: at least that remains the impression from the epigraphic evidence which generally depicts the well-to-do, although the labouring and servile classes are likely to have been of native origin.[1]

The Romans appear to have made good use of the seafaring talents of the Illyrians, some of whom may have made a significant contribution to Augustus' decisive victory at Actium in 31 BC. In the course of the civil wars that followed the death of Nero in AD 68 we learn that the imperial fleet stationed at Ravenna consisted of recruits mainly from the Illyrian provinces Pannonia and Dalmatia, and that state of affairs is borne out by the epitaphs of sailors not only from Ravenna and other stations but also, though to a lesser degree, from the other major fleet based at Misenum on the Bay of Naples. It is interesting to observe in the recorded tribal origins that recruits were drawn not only from the coastal peoples but from those of the interior, such as the Maezaei in northwest Bosnia, and that the qualities demanded for the service were not necessarily of those brought up to the sea. During the Julio-Claudian and Flavian periods Illyrians were not enlisted in the legions, for which the citizenship was required, and legions stationed among the Illyrians continued to draw recruits from Italy or from the colonies established in the Danube region. On the other hand, one cannot rule out the possibility that several of

[1] Wilkes 1969, Suić 1971 (Bribir), 1976a.

those who appear on tombstones with Roman names and origins were in fact native Illyrians whose lack of legal qualification was suppressed by the recruiting officer desperate to make up his quota. There is no lack of evidence for the unpopularity of military service among the Illyrians.[2]

Native urbanization among the Illyrians gets under way with the Flavians. In Pannonia the Flavian municipia at Neviodunum and Andautonia appear to have been established among the predominantly Celtic communities of the Latobici and Varciani. Only later, in the reign of Trajan (AD 98–117), does the Roman citizenship begin to appear among the Illyrian communities of southeast Pannonia, the Andizetes, Scordisci and Breuci. Some of those who bear Trajan's family name Ulpius may be ex-soldiers or belong to their families, to whom the grant of Roman citizenship was normally extended. In Dalmatia the Flavian municipium at Scardona (Skradin) may have owed its existence to a settlement of ex-soldiers, including some from the legion at Burnum higher up the river Titus (Krka), where a new city had been organized by the reign of Hadrian. Among the Japodes of the Lika the chief settlement Arupium, attacked by Octavian in 35 BC, became the city of the region with Monetium and Avendo probably no more than villages on its territory. New Roman cities were created at Rider (Danilo), a major settlement of the Delmatae near Šibenik, and at several places in the interior, 'Old' Bistue (in the Rama valley), 'New' Bistue (in the Lašva valley near Travnik) and in the Drina valley at Rogatica and Skelani.[3]

The Flavian municipium Doclea near the Lake of Shkodër lay at the confluence of the rivers Zeta and Morača. At the now deserted site there are still visible remains of several buildings erected during the early years of the Flavian municipium. Within the walls, a triumphal gate led to a paved street flanked with statues of emperors. Near the centre lay the forum (60 by 55 m) to which were attached the basilica (for trials and large meetings) and the council chamber (*curia*). Across the street lay the civic baths and two classical temples, each in its own

---

[2] Vulpe 1925, Marin 1977 (Illyrians in Italy), Protase 1978 (in Dacia), Tacitus, *Histories* 3.12, 50 (Ravenna fleet), Starr 1941, 74–7.
[3] Mócsy 1974 (Pannonia), Wilkes 1969 (Dalmatia).

precinct, one of the official Dea Roma, the other to Diana. Several Latin inscriptions record magistrates and benefactors of the city's early years. The basilica was a gift from Flavius Fronto and his wife Flavia Terulla, dedicated to the memory of their 15-year-old son Flavius Balbinus, after he had held 'all the offices permitted to him by law'. Behind the Roman façade of new names and architecture we can recognize the heirs to the old Illyrian kings still pre-eminent in their kingdom. The inscribed base of Fronto's statue records that he had undertaken expensive offices not only in his native Doclea but also in several other Roman cities of the area, including two places which had once been colonies of Roman settlers.[4]

In the course of the second century AD most Illyrians belonged to a city of the Roman Empire, in the majority of cases based on the local unit (*civitas*) defined by the Romans following the conquest. Cities were organized for the plains (*polje*) inhabited by the inland Delmatae, including Delminium (near Duvno), Pelva (near Livno), Salvium (Glamoč), Novae (near Imotski) and Magnum (in the Čikola valley). In Popovopolje the Derae-mestae may have been incorporated within the new municipium at Diluntum (Ljubinje). Several cities were created in the more remote regions of northeast Dalmatia, including the mining centre at Domavia (Gradina), Malvesa (Skelani on the Drina) and the municipium S. (the name survives only in this abbreviated form) at Pljevlja in northern Montenegro. Another fortress of the Japodes attacked by Octavian in 35 BC, Metulum, which probably lay in the area of Josipdol, also became a city probably before the end of the second century. In Pannonia, Bassiana (Petrovci) was organized out of the Scordisci and Cibalae (Vinkovci) from the Cornacates, both places situated on the major roads of the Danube area. Other Hadrianic cities among the Pannonian Illyrians include that of the Jasi at the spa centre Aquae Balissae (Daruvar) in the Papuk hills. In Moesia Hadrian's only known foundation was Ulpianum (Gračanica near Priština), likely to have been closely linked with the mines (metalla Ulpiana) on mount Zegovac. Cities were also

---

[4] Wilkes 1969, Suić 1976a, Cermanović-Kuzmanović, Srejović and Velimirović-Žižić 1975 (cemetery).

organized at the strategic crossroads Naissus (Niš) and at two places in the Morava valley, Margum (Orašje), near the mouth, and Horreum Margi (Ćuprija), an important river crossing. In the south the new city at Sočanica in the Ibar valley, probably named municipium Dardanicum, was another 'mining town' connected with the local workings (*metalla Dardanica*).[5]

Most of these new cities were a means of concentrating local authority and resources along the major roads, within easy reach of central authority. When compared with other provincials the Illyrians were 'late developers' in the spread and reception of urbanization. The second century AD saw increasing interference in local affairs by the central authorities. The compulsion to undertake magistracies and other expensive civic offices was now intensified and 'office-dodgers' were pursued, as more and more of the wealthy strove to gain the precious exemptions from the burdens of local municipal office. It is hard to see any of these new cities, in which the natives were forced to concentrate their wealth, amounting to much more than another element in what was becoming regarded by the state as the essential fabric of government. Those local worthies who appear as magistrates will have become locked into a system of imperial requisitions and burdens for which they and their family property would be held accountable, especially when there was a war on, as there often was somewhere on the Danube frontier. Descendants of these Illyrians could only improve their condition by advancing higher within the system, and for most Illyrians the only real prospects lay with a career in the army.[6]

The new cities will have affected not only the upper classes who appear on Latin inscriptions holding municipal office but also the mass of the people whose life was still based on tribal relationships, a process of change which may have already begun among the southern Illyrians in the Hellenistic period. In the previous chapter we have seen how inscriptions and sculptures of the Roman period furnish valuable evidence for

[5] Wilkes 1969, Mócsy 1974. Also Pašalić 1967, Bojanovski 1988 (Bosnia-Hercegovina), Mirković 1968 (Moesia), Cvetković-Tomasević 1983 (Ulpiana), Baçe 1986 (Roman cities in Illyrian Albania).
[6] Millar 1983 (municipal burdens and exemptions).

the way of life and beliefs of native Illyrians. In the matter of assessing Romanization the persistence of native names and other traditions tends to be judged as an indication of the superficiality and weakness of Roman influence. Another view, advanced by the Hungarian scholar A. Mócsy, argues that the true picture is quite different. The existence of any sort of epigraphic and sculptural evidence must in itself be regarded as telling evidence for profound Roman influence. Roman influence was not present when there is no evidence of this sort, and many Illyrian communities fall into this category. In the matter of religious cults some have argued that Silvanus, whose worship was widespread among the Illyrians, was really a native deity and that his popularity down to the third century indicates a resistance to the official Roman pantheon, Jupiter, Juno, Minerva, Mars, etc. Some have discovered in the representations of Silvanus with an erect phallus a connection with pre-Roman fertility cults. Against this Mócsy responds that there is really nothing in the Illyrian version of Silvanus that is not also to be found in the original Italic version. Rather than being regarded as an assertion of native Illyrian identity the cult is expressive of standardized, colourless Latin-speaking Roman provincial culture. This was the cultural background of the unsophisticated but conscientious Illyrian emperors of the third and fourth centuries. The Roman epithets of Silvanus also indicate the range of his appeal to the rural Illyrians, Domesticus, a bearded countryman with the vine- or fruit-pruning knife, with his dog; Messor is Silvanus the protector of the harvest, and Silvestris, often with Diana and the Nymphs, is the rural woodland identity, including hunting.[7]

The Romans of Illyricum came to prominence in the Empire suddenly as a result of the civil war following the death of Commodus in AD 192. On 9 April 193 the governor of Upper Pannonia L. Septimius Severus was proclaimed emperor by his legions and within less than two months he was ruling in Rome. The new emperor dismissed the existing Praetorian Guard,

---

[7] Mócsy 1974. Local Silvanus: Rendić-Miočević 1967, 1979–80, 1975b (Delmatae), Cambi 1968 (Attis identity), Gunjača 1968–9 (Riditae), Bojanov-ski 1977–8, Paškvalin 1979 (Silvanus and Nymphs), 1985–6a, 1985–6b, Matijašić 1985 (Istria).

which was recruited mainly from Italy, and replaced it with a
new force of twice the size (over 10,000) drawn from the
Pannonian and adjacent provinces. Within a few years a new
legion, recruited from the same area, was stationed at Albanum
a few miles outside the capital. The impression made by the
troops of Severus on the people of Rome is described by the
historian Cassius Dio, Roman senator and eye-witness of these
events: 'Severus filled the city with a throng of motley soldiers
most savage in appearance, most terrifying in speech, and most
boorish in conversation' (75.2, 6). Unfortunately the soldiers
from Illyricum were a lasting presence in Rome, as new recruits
to the Guard continued to be drawn from the Danube lands,
a reward to the provincial soldiers for loyal service, with prospects of further promotion. The Romans as a whole did not
like them: 30 years after their arrival we hear of a night-
time assault on the jurist Ulpian, then head of the imperial
administration, and on another occasion a three-day battle
between the townspeople and the Guard ended only when the
worsted soldiery began setting fire to major buildings. Cassius
Dio himself was hounded out of the capital because he had
once been an unpopular governor of the soldiers' homeland.
To the Roman middle and upper classes the Danubians were
clumsy, stupid and uncultured – they lacked *humanitas* – while
writers were not slow to embellish older stereotypes of brutal
soldiery from current experience.[8]

Though he was a native of Lepcis Magna in Africa and
married to a Syrian princess, Severus and his regime were most
attentive to the army and its homeland which had put them in
power. At its beginning the Severan campaign had been blessed
by local native priests, while the personal links between the
imperial family and the frontier towns were fostered. After the
conclusive victory at Lyon in 197 over his western rival some
officers of the Severan army set up thanksgiving altars to the
Pannonian and Dalmatian mothers who had nurtured and
sustained the fighting power of the Danube legions. The pre-
eminence of that region in the Empire is signalled by the return
to currency of Illyricum, a regional rather than ethnic identity

[8] Mócsy 1974, Šašel 1982 (Genius Illyrici).

in the Empire, whose leading citizens were known as Illyriciani. The origin of this sense of identity within the Roman world is to be found in the years of warfare on the Danube against Germans and Iranian Sarmatians who sought to enter the Roman Empire during the reign of Marcus Aurelius (AD 161–180). After the devastation caused by the first attacks the emperor himself spent several seasons in Pannonia. Attacks were made on peoples across the Danube, possibly with a view to extending the Empire into Slovakia and the Hungarian plain, but in the reign of his son Commodus (AD 180–192) an even more elaborate cordon of forts and watchtowers was erected along the Roman bank of the river. Though there are signs of local disturbances, notably with 'bandits' in the southern Balkans, the Illyrian provinces enjoyed more than half a century of peace and rising prosperity.[9]

During the early decades of the third century the army of Illyricum became more reluctant to commit its strength elsewhere, while insisting that resources were contributed from other areas of the Empire to sustain the exposed frontier on the Danube. When that support was threatened the Illyriciani did not hesitate to establish their own emperor as a means of keeping their hold on the imperial support-system. After the end of the Severan dynasty in AD 235 the frontier began to be threatened by large numbers of migrating Goths. When this happened during the reign of Philip (AD 244–249), Pacatianus, the field commander at Sirmium, was made to assume an imperial authority by the local interests. He was replaced at Sirmium by Messius Decius, a well-connected Roman senator who came from a village near Sirmium. His reign acknowledged the Illyrian sense of identity, with coins bearing the legend 'virtus Illyrici', while he too was said to have been an unwilling usurper at Sirmium against the authority of Philip. For the next few years the central authority kept its hold over the Sirmium command until local power was again asserted following disasters in the reign of Valerian (AD 253–260) until his successor Gallienus (AD 260–268) regained control through a 'foreign' army drawn from Britain and Germany under his chief general

[9] Mócsy 1974.

Aureolus. At the same time the power of the Illyrian legions was acknowledged with series of coins bearing their names and titles.[10]

The Illyriciani rose from humble, often rural, backgrounds, through service in the army. One of the first to do so was Valerius Maximianus from Poetovio in Pannonia, who was promoted during the reign of Marcus Aurelius to command several legions and achieved the consulship. He was a 'man of action' and the record of his career includes winning a hand-to-hand combat with a tribal chief from across the Danube. In the next generation the first Danubian to become emperor was Maximinus (AD 235–238), generally known as the 'Thracian' but probably originating from near the Danube in Moesia on the border of the Illyrian lands. After completing a campaign in Germany he moved the army to Sirmium to face the looming danger from the Goths. In spite of his conscientious work on the frontiers the Roman establishment treated Maximinus as a usurper, affronted by his indifference to the Senate and by his incessant demands for money, and in AD 238 two senior senators were chosen as emperors. Maximinus then entered Italy but suffered humiliating failure in an attack on Aquileia and was rejected by his own troops.[11]

With the accession of M. Aurelius Claudius in AD 268 following his victory over the Goths at Naissus, the Empire came under the control of the leading Illyriciani at Sirmium. The new ruler came from southern Illyricum, either Dalmatia or Dardania, but his reign ended with his death from a plague at Sirmium in AD 270. Rejecting the Senate's proposal of Claudius' brother, the Illyriciani chose instead one of themselves, the formidable Domitius Aurelianus, probably a native of Sirmium. He ended the fragmentation of the Empire in the east by defeating Zenobia of Palmyra, and in the west by deposing the Gallic emperor.[12] His most decisive initiative was to abandon what was left of the province of Dacia and settle the Roman evacuees in a 'New Dacia' south of the Danube, in which the two legions of old Dacia were stationed. There must have been a judgement that the old conquest of Trajan was now

[10] Mócsy 1974.
[11] Syme 1973 (imperial origins).
[12] Mócsy 1974.

expendable in the interests of Illyricum. If the reign of Aurelian marked the high point of Illyrian power it was also the period when the regime of the Illyriciani moved from Sirmium to the centre, and the mobile armies, composed of many units with Illyrian titles, lost their close links with their Illyrian homelands. Aurelian was succeeded by Probus (AD 276–282), another native of Sirmium, who fell out of favour with the army when he began to talk openly of a return to a peace-time economy. He is said to have been killed by some of his own troops while engaged in planting vines on the Almus mons (Fruška Gora) north of his native Sirmium. The biographer implies that his death was caused by his expressed ambition to make the army redundant, a dangerous notion in any age: 'Soon there will not be a Roman soldier. The whole world will manufacture no weapons and there will be no requisitions of produce, the ox will be reserved for the plough and the horse be bred for peace. There will be no wars and no prisoners' (*Augustan History, Life of Probus* 20). The army chose another of the Illyriciani to succeed him. Carus, who may have come from Narona in Dalmatia, was another competent general but died on campaign in Persia after reigning only ten months. In the Autumn of 284 the army, while on its march back from the east, chose another of the Illyriciani, C. Valerius Diocles, later known as Diocletian, and the Roman Empire entered a new era.

Aged around 40 at his accession, Diocletian was another of the Illyriciani schooled and promoted by Aurelian, and had risen from a humble origin in Salona on the Dalmatian coast. When he sought a colleague to share the burdens of rule his choice fell on Maximianus, an old army comrade and a native of Sirmium. Dividing the many pressing tasks between them the two Augusti found their arrangement so successful that in AD 293 they chose two junior emperors or Caesars to assist them. Galerius and Constantius were both Illyriciani, probably from Aurelian's New Dacia. For 12 years this college of four, the Tetrarchy, ruled the Empire with increasing success, though their last years were marred by an ill-judged persecution of the Christians. Half a century later the historian Aurelius Victor pays a qualified tribute to their achievement.

Illyricum was the homeland of them all. For all their lack of culture, their upbringing in the hardships of the country and their military careers proved to be the best possible for the state. Whereas it is

common knowledge that high-minded and well-educated men tend
to be more ready to find fault, those with an experience of life's
hardships, while judging everyone by their merit, pay less attention
to such details. And they look up to Valerius [Diocletianus] as a
father, as one would to a mighty god. But the harmony of these
men was proof that their natural ability and use of sound military
experience, such as they had acquired under the command of Aurelian
and Probus, almost made up for their lack of noble character.
(*Liber de Caesaribus* 39.26–28)

The new regime made great changes in the running of the
Empire. Frontier armies and defences were strengthened; provinces were subdivided to make the civil administration more
effective; currency and taxation were reformed; and government intervention extended even to the regulation of service
and commodity prices, though that proved a failure. The
Tetrarchy was the climax of more than half a century of rule
by Illyriciani.[13]

Diocletian's plans for an orderly transmission of power
through the promotion of Caesars to Augusti foundered on
family ambition. After several years of confusion following the
retirement of Diocletian in AD 305, Constantine, the son of
Constantius Caesar, defeated Maxentius, the son of Maximianus Augustus, in a battle at the Milvian bridge on the outskirts
of Rome in AD 312. The battle, which decided who was to rule
in the west, was later famous for Constantine's use of the
symbol of Christianity, and was commemorated by the arch
erected in his honour at Rome. In AD 324 it was as the champion
of Christianity that Constantine was able to eliminate his rival
Licinius, in a battle which marked the victory of the western
Roman armies over those of the Danube lands. The house of
Constantine ruled until AD 363. In general they paid little
attention to Illyricum, although when new emperors had once
again to be appointed the army chose Illyriciani, Jovianus
from Singidunum (Belgrade) and then Valentinian from Cibalae
(Vinkovci) in Pannonia. Though regarded by the historian
Ammianus as the leader of an 'Illyrian clique', Valentinian paid
no special attention to the needs of his homeland. He did not

[13] Williams 1985.

reside at the old headquarters in Sirmium and made little response to petitions from his distressed fellow-countrymen during his visit in AD 375, the year of his death. Sirmium was no longer the vital hinge of the Empire but merely a peripheral region between east and west as the two halves began to move apart towards the end of the fourth century.[14]

Roman Illyricum ended on 9 August AD 378, when the emperor Valens and his armies were wiped out by the Goths in a battle at Adrianople in southeast Thrace. These, along with Alans and Huns, had been permitted to enter the Empire a few years earlier. Within a year a large number of the invaders moved west and took possession of a good deal of Roman Pannonia. They could not, like earlier settlers, be incorporated in the structure of Roman Illyricum. There were too many of them and they had no intention of being settled on marginal land as farmers and taxpayers. The Roman administration collapsed and the barbarians took to raiding other areas for the supplies they needed. The poet Claudian depicts Pannonia in these years as being in a state of permanent siege. St Jerome, an Illyrian who came from a town called Stridon near the border of Dalmatia and Pannonia, presents a distressing account of his native land. In AD 380 he writes that his home town was in ruins (*Famous Men* 65) and then a few years later that 'everything has perished' (*Commentary on Zephaniah* 1.676). Other writers of the period also refer to a devastated Illyricum. Early in the fifth century what remained of the overland route across Illyricum linking east and west was severed by further invasions. The roads were packed with refugees fleeing south to Italy and the Adriatic. On the Dalmatian coast their numbers and distressed condition became a problem for the authorities. The sense of finality felt at the time is reflected by the removal of martyrs' bones from shrines that would soon have to be abandoned to the most feared of all invaders, the Huns.[15]

The persistence of Roman place-names in several areas of Illyricum suggests the survival of Latin-speaking communities,

---

[14] Mócsy 1974.
[15] Claudian, *On Stilicho's Consulship* 2.191–207 (LCL vol. 2 p. 16), Mócsy 1974 (translation of martyrs).

notably in that region near the Danube where Aurelian had
settled the people moved out of Dacia. It was from these and
similar communities in the southern Balkans that emerged the
Vlachs and the Romanians, whose varieties of Romance language are descended from Latin-speaking pastoralists. In Dardania the old Roman city of Scupi (Skopje), destroyed by an
earthquake in AD 518, was abandoned as its Romanized population chose to remain in the surrounding hills, near to the
safety of hill-top refuges. The need for local security was upper-
most in the great programme of fortress building and reconstruction throughout Illyricum described in the sixth century
by Procopius. In the southern Balkans it was the dispersal of
the Latin-speaking population from the major centres which
led to a survival of Roman traditions in several remote areas.
In some places these changes involved the reoccupation of the
ancient Illyrian hill-forts. When the emperor Justinian sought
to re-establish Roman Illyricum in the sixth century AD, that
essential foundation of strategically placed cities in the valleys
created in the first and second centuries AD, linked by policed
roads and bridges, no longer existed. Alongside Latin the native
Illyrian survived in the country areas, and St Jerome claimed
to speak his 'sermo gentilis' (*Commentary on Isaiah* 7.19). In
Dalmatia many Illyrian names survived into the Middle Ages
but for Illyricum as a whole the invasions at the end of the
fourth century destroyed not only the structure of the Roman
province but possibly a good deal of the older native Illyrian
cultures which had survived within it. In the words of Mócsy
(1974, p. 358), the Illyrians, like the Celts and Thracians,
'dissolved in the sea of later conquerors, simply for the reason
that during the long period of Roman rule they had lost their
native culture and were unable to utilize their language as a
means to a political life of their own.' The question of Illyrian
survival and that of a continuity between them and the Albanians during the early Middle Ages will be considered in the
second part of this chapter.[16]

[16] Winnifrith 1987 (Vlachs); Scupi: *Chronicle of Count Marcellinus* AD 518
(MGH Chronica Minora 2, p. 100). Late Roman refugia: Bojanovski 1979
(Ključ, Bosnia), Cerova 1987 (Albania), Pahić 1981, Ciglenečki 1987
(Slovenia).

Medieval and modern Illyrians

When Leo was emperor in Constantinople (AD 457–474) three young Illyrian peasants escaped rural poverty by walking to the capital from their village of Bederiana in Dardania to join the army. When they arrived with nothing but some biscuit wrapped in their cloaks, their fine physique gained them admission to the guard. One of them, Justin, rose to command the Palace Guard and became emperor on the death of the aged Anastasius in AD 518. Justin (AD 518–527) and his nephew Justinian (AD 527–565) were the last Illyrian emperors and, like their predecessors of the third and fourth centuries, applied themselves to the task of ruling with energy and determination. Under Justinian the Empire recovered territories lost in the previous century, Africa from the Vandals and Italy from the Ostrogoths. The sixth-century Illyrians were, also like their predecessors, mocked for their lack of education, notably by Procopius who makes Justin a near illiterate. Justinian, who came from the neighbouring village of Tauresium, had been called by his uncle to the capital for his education and was soon managing affairs of state on the latter's behalf. The origin of the family in northern Dardania was later marked by the new city Justiniana Prima, on a ridge above the village of Caričin Grad in southern Serbia, 20 miles west of Leskovac. The walls enclose an area 500 by 215 metres, with an inner acropolis at the northwest. Internal arrangements were based on two streets flanked with colonnades, with a circular forum at the intersection. Most of the interior appears to have been taken up with several churches, some of which had mosaic decoration. Justiniana Prima was made the seat of the archbishop of Dardania and was granted many privileges by a law issued in AD 535.[17]

The northern regions of Roman Illyricum, the old province Pannonia, were occupied by Avars and Lombards, but southern Illyricum remained an important source of manpower for the

---

[17] Procopius *Secret History* 6.2 (Justin), Kondić and Popović 1977 (Justiniana Prima).

imperial army. Most of the reconquests in the western Mediterranean were achieved by troops from the southern Balkans.
The security of these homelands was now based on local strongholds, either new or refurbished, many of which are listed by
Procopius in his work *Buildings*. Although the historian credits
Justinian with the new fortifications, they were the result of a
reconstruction begun probably by Anastasius. The network of
small forts, whose construction will have been a burden on
local communities, represented a passive defence from a basis
of limited control over the countryside. Below Singidunum
(Belgrade) the Danube was intensively fortified. A new city
Justinopolis was created in Dardania and the defences of Ulpianum, Naissus and Serdica were repaired. In the southern
Balkans 43 new forts were built and 50 existing ones repaired
in the provinces of Old and New Epirus, 46 in Macedonia and
a similar number in Thessaly. In spite of all these efforts,
according to Procopius in his hostile *Secret History* (18.20),
Illyricum was ravaged almost every year of Justinian's reign by
Huns and Slavs, causing many Roman casualties and so much
destruction that the place became another 'Scythian desert'.[18]

The migrations of the Slavs from the region of Poland began
early in the Christian era. By the fourth century they had
reached the old province of Dacia, where they were overrun
by the Huns. Early in the sixth century they moved across the
Danube in the direction of Epirus and Macedonia. By 536 they
had reached the Adriatic, in 548 Dyrrhachium, and in the
following years there are several reports of Slavs on the move
in Illyricum. Though hardly welcome, the newcomers were
not everywhere destructive raiders and made no challenge to
imperial authority. Some, it is true, were feared for their cruelty
and were said to leave behind a trail of corpses. Their weapons
were spears and the bow, sometimes using poisoned arrows.
They could cross major rivers but learned only later how to
take towns with ladders and machines. In the end it was the
dominance of the Turkic Avars in the Pannonian plain that
made the Slav raids such a threat to Illyricum during the later
decades of the sixth century, especially when the Avar khagan

[18] Procopius *Buildings* 4.1–4, V. Popović 1988 (Epirus Nova).

Baian captured Sirmium in 582 following a long siege. After some years of successful resistance Roman Illyricum finally disintegrated during the chaotic reign of Phocas (602–610), when large numbers of Slavs moved to occupy Macedonia and Thessaly. Most of mainland Greece was also overrun, and in 626 Avars and Slavs combined with Persia in an attack on Constantinople. In the West we learn from the *Letters* of Pope Gregory that Slavs were threatening Roman towns in Dalmatia, and in 611 they raided Istria. In or soon after 612 the Dalmatian cities of Salona, Narona, Doclea, Scardona, Risinium and Epidaurum were abandoned in favour of more protected places on the mainland or islands. By now the Slavs were free of Avar domination and began to form the groups from which the Slav states of the Middle Ages began to emerge.[19]

The earliest account of the Slavs who occupied Roman Illyricum was written by the emperor Constantine VII Porphyrogenitus, who died in 959. In his 'On Administering the Roman Empire', composed for his son Romanus, eight chapters describe the Slavs of Illyricum, with digressions on the early history of Croats and Serbs. He lists the surviving Roman communities along the coast, including Decatera (ancient Acruvium, modern Kotor), Ragusa (Dubrovnik), to which the inhabitants of Epidaurum had fled, Split (Aspalathos, Spalato), Diocletian's villa on the coast occupied by refugees from Salona, Tetrangourin (Tragurium, modern Trogir) and Diadora (Jader, modern Zadar), and on several islands in the Quarnero, Arbe (Rab), Vekla (Curictae, Krk) and Opsara (Osor). Constantine asserts that the settlement of Croats and Serbs had taken place with the acquiescence of the emperor Heraclius in the seventh century, as part of a scheme to expel the Avars, though most likely this was a later fabrication intended to bolster the claim of imperial authority over them. One modern theory holds that the two groups were not actually Slavs but perhaps a ruling minority of Iranian Sarmatian origin, similar to the Turkic

---

[19] Dvornik 1956, Toynbee 1973, 619–51, V. Popović 1978 (invasions), Kulišić 1979 (Slav paganism). During the siege a citizen of Sirmium wrote on a brick a prayer in Greek begging for God's deliverance from the Avars, Brunsmid 1893. Miletić 1989 (early Slav cemeteries in Bosnia-Hercegovina), Pasić 1975 (Vardar valley).

Bulgars, an alien elite later absorbed into the culture of their Slav subjects. Constantine's account of the Croats is a valuable primary source, listing eleven 'counties' (županias) and nine towns, of which three had been Roman centres, mainly in the south and near the Adriatic but, since it probably derives from a local Roman source, omits those communities of inland Dalmatia or Pannonia. The Serbs evidently arrived later and never reached the Adriatic, but are confined in their historic heartland of the upper Drina and its tributaries, Piva, Tara, Lim and Uvac, the upper Morava, Raška and Ibar. Between there and the Adriatic were the Zachlumi ('in behind the hills') who held the coast between Ragusa and the Neretva. Next to these on the south were the Terbuniotes of Trebinje in Popovo polje and the Kanalites of Konavle (near Dubrovnik). All three were connected with the Serbs and also are said to have settled there with the approval of Heraclius. Between these and the imperial territory around Dyrrhachium were Diocletiani, named from the then deserted city Dioclea (Doclea near Titograd). A reputation for piracy attached to the pagan Narentani, who controlled the coast north of the Neretva and most of the major islands.[20]

The new settlers did not strive to eradicate the existing Illyrian and Roman cultures, and several of their major settlements grew up on the sites of Roman cities. After more than three centuries of silence Latin-speaking communities begin to emerge, such as the 'road-travelling' Vlachs at the end of the tenth century, and several others are identified in medieval sources, Koutzovlachs, Morlachs, Cincars and Aroumani. Archaeological evidence has so far been unable to fill the gap between the end of Roman Illyricum and the tenth century. Few early Slav villages, with their hand-made pottery and cremation burials, have been identified in the Illyrian lands. Some Slavic material has been found on the sites of Roman cities and there are traces of an early settlement near Čapljina

---

[20] *Constantine Porphyrogenitus De Administrando Imperio*, ed. G. Moravcsik, trans. R. J. H. Jenkins, 2nd edn, Washington DC, 1967, and *Commentary* by R. J. H. Jenkins and others, London, 1962. The relevant chapters are 29–30 (Dalmatia), 31 (Croats), 32 (Serbs), 33 (Zachumli), 34 (Terbuniotes and Kanalites), 35 (Diocletiani) and 36 (Pagani or (N)arentani).

in the Neretva valley. It seems reasonable to assume that some of the local characteristics exhibited later by Slavs in the Illyrian lands were a consequence of assimilating existing local culture (see figure 36). The Illyrian heritage of the Adriatic Slavs is even today regularly invoked by Slovenes and Croats, while the Albanian claims to an Illyrian ancestry have encouraged Slavs to search for traces of their own Illyrian heritage. These include similarities in burial rites, stone-lined graves and the smashing of pottery; periodic redivision of land on the island Pag, similar to that reported for the pre-Roman Delmatae; use of a bread-making mould known in the Illyrian Iron Age; the tasselled Lika cap of the Japodes and the taste for tattooing which still survive in that area; and the possible descent of 'Mother Jana', forest goddess of the Balkan Slavs, from the Illyrian version of Silvanus. Medieval documents indicate the survival of Illyrian personal names, Licca from Licca/Licco, Batoia from Bato, Pletto from Plator, etc. In the mountainous areas the two medieval sources, the twelfth-century priest of Duklja (Dioclea) and Thomas the Archdeacon of Split, refer to the Svačičs (Snačičs), who were evidently of pre-Slav origin. The Illyrian contribution to Slav popular culture included several less easily documented examples: the 'circle' (kolo) dances of the southern Slavs which seem to resemble those on funeral monuments of the Roman era; the shepherd's panpipes, five pipes of unequal length clamped together, which appear on situlae and on some Roman reliefs of Silvanus; and some polyphonic musical patterns, confined to the Slavs of the Illyrian lands, which may be of ancient origin. Taken together, and there are probably several more examples which could be cited, they indicate a significant cultural inheritance but not necessarily an ethnic descent from Illyrians. In contrast a direct continuity from ancient Illyrians has been claimed, and contested, for the modern Albanians.[21]

Today's Albania occupies the ancient provinces of Praevalit-

---

[21] Slav fortresses: Burić 1987 (Bribir), Bosković, Mijović and Kovačević 1981 (Ulcinj). Illyrian survival: surveys in Benac 1969, Batović and Oštrić 1969, Brozović 1969 (language), Ljubinković 1969 (social organization and material culture), Stipčević 1977a, 72–6, 241–3 (music and dance), 261 note 110 (Svačičs), Suić 1967b, 103–4 (Pag), Rendić-Miočević 1949 (name survivals).

Figure 36 Early medieval stone relief with traditional native circles and Christian cross from near Sinj, Dalmatia

ana (in part) and Old and New Epirus. The condition of this region at the end of the Roman era is hard to assess, but there seems to have been a collapse of the inland towns which arose in the Hellenistic period, while the more secure coastal cities continued to enjoy a relatively prosperous existence. Some inland places were protected with the latest type of defences, including Scampis (Elbassan) on the Via Egnatia and Vig near Scodra. The damage caused by the passage of Alaric's Visigoths around AD 400 and Theodoric's Ostrogoths later in the same century may have been soon repaired. Their presence may have caused the building of several new hill-fortresses, such as Sarda overlooking the river Drin (see figures 37a and 37b). Dating of such places is not secure but the horseshoe-shaped towers and lack of brick in the construction point to a date after the fifth century AD. Around the same time the emperor Anastasius ensured the security of his native Dyrrhachium with a new perimeter of walls. Little is known of secular architecture, but several well-appointed Christian basilicas have been excavated. The provincial capital Scodra and Dyrrhachium were seats of the metropolitans, and there were bishops at Lissus, Doclea, Lychnidus (Ohrid), Scampis, Apollonia, Amantia, Byllis and Aulona. The population of this area were Latin-speaking provincials, in the interior mainly of Illyrian origin, but more cosmopolitan in the coastal towns. The demarcation between the areas of the Latin and Greek languages followed roughly the valley of the Shkumbin.[22]

The dispersal of Slavs in the southern Balkans following the unsuccessful siege of Thessalonica in 586 resulted in an occupation of Praevalitana and the region south of the Shkumbin, a distribution indicated by place-names of Slav origin. During the seventh and eighth centuries Dyrrhachium and the coast remained under imperial control but the old cities of Lissus and Scodra shrank to within their acropolis. The key evidence for the population of this period is the Komani-Kruja group of cemeteries (see figure 38a). Most are situated below fortresses and some have a church nearby. Their distribution

[22] Anamali 1986, V. Popović 1988; late cemeteries: Karaiskaj 1977–82 (Zgërdhesh, 3rd–4th cent.), Kurti 1976b (Mat valley).

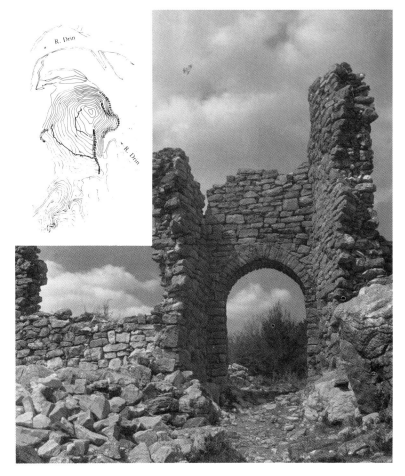

Figure 37 a) Plan of Sarda fortress, Albania
b) Gate of Sarda fortress

is centred on Dyrrhachium, and the general character of the
remains suggests communities that were town-based and Christian. In the opinion of several Albanian specialists these cemeteries represent evidence for a continuity between late Roman
Illyrians and the medieval Albanians. This view is contested by
Yugoslav scholars and the argument turns on the origins and
character of objects deposited with the burials. The graves,
made of rough stones sometimes with re-used brick, are mainly

Figure 38 a) Early medieval cemetery at Komani, near Shkodër, Albania, 7th–9th century AD

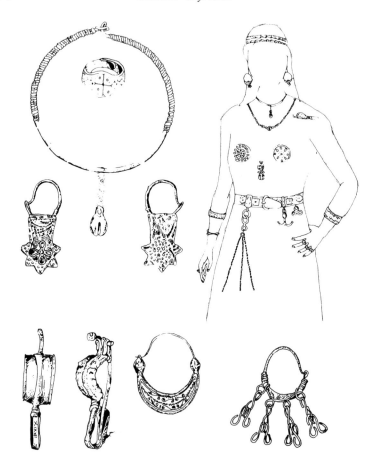

Figure 38 Continued
b) Ornaments and jewellery from Komani-Kruja burials, 7th–8th
century AD

orientated west–east, with the arms of some of the deceased
crossed on the chest in the Christian fashion. The plentiful
contents include pottery and glass, decorated in Byzantine style.
Jewellery includes filigree earrings, belt buckles, disc-brooches
with Christian ornament, small pectoral crosses and finger-
rings engraved with Greek words (see figures 38b and 38c).
Some of these objects were imports through Dyrrhachium but
others appear to be local imitation of Byzantine types, and are

Figure 38 Continued
c) Gold jewellery from Komani burials,
   6th–9th century AD

not paralleled elsewhere. Dating of many of the graves remains uncertain, while some contain several corpses, presumably from different generations. The cemeteries seem to have gone out of use by early in the ninth century, when the new military command (*Theme*) of Dyrrhachium came into existence.[23]

The Albanian case that the Komani-Kruja cemeteries represent a continuity of Illyrians rests on several arguments, notably the Illyrian character of the ornaments and the shapes of some grave-goods, hemispherical buttons, biconical beads,

[23] Anamali 1966, Prendi and Zheku 1983 (Lissus), Tatari 1984 (Durres), Mijović 1970 (Mijele near Lake of Shkodër), Andrea 1988 (Germenj), Dhima 1988 (skeletons), Spahiu 1985 (signet rings), Komata 1971b (medieval pottery). Critique of Albanian analysis: V. Popović 1984, 1988.

bracelets, the bronze hanging-fringes recalling Illyrian ornaments from the Mat valley. These comparisons are certainly valid, but the Albanian case is weakened by a highly improbable reconstruction of Illyrian history in this period. This makes the Illyrians recover their lost independence during the collapse of the later Roman Empire and reassert their ethnic identity through liberation from Greco-Roman dominance in material culture. This view regards the new fortifications in the area as measures against the independent Illyrians. Out of this population came the Arbëri of the tenth and eleventh centuries, represented by an early tumulus culture in southern Albania. The weakness of these arguments for an area where historical sources are non-existent seems obvious. There can surely be no doubt that the Komani-Kruja cemeteries indicate the survival of a non-Slav population between the sixth and ninth centuries, and their most likely identification seems to be with a Romanized population of Illyrian origin driven out by Slav settlements further north, the 'Romanoi' mentioned by Constantine Porphyrogenitus (*c*.32). This interpretation is supported by the concentration of Latin place-names around the Lake of Shkodër, in the Drin and Fan valleys and along the road from Lissus to Ulpiana in Kosovo, with some in the Black Drin and Mat valleys, a distribution limited on the south by the line of the Via Egnatia.[24]

The Albanian language, which belongs to the Indo-European group, has a distinctive vocabulary, morphology and phonetic rules which have engaged the attention of many philologists, of whom several have confidently proclaimed its origin from ancient Illyrian. In the Albanian vocabulary it is possible to detect something of the physical, social and economic conditions prevailing at the time of its formation, through the evidence of borrowing from other languages, including Latin and Slav. Those from the former relate to city-life, family

---

[24] Illyrian–Albanian continuity in material culture: Korkuti 1971, Vulpe 1976, Stipčević 1976 (symbols), Meksi 1976 (institutions), Gjergji 1971, 1976, Jubani 1970, Zozzi 1976 (dress and ornament), Tirtja 1976 (sun-worship), Sako 1976 (dance), Spahiu 1986 (ancient survivals in medieval Albanian cemeteries). Criticism of Yugoslav studies: Mirdita 1972, Buda 1982, but see now V. Popović 1988 (Romanized survival).

structure, agriculture, plants and fruits of the plains and marsh-lands. The smaller number of Slav loans relate to dwellings, agriculture and cattle-rearing. Plant names of Slav origin suggest that contacts took place when Albanians dwelt in the forest zone between 600 and 900 metres in altitude, while the words relating to the products of higher altitudes, including milk, are Albanian. This implies a pattern of seasonal movement between pastures, similar to that recorded for the Dalmatian Mavro-vlachs who journeyed to the Adriatic towns with cheese and wool to exchange for the invaluable salt. This pattern of existence explains the late entry of the Albanians in the historical record, during the years 1040 to 1080, when Arbanites are found serving in the imperial army. If the Komani-Kruja cemeteries represent a Romanized Christian population bordered by new Slav settlements on the north and south, then the ancestors of the historical Albanians were pastoral communities on the higher ground behind the plains. The tripartite linguistic division of the area has been recognized in some late medieval documents relating to the Shkodër region.[25]

We first learn of Albanians in their native land as the Arbanites of Arbanon in Anna Comnena's account (*Alexiad* 4) of the troubles in that region caused in the reign of her father Alexius I Comnenus (1081–1118) by the Normans. There seems to be no doubt that the root Alb- or Arb- is earlier than Shqip-, from which the modern name of the state (Shqipëria) derives, a name which appears only in the time of the Turkish invasions. We cannot be certain that the Arbanon of Anna Comnena is the same as Albanopolis of the Albani, a place located on the map of Ptolemy (3.12, 20) and also named on an ancient family epitaph at Scupi, which has been identified with the Zgërdhesh hill-fort near Kruja in northern Albania. Moreover, Arbanon is just as likely to be the name of a district – the plain of the Mat has been suggested – rather than a particular place. An indication of movement from higher altitudes in a much earlier period has been detected in the distribution of place-names

[25] Çabej 1958 (place-names), 1971, 1976, Anamali 1976a, Gjinari 1971, 1976, Luka 1977, Domi 1976 (Illyrian suffixes), Mansaku 1987 (early development of Illyrian), Katičić 1976a (Illyrian survival wider than Albanian), V. Popović 1988 (significance of loan-words in Albanian).

ending in -esh that appear to derive from the Latin -ensis or -esis, between the Shkumbin and the Mat, with a concentration between Elbassan and Kruja. This movement will have been another of the migrations from the hills similar to that which marked the Illyrians' entry into history at the beginning of the fourth century BC, and in that sense the migrants may be seen as their descendants. On the other hand, it is to be hoped that the unfortunate distortions which have marred outstanding progress in Albanian archaeology will soon be corrected. As new guide-books are demonstrating, the Albanian culture, as fascinating and varied as any in that quarter of Europe, is an inheritance from the several languages, religions and ethnic groups known to have inhabited the region since prehistoric times, among whom were the Illyrians.[26]

---

[26] Stadtmüller 1966, Anamali 1971, V. Popović 1988, Koch 1989 (guide-book).

Bibliography

Note: Publications in Serbocroat and Albanian are listed by titles of appended précis or summary.

Abramić, M., 1937. 'Über Darstellungen der Illyrier auf antiken Denkmälern', *Časopis za zgodovino in narodopisije* (Maribor) 32, 7–19.

Abramić, M., and Colnago, A., 1909. 'Untersuchungen in Norddalmatien', *JÖAI* 12, Beiblatt 12–112.

Alexander, J., 1965. 'The spectacle fibulae of southern Europe', *AJA* 69, 7–23.

——1972. *Jugoslavia before the Roman Conquest*, London.

Alföldy, G., 1961. 'Die Stellung der Frau in der Gesellschaft der Liburner', *AAnt. Hung.* 9, 307–19.

——1963. 'Cognatio Nantania: zur Struktur der Sippengesellschaft der Liburner', *AAnt. Hung.* 11, 81–7.

——1964a. 'Die Namengebung der Urbevölkerung in der römischen Provinz Dalmatia', *BzN* 15, 55–104.

——1964b. 'Des Territoires occupés par les Scordisques', *AAnt. Hung.* 12, 107–27.

——1965. *Bevölkerung und Gesellschaft der römischen Provinz Dalmatien*, Budapest.

——1966. 'Taurisci und Norici', *Historia* 15, 224–41.

——1969. *Die Personennamen in der römischen Provinz Dalmatia*, Heidelberg (*BzN* Beiheft 4).

——1974. *Noricum*, London.

Anamali, S., 1966. 'Le problème de la civilisation haute-médiévale albanaise à la lumière des nouvelles découvertes archéologiques', *SA* 3, 199–211.

——1970. 'Les villes de Dyrrhachion et d'Apollonie et leurs rapports avec les Illyriens', *SA* 7: 2, 89–98.

——1971. 'De la civilisation haute-médiévale albanaise', in Korkuti 1971, 193–9.

——1972. 'Amantie', *Iliria* 2, 67–148.

——1975. 'Podgradec', *Iliria* 3, 481–6.

——1976a. 'Des Illyriens aux Albanais (les anciens Albanais)', *Iliria* 5, 23–40.

——1976b. 'Données epigraphiques sur quelques cités de l'Illyrie du sud', *Iliria* 6, 131–7.

——1982. 'Les Illyriens et les villes de l'Illyrie du sud dans les inscriptions de la Grèce', *Iliria* 12: 1, 10–14.

——1985. 'Des Illyriens aux Albanais', *Iliria* 15: 1, 219–27.

——1986. 'Processus de transformation dans la région méridionale illyrienne aux Ier–IVe siècles', *Iliria* 16: 1, 5–41.

——1987. 'L'insurrection illyrienne des années 6–9 de n. ère', *Iliria* 17: 1, 5–23.

——1988. 'Deux ateliers de lampes estampillées à Byllis', *Iliria* 18: 1, 216–19.

Andrea, Z., 1975. 'Barç (Korcë)', *Iliria* 3, 415–20.

——1976a. 'La civilisation tumulaire du bassin de Korcë et sa place dans les Balkans du sud-est', *Iliria* 4, 133–55.

——1976b. 'Les tumuli de Kuç i Zi', *Iliria* 6, 165–233.

——1977–8. 'Les tumuli de Kuç i Zi', *Iliria* 7–8, 127–55.

——1985. 'A propos de la genèse et de la continuité de la culture de Mat à l'époque du Bronze', *Iliria* 15: 2, 163–74.

——1988. 'Tombes de périodes antique et médiévale à Germenj (distr. de Lushnje)', *Iliria* 18: 1, 169–97.

Andreou, I., 1985. (Illyrian helmet in Ioannina University), *Iliria* 15: 2, 281–4.

Archaeological Museum Pula 1986a. *Il movimento illirico in Croazia*, Catalogue 22, Pula.

——1986b. *Shipping and Seamanship in Istria in Classical Times*, Catalogue 23, Pula.

Arheološka Najdišča Slovenije 1975. (Archaeological Sites in Slovenia), SAZU (Arh. Inst.), Ljubljana.

Baçe, A., 1971. 'La ville fortifiée de Berat (Antipatreia)', *Monumentet* 2, 43–62.

——1974. 'La ville fortifiée de Karine', *Monumentet* 7–8, 25–54.

——1975. 'Les centres fortifiés du golfe de Vlore dans l'antiquité', *Monumentet* 10, 5–20.

——1979. 'Aperçu sur l'architecture des fortifications antiques dans nos pays', *Monumentet* 17, 5–45.

——1984. 'Aperçu sur la foi et l'architecture de culte chez les Illyriens', *Monumentet* 1984: 2, 5–32.

——1986. 'La structure urbaine des villes de l'Illyrie dans les années 168 av. n. ère – 212 de n. ère', *Iliria* 16: 1, 215–21.

Baçe, A., and Bushati, V., 1989. 'Aperçu sur l'habitation préhistorique et antique en Illyrie et en Epire', *Monumentet* 37: 1, 5–48.

Baçe, A., and Ceka, N., 1981. 'Les Stoas de la période urbaine illyrienne', *Monumentet* 22: 2, 5–54.

Bačić, B., 1970. 'Beiträge zur Kenntnis der urgeschichtlichen Burgfortifikation in Istrien', in Mirosavljević et al. 1970, 215–22.

Bakhuizen, S., 1986. 'Between Illyrians and Greeks: the cities of Epidamnos and Apollonia', *Iliria* 16: 1, 165–77.

——1987. 'The continent and the sea: notes on Greek activities in Ionic and Adriatic waters', in Cabanes 1987, 115–17.

Barfield, L., 1971. *Northern Italy before Rome*, London.

Bartosiwicz, L., 1985. 'Most na Soči: a preliminary faunal analysis at the Hallstatt period settlement', *AV* 36, 107–30.

Basler, D., 1971. 'Crvena Stijena, Petrovići, près de Nikšić', in Novak et al. 1971b, 145–6.

——1972. 'The Necropolis of Vele Ledine at Gostilj (Lower Zeta)', *WMBHL* 2, 5–125.

——1983. 'Palaeolitische Kulturen in der adriatischen Region Jugoslawiens', *GZMS* 38, 1–63.

Basler, D., Benac, A., Malez, M., Brunnacker, K., and Pamić, J., 1975. *Crvena Stijena*, Nikšić.

Batović, Š., 1958, 'Plattenfibel aus Kroatien (Hrvatska)', *Germania* 36: 3–4, 361–72.

——1965. 'Die Eisenzeit auf dem Gebiet des illyrischen Stammes der Liburnen', *AI* 6, 55–70.

——1968. 'Investigation of the Illyrian settlement at Radovin', *Diadora* 4, 53–74.

——1970. 'Excavation in (the) Liburnian settlement at Nin, 1969', *Diadora* 5, 33–48.

——1971a. 'Barice, Smilčić, près de Zadar: site néolithique', in Novak et al. 1971b, 83–7.

——1971b. 'Beretinova Gradina, Radovin, près de Zadar, site Liburne', in Novak et al. 1971b, 88–90.

——1973. 'Les vestiges préhistoriques sur l'archipel de Zadar', *Diadora* 6, 5–165.

——1974. 'Depôt de Jagodnja dans le cadre de la dernière phase de la culture liburnienne', *Diadora* 7, 159–245.

——1976a. 'Les problèmes de néolithique sur la côte est de l'Adriatique', Batović 1976d, 17–24.

——1976b. 'Probleme der Kultur der Eisenzeit an der östlichen Adriaküste', Batović 1976d, 89–112.

——1976c. 'Le relazioni culturali tra le sponde adriatiche nell'età del ferro', in Suić 1976b, 11–93.

——(ed.) 1976d. *Problèmes archéologiques de la côte Yougoslave de l'Adriatique, Actes (Materijali) XII: IXe congrès des archéologues Yougoslaves, Zadar 1972*, Zadar.

——1978. 'Bribir dans la préhistoire', in Rapanić 1978b, 9–23.

——1980a. 'L'eta del bronzo recente sulla costa orientale dell'Adriatico', *GCBI* XVIII/16, 21–62.

——1980b. 'Researches in the prehistory of Bribir', *Diadora* 9, 55–81.

——1984. 'Contributions aux études de la céramique corinthienne sur la côte orientale de l'Adriatique', *VAHD* 77, 37–62.

Batović, S., and Oštrić, O., 1969. 'Spuren des illyrischen Kulturerbes in unserer Volkskultur des Küstenraumes', in Benac 1969, 245–82.

Beaumont, R., 1936. 'Greek influence in the Adriatic before the fourth century BC', *JHS* 61, 159–204.

——1952. 'Corinth, Ambracia, Apollonia', *JHS* 72, 62–73.

Beck Managetta, G., 1897. 'Die botanischen Objekte aus dem Pfahlbaue von Ripač', *WMBH* 5, 114–23.

Benac, A., 1951. 'La nourriture des habitants préhistoriques de Bosnie et Herzegovine', *GZMS* 6, 271–9.

—— (ed.) 1964. *Vorillyrier, Protoillyrier und Urillyrier: symposium sur la délimitation territoriale et chronologique des Illyriens à l'époque préhistorique 15 et 16 mai 1964*, Sarajevo.

—— (ed.) 1967. *Symposium sur les Illyriens à l'époque antique, 10–12 mai 1966*, ANUBiH Publications Speciales V/2, Sarajevo.

—— (ed.) 1969. *Symposium: éléments ethniques preslaves dans les Balkans dans l'ethnogénie des Slaves du Sud, 24–26 Octobre 1968, Mostar*, ANUBiH CBI Publications Speciales XII/4, Sarajevo.

——1971a. 'Lisičići près de Konjic, site néolithique', in Novak et al. 1971, 60–3.

——1971b. 'Obre, près de Kakanj', in Novak et al. 1971, 66–9.

——1971c. 'Varos, site de la culture de Vinča', in Novak et al. 1971, 71–3.

——1971d. 'Zečovi, près de Prijedor: site préhistorique à plusières couches', in Novak et al. 1971, 78–81.

——1971e. 'Obre II: neolithic settlement of the Butmir group', *GZMS* 26, 5–300.

——1973. 'Obre I: neolithic settlement of the Starčevo and Kakanj culture', *GZMS* 27–8, 5–171.

—— (ed.) 1975a. *Agglomérations fortifiées illyriennes: colloque international, Mostar, 24–26 Octobre 1974*, ANUBiH CBI Publications Spéciales XXIV/6, Sarajevo.

——1975b. 'Quelques caractéristiques des agglomérations fortifiées dans la région des Delmates', in Benac 1975a, 81–91.

——1976 (1972). 'Apport à l'étude des processus ethnogénétiques et la délimitation territoriale des tribus illyriennes', *Iliria* 4, 105–12 [= *SA* 9, 173–85].

——1980. 'Problème de rétardation à l'époque transitoire du Néolithique à l'Age des Métaux dans le nord-ouest Balkans', *Diadora* 9, 45–54.

—— (ed.) 1984a. *Symposium: culture spirituelle des Illyriens (Herceg-Novi, 4–6 Nov. 1982)*, ANUBiH, CBI Publications Speciales LXVII/11, Sarajevo.

——1984b. 'Le culte des mortes dans la région illyrienne à l'époque préhistorique', in Benac 1984a, 133–52.

—— (ed.) 1985. *Agglomérations fortifiées illyriennes: gradinas des Delmates dans le polje de Duvno, Buško blato, et les poljes de Livno et Glamoč*, ANUBiH CBI Monographies LX/4, Sarajevo.

——1986. *Prehistoric Tumuli in Kupreško Polje*, ANUBiH CBI Monographies LXIV/5, Sarajevo.

——1987. Review of Islami et al. 1985, *CBI* XXV/23, 219–23.

——1988. 'Les Illyriens en Apulie', *GCBI* XXVI/24, 43–67.

——1990. 'Recently excavated Bronze Age tumuli in the Kupreško polje, Bosnia, Yugoslavia', *Antiquity* 64, 327–33.

Benac, A., and Čović, B., 1956. *Glasinac, 1: Bronzezeit*, Sarajevo.

——1957. *Glasinac, 2: Eisenzeit*, Sarajevo.

Benac, A., et al. (eds.), 1979a. *Praistorija Jugoslavenskih Zemalja I: Paleolitsko i Mezolitsko Doba*, ANUBiH, CBI, Sarajevo.

——1979b. *Praistorija Jugoslavenskih Zemalja II: Neolitsko Doba*, ANUBiH, CBI, Sarajevo.

——1979c. *Praistorija Jugoslavenskih Zemalja III: Eneolitsko Doba*, ANUBiH, CBI, Sarajevo.

——1983. *Praistorija Jugoslavenskih Zemalja IV: Bronzano Doba*, ANUBiH, CBI, Sarajevo.

——1987a. *Praistorija Jugoslavenskih Zemalja V: Želježno Doba*, ANUBiH, CBI, Sarajevo.

Bereti, V., 1977–8. 'Les fouilles à Triport', *Iliria* 7–8, 285–92.

——1985. 'Une agglomération illyrienne à Triport de Vlore', *Iliria* 15: 2, 313–20.

——1988. 'Coupes antiques découvertes dans le site de Triport', *Iliria* 18: 2, 105–19.

Bintliff, J., and Gaffney, V., 1988. 'The Ager Pharensis/Hvar project 1987', in Chapman et al. 1988, 151–75.

Blavatsky, V., 1966. 'Fondation de l'Apollonie illyrienne', *VAHD* 68, 143–6.

——1971. 'Apollonia et les Illyriens (avant 229 av. notre ère)', in Novak et al. 1971, 235–9.

Boardman, J., and Hammond, N. G. L. (eds.), 1982. *The Expansion of the Greek World, Eighth to Sixth Centuries* BC, Cambridge Ancient History, 2nd edn, vol. III, pt. 3, Cambridge.

Boardman, J., Edwards, I. E. S., Hammond, N. G. L., and Sollberger, E. (eds.), 1982. *The Prehistory of the Balkans; and the Middle East and the Aegean World, Tenth to Eight Centuries BC*, Cambridge Ancient History, 2nd edn, vol. III, pt. 1, Cambridge.

Bodinaku, N., 1975. 'Pazhok (Elbassan)', *Iliria* 3, 407–14.

——1982. 'La nécropole tumulaire de Pazhok (Fouilles de 1973)', *Iliria* 12: 1, 49–101.

——1984. 'Fibules "en archet" de bronze de la période du fer ancien', *Iliria* 14: 2, 47–58.

Boessneck, J., and Stork, M., 1972. 'Tierknochenfunde aus einer Siedlung des 9/8 Jahrhunderts v. Chr. in Bosnien-Herzegowina', *WMBHL* 2, 127–60.

Bojanovski, I., 1974. *Système routier de Dolabella dans la province romaine de Dalmatie*, ANUBiH CBI Monographies XLVII/2, Sarajevo.

——1975. 'Nouvelle confirmation épigraphique de Delminium dans le champ de Duvno', *WMBHL* 5, 41–56.

——1977–8. 'Nouveaux monuments représentant la communauté cultuelle de Silvain, provenant de Glamočko polje', *VAMZ* 9–10, 115–32.

——1978a. 'Contributions à la topographie des communications et des agglomérations romaines et préromaines dans la province romaine de Dalmatia, II: La voie préhistorique et romaine Narona-plaine de Sarajevo avec les agglomérations limitrophes', *GCBI* XVII/15, 51–125.

——1978b. 'Récentes trouvailles épigraphiques romaines provenant de la plaine de Glamoč', *GZMS* 33, 115–26.

——1979. 'Refuge tard-antique à Gornje Vrbljani près de Ključ (Bosnie occidentale)', *GZMS* 34, 105–26.

——1988. *Bosnie et Herzegovine à l'époque antique*, ANUBiH CBI Monographies LXVI/6, Sarajevo.

Bolta, L., 1966. 'Restes materiels des celtes aux environs de Celje', *AV* 17, 375–89.

Bonačić-Mandić, M., 1987. 'The coins of Faros from the Machiedo Collection in the Archaeological Museum of Split', *AV* 38, 393–405.

Bosković, D., Mijović, P., and Kovačević, M., 1981. *Ulcinj* I, Beograd (Institute of Archaeology Monographs 16).

Bosworth, A., 1981. 'The location of "Pellion" (Arrian, *Anabasis* i 5.5)', in Dell 1981, 87–97.

Bousquet, J., 1974. 'Une épigramme funéraire grecque de Dardanie', *ŽA* 24, 255–7.

Bouzek, J., 1974. 'Macedonian Bronzes: their origins, distribution and relation to other cultural groups of the Early Iron Age', *Památky Arheologické* LXV: 2, 278–341.

Božić, D., 1981a. 'Relative Chronologie der jüngeren Eisenzeit im Jugoslawischen Donauraum', *AV* 32, 315–47.

——1981b. 'Die spätlateinzeitlichen Astralgurtel vom Typ Beograd', *Starinar* 32, 47–56.

Braccesi, L., 1977. *Grecità Adriatica: un capitolo della colonizzazione greca in occidente*, 2nd edn, Bologna.

Brodar, S. and Brodar, M., 1983. *Die Höhle Potočka Zijalka: eine hochalpine Aurignacjägerstation*, Ljubljana (Institute of Archaeology vol. 13).

Brozović, D., 1969. 'L'installation des slaves et leurs contacts avec les autochthones à la lumière des recherches linguistiques', in Benac 1969, 129–40.

Brukner, B., 1971. 'Gomolava à Hrtkovci, site préhistorique à plusières couches: recherches et résultats', in Novak et al. 1971, 175–6.

Brukner, B., Jovanović, B., and Tasić, N., 1974. *Vojvodina in Prehistory*, Novi Sad (Society of Archaeology of Yugoslavia).

Brunšmid, J., 1893. 'Ein griechische Ziegelinschrift aus Sirmium', Eranos Vindobonensis, Wien, 331–3.

Brušić, Z., 1976. 'Agglomérations fortifiées ("Gradina") dans la région de Šibenik', in Batović 1976d, 113–26.

——1978. 'Trouvailles préhistoriques et de la haute antiquité dans les environs de Šibenik', in Rapanić 1978b, 25–34.

——1988. 'Hellenistic relief pottery in Liburnia', *Diadora* 10, 19–63.

Buda, A., 1976. 'Les Illyriens du sud: un problème de l'historiographie', *Iliria* 4, 39–53.

——1982. 'L'ethnogenèse du peuple albanais à la lumière de l'histoire', *SH* 36 (19): 3, 169–89.

—— (ed.), 1984. *Problems of the Formation of the Albanian People, their Language and Culture*, Tirana.

Budina, D., 1971. 'L'appartenance ethnique illyrienne des tribus épirotes', in Korkuti et al. 1971, 111–29.

——1976. 'Oricum: à la lumière des données archéologiques', in Suić 1976b, 255–63.

——1985. 'Le place et le rôle d'Antigonée dans la vallée du Drinos', *Iliria* 15: 1, 160–5.

Buonopane, A., 1980. 'Un cippo liburnico conservato presso il museo archeologico al Teatro Romano di Verona', *VAHD* 74, 47–54.

Burić, T., et al. 1987. *Bribir in the Middle Ages*, Split (Museum of Croatia: Archaeological Monuments).

Burton, R. F., 1874. 'Notes on the castellieri or prehistoric ruins of the Istrian peninsula', *Anthropologia* 1, London Anthropological Society.

Cabanes, P., 1976. *L'Épire de la mort de Pyrrhos à la conquête romaine (272–167)*, Paris.

—1986. 'Les modifications territoriales et politiques en Illyrie méridionale et en Épire, au IIIe siècle et dans la première moitié du IIe siècle av. n. ère', *Iliria* 16: 1, 75–99.

—(ed.) 1987. *L'Illyrie méridionale et l'Épire dans l'antiquité: actes du Colloque international de Clermont-Ferrand (22–25 octobre 1984)*, Clermont-Ferrand.

—1988a. *Les Illyriens de Bardylis à Genthios IV–II siècles avant J.-C.* (Regards sur l'histoire), Paris.

—1988b. 'Le développement des villes en Illyrie méridionale à partir du IVe siècle avant J.-C.', *Bulletin de la Société nationale des Antiquaires de France* (8 juin), 198–221.

—1988c. 'Recherches Archéologiques en Albanie 1945–86', *Rev. Arch.* 1986: 1, 107–42.

Çabej, E., 1958. 'Le problème de l'autochtonie des Albanais à la lumière des noms de lieux', *BUST* 1958: 2, 54–66.

—1971. 'L'Illyrien et l'Albanais', in Korkuti et al. 1971b, 41–52.

—1976. 'Le problème du territoire de la formation de la langue albanaise', *Iliria* 5, 7–22.

Čače, S., 1976. 'Les problèmes de la répartition et de la stratigraphie des toponymes préromaines et les recherches archéologiques', in Batović 1976d, 133–47.

—1988. 'Colentum insula (Plinio Nat. Hist. 3, 140)', *Diadora* 10, 65–72.

Čače, S., and Jurić, R., 1975. 'Notes sur les monuments archéologiques des environs de Metković', *Diadora* 8, 149–65.

Cambi, N., 1968. 'Silvanus-Attis: an example of cult syncretism', *Diadora* 4, 131–42.

—1975. 'Sarcophages antiques de la Lika', in Rapanić 1975, 75–83.

—1980. 'Venus Anzotica of Aenona', *Diadora* 8, 273–88.

—1984. 'Monuments sepulchraux du caractère anthropomorphe chez les Illyriens', in Benac 1984a, 105–18.

Cambi, N., Kirigin, B., and Marin, E., 1981. 'Recent archaeological excavations of Hellenistic necropolis of ancient Issa (1976 and 1979): preliminary report', *VAHD* 75, 63–83.

Ceka, H., 1971. 'Le trésor numismatique de Jubicë (Koplik-Shkodër)', *Iliria* 1, 83–103.

—1972a. *Questions de numismatique illyrienne avec un catalogue des monnaies d'Apollonie et de Durrhachium*, Tirana.

—1972b. 'Le trésor numismatique de Bakërr (Fieri)', *SA* 9: 1, 49–68.

—1976a. 'À propos de certaines questions de l'histoire des Illyriens à la lumière des données numismatiques', *Iliria* 4, 289–93.

——1976b. 'Le buste du roi Genthius ou une figure de mythologie illyrienne?', *Iliria* 6, 143–7.

——1976c. 'Les drachmes faux et imités de Dyrrhachium et d'Apollonie', in Suić 1976b, 309–12.

——1984. 'Réflexions sur la géographie historique de l'Illyrie méridionale', *Iliria* 14, 1, 15–26.

Ceka, N., 1970. 'La place et le rôle des Parthins dans l'Illyrie méridionale dans les siècles III–I avant notre ère', in Kostallari et al. 1970: 2, 421–7.

——1972. 'La ville illyrienne de la Basse-Selcë', *Iliria* 2, 167–215.

——1975a. 'Les constructions sépulchrales des cités illyriennes', *Monumentet* 9, 35–53.

——1975b. 'Les centres fortifiés des Amantins', *Monumentet* 10, 21–62.

——1975c. 'Traits de la civilisation urbaine illyrienne', in Benac 1975a, 137–48.

——1976. 'Les tombes monumentales de la Basse-Selcë', *Iliria* 4, 367–79.

——1977–8. 'Agglomérations protourbaines d'Illyrie du Sud', *Iliria*, 7–8, 249–62.

——1982. 'Timbres antiques trouvés dans la contrée entre Aous et Genusus', *Iliria* 12, 103–30.

——1983. 'La naissance de la vie urbaine chez les Illyriens du Sud', *Iliria* 13: 2, 135–92.

——1984. 'Le Koinon des Bylliones', *Iliria* 14: 2, 79–89.

——1985a. 'Les fortifications préhistoriques illyriens: les anciennes fortifications (l'époque néolithique, enéolithique et celle du bronze)', *Monumentet* 1985: 1, 27–58.

——1985b. 'La civilisation protourbaine illyrienne', *Iliria* 15: 1, 111–50.

——1985c. 'Aperçu sur le développement de la vie urbaine chez les Illyriens du Sud', *Iliria* 15: 2, 137–61.

——1986. 'Les fortifications préhistoriques illyriennes II: Les fortifications de la période protourbaine', *Monumentet* 31–2: 1, 49–84.

——1987a. 'Le Koinon des Bylliones', in Cabanes 1987, 135–49.

——1987b. 'Inscriptions Bylliones', *Iliria* 17: 2, 49–21.

——1987c. 'L'architecture de l'agglomération illyrienne de Margël-liç', *Monumentet* 33–4, 5–25.

Ceka, N., and Papajani, L., 1971. 'La route de la vallée du Shkumbin dans l'antiquité', *Monumentet* 1: 1, 44–59.

Cermanović-Kuzmanović, A., 1973. 'Die römisch-illyrischen Skulpturen aus Komini', *Antike Welt* 4: 2, 2–9.

——1978. 'Die römisch-illyrische Skulptur aus Komini', ŽA 28, 325–30.

——1980. 'Vorrömische Elemente in der Kultur des municipiums S . . . im Dorfe Komini', ŽA 30, 227–32.

Cermanović-Kuzmanović, A., Srejović, D., and Marković, C., 1972. *Necropoles romaines à Komini près de Pljevlja (Municipium S. . .)*, Inv. Arch. Jug. (fasc. 15), Y139–148.

Cermanović-Kuzmanović, A., Srejović, D., and Velimirović-Žižić, O., 1975. *The Roman Cemetery at Doclea*, Cetinje.

Cerova, Y., 1987. 'La forteresse de Qafa dans la région de Sulova', *Iliria* 17: 2, 155–85.

Chapman, J., and Shiel, R., 1988. 'The Neothermal Dalmatia project: archaeological survey results', in Chapman, Bintliff, Gaffney and Slapšak 1988, 1–30.

Chapman, J. C., Shiel, R. S., and Batović, S., 1987. 'Settlement patterns and land-use in Neothermal Dalmatia', *JFA* 14: 2, 127–46.

Chapman, J. C., Bintliff, J., Gaffney, V. and Slapšak, B., 1988. *Recent Developments in Yugoslav Archaeology*, BAR International Series 431, Oxford.

Ciglenečki, S., 1987. *Hohenbefestigungen aus der Zeit vom 3. bis 6. Jh. im Ostalpenraum*, Ljubljana (SAZU Inst. Arch.).

Cimochowski, W., 1976 (1973). 'Die sprachliche Stellung des Balkanillyrischen im Kreise der indogermanischen Sprachen', *Iliria* 5, 49–59 [= *SA* 10: 1, 137–53].

Čović, B., 1961–2. 'Eisenzeitgräber aus Crvenica bei Duvno', *VAHD* 63–4, 25–8.

——1962. 'Die Wallburgsiedlung auf der Kekica glavica', *GZMS* 17, 41–61.

——1971a. 'Gornja Tuzla', in Novak et al. 1971, 57–8.

——1971b. 'Pod près de Bugojno, site préhistorique à plusières couches', in Novak et al. 1971, 69–70.

——1975a. 'Die Befestigungen und befestigte Siedlungen des Glasinacer Gebietes', in Benac 1975a, 93–101.

——1975b. 'Pod bei Bugojno, eine befestigte Siedlung der Bronze und Eisenzeit in Zentralbosnien', in Benac 1975a, 121–9.

——1975c. 'Fund prähistorischen Schmucks aus Otok (Vitina)', *WMBHL* 5, 5–17.

——1975d. 'Zwei spezifischer Typen der westbalkanischen Bogenfibel', *WMBHL* 5, 19–39.

——1977. 'Velika Gradina im Dorf Varvara', *GZMS* 32, 5–175.

——1979. 'Fürstengräber des Gebietes von Glasinac', *Rites d'inhumation chez les Illyriens*, Beograd, 143–69.

——1980a. 'La prima e media età del bronzo sulle coste orientali dell'Adriatico e sul suo retroterra', *GCBI* XVIII/16, 5–20.

——1980b. 'Die Anfänge der Eisenmetallurgie im nordwestlichen Balkan', *GCBI* XVIII/16, 63–79.

——1980–1. 'Einige Bemerkungen zur Chronologie des Bronzezeitalters des Glasinac Gebiets', *GZMS* 35–6, 99–140.

——1984a. 'Das prähistorische Bergbauwesen und die Metallurgie in Bosnien und der Herzegovina', *GCBI* XXII/20, 111–44.

——1984b. 'Die Kunst der Spätbronze- und älteren Eisenzeit an der östlichen Adriaküste und in deren Hinterland', in Benac 1984a, 7–40.

Čović, B., and Gabrovec, S., 1971. 'Âge du fer', in Novak et al. 1971, 325–49.

Čremošnik, I., 1957.'Les symboles populaires sur les monuments romains dans nos régions', *GZMS* 12, 217–34.

——1963. 'Trachtendarstellungen auf römischen Denkmälern in Bosnien und der Herzegowina', *GZMS* 18, 103–25.

——1964. 'Die einheimische Tracht Norikums, Pannoniens und ihrer Vorbilder', *Latomus* 23, 760–73.

——1968. 'Die Darstellungen des 'orans' auf römischen Denkmälern in Jugoslawien', *AV* 19, 149–55.

Črnobrnja, N., 1983. 'Types of Scordiscan minimi in the collection of the Museum of the City of Belgrade', *AI* 20–1, 89–90.

Crossland, R. A., 1982. 'Linguistic problems of the Balkan area in the late prehistoric and early classical periods', in Boardman, Edwards, Hammond and Sollberger 1982, 834–49.

Crossland, R. A., and Birchall, A., (eds.) 1973. *Bronze Age Migrations in the Aegean: archaeological and linguistic problems in Greek prehistory*, London.

Ćus-Rukonić, J., 1980–1. 'Alcuni reperti preistorici nella collezione archeologica di Ossero', *Histria Archaeologica* (Pula) 11–12, 5–15.

Cvetković-Tomasević, G., 1983. 'Ulpiana, fouilles archéologiques au centre et dans la partie méridionale de la ville antique', *Saopštena* 15, 67–94.

Daicoviciu, C., 1958. 'Les "castella Dalmatarum" de Dacie', *Dacia* 2, 259–66.

D'Andria, F., 1986. 'Nuovi sulle relazioni tra gli Illiri e le popolazioni dell'Italia meridionale', *Iliria* 16: 1, 43–55.

Dautaj, B., 1972 (1965). 'La cité illyrienne de Dimale', *Iliria* 2, 149–65 [= *SA* 2: 1, 65–71].

——1976a. 'Dimale à la lumière des données archéologiques', *Iliria* 4, 385–409.

——1976b. 'Aspects de la vie économique à Dimal', *Iliria* 6, 149–63.

——1984a. 'Données numismatiques de Dimal', *Iliria* 14: 1, 131–69.

——1984b. 'Les stoas de Dimale', *Monumentet* 1984: 2, 33–56.

——1986. 'L'organisation politique et sociale de la Koine de Dimale durant les III–II siècles av. n. ère', *Iliria* 16: 1, 101–11.

Dautova-Ruševljan, V., 1975. 'Excavations to protect underwater deposit of amphorae on island Rab', *Diadora* 8, 89–102.

Degmedžić, I., 1967. 'Das Nord- und Ostgebiet der Illyrier', in Benac 1967, 55–61 [= *VAMZ* 3/1968, 53–62].

Degrassi, A., 1970. 'Culti dell'Istria preromana e romana', in Miro-savljević et al. 1970, 615–32.

Dell, H., 1967a. 'Antigonus III and Rome', *Classical Philology* (Chicago) 62, 94–103.

——1967b. 'The origin and nature of Illyrian piracy', *Historia* 16, 344–58.

——1970a. 'Demetrius of Pharus and the Istrian war', *Historia* 19, 30–8.

——1970b. 'The western frontier of the Macedonian monarchy', in Laourdas and Makaronas 1970, 115–26.

——1977. 'Macedonia and Rome: the Illyrian question in the early second century BC', *Ancient Macedonia* II, Thessaloniki, 305–15.

—— (ed.) 1981. *Ancient Macedonian Studies in Honour of Charles F. Edson*, Thessaloniki.

Deniaux, E., 1988. 'Ciceron et la protection des cités de l'Illyrie du sud et d'Épire (Dyrrachium et Buthrote)', *Iliria* 18: 2, 143–55.

Dhima, A., 1982. 'Un crâne illyrien découvert à Liqeti (Skraper)', *Iliria* 12: 2, 233–7.

——1983. 'Notes anthropologiques sur la formation du peuple albanais', *Iliria* 13: 1, 251–60.

——1985a. 'Materiels squelettiques de la necropole de Dyrrachium', *Iliria* 15: 1, 245–70.

——1985b. 'Aperçu sur les traits anthropologiques des Illyriens', *Iliria* 15: 2, 292–301.

——1987. 'Matériaux ostéologiques découverts au tumulus de Rapcka', *Iliria* 17: 2, 123–54.

——1988. 'Recherches anthropologiques sur le cimetière de Koman', *Iliria* 18: 2, 177–211.

Dibra, M., 1981. 'Un dépôt d'instruments de travail illyriens du village Melgush dans le district de Shkodra', *Iliria* 11: 1, 235–8.

Djuknić, M., and Jovanović, B., 1966a. *Illyrian Princely Necropolis at Atenica*, Čačak (National Museum).

——1966b. 'Illyrian princely tombs in western Serbia', *Archaeology* (Boston, Mass.) 19: 1, 43–51.

Djurić, N., Glišić, J., and Todorović, J., 1975. *Romaja: the Prehistoric Necropolis*, Prizren and Beograd (Dissertations and Monographs 17).

Dobruna-Salihu, E., 1982. 'La typologie des monuments sépulchraux de la période romaine en Kosovo', *Iliria* 12: 2, 197–232.

——1987. 'Les stèles sépulchrales de l'époque romaine dans le terri-toire du Kosovo: architectonique et plastique', *AV* 38, 193–205.

Domi, M., 1976 (1973). 'Suffixes illyriens en Albanais: concordances et parallelismes', *Iliria* 5, 93–8 [= *SA* 10: 1, 127–35].

——1983. 'Problèmes de l'histoire de la formation de la langue albanaise, résultats et tâches', *Iliria* 13: 1, 5–38.

Drechsler-Bižić, R., 1951. 'Boucles préhistoriques de Bosnie et Herzegovine', *GZMS* 6, 281–300.

——1958. 'Die Siedlung und die Gräber der vorgeschichtlichen Iapoden in Vrebac', *VAMZ* 1, 35–60.

——1961. 'Ergebnisse der in den Jahren 1955/56 durchgeführten Ausgrabungen in der japodischen Nekropole von Kompolje', *VAMZ* 2, 67–114.

——1966. 'Les tombes des Japodes préhistoriques a Kompolje', *Inv. Arch.* Y79–Y88.

——1968. 'Japodische Kappen und Kopfbedeckungen', *VAMZ* 3, 29–51.

——1970. 'Ein latènezeitliches Grab aus Trošmarija', in Mirosavljević et al. 1970, 243–50.

——1971. 'Crkvina, Kompolje, près de Otočac, nécropoles des Japodes', in Novak et al. 1971, 94–6.

——1972–3. 'Gräberfelder vorgeschichtliche Iapoden in Prozor bei Otočac', *VAMZ* 6–7, 1–54.

——1975a. 'Frühbronzezeitliche Tumuli in Lički Osik', *VAMZ* 9, 1–22.

——1975b. 'Le territoire de la Lika depuis le bronze ancien jusqu'à l'arrivée des romains', in Rapanić 1975, 19–37.

——1975c. 'Caractéristiques des agglomérations fortifiées dans la région centrale des Iapodes', in Bènac 1975a, 71–9.

——1986. 'Siedlungsfunde von einigen Wallburgen in der Provinz Lika', *VAMZ* 19, 107–27.

——1988. 'Zwei interessante Funde aus dem japodischen Gräberfeld in Prozor', *VAMZ* 21, 17–33.

Dukat, Z., and Mirnik, I., 1976. 'Pre-Roman coinage on the territory of modern Yugoslavia', *Bulletin of the Institute of Archaeology* (London) 13, 175–210.

——1983–4. 'The aureus of Quintus Cornificius', *VAMZ* 16–17, 91–3.

Dular, J., 1978. 'Tierkopfschmuck aus Gefässen in der Hallstattzeit in Slowenien', *AV* 29, 85–94.

——1982. *Die Grabkeramik der älteren Eisenzeit in Slowenien*, Ljubljana (Institute of Archaeology Monograph 12).

——1983. 'Die Hügelgräbernekropole in Loka bei Črnomelj', *AV* 34, 219–30.

Dumitrescu, V., 1976. 'Une enclave illyrienne au sud-ouest de la Roumanie datant du premier âge du fer', *Iliria* 4, 223–5.

Dušanić, S., 1977a. 'Two epigraphical notes', *ŽA* 27, 179–90.

——1977b. 'Aspects of Roman Mining in Noricum, Pannonia, Dalmatia and Moesia Superior', *Aufstieg und Niedergang der röm-*

ischen Welt, ed. H. Temporini and W. Haase, Berlin and New York, II Principat, vol. 8, 52–94.

Dvornik, F., 1956. *The Slavs: their early history and civilization*, Boston.

Eggebrecht, A., (ed.) 1988. *Albanien: Schätze aus dem Land der Skipetaren*, Mainz.

Ercegović, S., 1961. 'Ein keltisches Reitergrab aus Gardoš in Zemun', *VAMZ* 2, 125–37.

Ercegović-Pavlović, S., and Kostić, D., 1988. *Les monuments et les sites archéologiques dans la région de Leskovac*, Leskovac and Beograd (Institute of Archaeology Monographs 20).

Faber, A., 1976. 'Contribution à la chronologie des fortifications dans l'Illyricum littoral', in Suić 1976b, 227–46.

——1984. 'Beitrag zur Kenntnis der Architektur der Grabhügel auf dem Balkan', in Benac 1984a, 171–88.

Fadić, I., 1988. 'Round Liburnian tombstone from Verona (CIL V 2200, 8852, CIL III 2190)', *Diadora* 10, 73–88.

Fiala, F., 1899. 'Das Flachgräberfeld und die prähistorische Ansiedlung in Sanskimost', *WMBH* 6, 62–128.

Filip, J., (ed.) 1971. *Actes du VIIe congrès international des sciences Préhistoriques et Protohistoriques, Prague 21–27 août 1966*, Prague.

Filow, B., 1927. *Die archäische Nekropole von Trebenischte am Ohride-See*, Berlin and Leipzig.

Fistani, F., 1983. 'L'agglomération fortifiée illyrienne de Kratul', *Iliria* 13: 1, 109–17.

Foltiny, S., 1970. 'Zwei Feuerbocke aus dem Ringwall von Stična in Slowenien', *Mitteilungen der Anthropologischen Gesellschaft in Wien* 100, 158–61.

Franke, P., 1955. *Alt-Epirus und das Königtum der Molossier*, Kallmünz Opf.

——1976 (1972). 'Einige Probleme und Aufgaben der illyrischen Numismatik', *Iliria* 4, 295–9 [= *SA* 9: 2, 223–8].

Frashëri, K., 1975. 'Recherches sur les cités pénestiennes', *SH* 29 (12): 4, 135–58.

Frey, O.-H., 1966. 'Die Ostalpenraum und die antike Welt in der frühen Eisenzeit', *Germania* 44: 1, 48–66.

——1973. 'Bemerkungen zur hallstattischen Bewaffnung im Südostalpenraum', *AV* 24, 621–36.

Frey, O.-H., and Gabrovec, S., 1969. 'Zur latènezeitlichen Besiedlung Unterkrains: erste Ergebnisse der Ausgrabungen im Ringwall von Stična', *AV* 20, 7–26.

——1971. 'Zur Chronologie der Hallstattzeit im Ostalpenraum:

Bologna – Este – Sv Lucija – Dolenska (Unterkrain) – Hallstatt', in Novak et al. 1971, 193–218.

Gabričević, B., 1953. 'Deux communautés illyriennes dans les environs de Vrlika', *VAHD* 55, 103–19.

——1980. 'The beginnings of Roman provincial art in Liburnia', *Diadora* 9, 251–71.

——1983. 'Nécropole antique de Sinj: contributions aux recherches sur les croyances primitives', *VAHD* 76, 5–101.

Gabrovec, S., 1964–5. 'Die Hallstattkultur Sloweniens', *AV* 15–16, 21–63.

——1966a. 'Zur Hallstattzeit in Slowenien', *Germania* 44, 1–48.

——1966b. 'Zur Mittellatènezeit in Slowenien', *AV* 17, 169–242.

——1966c. 'Die Latènezeit in Oberkrain', *AV* 17, 243–70.

——1970. 'Die Zweischleifigen Bogenfibel: ein Beitrag zum Beginn der Hallstattzeit am Balkan und dem Südostalpen', *GCBI* 6, 5–65.

——1973. 'Der Beginn der Hallstattzeit in Slowenien', *AV* 24, 338–87.

——1975a. 'Überblick über eisenzeitliche Befestigungen in Slowenien', in Benac 1975a, 59–70.

——1984. 'Die Kunst der Illyrier im vorgeschichtlichen Zeitraum', in Benac 1984a, 41–64.

Gabrovec, S., and Svolšjak, D., 1983. *Most na Soči (S. Lucia) I: storia delle richerche e topographia*, Ljubljana (Katalogi in Monographia 22).

Gabrovec, S., Frey, O.-H., and Foltiny, S., 1970. 'Erster Bericht über die Ausgrabungen im Ringwall von Stična', *Germania* 48, 12–33.

Garašanin, D., 1960. 'Illyrischer Silberschmuck aus Umčari', *Starinar* 11, 86–92.

——1976 (1973). 'Les tombes tumulaires préhistoriques de la péninsule balkanique et leur attribution ethnique et chronologique', *Iliria* 4, 249–52 [= *SA* 10: 1, 179–84].

——1976. 'Consideration sur la chronologie de l'âge du fer II en Macedoine à la lumière des découvertes de Radanje', *MAA* 2, 135–41.

Garašanin, D., and Daicoviciu, H., et al. (eds.) 1971. *The Illyrians and Dacians*, Beograd (National Museum).

Garašanin, D. and Garašanin, M., 1971a. 'Radanje-Krivi Dol près de Štip, nécropole de l'Âge du Fer', in Novak et al. 1971, 144.

——1971b. 'Belotić-Bela Crkva, nécropole tumulaire de l'Âge du Bronze', in Novak et al. 1971, 168–70.

——1979. *Supska 'Stublina': vorgeschichtliche Ansiedlung der Vinča-Groupe*, Beograd (National Museum).

Garašanin, M., 1954. 'Zur Zeitbestimmung des Beginns der Vinča-Kultur', *AI* 1, 1–6.

——1966. 'Moenia Aeacia', *Starinar* 17, 27–36.

——1970. 'Ad Arrian I 4. 6.', in Mirosavljević et al. 1970, 393–7.

——1973a. *La préhistoire sur le territoire de la République socialiste de Serbie*, vols 1–2. Belgrade.

——1973b. 'Ethnographic problems of the Bronze Age in the central Balkan peninsula and neighbouring regions', in Crossland and Birchall 1973, 115–28.

——1973c. 'Les principaux problèmes de la préhistoire du sud-est européen', *Balkan Studies* 14: 1, 3–11.

——1975a. 'Zu den Problemen Makedonischer Vorgeschichte', *MAA* 1, 9–24.

——1975b. 'Agglomérations fortifiées dans la région frontière de l'est du territoire illyrien', in Benac 1975a, 113–20.

——1976. 'Les Illyriens au Montenegro à la lumière des découvertes archéologiques', *Iliria* 4, 319–25.

——1980. 'L'historiographie yugoslave sur l'état illyrien (à propos de la communication de Ali Hadri dans Iliria IV, Tirana 1976)', *G CBI* XVIII/16, 207–10.

——1982a. 'The Eneolithic period in the Central Balkan area', in Boardman, Edwards, Hammond and Sollberger 1982, 136–62.

——1982b. 'The Early Iron Age in the Central Balkan Area 1000–750 BC', in Boardman, Edwards, Hammond and Sollberger 1982, 582–618.

——1984. 'Rites funéraires illyriens à l'époque romaine', in Benac 1984a, 153–64.

——1988a. 'Formations et origines des Illyriens', in Garašanin, M., 1988b, 81–144.

—— (ed.) 1988b. *Les Illyriens et les Albanais: série de conferences tenues du 21 mai au 4 juin 1986*, Beograd (Serbian Academy of Arts and Sciences).

Gavela, B., 1952. *L'oppidum celtique Židovar*, Beograd (University of Beograd).

—— 1969. 'Sur les problèmes ethniques de la culture celtique à Židovar', *Starinar* 20, 119–27.

——1975a. 'Études méthodologiques sur la stratification archéologique, chronologique et ethnique de Židovar', *AI* 13, 39–44.

——1975b. 'Rois et états celtiques dans les Balkans (essai critique sur l'historiographie antique et moderne se rapportant aux Celtes balkaniques)', *GCBI* XIV/12, 61–8.

Georgiev, Z., 1978. 'A new Hallstatt find in the vicinity of Kumanovo', *MAA* 4, 69–70.

——1988. 'Handmade vessels from the necropoles at the lower course of the Vardar river', *MAA* 9, 65–81.

Gjergji, A., 1971. 'Eléments vestimentiaires communs des tribus illyriennes et leur continuation dans nos costumes populaires', in Korkuti et al. 1971, 151–71.

——1976. 'L'ornementation populaire albanaise et ses précédents illyriens', *Iliria* 5, 211–24.

Gjinari, J., 1971. 'De la continuation de l'illyrien en albanais', in Korkuti et al. 1971, 173–81.

——1976. 'À propos de l'article postponé de l'albanais sous l'aspect des rapports linguistiques illyro-albanais', *Iliria* 5, 99–103.

Gjoncegaj, S., 1977–8. 'Le monnayage d'Amantie', *Iliria* 7–8, 83–112.

——1984a. 'La circulation des monnaies de Corcyre dans l'Illyrie méridionale', *Iliria* 14: 1, 171–80.

——1984b. 'La circulation des monnaies de l'Épire dans les centres illyriens', *Iliria* 14: 2, 124–8.

——1986. 'La circulation des monnaies étrangères en Illyrie du Sud au cours des VI–I siècles av. n. ère', *Iliria* 16: 1, 145–54.

Glogović, D., 1979. 'Daunian pottery in Istria', *Histria Archaeologica* (Pula) 10: 1, 57–77.

——1988. 'Two part snake-like fibulae from Yugoslavia', *Diadora* 10, 5–18.

Gnirs, A., 1925. *Istria Praeromana*, Karlsbad.

Govedarica, B., 1978. 'Nouvelles contributions archéologiques aux recherches des tumulus dans la région de Glasinac', *GCBI* XVII/15, 15–35.

——1980–1. 'Die frühbronzezeitliche Ansiedlung von Veliki Gradac auf Privala', *AI* 20–1, 43–5.

——1982. 'Beiträge zu einer kulturellen Stratigraphie prähistorischer Wallburgsiedlungen in südwest Bosnien', *GCBI* XX/18, 111–88.

——1989. *L'Âge du Bronze ancien dans la région de l'Adriatique de l'est*, ANUBiH CBI Monographies LXVII/7, Sarajevo.

Grbić, M., 1971. 'Illyrische Kunst (Zusammenfassung)', in Filip 1971, 956–7.

Grmek, M., 1949. 'Iris Illyrica', *Lijecnički Vjesnik* (Zagreb) 71: 2, 63–4.

——1950. 'Les boissons enivrants et les poisons chez les anciens Illyriens', *Farmaceutski Glasnik* (Zagreb) 6: 3, 33–8.

Gunjača, Z. 1968–9. 'The relief of Silvanus Messor found at ancient Rider', *VAHD* 70–1, 177–86.

Guštin, M. 1973. 'Cronologia del gruppo preistorico della Notranjska (Carniola Interna)', *AV* 24, 461–506.

——1978. 'Typologie der eisenzeitlichen Ringwalle in Slowenien', *AV* 29, 100–21.

——1984. 'Die Kelten in Jugoslawien: Übersicht über dem archäologische Fundgut', *JRGZM* 31, 305–63.

Hadri, A., 1976. 'L'historiographie yougoslave sur l'état illyrien', *Iliria* 4, 273–9.

Hammond, N., 1966. 'The Kingdoms in Illyria circa 400–167 BC', *Annual of the British School at Athens* 61, 239–53.

——1967a. 'Tumulus-Burial in Albania, the Grave Circles of Mycenae, and the Indo-Europeans', *Annual of the British School at Athens* 62, 77–105.

——1967b. *Epirus*. Oxford.

——1968. 'Illyris, Rome and Macedon in 229–205', *JRS* 58, 1–21.

——1970. 'The archaeological background to the Macedonian Kingdom', in Laourdas and Makaronas 1970, 53–67.

——1972. *A History of Macedonia*, 1: *Historical Geography and Prehistory*. Oxford.

——1973. 'Grave Circles in Albania and Macedonia', in Crossland and Birchall 1973, 189–94.

——1974a. 'Alexander's campaign in Illyria', *JHS* 94, 66–87.

——1974b. 'The western part of the Via Egnatia', *JRS* 64, 185–94.

——1976 (1973). 'Tumulus-burial in Albania and problems of ethnogenesis', *Iliria* 4, 127–32 [= *SA* 10: 1, 169–77].

——1977. 'The campaign of Alexander against Cleitus and Glaucias', *Ancient Macedonia II*, Thessaloniki, 503–9.

——1981. 'The western frontier of Macedonia in the reign of Philip II', in Dell 1981, 199–217.

——1982a. 'Illyris, Epirus and Macedonia in the Early Iron Age', in Boardman, Edwards, Hammond and Sollberger 1982, 619–56.

——1982b. 'Illyris, Epirus and Macedonia', in Boardman and Hammond 1982, 261–85.

——1989. 'The Illyrian Atintani, the Epirotic Antintanes and the Roman Protectorate', *JRS* 79, 11–25.

Hammond, N., and Griffith, G., 1979. *A History of Macedonia*, 2: *550–336 BC*, Oxford.

Hammond, N., and Walbank, F., 1988. *A History of Macedonia*, 3: *336–167 BC*, Oxford.

Harding, A. F., 1976 (1972). 'Illyrians, Italians and Mycenaeans: Trans-Adriatic contacts during the Late Bronze Age', *Iliria* 4, 157–62 [= *SA* 9: 2, 215–21].

Hatzopoulos, M., 1987. 'Les limites de l'expansion Macédonienne en Illyrie sous Philippe II', in Cabanes 1987, 81–94.

Hidri, H., 1983. 'Fouilles de 1977 dans la nécropole de Dyrrah (secteur des collines de Dautes)', *Iliria* 13: 1, 137–80.

—— 1986. 'La production de la céramique locale à Durrachium durant les siècles VI–II av. n. ère', *Iliria* 16: 1, 187–95.

——1988. 'Coupes découvrées en relief de Durrachium', *Iliria* 18: 1, 75–89.

Holder, A., 1896–1914. *Alt-celtischer Sprachschatz* 1–3, Leipzig.

Hoti, A., 1982. 'La nécropole tumulaire de Bardhoc dans le district de Kukës', *Iliria* 12: 1, 15–48.

———1986. 'Le tumulus V et VI de Këneta', *Iliria* 16: 2, 41–70.

Hoxha, G., 1987. 'Vestiges relatifs au Bronze Age ancien dans la forteresse de Shkodra', *Iliria* 17: 1, 71–81.

Ilakovac, B., 1978. 'Inscribed Stone', *ŽA* 28, 373–6.

Ilievski, P., 1975. 'Illyrian personal names in the Mycenaean-Greek onomasticon?', *ŽA* 25, 413–21.

Irmscher, J., 1986. 'Illyrien und Illyrier in der Vorbereitung befindlichen "Einleitung in der klassischen Altertumswissenschaften"', *Iliria* 16: 1, 223–5.

Islami, S., 1970. 'La citadelle illyrienne de Xibri', in Kostallari et al. 1970, 385–90.

———1972a. 'Naissance et développement de la vie urbaine en Illyrie', *Iliria* 2, 7–23.

———1972b. 'La ville illyrienne à Zgerdhesh de Kruje', *Iliria* 2, 217–37.

———1972c. 'Le monnayage de Skodra, Lissos et Genthios (essai d'une revision du problème)', *Iliria* 2, 379–408.

———1974. 'L'état illyrien et ses guerres contre Rome (231–168 avant notre ère)', *Iliria* 3, 5–48.

———1975. 'Zgerdhesh (fouilles archéologiques 1973)', *Iliria* 3, 425–32.

———1976a (1972). 'L'état illyrien, sa place et son rôle dans le monde méditerranéen', *Iliria* 4, 71–87 [= *SA* 9: 2, 77–103].

———1976b. 'Problèmes de chronologie de la cité illyrienne', *Iliria* 6, 107–12.

———1981. 'La cuirasse illyrienne', *Iliria* 11: 2, 46–50.

———1984. 'La cité en Illyrie et en Épire (analogies et particularités)', *Iliria* 14: 2, 11–17.

Islami, S., Anamali, S., Korkuti, M., and Prendi, F., 1985. *Les Illyriens: aperçu historique*, Tirana.

Janakievski, T., 1976. 'A contribution to the question of the location of the antique settlement Nicaea, a station on the Via Egnatia', *MAA* 2, 189–204.

Janković, D., 1981. *La partie danubienne de la région d'Aquis au VIe et au début du VIIe siècle*, Beograd (Inst. Arch. Materiaux vol. 5).

Jelavich, B., 1983. *History of the Balkans*, 1: *Eighteenth and Nineteenth Centuries*; 2: *Twentieth Century*. Cambridge.

Jevtić, M., 1983. *The Early Iron Age Pottery of the Central Balkan Region*, Beograd (Univ. Centre Arch. Res. vol 2).

Jireček, K., 1901–4. *Die Romanen in den Städten Dalmatiens während des Mittelalters*, Wien (Denkschr. Akad. Wien 48/3, 49/1. 2.).

Jovanović, A., 1989. 'Ein Beitrag zur Erforschung der Gürtelplatten vom illyrischen Raum', *GCBI* XXVII/25, 115–33.

Jovanović, B., 1971. *Metallurgy of the Eneolithic Period in Yugoslavia*, Beograd (Archaeological Institute, vol. 9).

——1973–4. 'Eléments de l'art des Scordisques', *Starinar* 24–5, 17–31.

——1977–8. 'La significance de la céramique dace dans les agglomérations des Scordisques dans le podunavlje', *Starinar* 28–9, 9–17.

——1982. *Rudna Glava: der älteste Kupfergebau im Zentral Balkan*, Bor and Beograd (Museum für Bergbau und Hüttenwesen, Arch. Inst. 17).

Jovanović, B., and Jovanović, M., 1988. *Gomolava: late La Tène settlement (Gomolava 2)*, Novi Sad and Beograd.

Jovanović, B., and Popović, P., 1981. 'Bibliographie de la période La Tène en Yougoslavie (1945–1975)', *Études Celtiques* 18.

Jubani, B., 1967. 'Trois pendentifs illyriens, leur signification et leur évolution', *SH* 21: 3, 173–83.

——1970. 'La Xhublete (Cotte) albanaise, témoin de l'ancienneté du peuple albanais', in Kostallari et al. 1970, 291–307.

——1972a. *Bibliographie de l'archéologie et de l'histoire antique de l'Albanie (1945–1971)*, Tirana.

——1972b. 'La céramique illyrienne de la cité de Gajtan', *Iliria* 2, 409–50.

——1972c. 'Monnaies illyriennes à ethnikon de Labiatan découvertes à Kukës', *SA* 9: 1, 69–75.

——1982. 'Les tumulus de Kruma (district de Kukesi)', *Iliria* 12: 2, 147–95.

——1983. 'Les tumulus Illyriens de Këneta', *Iliria* 13: 2, 77–133.

——1985. 'Traits de la culture illyrienne dans la région de la Dardanie', *Iliria* 15: 2, 211–22.

——1986a. 'Sur la nouvelle détermination ethnique des tumuli de Suhareskë (Kosove)', *SA* 1986: 1, 187–98.

——1986b. 'L'habitat illyrien de "Kodra e Pazarit" à Perlati de Mrdita', *Iliria* 16: 2, 139–50.

Jubani, B., and Ceka, N., 1971. 'Fouilles dans la cité illyrienne de Rosuje (Tropoje)', *Iliria* 1, 49–68.

Kaca, I., 1981. 'Trois agglomérations illyriennes dans le district de Dibra', *Iliria* 11: 1, 255–61.

Karaiskaj, G., 1976. 'Les fortifications illyriennes du premier âge du fer dans les environs de Korcë', *Iliria* 4, 197–221.

——1977. 'Les fortifications préhistoriques en Albania', *Monumentet* 14, 19–40.

——1977–8a. 'La nécropole des IIIe et IVe siècles dans la ville illyrienne de Zgërdhesh', *Iliria* 7–8, 201–16.

——1977–8b. 'L'agglomération fortifiée préhistorique de Marshej', *Iliria* 7–8, 263–7.

Karouškova-Soper, V., 1983. *The Castellieri of Venezia Giulia, Northeastern Italy (2nd–1st millennium* BC*),* Oxford (BAR International Series 192).

Kastelić, J., 1960. 'A new type of the diadem from the Hallstatt period in Slovenia', *Situla* (Ljubljana) 1, 3–26.

Katičić, R., 1962. 'Die illyrischen Personennamen in ihrem südöstlichen Verbreitungsgebiet', *ŽA* 12, 95–120.

——1963a. 'Das mitteldalmatinische Namengebiet', *ŽA* 12, 255–92.

——1963b. 'Illyrii proprie dicti', *ŽA* 13, 87–97.

——1964. 'Namengebiete im römischen Dalmatien', *Die Sprache* 10, 23–33.

——1965. 'Zur Frage der keltischen und pannonischen Namengebiete im römischen Dalmatien', *GCBI* 1, 53–76.

——1966a. 'Nochmals Illyrii proprie dicti', *ŽA* 16, 241–4.

——1966b. 'Die keltischen Personennamen in Slowenien', *AV* 17, 146–68.

——1970. 'Illyricus Fluvius', in Mirosavljević et al. 1970, 385–92.

——1976a (1972). 'L'anthroponymie illyrienne et l'ethnogenèse des Albanais', *Iliria* 5, 79–82 [= *SA* 9: 2, 269–74].

——1976b. *Ancient Languages of the Balkans* (Trends in Linguistics 4: 5), The Hague and Paris.

——1976c. 'Illyro-Apenninica', in Suić 1976b, 177–83.

——1977a. 'The Paeonians and their language', *ŽA* 27, 25–31.

——1977b. 'Die Encheleer', *GCBI* 15, 5–82.

——1980. 'Die Balkanprovinzen', *Die Sprache im römischen Reich der Kaiserzeit: Kolloquium vom 8 bis 10 April 1974*, Köln and Bonn, 103–20.

——1984. 'Die Sprache der Illyrier', in Benac 1984a, 253–64.

——1988. 'Antenor an der Adria', *GCBI* XXVI/24, 5–23.

——1989. 'Diomedes an der Adria', *GCBI* XXVII/25, 39–78.

Kilian, K., 1973. 'Zu geschnurten Schienen der Hallstattzeit aus der Ilijak-Nekropole in Bosnien', *Germania* 51: 2, 528–35.

——1975. 'Trachtzubehör der Eisenzeit zwischen Ägäis und Adria', *PZ* 50, 9–140.

——1976. 'Zur Früheisenzeit in Albanien', *Iliria* 4, 191–6.

——1985. 'L'Albanie méridionale à l'âge du bronze récent', *Iliria* 15: 2, 175–8.

Kilian-Dirlmeier, I., 1984. 'Die Nadeln der Eisenzeit in Albanien', *Iliria* 14: 1, 85–109.

Kirigin, B., and Marin, E., 1985. 'Excavation in Hellenistic cemetery Martvilo', *VAHD* 78, 45–72.

Kirigin, B., and Popović, P., 1988. 'Maslinovik: a Greek watchtower in the Chora of Pharos', in Chapman, Bintliff, Gaffney and Slapšak 1988, 177–89.

Kitanoski, B., 1983. 'A contribution concerning internment in the early periods of Pelagonia', *AI* 20–1, 51–5.

Knez, T., 1974. 'Neue hallstattzeitliche Pseudokernoi aus Novo Mesto', *Antike Welt* 5: 4, 53–4.

——1976. 'Figural verzierte Situlen aus Novo Mesto', *Antike Welt* 7: 1, 32–8.

——1978. 'Ein späthallstattzeitliches Fürstengrab von Novo Mesto in Slowenien', *Germania* 56: 1, 125–49.

——1980a. 'Situlenkunst in Slowenien', *Antike Welt* 11: 2, 52–9.

——1980b. 'Novo Mesto in der Vor- und Frühgeschichte', *AV* 31, 65–79.

——1983. 'Denkmäler der Situlenkunst in Slowenien: Fundkatalog und Bibliographie', *AV* 34, 85–105.

——1984. 'Situlenkunst in Jugoslawien', in Benac 1984a, 89–104.

Knez, T., and Szabo, M., 1983. 'Ein keltischer Kantharos aus Novo Mesto', *AI* 20–1, 80–8.

Koch, G. 1989. *Albanien: Kunst und Kultur im Land der Skipetaren*. Köln.

Komata, D., 1971a. 'Un four antique dans Kuçi Zi', *Iliria* 1, 263–8.

——1971b. 'Traits de la céramique médiévale en Albanie', in Korkuti et al. 1971b, 217–39.

——1984. 'Un buste de femme à l'habillement illyrien', *Iliria* 14: 2, 129–30.

Kondić, V., and Popović, V., 1977. *Caričin Grad: site fortifié dans l'Illyricum Byzantin* (Galerie de l'Académie Serbe des sciences et des arts 33), Beograd.

Korkuti, M., 1971. 'L'agglomération préhistorique de Tren', *Iliria* 1, 31–47.

——1975. 'Fouilles archéologiques à Dunarec', *Iliria* 3, 395–400.

——1976. 'À propos des agglomérations fortifiées illyriennes de la première période du fer dans le territoire de l'Albanie', in Suić 1976b, 199–212.

——1981. 'Le tumulus de Patos', *Iliria* 11: 1, 7–55.

——1982. 'À propos de l'ethnogenèse des Illyriens', *Iliria* 12: 1, 174–90.

——1983a. 'L'habitat néolithique de Kolschi', *Iliria* 1983: 2, 11–75.

——1983b. 'Geschichte und Kultur Albaniens im vorgeschichtlichen Zeit', *Antike Welt*, Sondernummer, 3–11.

——1987. '25 ans de recherches sur le Néolithique et la Chalcolithique en Albanie (1961–1986)', *Iliria* 17: 2, 5–19.

Korkuti, M., and Andrea, Z., 1975. 'La station du Néolithique moyen à Cakran de Fieri', *Iliria* 3, 49–107.

Korkuti, M., et al., 1971. *Shqipëria Arkeologjikë*, Tirana.

——1972. 'La nécropole de Gajtan', *Iliria* 2, 451–66.

——1973. 'Les agglomérations fortifiées illyriennes de la première période du fer en Albanie', *SH* 27 (10): 3, 107–31.

——1975. 'Fouilles archéologiques à Dunavec', *Iliria* 3, 395–400.

Korošec, J., 1958. *The Neolithic Settlement at Danilo Bitinj: the results of excavations performed in 1953*, Zagreb (Yugoslav Academy of Arts and Sciences).

——1964. *Danilo und die Danilo-Kulturgruppe*, Ljubljana (Philosophical Faculty of the University).

Kos, P., 1986. *The Monetary Circulation in the Southeastern Alpine Region ca. 300 BC–AD 1000*, Ljubljana (Situla 24, National Museum).

Kosorić, M., 1976. *Cultural, Et[h]nical and Chronological Problems of the Illyrien Necropoles in the Drina Basin*, Tuzla (Dissertations and Monographs 18, Archaeological Society of Yugoslavia).

Kostallari, A., et al., 1970. *Deuxième Conférence des Études Albanologiques à l'occasion du 5e centenaire de la mort de Georges Kastrioti-Skanderbeg, Tirana 12–18 janvier 1968*, vols. 1–2, Tirana.

Kozličić, M., 1980–1. 'Surveys of ships on coins of the Daors tribe', *GZMS* 35–6, 163–88.

Krahe, H., 1925. *Die alten balkanillyrischen geographischen Namen*, Heidelberg.

——1929. *Lexicon altillyrischer Personennamen*, Heidelberg.

——1955–8. *Die Sprache der alten Illyrier* 1–2, Wiesbaden.

Kučan, D., 1984. 'Kulturpflanzen aus Pod bei Bugojno, Zentralbosnien (Hallstatt- u. La Tène-Zeit)', *Plants and Ancient Man: proceedings of the 6th symposium of the International Work Group of Palaeoethnobotany*, ed. W. Van Zeist and W. Casparie, Boston, 247–56.

Kučar, V., 1979. 'La nécropole préhistorique de Beram', *Histria Archaeologica* (Pula) 10: 1, 85–131.

Kulišić, S., 1979. *Ancienne religion slave à la lumière des recherches récentes: particulièrement balkaniques*, ANUBiH CBI Monographies LVI/3, Sarajevo.

Kurti, D., 1971. 'Vestiges de civilisation illyrienne dans la vallée de Mati', in Korkuti et al., 1971, 147.

——1976a. 'Nouveaux éléments sur la civilisation illyrienne des tumuli de Mati', *Iliria* 4, 237–48.

——1976b. 'La civilisation de la Basse Antiquité à Mati: chaînon intermédiaire entre la civilisation illyrienne et la civilisation albanaise', *Iliria* 5, 309–15.

——1979. 'Forteresses et citadelles inconnues dans le district de Mat', *Monumentet* 18, 77–92.

——1983. 'Les tumuli de Burrel', *Iliria* 1983: 1, 7–55.

——1985. 'Aperçu sur les tumulus illyriens de Burrel à Mat', *Iliria* 15: 2, 205–10.

——1987. 'Les tumuli IV, V, VI, VII de Burrel', *Iliria* 17: 1, 85–103.

Kurz, K., 1967a. 'Zum Charakter der Geldwirtschaft im Japodengebiet', *AV* 20, 259–69.

——1967b. 'Zur Ethnizität der Japoden', *LF* 90, 259–69.

Kuthmann, H., 1966. 'Salz zum Wurzen', *Archäologischer Anzeiger* (Berlin), 406–10.

Lahi, B., 1988. 'Le site fortifié de Beltoje', *Iliria* 18: 2, 69–92.

Lahtov, V., 1965. *Das Problem der Trebenište-Kultur*, Ohrid (National Museum).

Laourdas, B., and Makaronas, C. (eds.), 1970. *Ancient Macedonia: papers read at the First International Symposium held in Thessaloniki, 26–29 August 1968*, Thessaloniki.

Lazić, M., 1989. *The Topography and Typology of Prehistoric Barrows in Serbia and Montenegro.* Beograd (University of Belgrade, Centre for Archaeological Research, vol. 9).

Leković, V., 1980. 'Contribution à l'étude de la culture de l'âge du fer au Montenegro', *GCBI* XVIII/16, 81–90.

Lera, P., 1975. 'Symize (Korcë)', *Iliria* 3, 473–9.

Levi, M., 1973. 'Le cause della guerra romana contro gli illiri', *La Parola del Passato* 28, 317–25.

Lisičar, P., 1973. 'Cenni sulla ceramica antica: contributo allo studio della protoistoria dell'Adriatico orientale', *AI* 14, 3–27.

Ljubinković, M., 1969. 'Le problème de la continuité Illyres-Slaves', in Benac 1969, 201–15.

Lučić, J., 1966. 'Sur les migrations des Ardiéens, peuple illyrien', *ŽA* 16, 245–54.

Luka, D., 1977. 'Propos de quelques comparaisons des suffixes de l'Illyrien avec ceux de l'Albanais', *SF* 31 (14): 2, 67–76.

McPherron, A., and Srejović, D. (eds.), 1988. *Divoštin and the Neolithic of Central Serbia*, Pittsburgh (University) and Kragujevac (Museum), Ethnographic Monographs 10.

Majnarić-Pandžić, N., 1974. 'Der Goldfund aus Orolik bei Vinkovci', *AI* 15, 21–6.

——1978. 'Überblick der Erforschung der latènezeitlichen-keltischen Kultur im Nordkroatien', in Rapanić 1978a, 149–58.

Malez, M., and Osole, F., 1971. 'Paléolithique et Mesolithique', in Novak et al. 1971, 254–64.

Malinowsky, T., 1971. 'Über den Bernsteinhandel zwischen den südöstlichen baltischen Ufergebieten in dem Süden Europas in der frühen Eisenzeit', *PZ* 46, 102–10.

Maly, K., 1904. 'Fruchte und Samen aus dem prähistorischen Pfahlbau von Donja Dolina in Bosnien', *WMBH* 9, 165–70.

Manastirli, V., 1976. 'Les tombes monumentales de la zone de Mokër (district de Podgradec)', *Monumentet* 12, 49–51.

Mano, A., 1975. 'Le commerce et les artères commerciales en Illyrie du sud', in Benac 1975a, 165–73.

——1976a (1973). 'Les rapports commerciaux d'Apollonie avec l'arrière-pays illyrien', *Iliria* 4, 307–16 [= *SA* 10: 1, 185–94].

——1976b. 'Commerce et artères commerciales en Illyrie du sud', *Iliria* 6, 119–24.

——1977–8, 'Considérations sur la nécropole d'Apollonie', *Iliria* 7–8, 71–82.

——1986. 'Les rapports économiques et politiques des Hellènes avec les Illyriens (Ve–IIIe siècle av. n. ère)', *Iliria* 16: 1, 155–63.

Mano-Zissi, D., 1973. 'Die autochtone Bevölkerung West- und Zentralbalkans und des südlichen Mitteldonaugebietes und ihre kulturelle Beziehungen zur griechischen Zivilisation', *Actes du VIIIe congrès international des sciences préhistoriques et protohistoriques, Beograd 9–15 Septembre 1971*, Beograd, vol. 3, 163–74.

Mano-Zissi, D., and Popović, L., 1969. 'Der Fund von Novi Pazar (Serbien)', *BRGK* 50, 191–208.

Mansaku, S., 1987. 'Onomastique et histoire de la langue albanaise', *SA* 1987: 1, 85–96.

Marchesetti, C., 1903. *I castellieri preistorici di Trieste e della regione Giulia*, Trieste.

Margetić, L., 1971. 'Il decreto della fondazione di una colonia greca sull'isola di Korcula', *ŽA* 21, 189–204.

Marić, Z., 1964a. 'Donja Dolina', *GZMS* 19, 5–82.

——1964b. 'Problèmes des limites septentrionales du territoire illyrien', in Benac 1964, 177–213.

——1971a. 'Die japodischen Nekropolen in Unatal', *WMBHL* 1, 13–96.

——1971b. 'Vis, près de Derventa, site préhistorique à plusières couches', in Novak et al. 1971, 76–8.

——1975a. 'La frontière orientale des Japodes', in Rapanić 1975, 39–44.

——1975b. 'Fortificazioni prehistoriche e protohistoriche nel territorio di Daorsi', in Benac 1975a, 103–11.

——1976. 'Ošanići: centro della tribu illirica di Daorsi', in Suić 1976b, 247–54.

——1978. 'The hoard found at the Illyrian town of Daors', *GZMS* 33, 23–113.

——1979a. 'Archäologische Forschungen auf der Gradina oberhalb des Dorfes Ošanići bei Stolac im Jahre 1963', *WMBHL* 6, 5–59.

——1979b. 'Archäologische Erforschung der Akropolis der illyrischen Stadt Daors. auf der Gradina in Ošanići bei Stolac von 1967–1972', *WMBHL* 6, 61–181.

——1979c. 'Münzen aus dem dritten und zweiten Jahrhundert v. u. Z. von Gradina in Ošanići bei Stolac', *WMBHL* 6, 183–204.

——1979d. 'Neu entdeckter Belag einer Gürtelplatte auf der Gradina von Ošanići bei Stolac', *WMBHL* 6, 205–10.

——1979e. 'Bronzene Gussformen aus der Stadt Daors. oberhalb des Dorfes Ošanići bei Stolac', *WMBHL* 6, 211–42.

Marijan, B., 1985–6. 'Iron Age Communal Grave from Vašarovine near Livno', *GZMS* 40–1, 23–38.

Marijanović, B., 1984. 'Les recherches finales de l'Acropole sur Gradina a Ošanići', *GZMS* 39, 11–22.

Marin, E., 1977. 'Zur Forschung des illyrischen Namenguts auf der Apenninischen Halbinsel', *ŽA*, 411–41.

Marković, C., 1984. 'Schmuckgegenstände aus dem Fürstengrab in Lisijevo polje bei Ivangrad', in Benac 1984a, 81–7.

——1985. *The Neolithic of Montenegro*, Beograd (University Centre for Archaeological Research vol. 5).

Marović, I., 1961–2. 'Einige Funde aus der Hallstattperiode in Dalmatien', *VAHD* 63–4, 5–23.

——1963–5. 'Eisenzeitliche Gräber in Zaganj bei Šumartin auf der Insel Brač', *VAHD* 65–7, 5–26.

——1970. 'Einige unveröffentlichte silberne gegenstände aus dem liburnischen Gebiet im archaeologischen Museum in Split', in Mirosavljević et al. 1970, 265–84.

——1975. 'Salone dans la préhistoire', in Rapanić 1975, 9–22.

——1976a. 'Les résultats des fouilles dans les tumuli autours de la source du fleuve Cetina en 1953, 1954, 1958, 1966, et 1968', in Batović 1976d, 55–75.

——1976b. 'L'elmo greco-illirico', in Suić 1976b, 287–300.

——1979. 'Résultats du sondage archéologique de Gospodska pećina, proche de la source de la Cetina', *VAHD* 72–3, 13–50.

——1981. 'Contributions à la connaissance de l'Âge du Bronze en Dalmatia', *VAHD* 75, 7–61.

——1985. 'Excavation at Stone Barrows at Bogomolje (the island of Hvar)', *VAHD* 78, 5–35.

Marović, I., and Nikolanci, M., 1968–9. 'Four tombs of Viča Luka cemetery, Brač (found 1908)', *VAHD* 70–1, 5–55.

Martinović, J., 1966. 'Nouveaux éléments dans l'interpretation des chapitres 24 et 25 du Periple de Pseudo-Scylax', *Starinar* 17, 107–17.

Mason, P., 1988. 'The social context of the introduction of iron in the Early Iron Age of Slovenia', in Chapman et al. 1988, 211–23.

Masson, O., 1987. 'Quelques noms illyriens', in Cabanes 1987, 115–17.

Matejčić, R., 1968. 'Die Schutzausgrabung der liburnische Nekropole über des Ortes Lopar am Insel Rab', *Diadora* 4, 74–84.

Matijašić, R., 1985. 'Il Silvano di Pinguente: un nuovo ritrovamento dall'Istria settentrionale', *AV* 36, 187–94.

May, J., 1946. 'Macedonia and Illyria 217–167 BC', *JRS* 36, 48–57.

Mayer, A., 1957–9. *Die Sprache der alten Illyrier 1–2*, Wien (Schriften der Balkankommission, linguistische Abteilung Heft 15).

Medini, J., 1975. 'Certains aspects du développement des religions antiques sur le territoire des Japodes', in Rapanić 1975, 85–95.

——1984. 'Latra: Dea Neditarum', in Benac 1984a, 223–43.

Medović, P., 1978. *Die relative Chronologie der Siedlungen der älteren Eisenzeit im Jugoslawischen Donaugebieten*, Beograd (Dissertations Monographs 22).

Meksi, V., 1976. 'À propos de certaines institutions juridiques communes aux Illyriens et aux Albanais', *Iliria* 5, 317–19.

Mema, S., 1986. 'Idées sur la langue Albanaise chez les voyageurs anglais de première moitié du XIXe siècle', *SA* 1968: 2, 167–85.

Mendjušić, M., 1985. 'Bribir: Late Iron Age Cemetery', *Arheološki Pregled* 26, 79.

Migotti, B., 1986. 'Greek-Hellenistic pottery from Stari Grad on the island of Hvar', *VAMZ*, 19, 147–77.

Mihovilić, K., 1979. 'Il castelliere punta castello presso Medolino', *Histria Archaeologica* (Pula) 10: 1, 37–51.

Mijović, P., 1970, 'Les objects de parure de Mijele et les croyances de culte', *Starinar* 21, 59–69.

Mijović, P., and Kovačević, M., 1975. *Villes fortifiées et forteresses au Montenegro*, Beograd and Ulcinj (Institute of Archaeology Monographs).

Mikić, Z., 1978. 'Neue anthropologische Beiträge zur Untersuchungen der Grabhügel auf der Glasinacer Hochebene', *GCBI* XVII/15, 37–49.

——1981. *L'état et les problèmes de l'anthropologie physique en Yougoslavie: les périodes préhistoriques*, ANUBiH CBI Publications Spéciales LII/9, Sarajevo.

Mikulčić, I., 1966. *Die Geschichte Pelagoniens im Lichte der Bodenfunde: von der ägaischen Wanderung bis Augustus*, Skopje and Beograd (Dissertations vol. 3).

——1971. 'Pélagonie du sud, nécropoles archaiques', in Novak et al. 1971, 142–3.

——1973. 'Das vorgeschichtliche Stratum auf der Burg Kale in Skopje und Problem der Eisenzeit in Süddardanien', *Actes du VIIIe congrès international des sciences préhistoriques et protohistoriques, Beograd 9–15 september 1971*, Beograd, vol. 3, 179–85.

——1976. 'Die Lage von Bylazora', *Godišen Zbornik Filosofski Fakultet Skopje* 28: 2, 149–65.

——1985. 'Zur Topographie des vorrömischen Stobi', *Godišen Zbornik Filosofski Fakultet Skopje* 12 (38), 101–17.

Miletić, N., 1989. 'Frühslawischen Nekropolen in Bosnien und Herzegovina: komparative Betrachtungen', *GZMS* 44, 174–94.

Millar, F., 1983. 'Empire and City, Augustus to Julian, Obligations, Excuses and Status', *JRS* 73, 76–96.

Milošević, A., 1986. 'Zwei Hortfunde von Eisenwerkzeugen aus dem Gebiet der Delmater', *AV* 37, 97–127.

Mirdita, Z., 1972. 'La base illyrienne de l'ethnie albanaise: aspects de la question', *SA* 9: 1, 41–8.

——1975. 'Intorno al problema dell'ubicazione e della identificazione di alcuni agglomerati Dardani nel tempo preromano', in Benac 1975a, 201–16.

——1976. 'À propos de la romanisation des Dardaniens', *Iliria* 5, 143–50.

——1981. 'Le matériel épigraphique, son importance et ses limites pour connaître les structures ethniques, politiques et sociales en Dardanie des temps de Rome', *SH* 35 (18): 3, 201–22.

——1982. 'Neugefundene Inschrift in Kačanik (Kosovo)', *AI* 33, 79–83.

Mirković, M., 1968. *Römische Städte an der Donau in Obermösien*, Beograd (Archaeological Society of Yugoslavia, Dissertations vol. 6).

——1969. 'Die südillyrischen Stämme im illyrischen Kriege Octavians in den Jahren 35–33 v. u. Z.', *ŽA* 18, 113–27.

Mirnik, I., 1982. 'Coin hoards from Croatia, III: the hoard of African bronze coins and aes rude from Stikada', *VAMZ* 15, 149–67.

——1989. 'Circulation of North African, etc., currency in Illyricum', *AV* 38, 369–92.

Mirosavljević, V., 1971. 'Jamina Sredi, dans l'île de Cres, site préhistorique à plusières couches', in Novak et al. 1971, 102–5.

Mirosavljević, V., et al. (eds.), 1970. *Adriatica Praehistorica et Antiqua: miscellanea Gregorio Novak dicata*, Zagreb.

Mladin, J., 1966. *Kunstdenkmäler von vorgeschichtlichen Nesactium*, Pula (Arh. Muz. Istr.).

——1974. 'Bronzegefässe und Bronzehelme aus Istrien', *Diadora* 7,

——1980. 'Urgeschichtliche Kleinplastik im Archäologischen Museum Istriens in Pula', *Diadora* 9, 165–95.

Mócsy, A., 1959. *Die Bevölkerung von Pannonien bis zu den Markommannenkriegen*, Budapest.

——1966. 'Die Vorgeschichte Obermoesiens im hellenstichen-römischen Zeitalter', *AAnt. Hung.* 14, 87–112.

——1967. 'De lingua Pannonica', in Benac 1967, 195–200.

——1970. *Gesellschaft und Romanisation in der römischen Provinz Moesia Superior*, Amsterdam.

——1974. *Pannonia and Upper Moesia: a history of the Middle Danube provinces of the Roman Empire*, London.

——1983. 'The civilized Pannonians of Velleius', in *Rome and her Northern Provinces: papers presented to Sheppard Frere*, ed. B. Hartley and J. Wacher, Gloucester, 169–75.

Morgan, M., 1971. 'Lucius Cotta and Metellus: Roman campaigns in Illyria during the late second century', *Athenaeum* 49 (59), 271–301.

Munro, R., 1900. *Rambles and Studies in Bosnia-Herzegovina and Dalmatia*, 2nd edn, Edinburgh and London.

Myrto, H., 1984. 'Un cimetière antique dans le village de Vrin', *Iliria* 14: 1, 215–23.

——1986. 'Problèmes de l'histoire antique d'Epidamne', *SH* 1986: 2, 129–46.

Nagy, T., 1970. 'Der Aufstand der pannonisch-delmatinischen Völker und die Frage der Zweiteilung Illyricums', in Mirosavljević et al. 1970, 459–66.

Neméskeri, J., 1986. 'Les traits anthropologiques et démographiques des Illyriens', *Iliria* 16: 1, 299–305.

Neméskeri, J., and Dhima, A., 1988. 'Essai de reconstitution paléobiologique de la population apolloniate du Ie–IIIe siècles de n. ère', *Iliria* 18: 1, 119–55.

Nikić, D., 1983. 'Contribution à l'étude des voies de communications préromaines et romaines sur la région de Livno, Glamoč et Duvno', *GCBI* XXI/19, 229–50.

Nikolanci, M., 1968–9; 'Notes sur les vases corinthiens de Vis (Issa)', *VAHD* 70–1, 149–57.

——1976a. 'Les grecs adriatiques en tant que périphérie du monde hellénique', in Batović 1976d, 149–68.

——1976b. 'Les importations de l'Asie Mineure dans l'Adriatique oriental', in Suić 1976b, 273–86.

——1980. 'New and old Greek inscriptions in Dalmatia', *Diadora* 8, 205–27.

Novak, G., 1955; *Prehistoric Hvar*, Zagreb.

——1971. 'Markova Spilja dans l'île de Hvar', in Novak et al. 1971,

Novak, G. et al. (eds.), 1971. *Époque préhistorique et protohistorique en Yougoslavie: recherches et résultats*, Beograd.

Oreč, P., 1977. 'Agglomérations préhistoriques et tumulus sépulchraux dans les environs de Posušje, Grude et Listica (Herzegovinie occidentale)', *GZMS* 32, 181–291.

——1987. 'Trois lieux sacres préhistoriques (temples) à Posušje et à Ljubuški', *GCBI* XXV/23, 189–200.

Orlić, M., 1986. *Antique Ship near the Island of Ilovik*, Zagreb (Cultural Monuments of Croatia).

Osmani, Y., 1988. 'Un casque illyrien découvert à Durrës', *Iliria* 18: 1, 209–10.

Pahić, S., 1973. 'Fundstätten der frühen Eisenzeit im Slowenischen Drauland', *AV* 24, 521–43.

——1981. 'Brinjeva gora 1953', *AV* 32, 71–143.

Pajakowski, W., 1980. 'Wer waren Illyrii proprie dicti und wo siedelte man sie an', *GCBI* XVIII/16, 91–162.

——1981. *Illyrier – Illurioi – Illyrii proprie dicti. Wohnsitze und Geschichte: Versuch einer Rekonstruktion*, Poznan (Seria historica 87).

Palavestra, A., 1984. *Princely Tombs during the Early Iron Age in the Central Balkans*, Beograd (Serbian Academy Institute of Balkan Studies, special edition 19).

Panciera, S., 1956. 'Liburna: rassegna delle fonti, caratteristiche della nave, accezioni del termine', *Epigraphica* (Rome) 18, 130–56.

Papajani, L., 1976a. 'La cité illyrienne de Klos', *Iliria* 4, 411–22.

——1976b. 'Monnaies découvertes dans la cité illyrienne de Klos (avec un catalogue sur les frappés monétaires de la cité de Byllis)', *Iliria* 6, 259–73.

——1977. 'Les travaux de restoration effectués dans la ville illyrienne à Zgërdhesh', *Monumentet* 14, 5–18.

——1979. 'Le théâtre de la ville illyrienne à Klos de Mallakaster et les travaux de restoration qui y sont effectués', *Monumentet* 18, 43–55.

Papazoglu, F., 1961. 'Heraclée des Lyncestes à la lumière des textes littéraires et épigraphiques', *Heraclea I*, Bitola.

——1963. 'Sur le territoire des Ardiéens', *Recueuils de travaux de la Faculté de philosophie* (Belgrade), 7: 1, 71–86.

——1967. 'L'organisation politique des Illyriens à l'époque de leur indépendence', in Benac 1967, 11–31.

——1970a. 'Les Autariates et Lysimaque', in Mirosavljević et al. 1970, 335–46.

——1970b. 'Inscription hellénestique de Lyncestide', *ŽA* 20, 99–113.

——1970c. 'Quelques problèmes de l'histoire épirote: à propos du

——1974. 'Sur la monnaie illyrienne au nom de Redon', *ŽA* 24, 258–60.

——1978. *The Central Balkan Tribes in the Preroman Times: Triballi, Autariatae, Dardanians, Scordisci and Moesians*, Amsterdam.

——1986. 'Politarques en Illyrie', *Historia* 35, 438–48.

Parović-Pešikan, M., 1964. 'Les Illyriens au contact des Grecs', *AI* 5, 61–81.

——1976. 'Neueste Forschungen in der Boka Kotorska mit besonderer Hinsicht auf das Problem illyrischer und vorillyrischer Beziehungen zur Adrias', in Batović 1976d, 77–87.

——1977–8. 'Les recherches archéologiques à Boka Kotorska', *Starinar* 28–9, 19–67.

——1978. 'Greek alphabetic inscription from Lipljan', *AI* 19, 35–41.

——1980. *L'arrière-pays montagneux de Risinium*, Beograd and Nikšić (Institute of Archaeology Monographs vol. 15).

——1980–1. 'Finds of Mycenaean pottery imported into Macedonia', *AI* 20–1, 56–61.

——1982. 'La machaira grecque et le problème des épées recourbées', *GCBI* XX/18, 25–51.

——1983. 'The finds from Čungar and the problem of Italic import into the hinterland of the Adriatic', *AI* 22–3, 70–5.

——1985. 'Des aspects nouveaux de l'expansion de la culture grecque dans les régions centrales des Balkans', *Starinar* 36, 19–49.

——1985–6. 'Greco-Italic and Hellenistic vases in the Zemaljski Muzej Sarajevo Collection', *GZMS* 40–1, 39–56.

——1986. 'Les formes grecques de la céramique de l'âge du fer ancien', *Starinar* 37, 25–39.

Pašalić, E., 1967. 'Problèmes du développement économique à l'intérieur de la province romaine de Dalmatia', in Benac 1967, 111–37.

Pašić, R., 1975. 'Fouilles préhistoriques à Demir Kapija', *Starinar* 26, 155–8.

Pašić-Vinčić, R., 1970. 'Explorations archéologiques sur la localité "Orlova Čuka" près du village Star Karaorman (region Štip)', *Starinar* 21, 129–134.

Paškvalin, V., 1979. 'Nymphée antique à Putovići près de Zenica', *GZMS* 34, 55–84.

——1985–6a. 'Deux reliefs avec la representation du dieu Liber en Bosnie du sud-ouest', *GZMS* 40–1, 61–70.

——1985–6b. 'Le relief de Silvanus provenant de Volari près de Šipovo', *GZMS* 40–1, 71–7.

Patsch, C., 1900. 'Archaeologische-epigraphische Untersuchungen zur Geschichte der römischen Provinz Dalmatien, IV: Die Japoden', *WMBH* 7, 33–62.

——1904. *Das Sandschak Berat in Albanien* (Schriften der Balkankommission, Antiquarische Abteilung, Heft 3), Wien.

——1922. *Die Herzegowina einst und jetzt* (Historische Wanderungen im Karst und an der Adria 1: Osten und Orient, 2 Reihe neue Folge 1), Wien.

Peroni, R., 1976. 'La "koine" adriatica et il suo processo di formazione', in Suić 1976b, 95–115.

Petrić, N., 1978. 'La "gradina" grad à Nakovana, sur la presqu'île de Pelješac', in Rapanić 1978b, 35–48.

——1979. 'Tumuli de Hvar', *VAHD* 72–3, 67–78.

——1980. 'Aggiunta alle nozioni sulla ceramica geometrica apula sulla costa orientale dell'Adriatico', *Diadora* 9, 197–203.

Petrova, E., 1980. 'Illyrian drachms in the Archaeological Museum (Skopje)', *MAA* 6, 55–62.

——1983–4. 'The epichoric names on the inscriptions at Scupi', *MAA* 9, 127–31.

Petrović, J., 1984. *Gomolova*, Novi Sad (Vojvodina Museum).

Petru, P., 1968. 'Die ostalpinen Taurisker', *AV* 19, 357–73.

——1973. 'Società illirica occidentale come oppare effigiata sulle situle di Vače e Magdalenska gora', *AV* 24, 874–82.

Picard, O., 1986. 'Illyriens, Thraces et Grecs: la monnaie dans les rapports entre populations grecques et non-grecques', *Iliria* 16: 1, 137–41.

Pisani, V., 1976 (1972). 'Gli illiri in Italia', *Iliria* 5, 67–73 [= *SA* 9: 2, 259–68].

Polomé, E. C., 1982. 'Balkan languages (Illyrian, Thracian and Daco-Moesian)', in Boardman, Edwards, Hammond and Sollberger 1982, 866–88.

Popović, L., 1956. *Catalogue des objects découverts près de Trebenište*, Beograd (National Museum).

——1975. *Archaic Greek Culture in the Middle Balkans*, Beograd (National Museum).

Popović, M., 1982. *The Fortress of Belgrade*, Beograd (Archaeological Institute Monographs vol. 18).

Popović, P., 1976. 'Le trésor de drachms d'Apollonia à Čelopek près de Peć', *Starinar* 27, 175–9.

——1978. 'Les débuts du monnayage barbare dans les régions centrales des Balkans', *AI* 19, 26–30.

——1987. *Le monnayage des Scordisques: les monnaies et la circulation monétaire dans le centre des Balkans IVe–Ier s. av. n. è.*, Beograd and Novi Sad.

Popović, V., 1978. 'La descente des Koutrigours, des Slaves et des Avars vers la mer Egée', *CRAI* 1978, 596–648.

——1984. 'Byzantins, Slaves et Autochtones dans les provinces de Prévalitane et Nouvelle Epire', *Villes et peuplement dans l'Illyricum Protobyzantin: actes du colloque organisé par l'École Française de Rome (Rome, 12–14 mai 1982)*, Rome, 181–243.

——1988. 'L'Albanie pendant la basse Antiquité', in M. Garašanin, 1988b, 251–83.

Poulianos, A., 1976. 'About the origin of the Albanian [Illyrians]', *Iliria* 5, 261–2.

Pounds, N. J. G., 1969. *Eastern Europe*, London.

Praschniker, C., and Schober, A., 1919. *Archaeologische Forschungen in Albanien und Montenegro* (Schriften der Balkankommission, Antiquarische Abteilung Heft 8). Wien.

Prendi, F., 1975a. 'Un aperçu sur la civilisation de la première période du fer en Albanie', *Iliria* 3, 109–38.

——1975b. 'Aspects de la vie sociale, économique et culturelle de Lissus', in Benac 1975a, 149–63.

——1976a (1972). 'L'urbanisation de l'Illyrie du sud à la lumière des données archéologiques (V–IIe siècles avant notre ère)', *Iliria* 4, 89–100 [= *SA* 9: 2, 105–23].

——1976b. 'Le Néolithique et l'Enéolithique en Albanie', *Iliria* 6, 21–99.

—— 1977–8. 'L'âge du Bronze en Albanie', *Iliria* 7–8, 27–58.

——1981. 'Deux inscriptions de constructions de la ville Illyrienne de Lissus', *Iliria* 11: 2, 153–63.

——1982. 'The Prehistory of Albania', in Boardman, Edwards, Hammond and Sollberger 1982, 187–237.

——1984. 'Un depôt de hâches préhistoriques à Torovice de Lezha', *Iliria* 14: 2, 19–34.

——1985a. 'Unità e singolarità nella cultura illirica dell'età del ferro nel territorio dell'Albania', *Iliria* 15: 1, 63–92.

——1985b. 'À propos de la formation de la civilisation et de l'ethnie illyriennes sur le territoire de l'Albanie durant l'époque du bronze et au debut de celle du fer', *Iliria* 15: 2, 101–17.

——1988. 'Les recherches archéologiques dans le domaine de la civilisation pré- et protohistorique en Albanie', *Iliria* 18: 1, 5–25.

Prendi, F., and Andrea, Z., 1981. 'Nouvelles données sur le Néolithique en Albanie', *Iliria* 1981: 2, 15–40.

Prendi, F., and Budina, D., 1972. 'Fouilles 1960 dans la forteresse d'Irmaj (Gramsh)', *Iliria* 2, 25–66.

Prendi, F., and Zheku, K., 1971. 'Lissus à la lumière des plus récentes données archéologiques', *Monumentet* 2, 7–23.

——1972. 'La ville illyrienne de Lissus, son origine et son système de fortifications', *Iliria* 2, 239–68.

——1983. 'Continuité ethnoculturelle illyro-albanaise dans la ville de Lissus', *Iliria* 13: 1, 204–8.

——1986. 'Considération sur le développement urbain de Lissus (fin du IVe–Ier siècles av. n. ère)', *Iliria* 16: 1, 57–66.

Protase, D., 1978. 'Les Illyriens en Dacie à la lumière de l'épigraphie', *GCBI* XVII/15, 127–35.

Protić, G., 1985. 'Prehistoric finds from the island of Vis', *VAHD* 78, 37–44.

Puš, I., 1976. 'The impregnating of prehistoric pottery', *AI* 17, 21–2.

——1978. 'Anthropomorphic pendants from Ljubljana', *AV* 29, 46–54.

——1982–3. 'Das vorgeschichtliche Emona und seine Einwohner', *AI* 22–3, 21–7.

Pušić, I., 1971. 'Lipci-Morinja près de Risan, dessins préhistoriques', in Novak et al. 1971b, 147–51.

——1976. 'Vestiges préhistoriques et résultats des recherches dans le Boka Kotorska', in Batović 1976d, 127–32.

Radić, I., 1988. 'On finds of ancient ship-altars from the eastern Adriatic sea', *VAMZ* 21, 35–56.

Radimsky, W., 1895. 'Die Nekropole von Jezerine in Pritoka bei Bihać', *WMBH* 3, 39–218.

Radimsky, W. et al., 1897. 'Der prähistorischer Pfahlbau von Ripač bei Bihać', *WMBH* 5, 29–123.

Radmilli, A., 1970. 'The island of Lastovo (Lagosta) from Prehistory to the Roman era', in Mirosavljević et al. 1970, 439–46.

Rapanić, Ž. (ed.), 1975. *Quelques questions archéologiques sur la Lika: réunion scientifique Otočac 22–24 ix 1974*, Split (Archaeological Society of Croatia vol. 1).

——1978a. *Archäologische Forschungen in nordwestlichen Kroatien: Tagung Varaždin 22–25 x 1975*, Zagreb (Archaeological Society of Croatia vol. 2).

——1978b. *Nouvelles recherches archéologiques en Dalmatie: réunion scientifique Vodice 10–13 v 1976*, Split (Archaeological Society of Croatia vol. 3).

—— (ed.) 1984. *La région de la Cetina depuis la préhistoire jusqu'à l'arrivée des Turcs: réunion scientifique Sinj, 3–6 vi 1980*, Split (Archaeological Society of Croatia vol. 4).

Raunig, B., 1971a. 'Die japodische Nekropole auf der Crkvina in Golubić', *WMBHL* 1, 97–116.

——1971b. 'Fragment einer japodischen Urne aus Golubić bei Bihać', *WMBHL* 1, 97–116.

——1974. 'Monuments de pierre funéraires et cultuels Japodes', *Starinar* 23, 23–51.

——1975. 'Monuments funéraires et religieux en pierre des Japodes', in Rapanić 1975, 45–56.

——1980–1. 'Prähistorische Nekropole auf der Gradina im Dorf Ripač', *GZMS* 35–6, 141–62.

Rendić-Miočević, A., 1975b. 'Trois statuettes de Silvain illyrien provenant de la région des Delmates', *VAMZ* 9, 29–46.

——1984. 'La région des Ridites dans la plastique culturelle illyrienne', in Benac 1984a, 119–32.

Rendić-Miočević, D., 1948. *Illyrische Onomastik auf lateinischen Inschriften Dalmatiens*, Split (*VAHD* Supplement vol. 3).

——1949. 'Contribution à l'étude de notre onomastique du haut Moyen âge', *Starohrvatska prosvjeta (Ancient Croatian Culture)* 3rd series 1, 9–21.

——1956. 'Illyrica: zum Problem der illyrischen onomastischen Formel in römischer Zeit', *AI* 2, 39–51.

——1967. 'Problèmes de la romanisation des illyriens avec un regard particulier sur les cultes et sur l'onomastique', in Benac 1967, 139–56.

——1970a. 'Ionios "to genos Illurios" and the Graeco-Illyrian coinage' in Mirosavljević et al. 1970, 347–72.

——1970b. 'Some new fragments of the Greek inscription from Lumbarda', *VAMZ* 4, 31–44.

——1972–3. 'Monnaies des rois illyriens au Musée archéologique de Zagreb', *VAMZ* 6–7, 253–67.

——1975a. 'La Lika et la tradition anthroponymique des Japodes', in Rapanić 1975, 97–108.

——1975b. 'Quelques aspects de la continuité des agglomérations fortifiées illyriennes préantiques à l'époque romaine', in Benac 1975a, 47–58.

——1975c. 'La Lika et la tradition anthroponymique des Japodes', in Rapanić 1975, 97–108.

——1976a (1972). 'Le municipium Riditarum en Dalmatie: son patrimoine épigraphique et l'onomastique illyrienne', *Iliria* 5, 139–42 [= *SA* 9: 2, 229–34].

——1976b. 'Greci e illiri nell'Adriatico orientale alla luce delle fonti numismatiche', in Suić 1976b, 185–97.

——1979–80. 'Quelques aspects iconographiques et onomastiques de la communauté cultuelle "Pannonico-Illyrique" de Silvain', *VAMZ* 12–13, 105–23.

——1980. 'Cnidian colonisation on island Corcyra Nigra/Korčula', *Diadora* 9, 229–50.

——1981. 'Sur la typologie de la monnaie du "roi Monounios" et sur le problème de son identité', *GCBI* XIX/17, 97–123.

——1982. 'On some neglected aspects of the Iapodic urns', *VAMZ* 15, 1–10.

——1984. 'L'art des Illyriens à l'époque antique', in Benac 1984a, 65–80.

——1985. 'De nouveaux apports concernant les émissions à la légende Rhedon de l'atelier de Lissos', *VAMZ* 18, 45–56.

Renfrew, C., 1987. _Archaeology and Language: the Puzzle of Indo-European Origins_, London.

——1989. 'Models of Change in Language and Archaeology', _Transactions of the Philolological Society_ (London) 87: 2, 103–55.

Russu, I. I., 1969. _Illirii: istoria, limba şi onomastica, romanizarea_, Bucureşti (_Bibliotheca istorica_ 17).

Sakellarakis, J. A., and Marić, Z., 1975. 'Zwei Fragmente mykenische Keramik von Debelo brdo in Sarajevo', _Germania_ 53, 153–6.

Sako, Z., 1976 (1972). 'De la genèse de la danse Pyrrhique', _Iliria_ 5, 237–9 [= _SA_ 9: 2, 307–10].

Salmon, Pierre, 1986. 'L'image des Illyriens à Rome: étude de mentalité', _Iliria_ 16: 1, 203–11.

Šarić, I., 1975a. 'Urnes de pierre provenant de la Lika', in Rapanić 1975, 57–74.

——1975b. 'Les urnes japodiques en Lika', _VAMZ_ 9, 23–6.

——1983–4. 'The lid of the "Iapodic" ossuary', _VAMZ_ 16–17, 111–17.

Šašel, J., 1977a. 'L'anthroponymie dans la province romaine de Dalmatie', _L'onomastique latine: Paris 13–15 octobre 1975_, ed. H.-G. Pflaum and N. Duval (colloque internationale du CNRS 564), Paris, 365–83.

——1977b. 'Strabo, Ocra and Archaeology', _Ancient Europe and the Mediterranean: studies presented in honour of Hugh Hencken_, ed. V. Markotić, Warminster 1977, 157–60.

——1977c. 'Viae Militares', _Studien zu den Militärgrenzen Roms II: Vorträge des 10. internationalen Limeskongresses in der Germania Inferior_, Köln and Bonn, 235–44.

——1982. 'Zur Inschrift eines Zollbediensteten aus dem Stadtgebiet des obermösischen Ulpiana', _ZPE_ 49, 211–16.

——1989. 'Die regionale Gliederung in Pannonien', _Raumordnung im Römischen Reich: zu regionalen Gliederung in den gallischen Provinzen, in Rätien, Noricum und Pannonien_, ed. H. Gottlieb, München.

Schmidt, R., 1945. _Die Burg Vučedol_, Zagreb.

Schmitthenner, W., 1958. 'Octavians militärische Unternehmungen in den Jahren 35–33 v. Chr.', _Historia_ 7, 189–236.

Sedaj, E., 1986. 'Les tribus illyriennes dans les chansons homeriques', _SA_ 1986: 1, 157–72.

Simone, C. de, 1972. 'La lingua messapica: tentativo di una sintesi', _Le genti non greche della Magna Grecia (Atti dell'undicesimo convegno di studi sulla Magna Graecia, Taranto, 10–15 ottobre 1971)_, Napoli, 125–201.

——1976 (1973). 'Lo stato attuale degli studi illirici ed il problema della lingua messapica', _Iliria_ 5, 75–8 [= _SA_ 10: 1, 155–9].

——1977. 'Le inscrizioni della necropoli di Durazzo: nuove osservazioni', *Studi Etruschi* 45, 208–35.

——1986. 'Gli Illiri del sud: tentativo di una definizione', *Iliria* 16: 1, 239–42.

Simoska, D., and Sanev, V., 1976. *Pr[e]history in Central Pelagonia*, Bitola (National Museum).

Škegro, A., 1988. *Bibliographia Illyrica* (supplementum 1982–1987), ANUBiH publications spéciales LXXXVII/13, Sarajevo.

Slapšak, B., 1988. 'The 1982–1986 Ager Pharensis survey: potentials and limitations of "wall-survey" in Karstic environments', in Chapman et al. 1988, 145–9.

Slavković-Djurić, N., 1964. 'Tertres funéraires illyriens de Suva Reka', *Glasnik Muzeja Kosova i Metohije* (Priština) 9, 537–55.

Smith, R., 1988. 'Simulacra Gentium: the Ethne from the Sebasteion at Aphrodisias', *JRS* 78, 50–77.

Sokolovska, V., 1978. 'Archaeological excavations at Demir Kapija', *MAA* 4, 93–112.

——1979–82. 'Isar-Marvinci: the archaeological excavations in 1977 and 1978', *Zbornik Arheološka Muzeja Makedonija* 10–11, 9–23.

Sokolovska, V., and Mikulčić, G., 1985. 'Isar/Marvinci: Hellenistic and Roman cemetery', *Arheološki Pregled* 26, 81.

Spahiu, H., 1975. 'Berat', *Iliria* 3, 495–501.

——1983. 'Les murs d'enceinte de la forteresse de Berati (Résultats des fouilles de 1973–4 et 1978)', *Iliria* 13: 1, 119–35.

——1985. 'Nouvelles Bagues à l'inscription découvertes à Koman', *Iliria* 15: 1, 237–46.

——1986. 'Éléments de la tradition antique dans la culture des nécropoles du haut moyen age albanais', *Iliria* 16: 1, 263–71.

Srejović, D., 1971. 'Donja Brnjica, necropole de l'Âge du Fer Ancien', in Novak et al. 1971b, 171–3.

——1972. *Lepenski Vir: Europe's first monumental sculpture*, London.

——1973. 'Karagač and the Problem of the Ethnogenesis of the Dardanians', *Balcanica* (Belgrade) 4, 39–82.

——1980–1. 'A find from Lisijevo Polje near Ivangrad (Montenegro)', *AI* 20–1, 70–9.

——(ed.) 1984. *The Chipped Stone Industry from Vinča: excavations 1929–1934*, Belgrade (University Centre for Archaeological Research 4).

——1988. *The Neolithic of Serbia: Archaeological Research 1948–1988*, Belgrade.

Srejović, D., and Cermanović-Kuzmanović, A., 1987. *Roman Sculpture in Serbia*, Beograd (Serbian Academy Galeria 60).

Srejović, D., and Letica, Z., 1978. *Vlasac: a Mesolithic settlement in the Iron Gates*, Beograd (Serbian Academy Monographs DXII, Hist. vol. 5).

Stadtmüller, G., 1966. *Forschungen zur albanischen Frühgeschichte*, 2nd edn, Wiesbaden (Albanische Forschungen 2).

Stamati, F., 1981. 'La découverte des motifs d'ornement d'une cuirasse illyrienne au moyens des rayons X', *Iliria* 11: 2, 53–4.

Stančić, Z., and Slapšak, B., 1988. 'A modular analysis of the field system of Pharos', in Chapman et al. 1988, 191–8.

Stanko, J., 1987a. 'Etymologie du thème Messap-', *GCBI* XXV/23, 23–30.

——1987b. 'La Cimbriana illyrienne et quelques connexions linguistiques', *GCBI* XXV/23, 31–5.

——1988a. 'Quelques etymologies fausses', *GCBI* XXVI/24 25–36.

——1988b. 'Etymologies nouvelles illyriennes', *GCBI* XXVI/24, 37–42.

——1989. 'Quelques etymologies fausses II', *GCBI* XXVII/25, 145–66.

Stanković, S., 1986. *The Altars and Prosopomorphic Lids from Vinča*, Beograd (University Centre for Archaeological Research 7).

Starè, F., 1970. 'Darstellung der Geburt auf dem Pektorale aus Ulaka in Notranjsko (Innerkrain)', *VAMZ* 4, 13–30.

——1975. *Die Etrusker und der sudöstliche Voralpenraum, Razprave SAZU IX/3*, Ljubljana.

Starè, V., 1973. 'Kultstabe aus Šmarjeta', *AV* 24, 730–43.

——1976. 'Détermination chronologique des fibules naviculaires de Šmarjeta', *AV* 27, 97–119.

Starr, C., 1941. *The Roman Imperial Navy 31 BC–AD 324*, Ithaca, NY (repr. 1960, Cambridge).

Stipčević, A., 1960–1. 'Gli utensili degli Illiri', *Diadora* 2, 135–77.

——1963. *The Art of the Illyrians*, Milan.

——1966. *Gli Illiri*, Milan.

——1967. *Bibliographia Illyrica*, ANUBiH publications spéciales VI/3, Sarajevo.

——1976 (1973). 'Simbolismo illirico e simbolismo albanese', *Iliria* 5, 233–6 [= *SH* 27 (10): 2, 129–34].

——1977a. *The Illyrians*, trans. Stojana Čulić Burton, Park Ridge, NJ.

——1977b. *Bibliographie d'Archéologie antique en Yougoslavie I–II*, ANUBiH publications spéciales XXVI/7, Sarajevo.

——1978. *Bibliographia Illyrica (supplementum 1973–1977)*, ANUBiH publications spéciales XLII/8, Sarajevo.

——1981. *Symboles de culte chez les Illyriens: matériaux et contributions à la sistématisation*, ANUBiH CBI publications spéciales LIV/10, Sarajevo.

——1984a. *Bibliographia Illyrica (supplementum 1978–1982)*, ANU-BiH publications spéciales LXXVI/12, Sarajevo.

——1984b. 'Le culte de défunt heroisé dans la religion illyrienne', in Benac 1984a, 215–21.

——1986. 'Tout récit surs les Balkans commence par les Illyriens', *Iliria* 16: 1, 337–41.

Stojić, M., 1986. *Die Eisenzeit im Becken der Velika Morava*, Beograd and Svetozarevo (University Centre for Archaeological Research 8).

Suić, M., 1953. 'De situ magni lacus Naroniani in anonymi (Scylacis) Periplo', *GZMS* 8, 111–29.

——1955. 'The east Adriatic coast in the Periplus of Pseudo-Scylax', *Rad Jugoslavenske Akademije znanosti i umjetnosti* (Zagreb) 306, 121–81.

——1967a. 'Les frontières ethniques occidentales des Illyriens à la lumière des sources historiques', in Benac 1967, 33–53.

——1967b. 'Quelques données ethnologiques sur les Illyriens anciens dans les oeuvres des écrivains grecs et romains', in Benac 1967, 99–110.

——1971. 'Bribirska Glavica, Bribir, localité Liburne', in Novak et al. 1971, 93–4.

——1975. 'Approche scientifique et méthode de recherche des habitats autochtones sur le territoire illyrien', in Benac 1975a, 9–35.

——1976a. *Antički Grad na Istočnom Jadranu*, Zagreb.

—— (ed.) 1976b. *Jadranska obala u protohistoriji: kulturni i etnički problemi, simpozij, Dubrovnik 19–23 x 1972*, Zagreb (Archeological Institute).

——1976c (1973). 'Problèmes de palaeogenèse et d'urbanisation des centres illyriens', *Iliria* 4, 357–66 [= *SA* 10: 2, 105–16].

Svoljšak, D., 1973. 'Necropoli preistorica di Tolmin', *AV* 24, 397–415.

——1976. 'The prehistoric settlement at Most na Soči', *AI* 17, 13–20.

Syme, R., 1973. 'Danubian and Balkan Emperors', *Historia* 22, 310–16 [repr. in *Roman Papers* 3 (Oxford, 1984), 892–8].

Tasić, N., 1967. *Der Badener und Vučedoler Kultur-Komplex in Jugoslawien*, Beograd and Novi Sad (Archaeological Society of Yugoslavia, Dissertations vol. 4).

——1972. 'An Early Iron-Age collective tomb at Gomolava', *AI* 13, 27–37.

——1988. 'Einige Probleme der ethnischen Zugehörigkeit der Kulturen der älteren Eisenzeit im Gebiet Serbiens', *GCBI* XXVI/24, 69–79.

——1989. 'Mittlere Bronzezeit in Jugoslawischen Donauraum', *GCBI* XXVII/25, 91–102.

Tatari, F., 1977–8. 'Débris de céramique locale trouvés à Durrës', *Iliria* 7–8, 217–24.

——1984. 'Un cimetière du haut moyen-âge à Durrës', *Iliria* 14: 1, 227–45.

——1985. 'Constructions opus mixtum à Durrës', *Monumentet* 1985: 1, 87–93.

——1987. 'Une série de tombes des IIe–IVe siècles de n. ère dans la nécropole de Dyrrachium', *Iliria* 17: 1, 153–65.

——1988. 'Une maison antique sur la place parc "Rinia" à Durrës', *Iliria* 18: 1, 91–117.

Teržan, B., 1977. 'Die Certosafibel', *AV* 26, 317–536.

——1978. 'Über das Trachtzubehör auf Križna Gora', *AV* 29, 55–63.

——1984a. 'The amber from Debeli vrh above the village of Predgad', *AV* 35, 110–18.

——1984b. 'Die Tracht als kennzeichendes Element der alteisenzeit-lichen Gesellschaftsgruppen zwischen Drim und Devoll' (Romaja-Burrel-Kuç i Zi)', in Benac 1984a, 197–214.

——1985. 'Ein Rekonstruktionsversuch der Gesellschaftsstruktur im Doljensko-Kreiss der Hallstattkultur', *AV* 36, 77–105.

——1990. *The Early Iron Age in Slovenian Styria*, Ljubljana (National Museum, Catalogues and Monographs 25).

Teržan, B., Lo Schiavo, F., and Trampuž-Orel, N., 1984–5. *Most na Soči (S. Lucia) II: Die Ausgrabungen von J. Szombathy*, Ljubljana (National Museum Catalogues and Monographs 23, 1–2).

Težak-Gregl, T., 1981. 'Die Certosafibeln im japodischen Zentral-gebiet von Lika', *VAMZ* 14, 25–48.

Tirtja, M., 1976. 'Elément des cultes illyriens chez les Albanais (le culte du soleil)', *Iliria* 5, 241–60.

Toçi, V., 1965. 'Inscriptions et reliefs de la nécropole de Dyrrah (Dyrrhachium)', *SA* 2: 2, 49–99.

——1970. 'Données sur l'onomastique illyrienne à Dyrrhachium et dans d'autres centres de l'Albanie', in Kostallari et al. 1970, 2, 453–501.

——1976 (1972). 'La population illyrienne de Dyrrhachion à la lumière des données historiques et archéologiques', *Iliria* 4, 301–6 [= *SA* 9: 1, 77–84].

——1986. 'Données récentes sur l'onomastique illyrienne à Durra-chium', *Iliria* 16: 1, 123–35.

Todd, J., Eichel, M., Beck, C., and Macchiarulo, A., 1976. 'Bronze and Iron Age amber artifacts in Croatia and Bosnia-Hercegovina', *JFA* 3, 313–27.

Todorović, J., 1963. *Rospi Čuprija: nécropole de l'époque de La Tène à Beograd*, Belgrade (*Inv. Arch. Jug.* Y47–Y56).

——1967. 'Les nécropoles préhistoriques de Rospi Čuprija à Belgrade', *Starinar* 18, 193–200.

——1968. *Die Kelten in süd-ost Europa*, Beograd (Dissertations of the City Museum of Belgrade).

——1970. 'Les mouvements migratoires des Scordisques après 279 av. n. è', *AI* 11, 15–22.

——1971. 'Karaburma à Beograd: sites préhistoriques de différentes époques', in Novak et al. 1971, 179–80.

——1973–4. 'Une tombe double de guerriers scordisques à Ritopek', *Starinar* 24–5, 79–83.

Torr, C., 1895. *Ancient Ships*, Cambridge [repr. Chicago 1964, ed. with intro. by A. J. Podlecki].

Toynbee, A., 1973. *Constantine Porphyrogenitus and his World*, London.

Trbuhović, V., 1971. 'Die Illyrier als protohistorischer Volk', in Filip 1971, 861–4.

Trbuhović, V. and Trbuhović, L., 1970. *Donja Toponica: Dardanian and Slavic necropolis*, Beograd.

Tronson, A., 1984. 'Satyrus the Peripatetic and the marriages of Philip II', *JHS* 104, 116–26.

Truhelka, C., 1904 and 1909. 'Der vorgeschichtlicher Pfahlbau im Savebette bei Donja Dolina', *WMBH* 9, 3–156, and 11, 3–27.

Truhlar, F., 1981. 'Burgwalle: befestigte Siedlungen in Slowenien', *AV* 32, 530–8.

Turnock, David, 1988. *The Making of Eastern Europe: from the earliest times to 1815*, London and New York.

Untermann, J., 1961. *Die venetischen Personennamen*, Wiesbaden.

——1970. 'Venetisches in Dalmatien', *GCBI* 5, 5–22.

——1978. 'Veneti', *Realencyclopädie der classischen Altertumswissenschaft*, ed. Pauly-Wissowa, Suppl. vol. XV, col. 855–98.

Urleb, M., 1973. 'Die hallstattzeitliche Nekropole auf der Križna Gora bei Lož', *AV* 24, 507–20.

Valić, A., 1983. 'Vorgeschichtliche Grab- und Siedlungsfunde in Kranj: archaeologische Schutzgrabungen um die Pfarrkirche herum im J. 1972', *AV* 34, 129–39.

Vasić, R., 1967. 'The date of the Japod urns', *AI* 8, 47–57.

——1969. 'A contribution to the study of Iapod art', *Starinar* 20, 383–90.

——1972. 'Notes on the Autariatae and Triballi', *Balcanica* 3, 117–33.

——1973. *The Early Iron-Age cultural groups in Yugoslavia*, Beograd (Archaeological Institute Monographs 12).

——1974a. 'The decorated style of the sixth century BC in the north Balkans', *Actes du VIIIe congrès international des sciences préhistoriques et protohistoriques, Beograd 9–15 septembre 1971*, Beograd, vol. 3, 174–9.

——1974b. 'Bronzes from Titov Veles in the Benaki Museum', *ŽA* 24, 213–32.

——1975. 'A note on the lanceolate fibula', *AI* 16, 14–16.

——1976. 'Nouveaux éléments pour l'étude de l'âge du fer dans la vallée du Vardar', *Starinar* 27, 1–18.

——1977. *The Chronology of the Early Iron Age in the Socialist Republic of Serbia*, Oxford (BAR Supplementary Series 31).

——1977–8. 'Sur la datation des urnes Japodes', *Starinar* 28–9, 121–6.

——1981. 'Les débuts de l'âge du fer en Serbie', *Starinar* 32, 1–7.

——1982a. 'Contribution à l'étude des armes grecques en Yougoslavie', *GCBI* XX/18, 5–24.

——1982b. 'Ein Beitrag zu den Doppelnadeln im Balkanraum', *PZ* 57, 220–57.

——1982–3. 'Contribution to the study of "Illyrian" helmets in the north of Yugoslavia', *AI* 22–3, 76–80.

——1983. 'Greek bronze vessels found in Yugoslavia', *ŽA* 33: 2, 185–94.

——1985. 'A contribution to the study of "scharnier" fibulae in Yugoslavia', *GCBI* XXIII/21, 121–55.

——1986. 'Les tendances artistiques à l'âge du fer en Yougoslavie', *Starinar* 37, 1–24.

——1987. 'Beitrag zur Erforschung der Bogenfibeln mit viereckiger Fussplätte auf dem Balkan', *AV* 38, 41–68.

——1989. 'Une contribution à l'étude du groupe de Syrmie', *GCBI* XXVII/25, 103–13.

Vasiliev, V., 1983. 'Bermerkungen zum Transport von Bronzegefässen in der Antike', *AArch. Hung.* 35, 179–85.

Vasilijević, M., 1976. 'Les trouvailles de l'âge du fer ancien a Šabač', *Starinar* 27, 167–74.

Velimirović-Žižić, O., 1983. 'Poignard en bronze d'un tumulus près de Medun', *AI* 20–1, 40–2.

Veyvoda, V., 1961. 'Japodische doppelte Ziernadeln', *VAMZ* 2, 115–24.

Veyvoda, V., and Mirnik, I., 1971. 'Excavations of prehistoric barrows at Kaptol (Preliminary report)', *VAMZ* 5, 183–210.

——1973. 'Early Iron Age warrior graves from Kaptol near Slavonska Požega', *AV* 24, 592–610.

Vinski-Gasparini, K., 1968. 'Die ältesten Bronze-Eimer im jugoslawischen Donauraum', *VAMZ* 3, 1–27.

——1974. 'Die Violinbogenfibeln in Jugoslawien', *VAMZ* 8, 1–28.

——1978. 'Rückblick auf die Forschungen der späten Bronzezeit und der älteren Eisenzeit im nordlichen Kroatien', in Rapanić 1978a, 129–48.

Visona, P., 1985. 'Coins of Ballaios found in Italy', *VAHD* 78, 117–22.

Vreka, B., 1987. 'Trois inhabitations des IV–III siècles av. n. ère à Mashjezë', *Iliria* 17: 1, 117–34.

——1988. 'Plats hellénistiques à vernis noirs d'Apollonia', *Iliria* 18: 2, 121–41.

Vučković-Todorović, D., 1973. 'La céramique grecque et hellénistique dans l'est de la Yougoslavie', *Rev. Arch.* 1973, 39–52.

Vukmanović, M., and Popović, P., 1982. 'Les recherches de sondages des agglomérations fortifiées du type "Gradina" dans la région de la vallée de Vranje-Preševo (Serbie du Sud)', *GCBI* XX/18, 189–210.

Vulić, N., 1933. 'Neue Gräber in Trebenischte', *JÖAI* 28, 164–86.

Vulpe, R., 1925. 'Gli Illiri dell'Italia imperiale romana', *Ephemeris Dacoromana* 3, 129–258.

——1976 (1973). 'Considérations autour de l'origine illyrienne du peuple albanais', *Iliria* 5, 133–37 [= *SA* 10: 1, 199–205].

Walbank, F., 1976 (1973). 'Southern Illyria in the third and second centuries BC', *Iliria* 4, 265–72 [= *SH* 27(10): 1, 137–47].

——1977. 'The original extent of the Via Egnatia', *Liverpool Classical Monthly* 2, 73–4.

Wells, P. S., 1978. 'The excavations at Stična in Slovenia by the Duchess of Mecklenburg, 1905–1914', *JFA* 5, 215–26.

——1980. 'Magdalenska gora: ein Siedlungsplatz in Slowenien aus der Eisenzeit', *Antike Welt* 11: 3, 47–54.

Wilkes, J., 1969. *Dalmatia (History of the Roman Provinces)*, London.

——1976. 'Arthur Evans in the Balkans, 1875–1881', *Bulletin of the Institute of Archaeology* (London) 13, 25–56.

——1977. 'The population of Roman Dalmatia', *Aufstieg und Niedergang der römischen Welt*, ed. H. Temporini and W. Haase, Berlin and New York, II Principat, vol. 6, 732–66.

——1990. Review of Cabanes 1987 and Eggebrecht 1988, *AJA* 94, 502–4.

Williams, S., 1985. *Diocletian and the Roman Recovery*, London.

Winnifrith, T. 1987. *The Vlachs*, London.

Wiseman, J., 1973. *Studies in the History of Stobi I*, Beograd.

——1975. *Studies in the History of Stobi II*, Beograd.

Wiseman, J., and Aleksova, B., 1981. *Studies in the Antiquities of Stobi*, Titov Veles.

Woldřich, J., 1897. 'Wirbeltierfauna des Pfahlbaues von Ripač', *WMBH* 5, 79–113.

——1904. 'Wirbeltierfauna des Pfahlbaues von Donja Dolina in Bosnien', *WMBH* 9, 156–64.

Woodhead, G., 1970. 'The "Adriatic Empire" of Dionysius of Syracuse', *Klio* 52, 503–12.

Ylli, L., 1976. 'L'ancienne nécropole du village de Leshnje (Skrapar)', *Iliria* 6, 275–85.

Zaninović, M., 1961–2. 'Delminium. Some remarks on the location', *VAHD* 63–4, 49–55.

——1966. 'The Illyrian tribe of the Delmatae', *GCBI* IV/2, 27–92.

——1967. 'The Illyrian tribe of the Delmatae (II)', *GCBI* V/3, 5–101.

——1968. 'Burnum: from castellum to municipium', *Diadora* 4, 119–29.

——1973. 'The continuation of autochthonous settlements in the Graeco-Roman period in Dalmatia', *Actes du VIIIe congrès international des sciences préhistoriques et protohistoriques Beograd 9–15 septembre 1971*, Beograd, vol. 3, 185–94.

——1976a. 'The Illyrians and the grapevine', *GCBI* XIII/1, 261–72.

——1976b. 'Le relazioni greco-delmate sull'Adriatico', in Suić 1976b, 301–7.

——1978. 'New contributions to the archaeological topography of the island of Hvar', in Rapanić 1978b, 49–62.

——1982. 'Early hill-forts on central Dalmatian islands', *Actas: Union internacional de ciencias prehistoricas y protohistoricas X congreso, Mexico Oct. 19–24, 1981*, Mexico, 308–15.

——1983. 'Greek land-division at Pharos', *AI* 20–1, 91–5.

——1984a. 'Il culto di Libero sull'Adriatico orientale', in Benac 1984a, 245–52.

——1984b. 'New contributions to the archaeology of Pharos', *VAHD* 77, 93–101.

Zeqo, M., 1986. 'D'anciens témoignages de l'art à Durrës', *Iliria* 16: 1, 179–85.

Zheku, K., 1974. 'Restauration de la porte de la cité illyrienne de Lis', *Monumentet* 7–8, 7–24.

——1976. 'Problèmes relatifs à la restauration des systèmes de fortifications des villes illyriennes', *Monumentet* 12, 17–25.

——1977–8. 'Sur la typologie des fortifications préurbains illyriennes dans le territoire de l'Albanie', *Iliria* 7–8, 113–23.

——1980. 'La technique et les matériaux de construction des murs d'enceinte de villes illyriennes connues à ce jour dans notre pays', *Monumentet* 19, 131–60.

Živojinović, S., 1984. 'Branko Šlivić's study of human remains from Trebenishte graves and current anthropological views of this population', *Balcanica* 15, 45–54.

Zotović, L., 1984. 'Contribution à l'interprétation ethnique des sépultures de type Mala Kopasnica-Sase', in Benac 1984a, 165–70.

Zotović, M., 1972. 'Nécropole à Kremni et le besoin des recherches sur le territoire de l'Autariat', *Zbornik radova Narodnog Muzeja Čačak* 3, 1–10.

——1974. 'The necropolis in Pilatovići near Požega and some characteristics in the way of burying the dead', *AI* 15, 27–32.

——1984. 'Le tumulus du prince à Pilatovići près de Požega', in Benac 1984a, 189–96.

——1987. 'Problèmes de l'âge du bronze récent en Serbie occidentale à la lumière des découvertes à Krajcinovići près de Priboj', *GCBI* XXV/23, 51–62.

Zozzi, R., 1976. 'Traces archaïques dans les costumes traditionelles du peuple albanais', *Iliria* 5, 225–32.

Index

abortion, induced by plants, 221
Absyrtus, brother of Medea, 102
Acarnania, 104, 149; Acarnanians and Illyrians, 156, 160
Acelum (Asolo), settlement of Veneti, 183
Achaeans, 104; League, 157; against Illyrians, 160; Aetolians and Macedonians, 163; Achaea, Roman province, 210
Achelous, r., 103
Acroceraunia (Cape Linguetta), 104
Acrolissus, fortifications, 133; captured by Philip V, 166–7
Acruvium, in region of Illyria, 174; Roman settlement, 213
Actium, battle, 187, 255
Ad Picarias near Apollonia, asphalt deposits, 128
Adaeus of Beroea, envoy of Perseus, 172
Adria, 113
Adrianople, battle, 265
Adriatic, 32–3, 37, 39, 41, 45, 51, 56–8, 63, 68, 70, 84, 87; Greek trade and exploration, 91, 94–7, 102–3, 107, 119, 152; distrusted, 224
Adrion (Dinara), mt., 188
Aeacian Walls, Risinium, 136
Aeacides of Molossians, 124
Aeacus of Aegina, 136

Aegean migrations, 33, 36–8, 40; civilization, 104
A(e)gida (Koper), 185
Aegina, trade, 113
Aemilius Paullus, Roman commander in Illyria, 163–4
Aenona (Nin), 71, 101
Aepulo, king of Histri, 186
Aequum, Roman colony, 213
Aesculapius, cult of healing, 245, 247
Aetolia, Aetolians, 103–4; and Macedonia, 119, 148, 150; against Illyrians, 157–8; Macedonians and Achaeans, 163–4; Roman alliance, 167, 170
Agrianes, 122
agriculture, Illyrian, 220
Agrippa, admiral of Octavian, 187
Agron, king of Illyrians, 115, 129; victories, 157–8, 167
Aguntum, 77
Alans, in Pannonia, 265
Alaric, and Visigoths, 273
Albania, Albanians, 11–12, 20, 24–7, 30, 32, 35, 38, 41, 44, 46, 68, 70, 73–4, 87; imports, 92, 107–8; plain of, 125, 139; fortifications in, 194; Illyrian origins, 266, 271; language, 278; culture and origin, 280

Korčula, 51, 113
Koreta, 72
Korkuti, M., 11
Kosmaj, mt., 83–4
Kosovo: region, 11, 18–19, 20, 25–6, 45, 47–8, 68, 75, 86, 120; survival of Latin names, 278
Kotor, 15; Gulf, 99, 168; tombstones, 243
Kotschach, 76
Koutzovlachs, 270
Kozuf, mts., 18
Krahe, H., 69
Kraljevo, 20
Krapina, 28
Kriva Reka, 41
Krivodol, 35
Križna Gora, 63
Krk, is., 32, 101
Krka, r., 16, 56, 100–1
Krka (Slovenian), r., 22, 58
Krotinë, relief, 229
Kruja, place-names, 280
Kruma, 45
Kruševac, 20
Kuç i Zi, 47
Kukës, 19, 25, 45
Kumanovo, basin, 18–20
Kunovi Čuki, 49
Kupa, r., 58
Kushi, 41
Kvarner, gulf, 101, 185
kylices, 106

La Tène, 63, 137
Labeates, 99, 172; coins, 175, 180; Lacus, 177
Lagole di Calalzo, 76
Laianci, 77
Lakeland, Albania, 68
land-division, on Hvar, 115
Langarus, king of Agrianes, 122
Latin, language, 76; survival in Balkans, 266
Latobici, 81, 256; civitas, 217–18
Latra, Liburnian deity, 245
lead-working, 224
Lederata, 83

legions, Roman in Illyrian provinces, 211; recruitment, 255, 260
lekythoi, 106
lembus: Illyrian ship, 156, 163, 165, 172, 226; Macedonian, 165
lentils, grown by Illyrians, 220
Leo, emperor, 267
Lepcis Magna, home of Severus, 260
Lepenac, r., 18
Leskovac, 20
Leucas, battle, 164
Lezha, 14
Lias (Alos), 95
Lib, hill-fort, 192
Liber, deity, 247
liburna, ship, 111
Liburni, Liburnia, 39, 56–7, 64–5, 68, 70–1, 74–6, 84, 95–6, 98, 100–1, 110–11, 197–8; names, 76, 78; pirates, flocks, 183, 186; warships, 187; in Roman province, 209; civitates of, 216: settlements, 227; tombstone, 243, 253; Roman cities, 254
Licca (Licca/Licco), Illyrian name, 271
Licinius, rival of Constantine, 264
Licinius, Roman commander and Japodes, 201
life-expectancy, 220
Lika, plain, 57, 63–4, 70, 102; names, 79, 197–8, 201
Lim, r., 139, 270
lions, Illyrian symbol, 245
Lipci, near Risan, 29
Lisičići, 34
Lissus (Lezha), 114–15, 210; fortifications, 130, 133; limit of Illyria, 161–3; captured by Philip V, 168; base of Gentius, 173–4; coins, 175–7; Roman settlement, 213; bishop of, 273
Little Prespa, Lake, 17, 19, 47
livestock, Illyrian, 127, 220
Livno, plain, 188; relief, 228–9